Religion in the South
John B. Boles, Series Editor

The Roots of Appalachian Christianity

The Life and Legacy of Elder Shubal Stearns

Elder John Sparks

THE UNIVERSITY PRESS OF KENTUCKY

Publication of this volume was made possible in part by
a grant from the National Endowment for the Humanities.

Copyright © 2001 by The University Press of Kentucky
Paperback edition 2005
Scholarly publisher for the Commonwealth,
serving Bellarmine University, Berea College, Centre College of Kentucky,
Eastern Kentucky University, The Filson Historical Society, Georgetown
College, Kentucky Historical Society, Kentucky State University, Morehead
State University, Murray State University, Northern Kentucky University,
Transylvania University, University of Kentucky, University of Louisville, and
Western Kentucky University.
All rights reserved.

Editorial and Sales Offices: The University Press of Kentucky
663 South Limestone Street, Lexington, Kentucky 40508-4008
www.kentuckypress.com

09 08 07 06 05   5 4 3 2 1

"Ballad of the Goodly Fere" by Ezra Pound, from *Personae*, © copyright 1926 by
Ezra Pound. Reprinted by permission of New Directions Publishing Corp.

Library of Congress Cataloging-in-Publication Data

Sparks, John, 1961–
  The roots of Appalachian Christianity : the life and legacy of elder Shubal
  Stearns / John Sparks.
      p. cm.
  Includes index.
  ISBN 0-8131-2223-6 (alk. paper)
  1. Stearns, Shubal, 1706–1771. 2. Baptists—United States—Clergy—
Biography. 3. Appalachian Region—Church history—18th century.
I. Title.
BX6495.S77 S63 2001
286.'1'092—dc21   2001003412
Paper ISBN 0-8131-9128-9

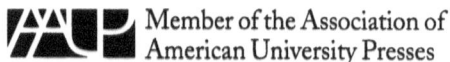

Member of the Association of
American University Presses

To my wife Sheila
and daughters Sarah and Amie;
to borrow a phrase from Shakespeare,
"The hopeful ladies of my earth";

and to Don Fraley and to the memory
of Elders J.T. Bailey, B.C. Ferguson, and
Scott Castle: the "Goodly Feres" of my youth

The Ballad of the Goodly Fere

Simon Zelotes speaketh it somewhile after the crucifixion.
"Fere," = shipmate or companion.

Ha' we lost the goodliest fere o' all,
For the priests and the gallows tree?
Aye, lover he was o' brawny men,
O' ships and the open sea.

When they came wi' a host to take Our Man
His smile was good to see.
"First, let these go!" quo' our Goodly Fere,
"Or I'll see ye damned," says he.

Aye, he led us out through the crossed high spears
And the scorn of his laugh rang free,
"Why took ye me not when I walked about
Alone in the town?," says he.

Oh, we drunk his "Hale" in the good red wine
When we last made company,
No capon priest was the Goodly Fere
But a man o' men was he.

I ha' seen him drive a hundred men
Wi' a bundle o' cords swung free,
That they took the High and Holy House
for their pawn and treasury.

They'll no' get him a' in a book I think,
Though they write it cunningly;
No mouse of the scrolls was the Goodly Fere
But aye loved the open sea.

If they think they ha' snared our Goodly Fere
They are fools to the last degree.

"I'll go to the feast," quo' our Goodly Fere,
"Though I go to the gallows tree."

"Ye ha' seen me heal the lame and blind,
And wake the dead," says he,
"Ye shall see one thing to master all,
'Tis how a brave man dies on the tree."

A son of God was our Goodly Fere
That bade us his brothers be.
I ha' seen him cow a thousand men.
I have seen him upon the tree.

He cried no cry when they drave the nails
And the blood gushed hot and free.
The hounds of the crimson sky gave tongue
But never a cry cried he.

I ha' seen him cow a thousand men
On the hills o' Galilee.
They whined as he walked out calm between
Wi' his eyes like the grey o' the sea,

Like the sea that brooks no voyaging
With the winds unleashed and free;
Like the sea he cowed at Genseret
Wi' twey words spoke suddenly.

A master of men was our Goodly Fere,
A mate of the wind and sea.
If they think they ha' slain our Goodly Fere
They are fools eternally—

I ha' seen him eat o' the honey-comb
Sin' they nailed him to the tree.

—Ezra Pound

Personae, 1926,
reprinted by permission of
New Directions Publishers, New York

Contents

List of Figures and Maps   x

Foreword by Loyal Jones   xi

Introduction   xv

The Covenant Owners: 1706–1740   1

Rude Awakening: 1740–1751   15

The "Garding in Closed": 1751–1754   34

Chance and Providence: 1754–1755   48

Chamomile: 1755–1765   72

Meshech: 1765–1771   109

Requiem: 1772–1801   181

The Legacy of the Goodly Fere: 1801–2001   199

Afterword: I, The Preacher   291

Notes   295

Selected Bibliography   307

Index   313

Figures and Maps

Figures

Exterior of Sandy Creek Church   106

Interior of Sandy Creek Church   106

Maps

The Journey of the Stearns Family   52

The Beginning of the Stearns Movement   102

Uplanders' Principal Migratory Routes   177

Foreword

I first encountered Elder John Sparks in the Forum section of the *Louisville Courier Journal* at Christmastime, 1993. He was responding to an article about Episcopalian bishop John Shelby Spong's controversial book, *Born of a Woman*, in which the bishop questions the divinity of Jesus. Elder Sparks, in his letter, pointed out the anomaly of Spong's position of power, influence, and income while doubting the validity of the central belief that lifted him to prominence. I was impressed with Sparks's clarity of thought, gracefully presented. I looked up his post office, Offutt, and found it to be in Johnson County, in Eastern Kentucky. My populist blood quickened. To me, we had here a David making a direct hit on a Goliath again! I was at the time interviewing a range of Appalachian Christians for a book on Appalachian religion, and so I contacted Elder Sparks to ask for an interview. He surprised me by saying that he had read an essay of mine while he was a student at Pikeville College. He graciously agreed to an interview but then asked if I would look over a manuscript he was working on about the history of Baptists.

I agreed, of course, and was impressed by what he had written. Not only did he know Baptist history, he was a good writer as well. His sentences were carefully crafted, reflecting a wry (perhaps Calvinist) sense of humor and a strong faith. I encouraged him in his work and suggested persons and places that he might send it to for publication. I saw that he had much to offer others in understanding the abiding faith of people such as he serves as a pastor.

In March of 1994, I visited his home where I was warmly welcomed by him—much younger than I had imagined—and by his wife Sheila and their then-small daughters Sarah Ann and Amie. We did a two-hour interview, and I later quoted him in several places in my book *Faith and Meaning in the Southern Uplands* (University of Illinois Press, 1999). I was particularly interested in his own beliefs among those espoused by other Baptists in the region. He had grown up in the Freewill Baptist Church and was ordained there as a preacher at an early age, but he eventually had trouble with some Freewill doctrines and with what he saw as "overpersuasion" by some of the preachers who relied heavily on

Romans 10 ("For with the heart man believeth unto righteousness; and with the mouth confession is made unto salvation"). The emphasis on confession with the mouth, he thought, sometimes led to long altar calls urging the sinner to make a confession of faith. This at times led to people confessing before they were ready and backsliding later. His doctrinal concerns led him to the United Baptists, the church of his grandparents, who stressed salvation by the grace of God, emphasizing the work of the Spirit rather than the work of preachers.

So Sparks was interested in how the United Baptists came to be as they are, but in his reading of new books on Appalachian religion, such as Deborah Vansau McCauley's *Appalachian Mountain Religion: A History* (University of Illinois Press, 1995) and Howard Dorgan's *Giving Glory to God in Appalachia: Worship Practices of Six Baptist Subdenominations* (University of Tennessee Press, 1987), he began to think wider than just Baptist history.

Sparks had long been fascinated by the ministry of the eighteenth-century Separate Baptist preacher Elder Shubal Stearns and his influence on Baptist history. As he looked closer at Stearns, however, he came to believe that Stearns had influenced all Appalachian religious groups and thus might be called the father of Appalachian religion.

Stearns, born in Massachusetts in 1706, was at first a New Light Congregationalist in Connecticut ("New Light" meaning he scorned church creeds as man-made and believed in the possibility of universal, rather than limited atonement), but he soon decided that immersion of adult believers was the only true baptism, and thus he asked for and received ordination from the Baptists. Stearns decided that his call was to minister to people on the frontier who had largely outrun their churches. His ministry took him to Virginia and then to the Piedmont of North Carolina, where he established the Sandy Creek Baptist Church and served it as pastor for sixteen years. His energy and that of others he inspired led to the formation of the Sandy Creek Association of forty-two Separate Baptist churches in North Carolina and Virginia, and other Baptist churches resulted in the years to come. Yet Stearns' name is largely unknown except to Baptist historians, and when mentioned by others, he has usually rated only a paragraph, a sentence, or a footnote.

It was Stearns's doctrine, his preaching style, and his zeal that fascinated Sparks and led to his belief that Stearns was a far greater influence on the religion of Appalachia and the areas surrounding it than other religious historians had noticed. He makes much of the little preacher's expressive eyes, his animation, and especially the high-pitched, rhythmic whine of his preaching chant. Sparks and Howard Dorgan (a speech teacher) have long been fascinated with the Appalachian preaching style that is shared by many of the rural churches of several denominations, and they realize that it, along with the singing styles and the tunes themselves, is learned in the oral tradition and passed on through the generations.

Shubal Stearns was a major purveyor of a populist religion aimed at the religion-starved frontier people. It was a religion available to all, the learned or the illiterate, the well-to-do or the lean poor, man or woman, and children, too, at an earlier age than the old Calvinists would have thought proper. The gospel was preached with a desperate zeal to get the attention of sinners before they stumbled into an everlasting hell. That zeal also touched the equally desperate longings of some of the old Calvinists in the Presbyterian and Regular Baptist folds, causing them to follow the bright eyed-preacher into a faith that was more optimistic than that offered by their predestinarian churches. Spiritually needy people in the mountains and elsewhere have continued to follow Stearns's successors down through the years, not only in the Separate, Freewill, Southern, and largely unaffiliated Missionary Baptist churches but also in the many other churches that have adopted Stearns's New Light doctrine and his energetic and zealous way of proclaiming it. This influence, according to Sparks, reached all of the non-mainline churches of the region, including the later Pentecostal-Holiness groups.

This is an important book because it fully examines the ministry of Shubal Stearns and is well-presented and documented. Such books usually come from remote scholars at a university, especially if published by a university press. This book is important because it comes from a practicing preacher living among people who share some of the same characteristics of Stearns's congregants: being relatively isolated from mainline society, leading sometimes hard lives, feeling a need of the gospel, and looking for choices in doctrine. Sparks, like other old-time Baptists, does not receive a salary from his congregation. He compares himself to the old "farmer-preachers" such as Shubal Stearns, although he calls himself a "technician-preacher," since he supports his family as a laboratory technician in a hospital. This book then is a labor of love, wrenched out of long and difficult study through mail orders, interlibrary loans, and the Internet. It is a product of a limited portion of days that required exacting tests in a laboratory, pastoral and preaching duties, and the considerable efforts of a caring husband and father. Sparks would be a remarkable man if he were spending most of his time on scholarly pursuits. That he could do such a fine piece of work in addition to the many other demands on his time and energy makes him even more remarkable. The main point, though, is that the book stands on its own, even if its author has produced it while leading a useful and meaningful life doing other things, related though they be.

I'm pleased that I had the good sense to suggest to John Sparks that he send this book to the University Press of Kentucky and more pleased that the editors, the readers, and the board looked on it with favor for publication. I am honored to have had a small part in bringing it to the reading public.

—Loyal Jones

Introduction

IN SEARCH OF THE GOODLY FERE

> Your society are much more like other folks now than they were when I was young. Then there was a company of them in the back part of our town, and an outlandish set of people they certainly were. You yourself would say so if you had seen them. As it was told to me, you could hardly find one among them but was deformed in some way or other. Some of them were hare-lipped, others were blear eyed, or humpbacked, or bowlegged, or clump footed; hardly any of them looked like other people. But they were all strong for plunging and let their poor ignorant children run wild, and never had the seal of the covenant put on them.
> —a "very honest and candid" old Southern lady to Baptist historian David Benedict, ca. 1810

As North Carolina native and Appalachian scholar Loyal Jones once noted, no group in the United States has aroused more suspicion and alarm among mainstream Christians than have Appalachian Christians, and never have so many Christian missionaries been sent to save so many Christians as in central and southern Appalachia.[1] The character of Appalachian religious beliefs has been the subject of a multitude of studies by both academics and theologians, and the issue is made more confusing by the different perceptions of the writers and the varying viewpoints taken. In most "mainstream" American Protestant as well as some academic literature, Appalachian religious values are generally stereotyped as bizarre, barbaric holdovers from days of yore, loud, emotional, fatalistic and superstition-based, with the ultraconservative and traditional Primitive and other "Old School" Baptists at one extreme or the snake-handling minority of the independent Pentecostal subgroubs at the other portrayed as the quintessential expressions of Appalachian faith. The prejudices that have arisen from this kind of cruel, unthinking characterization are legion, and for better or worse Appalachia's people may always be stuck with this image in some circles.

Fortunately, at least some independent academic scholars, including Jones, Howard Dorgan, and Deborah Vansau McCauley, have been more objective and sympathetic. McCauley, in her comprehensive *Appalachian Mountain Religion: A History* (University of Illinois Press, 1995), makes a strong, well-documented case for an idea that has been long suspected by many native Appalachian Christians themselves: that the emotional, personal, experience-based religiosity that has come to be regarded as characteristic of the region was once shared by a large portion of the population of the early United States and later supplanted in other areas by the development of the large, nationally based denominations for the sake of progress, the advent of nineteenth-century American rationalism and a broadened worldview. In other words, then, the mainline denominational writers who look down their noses on Appalachian Christianity are, whether they know it or not, snubbing their own heritage, and the missionaries they send to Appalachia are, rather than converting benighted pagans, meeting Christians of the type many of their own ancestors used to be.

As an Appalachian myself and a country preacher to boot, I hope that the reader will not take me too much to task for being subjective on this point. I'd enthusiastically subscribe to McCauley's thesis no matter how much or how little scholarly weight it carried. The question remains, though, if indeed Appalachian Christianity is largely an older expression of the faith since discarded by America at large, what were the factors that made this supposed early American faith the entity that it was, and why has it endured so strongly in this region?

For whatever an unschooled opinion is worth, *Appalachian Mountain Religion: A History* makes the most extensive effort yet attempted to answer this question. McCauley does an exceptional job of tracing the basic outline of the history. Our ancestors who first settled in the southeast were a small Duke's mixture of religious influences depending upon their own respective ethnic backgrounds, including Highland, Lowland, and Ulster Scottish Presbyterians; Anglican Churchmen; German Dunkards, Moravians, and Lutherans; and English and Welsh Baptists, yet within a generation or two the great majority of these backwoods families had gone over, as it were, either to the Baptists or to the Methodists who had finally made a full separation from the Anglican (Episcopal) Church in 1784. In the nineteenth century, denominationalism took a stronger and stronger hold. The Baptists split to one side or the other over various issues resulting in the organization of the Disciples of

Christ as well as various pro- and anti-mission factions that retained the name of Baptist, and as the Methodist denomination became more and more centralized on a national level, its influence gradually waned in the mountains, replaced in large part by Pentecostal groups who were themselves the product of both heavy Methodist and Baptist influence. The problem with McCauley's work—and again I must stress that this is an unschooled opinion—is that much of the early "history" actually takes the form of a sociology text rather than a pure historical account, and although a good many names of individuals important to Appalachian religious history are dropped, the emphasis seems to be on the process rather than historical events. The settlers came to this country from diverse cultures of "Scotch-Irish sacramental revivalism" and Old World pietism; they found this compatible with the "Baptist revival culture" they found on the Southern frontier; later on, still as Baptists, they embraced elements of Methodist "plain-folk camp-meeting religion," and so on and so on. The book does make an abrupt, rather surprising and refreshing change about halfway through with a diamond-hard factual account of the origins of the Church of God (Cleveland, Tennessee), perhaps the most widely known denomination of Appalachian origin, which McCauley traces to its roots in one United Baptist church in western North Carolina. McCauley provides warm, detailed historical information about this faith's earliest preachers as well, but unfortunately, and yet perhaps understandably, such minute detail is the exception rather than the rule; so many faiths in the mountains like the Church of God can trace themselves to the early Baptists, or at least to the Presbyterians who were proselytes to the Baptist cause, but only that far back. We are left, then, with a bit of Old World pietistic tradition, "Scotch-Irish sacramental revivalism," the "Baptist revival culture" and "plain-folk camp-meeting religion," almost like an old Appalachian ballad of uncertain authorship that has been preserved and rediscovered a continent and several generations away from the Scottish border country, telling of events that really happened but with something of the aura of legend.

For Appalachian people as well as outsiders interested in the region, this vague, quasi-legendary, balladlike approach to the origins of Appalachian religious culture presents something of a disadvantage. It lays the field wide open for any "inside" regional denomination so disposed to put its particular spin on history, however flawed and fanciful its speculations might be. All agree that the first "in" as regional denominations were the Presbyterians, Baptists (both English and German Dunkard varieties), and Methodists, but from later groups such as the Disciples of Christ and the various branches of Pentecostalism, we are more apt to find emotional diatribes full of pathos about how their reforming ancestors in the faith were abused by the older, hidebound parent denominations than accurate history. In their turn, the Baptists have often acted on par; not all, but all too many mountain Baptist churches subscribe to the "Old Landmarker" school of thought introduced to the Appalachians from the west in the 1850s that purports to show an unbroken apostolic chain of Baptist churches all the way back to John the Baptist himself, thus portraying the Baptist sect as "the only true Gospel church." The Landmarkers have rewritten history to suit themselves and their followers, and although most of their claims are easily exploded by the most basic objective historical research, they, when seen in company with the biased secular writers who insist on portraying Appalachian religion as nothing more than ignorance- and poverty-based emotionalism, have added a second strike to the study of Appalachian religious history. It will be demonstrated that even some academics have been misled by certain portions of Old Landmarker tradition, perhaps mistaking it for authentic folklore and believing there is data no more substantial than Old Landmarkism to go on.

When both academic sociological jargon and denominational propaganda are stripped away from the folklore, we find that tragically little remains. But the little that is left is very important indeed. In its most basic and untainted form and with little variation, the legend of the origins of Christianity in the Appalachians, accepted by most "inside" denominations but emphasized most particularly in all its points by the various Old School Baptist groups in the region, runs something like this: *Our faith and doctrine are that of the King James version of the Bible with nothing added to or taken away therefrom, and this faith was handed down to us by the Old Brethren who came here first, generations ago. The Old Brethren knew what was good and what was right and lived and died by it, and if this belief was good enough for the Old Brethren back then it's good enough for us now.* Even though the memory of the exact identity of these Old Brethren has faded from collective consciousness with the passage of time and chance and the legend is thus open to both academic/sociological and "Old Landmarker" interpretations, it's an honest piece of Appalachian folklore, transmitted orally from generation to generation and picking up "Old Landmarker" and other denominational variants as appendages along the way. Who, then, were these Old Brethren? Larger-than-life demigods who lived in a time when men were closer to the Lord, such as one might find in the ancient Celtic ballads our ancestors brought here with them from the Old Country? In a sense, perhaps, when one remembers that, however fanciful the story lines of these old ballads can get, many if not most contain at least a grain of historical truth at their hearts, and that, although the authorship of most has long since been forgotten, they each had an original version and an individual author. Though the powerful poem that appears at this book's beginning has all the appearances of an ancient translation of the Passion Story to the old Scots border ballad form, it was actually written in the twentieth century by an American rather than a Celt of several centuries ago; a complex, enigmatic but always an intense poet, both loved and hated in his own time and still the subject of controversy nearly three decades after his death. What, then, is the grain of historical truth at the heart of the Appalachian Old Brethren legend? And what poet, what seer, what author, despite whatever faults he may or may not have had and whatever controversies he may have generated intentionally or otherwise, gave the Appalachian people such a distinctively rough-edged, gritty, emotional, *Appalachian* vision of the Christ and the Gospel its Christians love and uphold?

The answers to these questions can be found neither in the sociological jargon of the academics nor the fanciful "reasoning" of the Old Landmarkers but buried and long ignored in the accounts of older American Baptist historians such as Isaac Backus, Morgan Edwards, and Robert B. Semple, and strangely enough in bits and pieces of the few historical accounts left behind regarding the defeat of an independent, radical colonial paramilitary group by the forces of the British Crown some years before the American Revolution began. The Old Brethren were a group of sixteen Baptists who migrated from New England to the Piedmont plateau of North Carolina not far from the central and southern Appalachian foothills in the middle years of the eighteenth century. In the historical record of their activities can be found not only the origins of each of the distinctively "Appalachian" worship practices scoffed at by mainline American Protestant denominations and studied by scholars but very nearly an entire history of the Appalachian people in capsule form. This volume is a biography of their leader, a man whose search for an ideal brought them all to the Carolina uplands and whose backwoods converts were wont to call—in direct disobedience to Christ's words in Matthew 23:9—their "Reverend Old Father." He was by no means a perfect man: he lacked the scholarship of a Calvin or a Luther, he was simple in some ways and complex in others, and he managed to stamp many of his own eccentricities upon the spiritual lives of his descendants in the faith. These sometimes perplexing, but warmly human, quirks made most Baptist historians more or less ashamed of him, and the very obscurity they created around his memory caused Deborah McCauley, in a five-hundred-plus page book, to devote no more than one small paragraph to his life and his work. Yet he was utterly moral, basically honest, and undoubtedly completely dedicated to that which he regarded as his divine calling; his story is one of much joy, much grief, and much of what Albert Camus referred to as human fate, in all its simplicity and grandeur. In a sense it is thus, in a very small portion, my own story, too, as well as that of every other mountain preacher I have ever known.

Away then, to the rocky hills of New England, across New York, Pennsylvania, and the panhandle of Maryland, up the Shenandoah and along the Blue Ridge through Virginia to an obscure grave in the North Carolina Piedmont and the dim memory of a loud, melodious, musical preaching cant and a pair of large, keen, piercing eyes . . .

1
THE COVENANT OWNERS
1706–1740

> I can recall nothing further back than this land, and Christianity.
> —Rimbaud, *A Season in Hell*

In Boston, Massachusetts in the month of January 1706 were born two men whose lives would touch multitudes of others and who would, each in his own way, leave his distinctive mark upon the course of American history. Both came from humble backgrounds and neither would ever receive much formal schooling; yet one would rise above his start as a "printer's devil" to become the first great American man of letters while the other, though never outgrowing the status of a lowly yeoman farmer, would in his own time be recognized as perhaps the second most effective Christian evangelist ever to preach on American soil. One was a confirmed skeptic, abandoning the Puritanism of his parents for the Deistic faith of the Enlightenment that held reason supreme and whose "self-evident truths" became the soul of the Declaration of Independence; the other just as consistently maintained a stubborn stance on the special revelation of God through Jesus Christ and in so doing converted the historical evolution of that same Puritanism into *the* faith of the American frontier. One, born on the seventeenth day of January, 1706, was of course the great Benjamin Franklin; the other, born eleven days later and who would become the founding father, as it were, of Appalachian Christianity, was Shubal Stearns.

His name, actually spelled *Shubael* ("captive of God") as found in a couple of soporific genealogies in the book of I Chronicles in English translations of the Old Testament, was already an old one in his family by the time of his birth, and its very obscurity and its definition may indicate that his English ancestors were Puritans, who as a rule were great fans both of obscure Scripture texts and names from an early date. The first male American members of the family, the brothers Shubael and Isaac Stearns, had come to the Massachusetts Bay Colony not long after settlement had begun there on the English ship *Arbella* from Nayland in Suffolk, England; this first Shubael Stearns died young, leaving his children in the care of Isaac, and family records are somewhat unclear as to which sons and daughters belonged to whom. For the next four generations the family seemed to center itself in and around the periphery of Boston. Charles Stearns, son of Shubael or Isaac, was admitted as a freeman in Watertown in 1646, but by the time his son Shubael was born on September 20, 1655, to him and his second wife, Rebecca Gibson, he had evidently moved to or near Cambridge. Charles died at Salem in 1696, not long after the notorious witch trials. The second Shubael Stearns married Mary Upton on April 27, 1682, and lived a long life that came to its end at Lynn, Massachusetts, on September 2, 1734. Shubael's and Mary's oldest son, also a Shubael, was born on August 9, 1683; he married Rebecca Sanford Lariby on December 28, 1704, and their oldest son, born as noted at Boston on January 28, 1706, is the subject of our study—although ultimately, his initial followers came to include his parents as well as most of his brothers and sisters. By the time of his birth the family's rate of literacy may have degenerated somewhat; though all his ancestral namesakes down to his father are noted by the correct biblical spelling of the appellation, he himself consistently signed his first name as Shubal and seems to have pronounced it as the spelling indicated. As to the pronunciation of his surname, many of his brothers' descendants in the South now spell it as *Starnes*, and given the state of flux American regional dialects were in during his lifetime, that is probably the very way it sounded.[1] Though perhaps unusual, the distinctive mispronunciations somehow seem appropriate.

This much we know of Shubal Stearns's heritage and family; pitifully little compared to that of Benjamin Franklin, who provided his illegitimate son with an autobiography that has gone on to become an American classic. Stearns himself left no autobiography or any other writings save a few personal letters that dealt almost exclusively with his ministerial labors. But then again, Stearns and Franklin have something in common here. Franklin wrote in his autobiography only that which he wished to reveal of himself to his son, candid in parts though it is, and autobiographers nearly always present themselves as they think they should be, rather than exactly as they are. With only one exception, all of the few accounts of Stearns's life have been penned by denominational historians who likewise conveyed more of the character they thought Stearns ought to be, rather than an actual portrait of the man himself.

Nonetheless, the beginnings of an understanding of Shubal Stearns may be gleaned from an examination of the social and religious environment in which he was born, raised, and spent more than half his life—the culture of Puritanism and that of the religious dissent that had come into existence around it.

Defined in its simplest terms, Puritanism was a collective effort to "purify" the Established Church in England from all Roman Catholic influence using as a guide the Scriptures and the five-point theological system of French reformer John Calvin, with its "tulip" acronym: total depravity of the human race through sin, unconditional election to salvation by the grace of God through Jesus Christ by individual predestination, limited atonement through Christ's blood only to those elected, the irresistible call of God to the elect, and the perseverance of the elect in their salvation, through grace, to glory. Brought to England shortly after the death of Bloody Mary by Protestant exiles who had been exposed to Calvin's teachings in Europe, Puritanism had two types of adherents at first. Those who wanted to replace Crown-appointed bishops with elected councils of elders or presbyters were called Presbyterians; others, who advocated a system by which each individual congregation governed itself, were known as Independents or Congregationalists; and after a few years, this latter school of thought produced a radical fringe that wanted to make a complete break with the English Church and who were thus called Separatists. Though Presbyterianism became the Established Church of Scotland, the English Puritans were always a minority party, gaining power during the English Civil War and Cromwell's rule only to lose it after the Restoration, and over the years great numbers had migrated to New England. The original Plymouth Colony of 1621 was first established by Separatists, but the later and more prosperous Massachusetts Bay Colony established a state faith along Independent Puritan lines, held together by the power of the clergy in a self-proclaimed theocracy—which, of course, like all other such claims before and since, proved to be something less than its ideal.

It was into this so-called theocracy that Shubal Stearns was born in 1706, although the faults and limitations of the system had already been cruelly demonstrated by the Salem witch trials of fourteen years before. As dissenters to established Anglicanism in the old country, the Puritans had worked patiently and consistently for recognition of their rights, but as the Established Church themselves in most of New England, the Independents were every bit as cruel to those who disagreed and dissented with them as the bishops of the Church of England had been to them. The Puritans were a dour bunch, utterly convinced that they possessed the truth, the whole truth, and nothing but the truth, and although the Presbyterian and Congregational branches of the faith treated one another and even Calvinistic Anglicans with respect, they had scant tolerance for other dissenters, fining them, beating them, and even banishing them from the colonies where they held control, sometimes on the slightest of pretexts.

Of these minority dissenters, the small sect known as the Baptists had one of the most unhappy lots, their persecution from the Puritans exceeded perhaps only by that which was thrown at the Quakers. Though they could trace their ideological roots partially to such Scripture-oriented groups as the Lollards, Waldensians, and even the ancient Donatists, they were actually an extreme left-wing party within the larger Puritan movement whose members had taken the position that the Church of Jesus Christ, as a visible structure, was a community of consenting believers over whose consciences neither king nor government held any power. In the process of their organization as a sect and the development of their thought, which was regarded as dangerously radical by nearly every other contemporary religious group, the Baptists had adopted some, but certainly not all, of the beliefs and practices of the Dutch Mennonites who were themselves the inheritors of the traditions of the earlier German Anabaptists.

As a rule, the first British Baptists emphasized literal Scriptural interpretation over episcopal or conciliar tradition; religious liberty with complete separation of church and state; personal responsibility for sin that was not removed by penances, rites, and sacraments but only by the blood of Christ; and a congregation composed of individual adult professors of faith with each member voluntarily submitting himself to membership by the example of believer's baptism. Though the earliest English Baptist churches appear to have begun by using affusion (pouring water over the heads of those baptized as opposed to sprinkling), by 1641 the rite of total body immersion, as advocated by Mennonite patriarch Menno Simons and introduced to the Baptists by the Rhynsburger or Collegiant Mennonites in Holland, had become their accepted norm because of its resemblance to "burial and riseing again."[2] Even so, the English Baptists by and large had rejected many fundamental articles of Mennonite piety such as the Dutch group's refusal to take oaths, bear arms for civil defense, or participate in public affairs, and soon they managed to distance themselves equally from Catholics, Anglicans, Puritans, and European Pietists alike. The larger Puritan groups evidently regarded them something like half-witted cousins rather than brothers in dissent.

They had experienced the severe ire of James I and the Anglican hierarchy, and in fact the last man ever burned at the stake in England for heresy was Edward Wightman, condemned by King James for, among other things, "the errors of the Anabaptists" a year after the Bible translated in the King's name was published.[3] Some denominational records show that Wightman was a Baptist, others a Separatist with Baptist leanings; given the time of his execution, the latter claim is probably the correct one. During the ups and downs of England's Civil War, Baptists gained some respect and enjoyed a respite from persecution during Cromwell's time, but intolerance was restored with the government of Charles II and continued up to the time of the Glorious Revolution when the Act of Toleration for Protestant Dissenters was passed. It was in these years that many British Baptists began to emigrate to the colonies, and some did find a safe haven in those religiously tolerant enclaves such as Pennsylvania, established by the Quaker William Penn, and Rhode Island, founded by Roger Williams who had himself been exiled from Massachusetts by the intolerant Puritans. Others, settling in the Massachusetts and Connecticut of Shubal Stearns's childhood and youth, or in Virginia, whose leadership stood fast on conventional Anglicanism and seemed incapable of implementing all the liberties of the Toleration Act, found their new environment little better than their old one.

In spite of the unifying effect that mutual persecution would be expected to have on those persecuted, even at this early date not less than three distinct Baptist subgroups existed within the Nonconformist community of both Great Britain and America. The oldest of these, and certainly the one closest to Mennonite doctrinal and practical outlook, was known as the General Baptist sect because, unlike Calvinists, the Generals believed that the atonement of Christ's blood was accessible to all through repentance and faith. Though the belief is popularly called Arminianism from Jacobus Arminius, its most famous early Protestant advocate, it was known among Mennonites and other Anabaptist sects both in Europe and in England where some emigrated and preached before Arminius was ever born. By and large the early General Baptists preferred extemporaneous sermons over written texts that might hinder the influence of the Holy Ghost on a preacher, justifying their view on the grounds that "Jesus of Nazareth closed the sacred scroll before he began to preach."[4] Many, many years would pass before any General Baptist congregation either in England or America would even consider requiring its ministers to undergo formal theological training, much less think of organizing a seminary of their own. Moreover, initially the General Baptists did not believe in hymn singing as a part of worship, and most congregations observed four distinct ordinances in addition to a believer's immersion and the standard Protestant Lord's Supper or communion: imposition, or the laying on of hands after baptism as per Acts 19 and other biblical references; foot washing as described in John 13; the love or charity feast of I Corinthians 11 and the Book of Jude; and the anointing of the sick with oil as commanded in the fifth chapter of James.

In spite of the ups and downs of Stuart rule and the English Civil War, the General Baptists expanded rapidly from their London base all across southern and central England. By the year 1651 they had formed a thirty-congregation association of churches in the midland counties and later on even a national General Assembly. The first General Baptist church on the American continent was gathered by Ezekiel Holliman and Massachusetts exile Roger Williams. Though Williams did not long remain a Baptist, the church endured, and with three other small congregations formed from its evangelistic efforts it helped to organize the very first American Baptist association, the Rhode Island Yearly Meeting of General Baptists, in 1670. By 1729 the Yearly Meeting had expanded to eight churches in tolerant Rhode Island, one in New York City, and even two apiece in Puritan-controlled Massachusetts and Connecticut. The entire group was served by eight ministers. After a period of experimentation with written creeds to settle obscure doctrinal differences, the majority of General Baptist adherents both in Britain and America developed a brief, nonspecific, Scripture-based statement of faith emphasizing the so-called Six Principles of Hebrews 6: repentance, faith, baptism, the laying on of hands, the resurrection of the dead, and eternal judgement. For this reason they earned the additional nickname of Six Principle Baptists.

"Arminian" and noncreedal in their outlook though they might have been, the General Baptists certainly were no independents by any stretch of the imagination. Perhaps from their Mennonite ideological antecedents they inherited some very strong thoughts about the powers of governing bodies outside the local congregation; though they recognized that each local church had rights, both in the Old World and New it was expected, even demanded, that local churches delegate much of their authority to their associations, and the Rhode Island Yearly Meeting and its British cousins usually exercised a strict control by council. Early General Baptist association life was described most vividly by historian Robert Torbet:

> Among General Baptists there was a stricter control over the churches than among [the other branches of Baptists].... For example, a careful watch was maintained over the young people. In order to maintain their identity and witness as Baptists, they required their young folks to be married within the Baptist communion on pain of suspension for violation of the rule. Thus the Association and Assembly meetings "became great opportunities for matchmaking." Such practices as cockfighting, dancing and gambling were denounced.... Immorality and the slave trade were consistently looked upon as grievous sins ... discipline was strict. In a very real sense, General Baptists had developed in their organizational life a denominational consciousness which was felt by all its members. Indeed, it has been observed that their church order, to some degree, was more presbyterian than congregational in character.[5]

Of the eight General Baptist ministers laboring in the New England of Shubal Stearns's youth perhaps none was more intrepid than Valentine Wightman, great-grandson of the old martyr Edward Wightman mentioned earlier. Wightman gathered the first, and for many years the only, Baptist church in Connecticut at the southern seacoast town of Groton in 1705. A native of North Kingstown, Rhode Island, Wightman had been raised up to the ministry and ordained—if the American General Baptists' records are to be believed in this particular, and they do smack of a possible clerical error here—at the tender age of fifteen in 1696.[6] In spite of the oppressive rule of Governor Gurdon Saltonstall, Wightman remained a quiet, consistent practitioner of civil disobedience, although initially he was forced to post a two-hundred-pound bond even to stay in Groton. His efforts eventually earned the Connecticut Baptists a measure of relief from the colony's ecclesiastical taxes under Saltonstall's successor, Joseph Talcott. After more than two decades of nearly solitary ministerial labor at Groton, interspersed by occasional visits from Rhode Island preachers and one interesting brief escapade with a traveling evangelist named Paul Palmer that will be discussed later, Wightman finally gained a permanent colleague, Stephen Gorton, when he helped to organize a second Connecticut Six Principle church at nearby New London in 1726 and a third at Wallingford, twelve miles from New London, in 1731. Valentine Wightman became a strong advocate of hymn singing in worship, and these three congregations were probably the first of their sect in America to break tradition with conventional General Baptist forms in introducing hymns and hymnbooks to their services; it is not known what type of hymns they sang at first, if not the conventional psalms of their neighboring Puritans.

Less numerous but certainly more radical than the General Baptists were the Sabbatarians or Seventh Day Baptists, who were doctrinally related to the earlier group but believed that the Sabbath should be observed on Saturday as per Mosaic law. Organized as a sect in England mainly from followers of the millennial group of its day, the Fifth Monarchy movement, the Sabbatarians gathered their first church in America at Newport, Rhode Island, in 1672 and from thence slowly expanded in to Pennsylvania, New Jersey, and Maryland. In their early years in America, the Sabbatarians of New England experienced perhaps more persecution than any other Baptist group for their refusal to conform to conventional Sunday observances, which were enforced as law in both Massachusetts and Connecticut. But at least in some cases maltreatment may have come as a result of some Sabbatarians' propensity—they *were* the descendants of a millennial group, after all, and proportionately zealous—to criticize, and on occasion even interrupt, the Sunday worship of other Christians.

Ultimately the largest and most successful of the three early Baptist sects was the group known in the British Isles as the Particulars, and in the colonies as the Regulars. Originally these were essentially Puritan Independents, complete with five-point Calvinist theology, who had repudiated their belief in infant baptism in favor of believers' immersion and the traditional concept of church and state for religious liberty. In light of the modern, right-wing, "old-timey" conservative connotations of the title of "Regular Baptist," however, the group was progressive, refined, and innovative and is in fact the ancestor of most modern American Baptist groups that bear the name including, to a certain extent, the Southern Baptist Convention. Ironically, this is the group that the Old Landmarkers most often try to link all the way back to Jerusalem by an apostolic succession as well, usually by contending that a group of ancient Old Landmark or sometimes Primitive Baptists stayed hidden in a remote corner of Wales for twelve to fifteen hundred years and then associating all anti-Papist activity they can find by Lollards, Waldensian immigrants from France, and even the bizarre Cathar cult of Provence and Languedoc with these same so-called ancient Baptists. Some bandy about such esoteric names as the preachers "Archer Flavin," "Telletsman" and "Aaron Arlington" in a sort of pseudo-genealogy of similarly named churches like "Timto," "Lima Piedmont," and "Pontifossi," from old Jerusalem to a church called Hill Cliffe in Wales that was actually organized about 1650 rather than the 987 AD that they claim; others prefer tracing the succession through a church at Olchon on the English-Welsh border near the estates of the famous Lollard martyr Sir John Oldcastle. Either way, not a single link in the supposed chain can be verified by historical records until the middle of the seventeenth century except those of wishful-thinking nineteenth- and twentieth-century Old Landmark writers. The group even makes a great number of blunders in tracing the alleged succession in its American branches as well.

So much for the Old Landmarkers for now, though unfortunately the author must allude to them again from time to time simply to display how they have corrupted historical tradition. The author hopes that he can give an accurate enough account of religious events in America during Shubal Stearns's life to expose the follies of Old Landmark contentions for the same time period, many of which have kept the study of Appalachian mountain religion in such confusion. The Particular/Regular Baptists were an identifiable body in London by 1644, when a group of seven local Particular churches drafted and published a fifty-article statement of their beliefs, advocating standard Puritan Calvinist theology with the exception of the Puritan church-state concept, and believers' immersion rather than infant baptism. This First London Confession, as it came to be called, set the stage for considerable denominational growth both in England and Wales during Cromwell's rise to and tenure in power. Cromwell was extremely tolerant of the Particulars, and many served honorably in his New Model Army where they carried Particular Baptist doctrine into Ireland and Wales as well as throughout England. The group's Welsh base did become exceptionally strong with amazing speed, and a great number of America's original Particular Baptist immigrants came from Wales and settled in tolerant Pennsylvania, New Jersey, New York, Delaware, and South Carolina. The first three Particular churches in America, however, were organized by former physician John Clarke, at Newport, Rhode Island, in 1644 and at Swansea and Boston in Massachusetts subsequently. Like the General and Sabbatarian Baptists, these early New England Particulars received their share and more of the heavy hand of Puritan discipline. One group, having left the main Massachusetts colony for its remote Maine district, was driven from there as well in about 1682 and subsequently established themselves at Charleston, South Carolina, where, in years to come, they were joined by an ever-increasing number of Welsh Particular immigrants.

Unlike the General Baptists, both the Particulars in Britain and the Regulars in America were staunch believers in a formally trained ministry and the use of prepared pulpit discourses. The English Particulars founded a Baptist college at Bristol at a surprisingly early date in their history as an organized denomination; some well-to-do colonial Regular congregations imported graduates of this institution to fill their own pulpits much as the New England Puritans depended on Harvard and Yale at the same time. In years to come the American Regulars would found their own schools at Hopewell, New Jersey, and at Providence, Rhode Island. Likewise the Regulars believed in a paid ministry as opposed to the General Baptist preachers' custom of earning their living at secular employment.[7] And along with the great majority of Protestant denominations both in the Old Country and the colonies, the Regulars made a strong stance on the religious education of children. Although Sunday schools in the modern sense did not yet exist, most faiths employed catechisms for their members' young to memorize, and evidence exists that the American Regulars endorsed such a document for the benefit of their own churches at an early date—quite possibly the very same catechism, *Milk for Babes* by the famous John Cotton, used by the mainline Puritans themselves.[8]

In the latter years of the seventeenth century and the early part of the eighteenth, two events in particular occurred to further define the British and American Calvinistic Baptists as a denomination. One was the formation in 1689 of an English General Assembly of Particular Baptists that endorsed the adoption and publication of a second London Confession of Faith. Far from being an original document such as the Confession of 1644, this second creed was actually a 1677 Baptist adaptation of the articles of faith developed by the Presbyterian Puritans in conjunction with the Long Parliament between 1643 and 1645, when it appeared that the English Civil War would cause the abolition of the Anglican episcopacy and Presbyterianism would take its place as the state religion. Though this never occurred, the Westminster Confession remained as the standard doctrinal statement of the Presbyterian Church, and its stepdaughter, the Second London Confession of the Baptists, provided the same service for the Particular/Regular Baptist family. There was, however, some disagreement as to how strong a Calvinism should be preached. The 1677/1689 Confession contained separate chapters or articles avowing equal belief both in "God's Decree," or foreordained election by grace (chapter 3), and man's free will and consequent individual accountability for his sins (chapter 9), allowing for a balance between the two equally biblical doctrines. Even so, all too many Particular ministers, notably Dr. John Gill and his followers, concentrated almost solely on "God's Decree" and refused even to address a sermon of repentance to sinners. Others emphasized the "free will" aspect of the doctrine or adopted a middle-of-the-road approach that allowed them to be almost as evangelistic as the General Baptists.

The second major defining act of the denomination in America occurred in 1707, with the organization of the Philadelphia Baptist Association from five Regular Baptist churches in Pennsylvania, New Jersey, and Delaware. Though small and hardly representative of all American Regular congregations at its inception, the Philadelphia Association grew very rapidly to include Calvinistic Baptist churches all the way from Nova Scotia to northern Virginia before fostering the establishment of other regional associations formed on the same organizational plan. Even though the General Baptists' Rhode Island Yearly Meeting antedated Philadelphia Association by thirty-seven years, many historians have mistakenly identified Philadelphia Association as the "mother" institution of American Baptists, perhaps at least in part from propaganda issued by the Regular Baptists and their descendants themselves.

Both the tiny scattering of Regular Baptist churches in Massachusetts and Rhode Island and the General Baptist Yearly Meeting were small albeit integral parts of the religious makeup of Shubal Stearns's New England, but for most of his early life it is doubtful that he was more than marginally aware of their existence. At the age of nine in 1715, he and his family moved from the outlying areas of Boston to a new, rural north central Connecticut village known as Tolland. The first Stearns's grant, in the name of Shubal's uncle John, was located in the hills about two miles east of Tolland's courthouse. Interestingly, this hilly section of Connecticut is within the northeast corner of the Appalachian range, and in Shubal's youth Tolland was rustic and rather backwoodsy even for that time and place. A large portion of the southern end of the township was claimed by the legatees of Joshua Uncas, sachem, or chief, of the Mohegan Indians later made famous by the exciting but distorted literary fantasies of James Fenimore Cooper, and by 1720 only twenty-eight white families including the Stearns had settled there. Though Shubal's father served at different occasions in such local offices as "proprietor clark" and selectman, the family was quiet and unremarkable, wresting its living from the rocky northern Connecticut soil along with their neighbors and attending Tolland's parish church—whose first minister, Rev. Stephen Steel, arrived from Hadley, Massachusetts in 1720 and kept charge of the Tolland parish literally throughout the remainder of Shubal's life in Connecticut[9]—with perhaps only a conventional form of piety.

In keeping with their original concept of a theocracy or Bible commonwealth, the original Puritan settlers had insisted on a conversion experience, in terms of Calvinistic doctrine, as a prerequisite to full church membership and consequently any responsible community position as well. The political weakening of the theocracy concept, though, coupled with a gradual cooling in religious fervor, had caused Puritan leaders in both Massachusetts and Connecticut to relax their standards. As historian James Tull has noted, they eventually came to view the conversion experience as an occurrence so inward and subtle that it could happen, possibly, without even being completely recognized by an individual. Consequently anyone who lived a respectable moral life, "owned" the church covenant in the periodic, quasi-revivalistic community purification rite celebrated for that purpose in every Puritan parish, and maintained a socially acceptable observance of church duties, was presumed to be converted.[10] Church membership was thus greatly boosted at the expense of spirituality. The problem was compounded by the adoption of the so-called Halfway Covenant as endorsed by premier Puritan clergyman Solomon Stoddard. The Halfway Covenant allowed at first limited, and later on full, church membership for all persons unconverted as well as converted with the reasoning that "persons baptized in infancy, even though not professing Christians, were connected somehow to the visible church and were capable of passing along to their children the same degree of membership that they themselves possessed."[11]

In 1708 the Connecticut General Court had ordered the churches in each county of the colony to send lay and clerical delegates to a conference at the township of Saybrook for the purpose of religious reform, but their deliberations apparently dealt only with matters of church governance. The resulting statement of their labors, known as the Saybrook Platform and enacted into law by the colony in October of that year, further established the Halfway Covenant by instituting a presbyterian church rule with ministerial associations to oversee and approve clerical ordinations, county organizations to enforce discipline within the churches under their care, and a General Association of ministers to supervise the whole of the colony's ecclesiastical affairs. Thus it appears that Shubal Stearns was baptized at his birth as an Independent and bred a Presbyterian, though the only difference between the two was a matter of church governments in the Massachusetts and Connecticut colonies—and really, the Halfway Covenant made the difference matter less.

On March 6, 1726/1727—in those days New Year was not celebrated in New England until March 25—Stearns married Sarah Johnston of Lexington, Massachusetts, perhaps having met her on a visit to his old grandfather at nearby Lynn; in any case, Tolland was so small and isolated one may speculate that many young men of his generation were forced to leave the township simply to find brides not related to them. Even so, first-cousin marriages were then common. Shubal settled down with Sarah in Tolland, undoubtedly on or near the original Stearns grant, as the head of his own household. Little is known of the couple's early domestic life, but although Shubal and Sarah never had any children of their own, Shubal's position as the eldest son of a large family in patriarchal New England probably gave him a close and perhaps almost paternal relationship with his younger brothers and sisters and their families. These included brothers Isaac, who married Rebecca Johnson or Johnston, possibly a sister of Sarah; Ebenezer, who married first Elizabeth Young and second Anna Field; Peter, who married Hannah Stinson, his first cousin; and sisters Rebecca Ruth, who married Jonathan Paulk or Polk; Elizabeth, who married Enos Stinson, another first-cousin union; Mary, who married Joseph Hatch; Sarah, who married Jeremiah Hatch, Joseph's brother; and Martha, the latter daughter being the "baby" of the family and twenty years younger than Shubal. Much evidence exists that Shubal and his baby sister were extraordinarily close, and more than any of his other siblings she may have seemed more like a daughter than a sister to him. Whatever his and Sarah's family status, though, they remained in Tolland as a simple farm couple—in fact, an Appalachian farm couple—and thus at the same point in time in which good old Ben Franklin had struck out for Philadelphia to make his name and fame as a printer, pamphleteer, journalist, philosopher, and political analyst, Shubal Stearns, at the same age, seemed destined—predestined, even— to a life and death in rural obscurity.

All that would change, however, with the development of an evangelical minority party within the Church of England known as the Methodists, the labors of a peculiar English evangelist named George Whitefield, and a mid-eighteenth-century phenomenon in the British dominions known as the Great Awakening.

2
RUDE AWAKENING
1740–1751

> It was a matter of speculation to me . . . to observe the extraordinary influence of his oratory on his hearers, notwithstanding his common abuse of them, by assuring them they were naturally half beasts and half devils.
>
> —Benjamin Franklin, of George Whitefield

Once, when speaking to his daughter advising her to keep up regular church attendance despite the imperfections she might encounter in ministers, Benjamin Franklin observed that pure water had often been known to issue from very dirty earth. One wonders whether Franklin, who was personally acquainted with George Whitefield and once let him take lodgings above his print shop in Philadelphia, might have been thinking of the famous Methodist revivalist when he penned the maxim, but this may be an unfair guess; there is every evidence that Franklin genuinely liked Whitefield, though he consistently resisted Whitefield's unceasing efforts to convert him from Deism.

Still, though evangelists are vital tools in any religious movement, both in ancient and modern times, they have often been known to be impulsive, quick on the draw, and temperamental, sometimes suffering persecution for poor judgment as much as or more than for the causes they espouse, and frequently leaving theological loose ends and questions behind them for calmer, more thoughtful ministers and laymen to clear up while they speed merrily off to their next field of labor. In this sense George Whitefield fit Franklin's metaphor perfectly; though without question he was the most successful evangelist ever to preach on the American continent and probably the primary catalyst for the explosive religious revival in Britain and its American colonies since called the Great Awakening, Whitefield was also one of the most quirky individuals anyone would ever care to meet. Slightly cross-eyed as the result of a childhood bout with measles, more than slightly prissy and effeminate perhaps from the lack of a strong father figure in his youth, George Whitefield combined an immense talent in public speaking and radically novel pulpit techniques with the habits of a finicky old maid, of whom it was once said that "he did not think he should die easy if his gloves were out of place."[1] The contradictions between his personal and public lives seemed unending: outwardly avowedly ready to suffer any type of persecution that the cold, sinful world might throw at a Christian minister, Whitefield was literally petrified at the mere thought of physical violence against his own person. He made no less than thirteen Atlantic crossings during the course of his ministry in a day when such trips were never taken for pleasure although he was equally terrified of shipwreck and drowning, once frankly confessing that his wife was braver aboard ship than he was. And although he consistently made dramatists and the theater a target of the hottest invective in his sermons, he himself had seriously studied drama in his youth and brought every bit of his considerable dramatic skill to the forefront when he was in the pulpit. The delicately built, physically cowardly evangelist was as bold as a lion once he assumed the stage, be it inside a cathedral or in the middle of an open field.

Along with Scottish Presbyterians Ralph and Ebenezer Erskine, the American Tennant brothers, and the Welsh Calvinistic Methodist Howell Harris, he very nearly made the words "revival" and "dissent" synonymous. Yet Whitefield, whose ministry both fed and was fed by the work of all these men, became the great revival's premier preacher while keeping his own labors within the borders—just barely—of the Church of England, with which he often quarreled but never broke his affiliation. His career was wildly successful but decidedly odd, and in one of its unusual twists and turns, Shubal Stearns found his life's calling—and this in spite of the fact that the only time Whitefield appears to have been advised of Stearns's work, the great preacher disowned any connection with it.

Born at Bristol, England in 1714, Whitefield was brought up by his widowed mother and older brothers and sisters and encouraged by them to prepare himself for a career in the Established Church. After a serious flirtation with the idea of becoming an actor instead—he excelled especially at the time-honored Shakespearean custom of dressing as a female and playing an actress's part, by his own admission often taking as many as three days to get himself in character for the role he was to play—he matriculated at Pembroke College, Oxford, as a "servitor" who earned much of his tuition by working as a lackey for wealthier, more nobly born students. Here he met the brothers John and Charles Wesley, who by this time had already organized their famous "Holy Club" at Oxford, dedicated to the spread of the Gospel at the university and the poor parts of town around it and from which would grow the great Methodist movement. In spite of his acting experience, Whitefield had been a conventionally observant Churchman most of his adult life, but after he met and heard the preaching of the Wesleys he experienced an extended period of despondency that both shocked and puzzled him. During this time he tried but failed to find spiritual peace in good works and self-mortification, but his depression was followed by an ecstatic conversion of the type that he and the Wesleys equated with the biblical reference in John 3 to being born again. Though the Wesleys and Whitefield would remain loyal if controversial Anglicans throughout their ministries, between themselves they would come to differ greatly in certain points of doctrine. The Wesleys were thorough Arminians who developed a sanctificationist, perfectionist theology that would form the basis for "Wesleyan" Methodism as well as its later descendant Holiness-Pentecostal movement, while Whitefield's "travail" and subsequent born-again experience made him a consistent Calvinist who saw no good in the human race except that imputed to it by God's grace. Still, Whitefield never did accept the "I" of the five-point Calvinist acronym; he felt that sinners were drawn to God through grace in Christ and that alone, but once that drawing occurred a sinner had the option of heeding it or resisting it. Consequently he was every bit as evangelistic as the Wesleys and perhaps even more so.

After completing his studies at Oxford in 1736, Whitefield was ordained by the Church as a deacon, the office just below that of elder or priest in the Anglican hierarchy, and he began his ministry along conventional lines. He was gifted with an extraordinarily loud, resonant voice, and he soon discovered that his forte as a preacher lay in using it to its full capacity with extemporaneous sermons into which he could work his dramatic talents, often even acting out the Scriptural roles of the biblical characters of whom he spoke. After making himself something of a minor sensation in temporary and guest preaching appointments across southern England, Whitefield accepted a missionary position in the new colony of Georgia, replacing the Wesley brothers who had filled the same mission for a brief, unfruitful season. At the Georgia mission Whitefield was much more successful than the Wesleys ever had been, and here in the New World he finally hit upon a plan for his life's work. He already had a burning desire to be a great, traveling evangelist, spreading the gospel of the New Birth wherever he went, and under his circumstances it almost seemed like a pipe dream; there was no such office in the Church of England, and he needed a specific assignment or station, called a "living," to be eligible for full ordination. Whitefield hit upon the idea of founding an orphanage in Georgia, with himself as director and several of his new Georgia friends as trustees to oversee the institution's mundane operations. He planned to assume the responsibility of soliciting funds for its operating expenses through itinerant preaching tours, thus opening the entire domain of the United Kingdom as a field for charitable contributions and, more importantly to him, born-again evangelism, while he technically maintained the "living" required for full Anglican ordination. As priest and director of a legitimate charitable enterprise of the Church he would be welcome, ostensibly, in any Anglican parish; as a Calvinist, equally welcome among Independent and Presbyterian Puritans; and as a Methodist, not in the later denominational sense of the word, he would proclaim and exhort in behalf of the New Birth in Christ wherever he went.

At the time Whitefield figured out his ministerial calling, Great Britain and its colonies were ripe for the kind of evangelism he represented. In Wales, Howell Harris, himself originally an Anglican with Calvinistic Methodist leanings, was beginning an itinerant ministry of the type Whitefield visualized, perhaps not so much with a specific "living" as simply the Welsh bardic tradition as its basis. In years to come, Whitefield would labor frequently with Harris in Wales and Scotland, and Harris played matchmaker between Whitefield and his Welsh bride, Elizabeth James. In Scotland, Ralph and Ebenezer Erskine gave revival a hypercalvinistic or extreme predestinarian flavor with the organization of their Associate, or Seceder, Presbytery, their main weapon the hundred-plus-years-old tradition of sacramental or communal revivals of which Deborah Vansau McCauley speaks so eloquently, and which Whitefield was to incorporate into his own services by closing them with the administration of the sacraments. In Pennsylvania and New York, William Tennent and his sons, inspired in part by the preaching of Dutch Reformed pastor Theodorus Frelinghuysen, had begun to emphasize the importance of experential conversion among their own middle-colony Presbyterian congregations. Even the old Halfway Covenant advocate Solomon Stoddard and his grandson and successor, Rev.

Jonathan Edwards of Northampton, Massachusetts, had given the old Puritan community covenant-owning ceremony a more revivalistic flair. Not long before Whitefield's ordination Edwards had led his parish at Northampton as well as several surrounding it through a dramatic series of meetings during which great numbers of backcountry New Englanders had claimed conversion in preparation to their annual "owning" of their covenant.

The Baptists of America also had at least one pre-Whitefield revivalist, although their experiences with him proved far from happy in most cases. The evangelist in question was Paul Palmer, mentioned in the last chapter in connection with Valentine Wightman in Connecticut, and almost no particulars are known of his life outside of his erratic ministry. Both his birth and death dates are unrecorded, although it is fairly certain he was a Maryland native, but he entered the stage of history with his baptism by Rev. Owen Thomas, pastor of the Philadelphia Association's Welsh Tract Church in Delaware. Palmer thus began as a Calvinistic Regular Baptist, but none of Philadelphia Association's records in connection with Welsh Tract Church ever mention his name and it is not likely that he preached much, if any, while he belonged there. Probably between 1710 and 1718, Palmer moved to Connecticut and later claimed to have been ordained there in 1720 or before;[2] as Valentine Wightman's Groton Church was the only Baptist congregation in the entire Connecticut colony at the time, and as the Rhode Island Yearly Meeting never disputed his claim although he gave the group ample cause to deny any connection with him if it truthfully could have done so, we must assume that Palmer had changed his affiliation to General Baptist, united with Wightman's church, and been ordained there by the older preacher and some of his Rhode Island colleagues. There were a great number of Palmers in the Groton/Stonington area, and he may have come there initially to visit relatives. After his ordination Palmer is supposed to have labored briefly in New Jersey and Maryland, baptizing nine people in the latter colony but not staying to organize a church, and soon after he settled in the northeastern corner of North Carolina, near the southeastern Virginia border. Here he joined forces with a small, struggling General Baptist church at Burleigh on the Virginia side, made up of mostly English immigrants and led by preachers Robert Nordin and Richard Jones. Between 1720 and 1727 he preached extensively in northeastern North Carolina, evidently organizing the first Baptist church in the colony there in the latter year. Before his death, which occurred most likely in the late 1730s or early 1740s, he seems to have taken part in the gathering of no less than fifteen more congregations in the area, which apparently met in a yearly conference much like the Rhode Island General Baptists' Yearly Meeting.

It was during this time at the end of his life that Palmer's erratic attitude towards his ministry became apparent. Nowhere is it recorded that he served a single one of these sixteen churches as pastor, evidently preferring to ordain young converts to the ministry, with some help from the Burleigh Church in Virginia, to fill pastoral posts while he concentrated on itinerant evangelism. Even here, though, he seems to have had no clear concept or philosophy of the message he was supposed to be preaching: from all available evidence he concentrated on the rite of immersion almost exclusively, baptizing candidates often simply upon their acceptance of the ordinance and a promise to "be more religious in the future." In addition, he very well may have employed the tactic known now in the rural American Southeast as "overpersuasion"—enthusiastically but overwhelmingly trying to talk candidates into making an oral profession of faith long before they felt ready to do so without his badgering. One of his subsequent North Carolina ministerial associates later indicated that Palmer's cadre of ministers were willing to baptize by firelight, lest their candidates should get out of the notion of it before morning.[3] Thus, though some of his converts were undoubtedly genuine, Palmer left behind him a great number of "dipped" individuals, perhaps even young children, who scarcely had any idea of what immersion and church membership implied. He even managed to stir up confusion during his one known trip back to New England, about 1730; while on the journey he helped ordain a preacher who went by the name of Henry Loveall, who later turned out to be an escaped convict from Long Island named Desolate Baker (yes, one name sounds as melodramatic as the other) and who used his position in the General Baptist ministry for several years as a cover for his real identity as well as additional questionable activities. Though Palmer was censured by the Rhode Island Yearly Meeting for this act, he nonetheless recommended Loveall/Baker to his Maryland acquaintances and converts, and the impostor actually organized the Maryland colony's very first Baptist church as well as another, on Opequon Creek near the Potomac River in what is now the eastern panhandle of West Virginia, before being discovered again and slipping off into obscurity. After Palmer's death, all of the churches he had been involved with except four or five in North Carolina had to apply to the Regular Baptists of Charleston and Philadelphia for aid in bringing their organization under control; the tiny remnant that stayed unaffiliated with the Regulars is now claimed by the modern National Association of Free Will Baptists as the southern branch of its ancestry.

We left George Whitefield ready to travel to England to get his "living" approved and be ordained by the Bishop of London, who was in control or "had the cure" of all the Anglican churches in the American colonies. Once this was accomplished, in January 1739, the burgeoning Great Awakening seemed to turn on Whitefield's own ministry as a fulcrum. The Bishop, thinking he had rid himself of one of the ringleaders of the increasingly vocal Methodist party in the Church by granting Whitefield's requests, soon had an awakening of his own—perhaps not a great one, but certainly rude. With his ordination and his living securely tucked under his belt, Whitefield immediately began a trial run in London of the evangelistic methods that would become hallmarks of the Great Awakening over the next thirty years, techniques not tailored to win the approval of conventional, conservative clergymen. It all began with the "St. Margaret's Affair" on February 4, 1739, when Whitefield was invited to preach in a London parish church by a group of "friends" who ostensibly had secured the parish rector's permission for the appointment. As it happened, though, these "friends" turned out to be "several lusty fellows" who, with or without Whitefield's knowledge, commandeered the pulpit for Whitefield while "the proper Preacher was lock'd into his pew."[4] The entire ludicrous proceeding prompted almost all the outraged rectors of the London parishes to close their pulpits to their flamboyant young colleague. Whitefield seized the opportunity to interpret their response as "persecution," publicize it for all it was worth, and begin holding outdoor "field" meetings where the "persecutions" of rectors, churchwardens, and the like could not reach him. These outdoor gatherings, similar to the sacramental revival gatherings that were already a tradition in Scotland and Ulster, quickly became an institution of New Birth evangelism and created a format to be copied first by Baptists, in ways that will be shown subsequently, by Presbyterians, and later by Methodists after the Wesleys' followers organized a denomination in their own right. Unfortunately, given their origin after the St. Margaret's Affair, they also gave the adversarial spirit between Whitefield's Methodism and mainline Anglicanism an avoidable, perhaps unnecessary boost.

After making an appointment for one of these meetings at a specified time and place, Whitefield and his Methodist friends would draw in and focus the crowd by singing some of the new evangelistic hymns penned by Charles Wesley, Isaac Watts, John Newton, and Augustus Montague Toplady and set to the music of then-popular and mostly minor- and modal-keyed broadside ballads. Though Whitefield may have scorned the high liturgy of the Church of England, one or more of these songs, whose lyrics almost always dealt with basic theological propositions, served as a powerful liturgy within themselves. The group would proceed to prayer, after which Whitefield, in roaring voice, would deliver an extemporaneous sermon based on one or more evangelical doctrines and that, often as not, would be copied in shorthand by a clerk for publication later. At the close of his sermons he would collect donations for his orphanage, but much more important to him was the opportunity to exhort sinners to pray for the experience of the New Birth in Christ. As an end to the services, Whitefield, perhaps unconsciously, again echoed the tradition of the Scotch-Irish Presbyterians by setting communion for the crowd, in which all those joyfully born-again were invited to participate as a means of declaring their newfound faith. With some variation, the essentials of Whitefield's methods have survived to this day as standard revival techniques.

After another whirlwind junket of southern English towns during which he continued to ruffle as many Anglican rectors' feathers as sermons he preached, Whitefield sailed back to Georgia to deliver funds and inspect the progress of his new orphanage. Before the year was out he had traveled northward as far as the middle colonies for another itinerant tour, continually adding increasingly vitriolic rhetoric against the Bishop of London and his adversaries in the St. Margaret's Affair to his fiery preaching. In Pennsylvania he met the Tennants and enjoyed great success among their conversion-oriented "New Side" Presbytery, which readily assimilated the fruits of his preaching into their own cause.

Up to this point Whitefield had caused no actual breach in the Established Church he represented except the making of more Methodists who, like him, regarded themselves as loyal Churchmen adhering to pure biblical doctrine rather than as schismatics out to establish a new denomination, and he interacted with the New Side Presbyterians similarly without incident. The last leg of this particular tour, though, a brief stopover in Williamsburg, Virginia, from December 14 to 16, 1739, proved entirely different and set the stage for all that would follow over the next few years. Whitefield's few Williamsburg meetings appear to have attracted listeners from as far as three and four counties away; many of these spread the news of the preacher's evangelistic Calvinism and his dynamic pulpit mannerisms within their own communities, kindling enough interest among the general population of eastern Virginia to inspire the widespread purchase and reading of the printed texts of some of his sermons. Thus provoked, a sizable group of small farmers and mechanics in the east central county of Hanover became dissatisfied with their traditional Anglicanism in spite of Whitefield's own standing in the Church. Led by one Samuel Morris, who is supposed to have been a bricklayer by trade, they built themselves a meetinghouse and began to absent themselves from their regular parish services to hear Morris read religious tracts and Whitefield's published sermons, and to ape his castigations of the mainline Anglican clergy for their "degeneracy." Quickly falling foul of the colonial authorities with such statements as their Whitefield-inspired suggestion that the Bishop of London might even be an "unconverted man," Morris and some of his followers were hailed into county court, fined, and called upon to give an account of their behavior. Had Whitefield been as dedicated a pastor as he was an evangelist, he might have made stalwart Anglican Methodists out of Morris's entire flock and things might have turned out differently; as it was, Morris and his followers were so uncertain of themselves apart from the reference point of their dissent that they hesitatingly described themselves as "Lutherans" simply because they recalled the name of Martin Luther as that of "a noted Reformer, and that his Doctrines were agreable [sic] to our Sentiments."[5]

In spite of sporadic government harassment, these self-proclaimed "Lutherans," who were hardly even aware of the existence of the established denomination of the same name, gradually spread their message and their "reading houses" into Goochland, Caroline, and Louisa Counties, but by the middle of 1743 all seemed to have had their fill of the simple "Lutheranism" with which their interest in Whitefield had left them. Morris and the others sent a party of men to the Blue Ridge to invite William Robinson, an evangelical Presbyterian missionary working among some Scotch-Irish immigrants there under license from Governor Gooch, to come and preach to them, and three or four years later the Tennents' New York Presbyterian Synod formally adopted the Morris group and sent Rev. Samuel Davies to be their permanent minister. Under Davies's guidance they finally got their "reading houses" licensed under Virginia law, although it appears that the colonial government made occasional efforts to suppress them at least until 1759. Although George Whitefield eventually learned of this group and more or less endorsed its actions, he had pretty much left his brave Virginia adherents to their own devices. Like a genial but thoughtless cowbird, he had dropped the fruits of his labor in a nest for someone else to raise and had sped merrily off to greener, uncultivated fields. We left him, as the reader will recall, in Williamsburg at the close of his 1739 preaching tour; after another trip back to Georgia and his orphanage he headed northward once again in 1740, this time for a series of meetings in New England.

Hyperbole allowed, the most accurate assessment of Whitefield's autumn 1740 New England tour relates that the region "had never seen anything like it before, except at the time of the general Earthquake."[6] The earlier Stoddard and Edwards revivals, based as they were on the "covenant-owning" New England community purification ritual, had paved the way for Whitefield's preaching both in Massachusetts and Connecticut, and Whitefield's Calvinistic Anglicanism made him welcome both in the Independent-controlled and the Presbyterian colony; initially he was received cordially, much as he had been in the middle colonies the previous year. Even so, the story of the St. Margaret's Affair had followed Whitefield to New England, and not long after he settled in to conduct his meetings in Massachusetts he was barred from a good many churches there. He compensated with the same retaliatory tactics that had borne so much fruit in and around London; however, this time his opponents were the hierarchy of mainline New England Congregationalism and Presbyterianism. In the process, the state churches of the New England colonies were turned literally inside out, with thousands of respectable Halfway Covenanters and perhaps even a number of ordained deacons, ruling elders, and ministers mourning their sins and lack of relationship with God to profess an ecstatic New Birth in Christ afterward.

Though Whitefield departed the region almost as quickly as he had the Middle Colonies the year before and did not return until 1746, the work characteristically developed a mind of its own. Many New England ministers caught the evangelistic fire, began to preach "experimental religion" after the manner of the great exhorter, and conducted their own itinerant tours. Within a year of Whitefield's visit, Gilbert Tennant came up from Pennsylvania to lead a second wave of revival meetings almost as dramatic as those of Whitefield himself. Tennant's work was supplemented by the spirited but haphazard work of the fiery, erratic James Davenport. Even Jonathan Edwards, who had tried to temper the enthusiasm generated during his own pre-Whitefield labors with exhortations toward reason and reflection and who was generally regarded as the best-educated minister in the New England of his day, found himself caught up in the effects of the Awakening. As a guest speaker at the Enfield, Connecticut, parish church on July 8, 1741, he read a written discourse he had preached before his flock at Northampton the previous summer with but little response or appreciation from his congregation. At Enfield, however, *Sinners in the Hands of an Angry God* made history, causing nearly the entire assembly to yell and shriek, roll in the aisles and crowd up into the pulpit to beg him to stop speaking.[7] Still alternately praised and condemned in the annals of American literature, the sermon is indeed an apt reflection of the feelings generated during the Awakening.

For his own part, Jonathan Edwards, though still extremely distrustful of emotionalism, consistently supported both Whitefield and the Great Awakening, having come to the conclusion that the Revival was "in general from the Spirit of God" despite many unsettling side effects.[8] Other high-ranking Massachusetts and Connecticut Puritans of the secular arm, especially those in Connecticut trying to enforce the regulations of the Saybrook Platform, were not so liberal. Many in power denounced the Revival as a travesty of the traditional, sober Calvinism they considered to be the foundation of the New England colonies. The Revival's proponents, of course, quickly developed an opposing attitude, condemning the Halfway Covenant, the Saybrook Platform, and all forms of New England clerical traditionalism as nothing more than God-and-mammon politics, and as in Hanover County, Virginia, the die was cast for a major rupture in the Established Faith. Some churches and members opted for a connection with the Tennents' New Side Presbyterian Synod in New York over the Saybrook Platform Presbyterianism of the Connecticut colony; already mentioned in connection with Whitefield's Virginia dissidents, the Synod had been organized from three middle-colony presbyteries about the time of Gilbert Tennent's first New England tour in 1741. Others, perhaps more numerous, probably more vocal and certainly more extreme, organized "New Light" or "Separate" churches after the Independent form throughout eastern Massachusetts and Connecticut, and the Separate Congregationalists took shape as a denominational entity within four years of the Revival's beginning.

The New Side Presbyterians, though at odds somewhat with their parent denomination, retained the original group's organizational structure in terms of synod- and presbytery-based church supervision and missionary outreach, even boasting their own theological seminary in the so-called Log College in New Jersey that would become Princeton University. The Separate Congregationalists were more like Samuel Morris's Virginia "Lutherans" in terms of structure, or lack thereof, but the Separates had a greater spirit of independence. Instead of springing up from the labors of only one local congregation, the New Light group pieced itself together haphazardly during the decade after Whitefield's tour, from schisms in literally hundreds of Puritan parish churches in which the Halfway Covenant and/or the Saybrook Platform had become stale forces in the wake of the Revival's emphasis on the New Birth. In addition, the Separates by and large dismissed the paid clergyman as "too lazy to work and too proud to beg . . . who jumps into commission with a Lye [sic] in his mouth that he is moved by the Holy Ghost, when his highest Aim is a fat living."[9] Whereas Morris had only read tracts and sermon texts before his followers until he could formally secure the preaching services of the Presbyterians, the more outspoken New Lighters began to raise up from their midst unsalaried and untrained "farmer-preachers," with little or no formal education but a great deal of commitment to their calling and to the rural flocks they led. In their ministrations to these new, independent, and autonomous Separate churches, the New Light farmer-preachers, augmented by perhaps 130 parish ministers also swept up in the New Light cause from a total of possibly 400 parishes, proudly declared that "their faith and practice [came] the nearest to that of the first planters of New England, of any churches . . . in the land."[10]

Ironically, though, this much-touted faith and practice—probably the first recorded religious reference for an "old-time way" in American history—was enunciated more clearly by the Separates' mainline clerical opponents in their condemnation of it than by the Separates in their own defense. Witness the letter published in 1744 by the Associated Ministers of the County of Windham, in the extreme northeastern portion of Connecticut, listing "some of the most considerable errors of the Separates":

> 1) That it is the will of God to have a pure church on earth, in this sense, that all the converted should be separated from the unconverted. 2) That the saints certainly know one another, and know

who are Christ's true ministers, by their own inward feelings, or a communion between them in the inward actings of their own souls. 3) That no other call is necessary to a person undertaking to preach the Gospel, but his being a true Christian, and having an inward motion of the Spirit, or a persuasion in his own mind, that it is the will of God that he should preach and perform ministerial acts; the consequence of which is, that there is no standing instituted ministry in the Christian Church, which may be known by the visible laws of Christ's Kingdom. 4) That God disowns the ministers and churches in this land, and the ordinances as administered by them. 5) That at such meetings of lay preaching and exhorting, they have more of the presence of God than in his ordinances, and under the ministration of the present ministry, and the administration of the ordinances in these churches.[11]

By the time these events had started to take place in New England, George Whitefield was already busy elsewhere, crisscrossing the Atlantic and preaching both in the Old World and the New at a lightning pace. He had met Howell Harris in Wales and the Erskine brothers in Scotland, and his preaching in both places in their company was as dynamic as it had been on his 1740 New England tour. In the meantime, the New England New Light preachers labored on, and although few if any could match Whitefield's dramatic flair, they compensated by developing a distinctive preaching cadence based largely on Whitefield's own emotive style and embellished by a singsong, almost hypnotic chant of "nasal quality."[12] The "New England Holy Tone," as it quickly came to be called, was given perhaps its best description by historian Robert Baylor Semple: "The Separates in New England had acquired a very warm and pathetic address, accompanied by strong gestures and a singular tone of voice. Being often deeply affected themselves when preaching, correspondent affections were felt by their pious hearers, which were frequently expressed by tears, trembling, screams, and exclamations of grief and joy."[13]

Though largely derided by modern historians, the New England Holy Tone was an effective means for a rural Separate Congregationalist evangelist to communicate his message of the New Birth in Christ—more often than not, according to the historians, with a repetitive, detailed account of his own born-again experience—to the rustic audience that comprised most of his field of labor. Interestingly, a chant style of preaching also seems to have followed the labors of Whitefield, as well as of Howell Harris in Wales, and probably as an effect of the same cause. Known as *hywl (hoo-ill)* from an ancient Welsh word that is best translated into English in this instance as "indescribable eloquence," the chant was not described in detail until 1876 by historian Erasmus Jones, but it had to have been a respected tradition among the rural Welsh by that year. Characterized by "spontaneously composed, spoken/sung/chanted sermons and executed in a minor key and usually marked by a great variety of intonations," *hywl* was more particularly noted by Jones as follows:

> The best description I can give of this peculiarity is this: it is the application of sentences in a chanting style to portions of the minor scale. The minister is never at a loss how to apply the words to the melody; they appear to run together as by mutual attraction. The sentence is started, for instance, on E minor. The minister has his own peculiar melody. It ranges there from the first to the fifth, often reaching the octave, and then descending and ending with sweet cadence on the key-note. I am sure that in the genuine *hywl* the intonations are always in the minor mode. The introduction and the deliberative parts are in the major, and the voice continues until the emotional point is reached; then it glides triumphantly into a thrilling minor, which generally continues to the close.[14]

The relationship between *hywl* and New England Holy Tone preaching, in terms of its significance to the ministry of Shubal Stearns, will be discussed later in this volume. For George Whitefield's part, by the time he returned to New England after his English, Welsh, Scottish, and additional colonial tours of 1741 through 1745, he was a changed man. An enthusiastic soul winner he was and would remain for the rest of his life: in his unflagging efforts to continue his evangelistic tours in support of his beloved orphanage, he ignored the steadily increasing symptoms of congestive heart failure that crept up on him, and he quite literally preached himself to death just short of his fifty-sixth birthday in 1770. He maintained his same broad ecumenism from first to last, whether preaching in the meetinghouses of nearly any sect that would permit him to do so or conducting his own spirited outdoor gatherings. However, by the time of Whitefield's second New England visit, he had been forced to take a hard look at his own motives and the consequences of his actions. He had preached in the middle colonies, Virginia, and New England believing that he represented a spiritual union of Christians of all denominations based on the experience of the New Birth in Christ, but his subsequent rocky relationship with the hypercalvinistic Erskine brothers and their ultrasectarian Scottish Seceder Presbytery had painfully impressed upon him the reality that he had played altogether too fast and loose with the tools of schism and sectarianism. The cause of born-again Christianity was flourishing now in all points where he had labored and along with it was an equal or greater measure of strife, hard feelings, and lack of Christian fellowship within the same fields of labor Whitefield had thought he could unite in one mind and one accord. His own wily, opportunistic accusations of persecution against himself and his ministry had been largely responsible for this state of affairs, coupled with the fact that he had given little or no thought for the pastoral care of his newly born-again converts. By now he realized his shortcomings quite as much as those who had initially opposed him. Reflecting upon his part in the beginnings of the Great Awakening, Whitefield sorrowfully noted: "Alas, alas. In how many things have I judged and acted wrong . . . Being fond of Scripture language, I have used a style too apostolical and at the same time I have been too bitter in my zeal. Wildfire has been mixed with it, and I find that I frequently wrote and spoke in my own spirit, when I thought I was writing and speaking by the assistance of the Spirit of God."[15] An outspoken and controversial preacher George Whitefield was and would remain, but henceforth he would always be scrupulously careful to temper his messages to discourage the type of religious schism and separation that had rocked both Virginia and New England in his wake during the early years.

Had not Whitefield been the flamboyant young peacock that he was during his early ministry, however, Shubal Stearns might have remained in the same obscure station in which we left him at the end of the previous chapter, and our story might never have taken shape. As it happened, though, he had been overpowered by Whitefield's preaching along with many of his relatives and neighbors—including his parents— and had experienced an ecstatic New Birth in Christ, and undoubtedly to good old Stephen Steel's indignation nearly the entire family had taken part in the formation of a Separate Congregational church in Tolland that Shubal now, in the tradition of an upright New Light farmer-preacher, served as Steel's rival pastor.

While as of yet he was no great evangelist, Stearns appears to have enjoyed a good reputation among the eastern Connecticut Separate community. Although few if any of his writings from this period survive, it is likely that the "errors" noted in the Windham Associated Ministers' letter quoted earlier, originating as it did from the county bordering Tolland, were the sum and substance of Stearns's own doctrinal outlook. A few historians believe that Stearns did not become involved in the New Light movement until Whitefield's second New England tour, but the weight of evidence appears to favor a 1740 conversion instead, perhaps with a ministerial ordination about the time of Whitefield's second visit. By 1746 Stearns was already deeply involved in a crusade to secure formal recognition for the Separate Congregational denomination by the Connecticut General Assembly and for legal sanction and protection under Great Britain's 1689 Toleration Act, a weighty matter that would not have been entrusted by the Tolland Separates to a new convert. The Assembly rejected petitions signed by Shubal Stearns and many other ministers both in 1746 and 1748 on the assumption, fair or not, that the New Light movement was headed and maintained by revolutionaries, but such legal persecution as the Separates were forced to endure was neither so lengthy or harsh as that perpetrated against earlier dissenter sects simply because of the sheer number of citizens involved in the dissent. It can be imagined, though, that Stearns himself at least received many a frosty look—and perhaps many a pulpit denunciation as well—from old Stephen Steel. In retrospect this seems sad; we will never know how well or how poorly Steel had gotten along with the Stearns family until the Great Awakening began, but he had begun his career in Tolland as a young man and had grown old there, and it is conceivable that they could have been close.

Stearns's wife Sarah appears to have been an equally enthusiastic Separate, as were his brothers Peter and Ebenezer, his sisters and brothers-in-law Enos and Elizabeth Stimson and Jonathan and Rebecca Polk, and even his parents. Martha, the "baby" of the family, was especially so, and it is perhaps a testimony of her oldest brother's fondness for her that he often let her take part in worship services in ways usually reserved for men. Described as "a lady of good sense, singular piety and surprising elocution," Martha "in countless instances melted a whole concourse into tears by her prayers and exhortations."[16] On June 23, 1747, Martha married Daniel Marshall, another New Light exhorter from the nearby town of Windsor and the son of Thomas and Mary (Drake) Marshall. Approximately the same age as Shubal Stearns and thus twenty-odd years older than Martha, Daniel Marshall had been wed previously to Hannah Drake, possibly a cousin, who had died relatively young and left him with one son, Daniel. Marshall himself had been converted at the age of twenty and had served the parish church at Windsor capably for many years as a deacon; he appears to have been industrious in a secular fashion as well, successfully managing a large, productive farm in the lower Farmington River valley. After his exposure to the Great Awakening, however, Marshall became as dedicated a New Light enthusiast as were so many in the Stearns family.

It is not known exactly when Daniel Marshall began preaching; he may have done a little exhorting even before the days of the Great Awakening in his office as deacon, as George Whitefield did in the first days of his missionary work. After the Whitefield revival, though, he and the Windsor church—or perhaps a schismatic faction—to which he belonged seem to have opted for the more organized but no less evangelistic New Side Presbyterian wing of the New Light movement over that of the Separate Congregationalists. At any rate, after 1747 Marshall and his young wife began a phenomenally active joint ministry that would endure through nearly forty years of labor together, the births of several children, and countless ups and downs. It began, oddly, with a then-common interpretation of certain biblical prophecies in light of the prejudices contemporary to the age. Several Old Testament prophets, including Ezekiel, Jeremiah, and Zechariah, as well as the Apostle John in the Book of Revelation, had spoken of a time in the distant future when all twelve tribes of the Nation of Israel should be united in peace and the worship of the Messiah. Believing that this wonderful era was near at hand and subscribing to the commonly held notion that the American Indians were the descendants of the Ten Lost Tribes of Israel, the Marshalls sold their fine farm and accepted a New Side missionary assignment to the Mohawks in the upper Susquehanna valley of Pennsylvania in order that their labors should hasten the millennial reign. Settling in an Indian village known as Onnaquaggy, Daniel and Martha began their work under the hardest of conditions, but their lives were brightened by the birth of their three oldest children as well as Daniel's—and probably also Martha's—"considerable success" at preaching.[17]

During this period Shubal Stearns may actually have considered encouraging his Tolland Separate flock to accept an affiliation with the New Side Presbyterians also, if for no other reason than that New Side membership would make for increased religious liberties for his parishioners. Despite the New England colonial governments' perceptions of the New Sides as revolutionaries and radicals, their acceptance of their parent group's doctrinal statement did ease their status in this regard. Stearns apparently owned a copy of the Presbyterians' Westminster Confession that was later passed down through one of his siblings' families as an heirloom; according to one source this document was still in existence in 1902 and bore evidence of being "well thumbed."[18] Even so, Stearns and most of his Separate contemporaries were extremely wary of accepting any written creed as such, preferring to uphold the Bible itself as their statement of faith than to limit themselves to the tenets of a man-made document, however Scripture-based those tenets might be. Though perhaps still as Calvinistic doctrinally as the Presbyterians even in their older Puritan form, the Separates' essential basis was the New Birth in Christ, and—at least at this point in time—the finer points of Calvinistic doctrine were as abstract to them as they had been to George Whitefield.

This relatively greater acceptance that the New Side Presbyterians enjoyed did give them a significant advantage over the Separates that may have prompted several other congregations of New England's Whitefield converts to join the evangelical Presbyterian faction: the creed-based institutions of the sect, like those of the Church of England that Whitefield had used so effectively for his own missionary purposes, made for greater coordination and thus greater freedom of movement for an intercolonial outreach than the Separates could ever know. The New Side Presbyterians' adoption of Samuel Morris's Virginia "Lutherans" is but one example of the fruits of this advantage. The loose confederation of independent churches that made up the Separate Congregational sect was limited, in many ways, to the cultural environment in which this faction of the New Light movement had sprung up, with little chance of organized outreach to other areas. While Daniel and Martha Marshall ministered to the Mohawks at Onnaquaggy, Shubal Stearns thus remained at Tolland with his flock, content for the time being perhaps with the thought that his New Birth preaching in and around his home was the sum and substance of his life. Little did he know that, in spite of the limits imposed upon him by the status of the Separate Congregationalists as well as his own outlook, within a few years he would enter a field of labor geographically larger than the entire settled area of New England and a period of wild, fevered preaching activity rivaling the work of George Whitefield and ending only with his own death. Before this state of affairs would unfold, however, Stearns's doctrinal perspectives were altered once again, slightly but significantly.

As the work of a famous evangelist had once changed the course of his life, so now would the labors of another itinerant, this time a man as petty and obscure as was Stearns himself: a crusty, outspoken young disciple of Valentine Wightman named Waitstill Palmer.

3

The "Garding in Closed"

1751–1754

> ... I being in the way, the LORD led me to the house of my master's brethren.
>
> —Genesis 24:27, King James version,
> a favorite text of Appalachian old-time Baptist preachers

In September 1743, in the aftermath of George Whitefield's heyday and during the most frenzied period of activity for his imitators, thirty-two-year-old Waitstill (or "Wait," as he was most commonly called) Palmer applied to the New London Ministerial Association for a license to preach in accordance with the guidelines of the Saybrook Platform. No evidence exists that Palmer, who was already deeply involved in the New Light movement, ever had any of the formal training expected of a clergyman of the mainline Connecticut State Presbyterian Church, and the application itself seems to have been gratuitously filed and a rebuff fully expected; like Whitefield before him, Palmer may have made the effort simply to be turned down so he could complain about persecution against himself afterward. At any rate, his application was rejected, and the young New Light exhorter and several of his friends in the parish churches of Stonington and North Stonington withdrew from the Established Faith to join the growing ranks of Separate dissenters within the colony. Rather than trying to gather another run-of-the-mill Separate congregation in Stonington, however, Palmer and his followers petitioned their old neighbor over in Groton, Valentine Wightman, for the ordinance of baptism by immersion and were organized by him as a Baptist church almost directly after their defection from the establishment. Shortly after the church's constitution, Palmer was ordained and installed as the flock's pastor.[1] Wightman and probably Stephen Gorton, still the closest other Baptist minister then available, officiated. This series of actions, which were considered radical even in those heady days and times, marked the beginning of a trend that would ultimately overshadow the work of both Separate Congregationalists and General Baptists in New England: the fusion of New Light evangelistic Calvinism and Baptist worship practice that came to cause the formation of a fourth American Baptist subdenomination, the Separate Baptists.

Though Palmer's Stonington Church was among the earliest Separate Baptist fellowships ever gathered, it is unlikely that it was the very first. That distinction probably goes to a Boston congregation that defected from the Regular Baptist church there during Whitefield's first New England tour. This body became so extremely Calvinistic that the famed British predestinarian Dr. John Gill presented it with a fine communion "set" and a valuable collection of books as a token of his endorsement of its doctrines. A small number of New England Separate Baptist churches were, like the Boston flock, breakaways from the three older Regular Baptist congregations active in New England before the Great Awakening, and some historians such as the Kentucky Baptist chronicler John Henderson Spencer were careful to emphasize this connection as the primary root of the Separate Baptist family tree. However, Spencer wrote in the 1880s for an audience that demanded pure Old Landmarkism served up consistently for breakfast, lunch, and dinner. While he certainly tempered the wind to suit the shorn lamb, even Spencer must have known that by far the greater percentage of early Separate Baptist churches were New Light Congregational and Presbyterian proselyte bodies, some adopting Baptist positions only by degrees over a period of years and most owing their growth and eventual success to the ministrations of the Rhode Island Yearly Meeting rather than those of the Regular Baptists, who took little or no interest in them until they had become a power in their own right.

The main reason for the great Separate Congregational reidentification with Baptist principles and practice was the conflict that ensued when the group, as a loose collection of independent churches determined to maintain that independence, attempted to reconcile some of its traditions and rites with the theology of the New Birth in Christ. If indeed true Gospel churches were to be composed only of born-again believers, the Separates reasoned, admission to both church membership and communion should be restricted to those who could honestly profess the experience of the New Birth. The baptism of infants, which technically made them members of the church under the sponsorship of their parents and godparents who were active church participants, seemed to deny such a strict scruple. Some Separate congregations wished to abandon infant baptism, others saw sufficient grounds to maintain it, and many were simply torn between their traditions and their theology. The denomination's loose, disjointed structure precluded any resolution to the disagreement that could be satisfactory to all parties. Into this melee entered the tough, resilient General Baptist itinerants such as old Wightman, who remained active as both pastor and evangelist until his death in 1747, his preacher son Timothy, his successor in the Groton pulpit Daniel Fiske, and their Rhode Island colleague Benjamin Pierce; when invited into Separate Congregational fellowships for preaching appointments, these men and others like them could and did make a strong case for the practice of believer's immersion as a prerequisite both for church membership and communion. Some congregations such as Wait Palmer's Stonington flock became Baptists outright, and others, such as the group at Middleboro, Massachusetts, pastored by Isaac Backus after his baptism by Benjamin Pierce, actually kept a foot in both immersionist and "pedobaptist" camps for some years, inviting the itinerants to immerse any of their members disposed toward the ordinance and yet maintaining infant sprinkling for those still inclined to it.

Actually, though, had the General Baptists handled this great state of flux in New England evangelism with a little more forethought than they did, they, rather than the Regular Baptists, might have successfully established their claim as premier spokesmen for the denomination in America, and in their own turn would have had revisionist historians attempting to trace their roots back to antiquity as the only biblical Christians. It has been noted already that the General Baptists were a close, standoffish little society both in the Old World and the New; though certainly more cosmopolitan than their Mennonite/Anabaptist antecedents, the Rhode Island Yearly Meeting still had strong overtones of an insular community of pietists. Likewise it has been noted that Paul Palmer's erratic and haphazard pre-Whitefield attempts at evangelism both in the middle colonies and the South had caused them no little embarrassment, though according to General Baptist historian Richard Knight, the Yearly Meeting did recognize the churches and the conference or association that Palmer gathered. The ministers of the Yearly Meeting of course took advantage of the wonderful opportunity that the Great Awakening gave for the advancement of the General Baptist cause, and their first efforts got the Separate Baptist movement on its true foundation. However, it soon came to an obvious case of Saul slaying his thousands and David his ten thousands; rather than leading the Separates docilely inside their close little community, the Generals looked on with increasing dismay as the Separates took General Baptist principle and practice and gave it their own distinctive flavor with their New England Holy Tone preaching and happy emotionalism, standing independently as a new group in their own right and actually leading many younger General Baptists away from the closeness of the Yearly Meeting. Moreover, the Separates seemed to gain the field in terms of doctrine as well, their then-popular Whitefield evangelistic Calvinism being adopted by increasing numbers of younger General preachers and then merged with the Generals' own traditional stance on the atonement. By the mid-1750s, Isaac Backus had even started referring to the churches of the Yearly Meeting in Rhode Island as Separate Baptist congregations and had voiced a prediction that all of the old General flocks would eventually become Separates.[2] Thus in 1758, the Yearly Meeting attempted to reestablish its own position and doctrinal stance by condemning its ministers' new and productive alliances with the New Light movement and challenging the Separate Baptists to join them or remain forever apart. If the group hadn't handled the affair in such an underhanded political way, the Generals might have brought the gambit off. As it was, and really as might have been expected from their heritage as tiny, insular communities of rural dwellers and urban small mechanics, the Generals took Daniel Fiske, old Wightman's successor in the Groton pulpit, made a scapegoat of him, crucified him, and held his example up as a warning to others. Witness the proceedings of the Yearly Meeting's 1758 general council session, in grammar, spelling, content, and overtones so hauntingly like a multitude of Appalachian old-time Baptist association minutes that this author has read. Fiske was charged with

> ... Joining in prair to God with som men that be not in Communion with our said Churches and had holden meetings with som of them in their Appointed places and attended thair meeting that wair so far from the True order of the Gospel of our Lord Jesus Christ that instid of Baptizing do in rume thairof a minister sprinkling of a littel Water on the heads of thair Members. The True Church of Jesus Christ thair four being considered as a Garding in closed, a Spring shut up, a fountain sealed and as one Aspoused to thair hed and husband Jesus Christ that all the members thairof may be presented as chaist virgens to Christ: The

said General Counsel meeting . . . withdraw thair communion from him untill he duly reform and make appeair to said Community a more chaist behaveyour to the Lord and walk with his Church and peopel in so sacred and spiritual Devotion. And thair was but two vote to the contrary.[3]

Perhaps the result of the Yearly Meeting's blatant railroading of Fiske could have been expected as well: meek obedience by most older members whose religious perspective had been shaped almost entirely by their community leaders, and rampant rebellion among the younger ones who had had a taste of successful labor in the Great Awakening. Most of the newer churches and congregants, already heavily influenced by and leaning toward the group the General Baptists now seemed to regard as the bastard children of their own "unchaist" ministers, simply withdrew from the Yearly Meeting over the next few years and went full-fledged into the Separate movement. Although General minister Wightman Jacobs did manage to gather a small new Yearly Meeting of General Baptist churches in eastern Connecticut's Windham County between 1750 and 1763, by 1770 even these congregations seem to have abandoned their union and become independent Separate Baptist churches as well.[4] The old church at New London, Connecticut, under the care of a young and evangelistic Rhode Islander named Joshua Morse after Stephen Gorton's ministry ended, left the old Yearly Meeting in 1760, and although the historic Groton flock, now under the leadership of Valentine Wightman's son Timothy after Daniel Fiske's harsh treatment at the hands of his Rhode Island brethren, stuck around until 1774, the congregation seems largely to have ignored its association's 1758 decision and proceeded to work with the Separates anyway.[5] In effect the old Yearly Meeting had become its own worst enemy; despite its members' and ministers' brave pre-Awakening dissenter stance and all the persecutions they had endured in New England, its 1758 decision to remain as "a Garding in closed" put it in the paradoxical position of the only organized American dissenter group actually to shrink in the aftermath of the Whitefield Revival. The Yearly Meeting carried on its work with only a handful of churches and ministers throughout the latter part of the eighteenth and all the nineteenth and twentieth centuries, and by 1977, the latest year for which the author has been able to obtain statistics for the group, the 307-year-old body had been reduced to three small congregations largely dependent on extradenominational aid to fill their pulpits and an organization based more upon the innovations of later Baptist groups than the institutions of its own history.[6]

During the same period that the General Baptists seemed bent on destroying their own influence, however, the Particular, or Regular, Baptists had tried the opposite tack and thus were growing by leaps and bounds. In 1742 the Philadelphia Association had published its own version of the Second London Confession with a small treatise of discipline attached, and the new document, called the Philadelphia Confession, set the standard for evangelistic Baptist Calvinism in the colonies for many years to come. Adopting a policy of inclusion toward the rapidly growing New England Separate Baptists, the Philadelphia Association recognized their legitimacy as independent Baptist churches and initiated a period of friendship with them until the Separates were finally ready to organize their own associations—under Philadelphia's friendly, but perhaps calculated influence, however, with the Philadelphia Confession as the standard of faith and doctrinal statement. The first such Separate-turned-Regular group was Rhode Island's Warren Association, organized with four churches at Providence in 1767; Isaac Backus was asked to be the clerk of the body's first session, and though he probably agreed with many or most of the articles of the Philadelphia Confession theologically, from a practical standpoint he was alarmed at the idea that the new association might try to assume the same strict church control as had the old General Yearly Meeting. After he arranged and prepared Warren's first minutes, he declared that he "did not see [his] way clear to join [the association] now, if ever." The association, under the leadership of Dr. James Manning, responded by spearheading a revision of Warren's constitution that included the stipulation that the association might not violate "the independency of particular churches, because it pretends to be no other than an *Advisory Council,* utterly disclaiming superiority, jurisdiction, coercive right, and infallibility."[7] Their fears of tyranny relieved, Backus's church and ten other likeminded Separate fellowships joined the Warren Association by 1772. Under similar circumstances the Stonington Association in Connecticut was organized in that year, with Joshua Morse as its first moderator.

Along the southern Atlantic coast, Philadelphia ministers and missionaries continued to act in the same progressive way. In 1751 the Charleston, South Carolina, Association was organized from the descendants of the old group run out of Maine in the 1680s as well as a good many Welsh and English immigrant congregations; to this as well as to Philadelphia itself were added most of the remnants of Paul Palmer's work in eastern North Carolina, reorganized in the 1750s as Regular Baptist churches and finally gathered in Quehuky, or Kehukee, Association in 1769. Even Henry Loveall/Desolate Baker's forlorn and mistreated flock in northern Virginia was reorganized and sustained by Philadelphia ministers, being admitted to that body in 1751 and later joined by a few other congregations in the Shenandoah basin that were all gathered in the Catoctin, or Ketocton, Association in 1766. Some of these actions will be discussed in more detail later in this work, but herein lies another, perhaps greater, paradox than even the one the General Baptists made for themselves: this post-Whitefield policy of inclusion and assimilation exercised by the American Regulars made them not only the supplanters of the General Baptists but the rewriters of history as well, as it was in Regular Baptist context that the Old Landmark movement first came into being, about a hundred years after the Philadelphia Confession was published, and at first mainly in the southwestern United States.

Meanwhile, with the passage of time and the waning of the Great Awakening, the Separate movement, both Congregational and Baptist, began to fade as well. Those churches still inclined to maintain infant baptism and reject immersion eventually were taken back into the folds of their respective state churches (Connecticut did not disestablish its state faith until 1818, Massachusetts not until 1833). Many of those Separate Baptist congregations that did not ally themselves with the Regular Baptists eventually joined Benjamin Randall's "Free Will Baptist Connexion," which was organized essentially on an Arminian theology, an "open" or nonrestricted communion, and a combination General Baptist/Quaker organizational structure by Randall in New Hampshire in 1780. Over time the Randall group grew out of New England to other regions of the United States, eventually combining with the few remnants of Paul Palmer's work not allied with the Regular Baptists; the group's modern entity, the National Association of Free Will Baptists, with its headquarters in Nashville, Tennessee, is probably the only multiregional American Baptist group that endorses the old General Baptist practice of foot washing as a part of the communion service. To return to the decline of the Separates, though, in the year 1817 the Groton Union Conference of Connecticut, formed in 1788 as the last remaining collection of mixed Separate immersionist and pedobaptist congregations, formally united with the Regular Baptists, and with its passing the great New Light–Separate movement became history.

Thus for his own part Wait Palmer, who was born in May 1711 and died at the ripe old age of 84 in 1795, was witness to a great deal of transformation among the New England Baptists between the beginning of his ministry in 1743 and the end of his life. As he was one of the very first actual Separate Baptist ministers, it would be pleasant to report that he was a key player in at least some of the events that brought stability, prosperity, and recognition to his adopted denomination, but it must be admitted that this was not Palmer's case. He may or may not have been related to Paul Palmer, the other noted disciple of Valentine Wightman who had moved to the southeastern Atlantic coast; be that as it may, Wait Palmer's own ministry had all the instability of Paul Palmer's with little comparable success. After Valentine Wightman's death, he appears to have worked more or less closely with both Timothy Wightman and Joshua Morse, and perhaps Daniel Fiske as well, at least for a time, but the relationship of his Stonington church to the Rhode Island Yearly Meeting in the years before Fiske was ousted is not known. Church records from Stonington during the period in question are completely nonexistent. Perhaps the Rhode Island General Baptists looked on the congregation simply as a branch of the old Groton church and regarded Stonington as being represented in the Yearly Meeting through the older congregation. This practice of churches having different "branch" or "arm" subcongregations in various locations was certainly a marked trait of late-eighteenth- and early-nineteenth-century American Baptists generally. On the other hand, Stonington Church could even have been an active member of the Yearly Meeting, the relationship ignored and forgotten as the Philadelphia Association and the Regular Baptists gained prominence in the territory. At any rate, Wait Palmer pastored the Stonington church for several years and apparently went on occasional itinerant preaching tours through eastern and central Connecticut as well; but it was known, and candidly admitted by his descendant Rev. Albert Palmer that

> Of Mr. Palmer's character little can be known ... and this we fear may be less favorable to him as a man, as a Christian, as a minister, than strict justice would demand. From all we have been able to gather respecting him, we should judge him to have been a man of strong and fixed prejudices, immovable in his decisions, and

somewhat austere and censorious in the exercise of his ministerial functions. He reproved with severity, and, without consulting consequences, followed out what he regarded as truth and duty. Still, his piety seems to have been of a mystical cast, which often . . . led him to renounce as wrong what was evidently right, and to hold as right what was evidently wrong.[8]

At least a portion of the latter observation appears to have been inferred from the record of a serious difficulty that arose between Palmer and his Stonington flock during the middle 1760s. Though he had carried on an itinerant ministry for several years already, after his wife's kinsman Eleazar Brown also began to preach at Stonington, Palmer once more petitioned, or perhaps demanded, permission from the church to "travel and preach the Gospel wherever God might open the way before him." The Stonington congregation readily gave its blessing to their pastor and his work, but after he had baptized Simeon Brown, founder of a second Baptist church in Stonington, in 1764, Palmer threw his own flock into confusion by suddenly demanding a stated salary for his services. The memory of the weight of the Saybrook Platform still being heavy on the members' minds, they responded by accusing him of being "actuated by a hireling spirit" and refused to pay him. Palmer then compounded the problem by professing to have received an "internal dismission" from the church, supposedly from God himself, and he pronounced the body to be dissolved; evidently God was taking Stonington Church away from its members for their sin in refusing to pay Palmer what he thought he was worth. Stonington Church apparently retained Eleazar Brown as its minister and seems to have exercised quite a bit of patience in trying to appease and reconcile the proud, stubborn Palmer, but after a solid year of his whiny, querulous insistence that God had dismissed him, as a brand plucked from the burning, and had then struck down the church on account of its refusal to pay him, the church had had enough. The congregation requested the assistance of Timothy Wightman and others in a council meeting, and after hearing Palmer's woeful tale—by now he admitted he had gone about the salary business wrongly, but he still insisted that God didn't want him to deal with Stonington Church anymore—the council recommended that Stonington strip Palmer of his ordained authority as an elder and exclude him from communion and fellowship, which they did.

After this Palmer appears to have drifted about the periphery of the

Baptist denomination for the rest of his life. Shortly after the resolution of the conflict at Stonington, he removed to Preston, Connecticut, began to hold worship services in his own home, and after a time gathered a small congregation there that seems to have been recognized later as a Baptist church. From there he migrated to Stephentown, New York, where he may have been restored to ordained status as a minister by the Shaftesbury Regular Baptist Association in the early 1780s. In the last years of his life, though, he returned to Stonington where he died and was buried, according to Isaac Backus having "not preached much for many years"[9] and evidently never having reconciled himself to the little church that had given him his start in the ministry, such as it was.

What turned out to be the high-water mark of Wait Palmer's career in the ministry was a journey he took up the Connecticut River valley about the middle of March 1751 to hold a series of meetings in Daniel Marshall's hometown of Windsor. Of course at this time, Daniel and Martha Marshall and their growing brood were away in the Susquehanna valley of Pennsylvania on their New Side Presbyterian mission to the Mohawks; but it appears that Shubal Stearns, his wife, his parents, and most of his brothers and sisters came over from Tolland to hear Palmer, and he succeeded in converting them all to Baptist views over the course of his meeting and immersed them there, probably near the confluence of the Farmington and Connecticut Rivers. Much as old Valentine Wightman had once done for him and his flock, Palmer then followed his new proselytes back to Tolland and organized a Separate Baptist church there on March 20. Though he could just as easily have enlisted the aid of Wightman Jacobs over in Windham, the next county from Tolland, Palmer then returned to the coast and brought back Joshua Morse from New London to assist him in Shubal Stearns's ordination as a Baptist minister exactly two months after the new Tolland church's constitution. Although Palmer and Morse may have given Stearns additional assistance in the ordination of deacons and the establishment of other offices in the Tolland church, their subsequent relationships with him are not clear. One Palmer cousin who will be introduced shortly did become one of Stearns's closest followers; they may have worked closely or merely intermittently with Wait Palmer or, in the vein of George Whitefield with his Virginia "Lutherans," not at all.

Be that as it may, with the aid of Palmer and Morse, Tolland now had a new Separate Baptist church, and Shubal Stearns was now a full-fledged Separate Baptist minister. Although he served the church (which, as has already been mentioned, had a majority of members directly related to him) in this capacity between 1751 and 1754 very little is known of his actual activities during his earliest period as a Baptist minister. Neither is it known whether the Tolland church ever joined up with Wightman Jacobs's little General Baptist Yearly Meeting over in Windham County, but there is a great deal of subsequent evidence to indicate that Stearns picked up much of his perspective on Baptist associational life from the General Baptists rather than the Regulars. Given his circumstances, the neighboring small Windham Yearly Meeting would have been the most obvious place where he would have been introduced to such an outlook. On the other hand, Wait Palmer, still probably working closely with Groton as well as Stonington in these early days before the Rhode Island Yearly Meeting lowered the boom on Daniel Fiske for his missionary activities among the Separate Congregationalists, could easily have given Stearns his associational outlook in a similar manner. This associational perspective will be discussed in much further detail later, but it is fairly certain that, where the Tolland church itself was concerned, Stearns implemented an eclectic mix of General Baptist, Separate Congregational, and even mainline standing-church Presbyterian tradition in his worship services. Whether or not this was a common practice among the Separate Baptists in the Connecticut Appalachians, the mix did become one of the hallmarks of his ministry.

Though most evangelical churches involved in the Whitefield Revival recognized only two "Gospel ordinances" as established by the New Testament, namely baptism and communion, Stearns and his followers vociferously contended for at least a half dozen more. Besides the two aforementioned, they included imposition or the laying on of hands after baptism, the washing of one another's feet and the "love feast" in addition to communion, and the anointing of the sick with oil (all General Baptist traditions); the appointment of "ruling elders" as enforcers of church discipline in addition to the ministers who were "teaching elders" (Presbyterian tradition), plus the recognition of the wives of elders and deacons as "eldresses" and "deaconesses" (pure Separate Congregational revivalism). In addition, Stearns and his congregation exhibited an extreme fondness for embracing one another and shaking hands when they felt moved by the Holy Spirit, and so they added to their list of rites the "kiss of charity" and the "right hand of fellowship," probably Separate practices though also known among the Anabaptists and other European Pietist antecedents of the Baptists. A variation of the old Puritan infant baptismal rite called "the devoting of children" or "dry-christening," which Shubal Stearns may even have invented himself, was added to the mix as well. In it, on parents' request he would take a young infant in his arms, ask God's blessing upon it and formally bestow its name upon it: in essence a christening without baptismal sprinkling.[10] And over the whole was laid the happy, open emotionalism of the Separates during worship, with its new hymnody and quasi-liturgy of evangelistic lyrics combined with secular, modal ballad melodies, the congregation's handshaking, hugging, laughing, shouting, and weeping both sustaining and sustained by the New England Holy Tone stridently being issued from the pulpit. As with so many aspects of his work, Stearns's preaching style must be discussed in more detail later; as much as any aspect of his worship services at Tolland heretofore mentioned, it defined who he was and the impression he made.

Doctrinally, from most available evidence it appears that Shubal Stearns was still a predictably mild Whitefield-style evangelistic Calvinist, but he was now exhibiting a strong General Baptist perspective as well. One questionable source does accuse him indirectly of preaching "the irresistible influence of the Spirit," a strongly Calvinistic precept, but it is almost certain that the accuser did not know Stearns personally and may have been relying on secondhand information or even gossip.[11] One problem for historians researching this matter is the fact that, in terms of his endorsement of a written creed or confession, Stearns still remained a true Separate; he declared himself to have taken the Bible itself as his confession and he needed no other, and though he did possess a copy of the old Westminster Presbyterian Confession, as has already been noted, there is no evidence that he ever used the document except for his own reading and intellectual exercise. Far more telling is the preamble of the short covenant that he almost certainly either wrote or dictated for another Baptist church he gathered and helped organize within five years of his own immersion. Copied at the church's reorganization in 1783, it reads verbatim as follows: "Believing the Old and New Testaments to be the perfect rule of life and practice and 2ly [*sic*] Repentance from dead works and 3ly Faith towards God and 4ly The doctrine of baptism and 5ly laying on of hands and 6ly The preservation of saints and 7ly the resurrection of the dead and 8ly Eternal judgement...."[12]

This brief statement was not copied by Stearns, and neither was the essence taken from the Westminster, First or Second London, or Philadelphia Confessions at all. It is a simple listing of the old General Baptists' Six Principles headed by a Separatist affirmation of the authority of Scripture and complemented by merely one Calvinistic article: that of the perseverance of the saints. Though he may have privately held other Calvinistic articles of belief such as election and foreknowledge, here again, the evidence is strong that Stearns was highly influenced, either directly by Wightman Jacobs in Windham or indirectly through the Stonington-Groton connection, by the old Rhode Island Yearly Meeting.

Perhaps the most remarkable aspect of the discipline Shubal Stearns and his followers upheld, and another indication of their being influenced by one or both of the two pietistic communities of General Baptists in New England, was his strict interpretation of certain portions of I Corinthians 11 and I Timothy 2 regarding proper dress and grooming for a Christian. Gaudy, bright, expensive, or even most light-colored clothing for either gender was frowned upon as unbecoming. Shoulder-length clubbed hair was the fashion for men in that day, and most evangelical ministers such as George Whitefield and even Separate Baptists like Isaac Backus were content to conform to it, topping the style off with a wig for dress occasions; Stearns and his male followers kept their hair close-trimmed about their ears, neck, and forehead in a manner that one historian compared to that of "Cromwell and his roundheaded chaplains." For their part, the women "cast away all their superfluities so that they were distinguished from others";[13] in that day it was unthinkable that a woman whether professing Christianity or not should cut or "bob" her hair except in the case of a serious illness.

Apart from the New Light Separate philosophy of the New Birth in Christ with its ecstatic conversion experience, the true cohesive force between Shubal Stearns and his Tolland church was probably his earthly relation to most of the members. By the early 1740s the older Shubael and Rebecca Stearns were approaching sixty, an old age for that day and time; if they were the patriarchs of the Stearns, their eldest son must certainly have been held in esteem as the family's chief counselor, especially, as is probably the case, if his mother and father deferred to his judgment. This is not to say that he tried to upstage them in power and influence in the family, though such occurrences certainly were not unknown. But it is more likely that the elder Stearns were simply proud of their minister son—after all, he now enjoyed a position of community power that, through their modest means, they themselves could never have made available to him if the Great Awakening had not occurred—

and their example of deferential respect influenced the rest of the family, immured in the traditions of clannish rural New England, to follow in the same direction. Thus, perhaps even unconsciously on Shubal Stearns's part, the concept of born-again Christians united under a patriarchal leader became a fundamental concept of his ministry as well.

Though the Tolland congregation's relationship to the old Six Principle Baptists can be thus far fairly accurately traced by its actions, it must be stressed here that there is no way we can now truly ascertain just how much that Stearns's flock had in common with other eastern Connecticut Separate Baptist churches in terms of specific detail. As has been noted, most like-minded New England congregations eventually adopted the Philadelphia Confession and joined forces with the Regular Baptists, and we know that the forms of worship advocated and practiced by Shubal Stearns and his members passed completely away from the New England religious scene many years ago—of course, before being reintroduced by many newer ethnic and Pentecostal denominations in the region more than a century later. Had Stearns stayed where he was, he might have followed convention, let his church discard its then-radical worship forms over time as so many other Baptist congregations did, and become a leader in the Warren Association when it was formed in 1767 (as his successor in the Tolland pulpit, Noah Alden, in fact did). As it happened, though, in the summer of 1754 he and a sizable portion of his congregation/family left Connecticut forever, on what many of his Tolland neighbors must have regarded either as a tremendous act of faith or an insane wild goose chase. Despite the fact that at forty-eight years of age he could have been classified as an old man in a time when life expectancy for males in America averaged less than forty-six years, Shubal Stearns felt it behooved him to leave the home of his youth and early manhood and join a growing number of northerners who had decided to seek their fortune in the new, undeveloped lands of the southern colonies. As he himself put it, God had given him a great and extensive work to do in the west.

4

CHANCE AND PROVIDENCE

1754–1755

> BEHOLD up yonder, brethering, a first-rate crotch for a packsaddle!
> —Separate Baptist preacher Joseph Craig,
> in the midst of a Shubal Stearns–style sermon
> during which he threw his head back and gazed up
> in the tree under which he was preaching

Morgan Edwards, Isaac Backus, Robert B. Semple, and David Benedict all relate essentially the same tale: Shubal Stearns and his congregation set great store by what they perceived as direct impressions of the Holy Spirit upon their consciences, and Stearns, listening to some of these instructions from Heaven, began to believe that God had laid a "great work in the west" upon his shoulders. He, his wife Sarah, and a number of his church members likewise dedicated to the pursuit of this great work accordingly left Tolland in August 1754, not knowing their ultimate destination but convinced that God was leading them. After a taxing journey they finally came to a stop on Opequon Creek in Berkeley County, Virginia (now in West Virginia), where either by chance or divine providence—the historians, all being Baptists, favor the latter—they met Daniel and Martha Marshall, who had had their Indian mission in Pennsylvania broken up by intertribal warfare and who had likewise wandered south unbeknownst to the Stearns party. The Marshalls also accepted Baptist principles and were immersed, and they joined Stearns and his other followers in a settlement in the Cacapon River valley of Hampshire County, Virginia (likewise in present-day West Virginia). Enjoying no ministerial success in this area, the group became dissatisfied and, acting on information sent by "friends" about a newly settled area in the uplands of central North Carolina where the inhabitants "had to go upward of a hundred miles to hear a sermon," they resolved to relocate there to spread the Gospel. They arrived in the North Carolina Piedmont, supposedly in the midst of an entire population of settlers virtually ignorant of the principles of Christianity, towards the end of November 1755. Immediately Shubal Stearns, with Daniel Marshall as his assistant, embarked upon a ministry successful beyond his wildest dreams—indeed, a complete fulfillment of God's promise to him of a great and extensive work in the west.

In those points that can be determined objectively, many particulars of the Baptist historians' accounts are accurate. In truth, though, the entire set of actions most probably began neither with Shubal Stearns nor Daniel Marshall but with a pair of their friends and church associates, Joseph and Priscilla (Avery) Breed. The Breeds had been residents of Groton, Connecticut, and may have belonged to Valentine Wightman's historic old General Baptist church there. However, Joseph's parents were state-church Puritans; Joseph's mother was a Palmer and he may have been a second or even first cousin of the man who had baptized the Stearns, and it is also conceivable that Joseph and Priscilla could have been members of the state church until the Whitefield Revival made Baptists out of so many of the Palmers. Joseph is known to have done some exhorting in the pulpit, though there is no record that he was ever ordained as a minister. Between family records and Morgan Edwards's notes the story is a little sketchy, but it seems that the couple were landowners at Groton, residing near Priscilla's parents until August 11, 1746,[1] when they pulled up stakes and moved southwest to Opequon Creek in northern Virginia, noted already as the location of the Stearns party's first stop eight years later. The reader also may remember that Opequon Creek was also the location of the unfortunate little General Baptist church that the escaped convict and Paul Palmer ordainee Desolate Baker, alias Henry Loveall, gathered in 1743 and soon after abandoned. It is probable that the Breeds joined this flock when they moved to Virginia, or perhaps a few years afterward; after withering with no ministerial help for several years, with the possible exception of the unordained Breed, it was finally reorganized in 1751 by Philadelphia Association missionaries as a Regular Baptist church and admitted to Philadelphia Association under the care of pastor Samuel Heaton. At any rate, whether they were yet acquainted with Shubal Stearns or not, Joseph and Priscilla Breed were the first members known to have been associated later with the Stearns party to have left New England for Virginia, and they seem to have blazed the trail for the chain of events that led the Stearns family there.

The events that brought the wandering Marshall family to the same northern Virginia location also must be examined. According to the brief biography of Daniel Marshall written by his and Martha's son Abraham, the idealistic missionary couple departed from Onnaquaggy very reluctantly, undoubtedly due to the dangers of the intertribal war that threatened but possibly at the behest of the New York Synod, which controlled the New Side Presbyterians' missionary operations, rather than by their own choice. They were reassigned to another Pennsylvania settlement known as Connagogig; Abraham Marshall's sole reference to this place, an obscure comment that at Connagogig his father had found it "much more difficult to benefit Scribes and Pharisees than Publicans and sinners,"[2] indicates that Daniel encountered at least some opposition there, most probably from white, more traditional Presbyterian elders who disdained his lack of formal education and his New England Holy Tone exhortations and under whom he felt uncomfortable as a missionary. In any case, the Marshalls seem to have left Connagogig quickly after this, and they, like the Breeds before them, appear simply to have drifted down Virginia way among a tide of other new settlers trying to find new land and opportunity, perhaps with some hazy and unfixed idea of finding another field of spiritual labor among their new neighbors. They arrived at Winchester, seat of government in the northern Virginia county of Frederick, as early as 1751 or as late as the spring of 1754, and apparently met the Breeds there; Joseph Breed did claim some land in Frederick County for which he was finally given a grant in 1755,[3] and it is probable that the two New England Yankee families fell in with one another spontaneously and easily. Their mutual heritage in the northeast would have sparked the friendship as much as their common evangelical interest, and it is just as likely that Joseph and Priscilla Breed, rather than Shubal Stearns himself, converted the Marshalls to Baptist principles and influenced them to be immersed and join the church at Opequon. At any rate, this the Marshalls did at some time before 1754, most probably 1753 as Abraham Marshall later declared that his father had been immersed in the forty-eighth year of his life.[4] Pastor Samuel Heaton officiated, and Daniel—and perhaps Martha as well—joined his own exhortations to those of Heaton, Breed, and neighboring minister John Garrett or Garrard.

Thus the journey of the Stearns family southwestward in 1754 proves to be just a little more complex and involved than a simple case of Shubal Stearns's receiving instructions from God. Though intercolonial postal services were slow, irregular, and often undependable, they were definitely well established by this time, and in years to come Stearns himself would maintain an infrequent but steady correspondence with his successor in the Tolland pulpit, Noah Alden. The Marshalls, though separated from the family for several years now, very probably wrote to Shubal Stearns or his parents at Tolland regularly through their tours at Onnaquaggy and Connagogig, and in turn the missionary couple would have learned of the family's 1751 Baptist conversion and perhaps pondered the question of immersion themselves even before they had left Pennsylvania. We cannot now know the exact sequence of events, but the extended Stearns family almost certainly kept up with Daniel's and Martha's activities by mail through Pennsylvania on into Virginia. It becomes apparent that Shubal Stearns's meditations on God's call to a great work in the west may have been heavily influenced by news that his baby sister and her missionary husband were now Baptists themselves and laboring for the cause again in a new, developing area with much potential for further settlement. We must admit, however, that these circumstances, though auspicious without divine intervention, in no way disprove Stearns's declaration of his calling either. The accounts are not contradictory.

In July 1754, then, Shubal Stearns baptized Noah Alden, like himself a former Separate Congregationalist preacher, and within a month left him in charge of his Tolland church when he left with his followers—all family members—to Virginia to join the Marshalls and to find the great work to which he believed he had been commissioned by God. Alden was ordained the next year by neighboring Baptist ministers and, as has been noted already, later became prominent in Warren Association. Besides Shubal and Sarah Stearns themselves, the group of pilgrims included Stearns's parents, old Shubael and Rebecca; brothers Peter and Ebenezer, with their wives Hannah and Anna; his sisters Elizabeth Stinson and Rebecca Polk and their husbands Enos and Jonathan; and also, apparently, Stearns's brother Isaac and his only daughter Hephzibah, neither of whom at this time were church members. Isaac's wife Rebecca, already mentioned as possibly Sarah Stearns's sister, may have died by this point, and Shubal and Sarah might have taken a hand in helping him and his parents raise Hephzibah; at any rate, Shubal and Sarah apparently looked after Isaac's needs during part of his life at least, as one scrap of evidence exists that Isaac might have become incapable, either physically or mentally, of caring for himself. Years later, when he made his will, Shubal made one special, poignant bequest: "To Isaac Stearns, my Dearly beloved brother, all my wearing cloaths of all sorts both inside and outside cloaths of all sorts of every kind."[5] The rest of Shubal's sisters evidently stayed in Tolland, but the author has been able to gather data on only one: Mary, who married Joseph Hatch and who did remain in eastern Connecticut several years before settling with her husband and family in Alstead, New Hampshire, about 1774.[6] There were thus thirteen adults, twelve of them church members, in the group. With minor children counted, the entire company might have ranged anywhere from fifty to one hundred persons depending on the size of the individual families.

After what must have been a long trip southwest—the historical accounts seem to imply that the party traveled overland by horse-drawn wagon, sled, and crude tree-limb "packsaddles," although it is possible they took a sloop from the port near Groton down the coast at least as far as Chesapeake Bay instead—the party arrived at Opequon Creek in the Shenandoah basin sometime in the fall of 1754 and were joyfully

THE JOURNEY OF THE STEARNS FAMILY, 1754-1755

reunited with Daniel and Martha Marshall and their children. John Garrard is likewise said to have received the Stearns with kindness, although it was never reported exactly what Samuel Heaton thought of all these New England New Lighters invading his church within a few years' time. Given the Regular Baptists' emphasis at that time on ministerial education and prepared pulpit discourses, add to that the difficulties a dissenter church could run into with the Virginia government regarding unlicensed, unsanctioned preaching as well as this church's previous heritage with the General Baptists and Henry Loveall/Desolate Baker, it is not likely that he would have received these Separate Baptists altogether gladly. Moreover there were, at this time, two other Regular congregations in the Shenandoah basin, one on Ketockton or Catoctin Creek under the care of Rev. John Marks and the other up the north fork of the Shenandoah on a tributary known as Smith and Lynville's Creek, not yet organized as a church but led by a tough old Yorkshireman named John Alderson.[7] Both ministers were considerably older than Shubal Stearns and Daniel Marshall, and Marks was reputed to have been an extremely cold and dry pulpit orator.[8] Alderson, whose son and namesake pioneered the Regular Baptist cause in what is now southwestern West Virginia and in the process used not a few of the evangelistic techniques employed by Stearns and Marshall, was perhaps less so, but at this point neither man would have been entirely friendly with a flock of shouting and weeping New Englanders whose spokesmen chanted and "barked" when they preached. Stearns and his whole party must really have stuck out like sore thumbs, and so accordingly they all soon decided to strike out on their own. Fellow New Englanders Joseph and Priscilla Breed followed, and in keeping with Stearns's prophecy about the great work in the west waiting for them, the party, now numbering sixteen church members, turned again to the west—due west, in fact. They tramped approximately thirty miles overland to a mountainous, unsettled wilderness on Cacapon River in present Hampshire County, West Virginia, and there stopped and spent the winter of 1754 and the spring of 1755 waiting for the prophecy to come true.

 The Stearns remained at their tiny Cacapon settlement at least until the summer of 1755, perhaps even cultivating land and raising a few crops as a supplement to the abundant wild game on which they must have subsisted, but up to this point the promised great and extensive work in the west must have been a terrible disappointment. Though indeed in "the west"—in fact as far west as one could safely travel in

Virginia in that day and time—Hampshire County was simply too far off the beaten track up the Shenandoah and along the Blue Ridge to attract many permanent settlers at this point. It actually was cleared and developed so slowly that no church whatsoever, Baptist or otherwise, could even be gathered there until after the outbreak of the Revolutionary War more than twenty years later.[9] To the west there existed only isolated military outposts, and at one of these a few hundred miles away near the forks of the Ohio, a Virginia regiment with a young, inexperienced but resolute colonel named George Washington had just touched off the French and Indian War. The Cacapon River area's chief advantage, which was of course enjoyed by the other Baptist congregations on the lower Shenandoah, was that its remoteness from the Virginia establishment in the colony's coastal plain or "Tidewater" region ensured their safety from much of the government harassment they surely would have received if they had settled closer to civilization. Tidewater social hierarchy was marked by royal governors who, ever since the pompous and land-greedy old aristocrat for whom Berkeley County had been named, tried to reproduce the same land- and gentry-based class structure found in the Mother Country. In time, Shubal Stearns's disciples would shake the genteel society of the Tidewater to its knees, but that set of circumstances was still a decade off. In late 1754 and early 1755, the Stearns party preached, sang, and rejoiced on Cacapon River—sadly for them, all by themselves.

One is tempted to wonder if Joseph Breed finally received his 1755 Frederick County land grant as the result of an attempt to resettle the party back closer to civilization, perhaps a forlorn admission that he suspected himself of being on a wild goose chase. We will never know for sure. If nothing else, though, Shubal Stearns and his other followers were firm and even stubborn in their faith, and even though by the spring of 1755 their efforts appeared to have been in vain, they remained undaunted. If their great and extensive work was not ordained to be in Hampshire County, or even anywhere else in the Virginia colony, it must lie elsewhere, and when Shubal Stearns got a report from his "friends," as the religious historians call them, of the newly settled and apparently religiously barren uplands of central North Carolina, they were not long in getting ready to hit the road again. As to the identity of the person or persons with whom Stearns had made friends, the historians are all rather vague. Edwards does not even mention the unnamed friends at all. Benedict and Semple do merely in passing, perhaps with the implication that they were migrants passing through the Shenandoah basin whom Stearns had met or to whom he had preached. Backus provides the additional detail that Shubal Stearns himself wrote Noah Alden from Hampshire County in a letter dated June 13, 1755, informing him that "some of their company were then settled in North Carolina" and had sent Stearns a letter advising him of the dire need there,[10] suggesting that Stearns, again acting on direct divine impression, had sent out his own scouts. It has already been noted that nothing in the available records directly contradicts the idea that Stearns may have had divine guidance here, even if the historians were selective about what they wrote, and thus Edwards, Semple, Benedict, and Backus all may have been at least partially right. However, the most reliable subsequent evidence indicates that the Shubal Stearns party's primary source of information about North Carolina was neither a nameless group of migrants nor his own picked scouts but a former agent for a defunct land company that had been based in Maryland and Pennsylvania. His name was Herman Husbands, and since his career and that of Shubal Stearns would become closely linked after Stearns and his followers left Hampshire County, his own biography merits attention.

Born in Cecil County, Maryland, on October 3, 1724, to William and Mary (Kinkey) Husbands, Herman Husbands was half Dutch, half English, and certainly one of the most complex, bizarre personalities ever to dance across the stage of North Carolina—and for that matter, American—history. The son of wealthy, slave-owning planters, Husbands was raised as an Anglican and received a good education under the sponsorship of his Dutch maternal grandfather, Herman Kinkey. At a relatively young age, he had been converted under the preaching of George Whitefield and the Tennants and had broken with the Church of England to join the New Side Presbyterians. However, in addition to being a child of the Great Awakening, he was also heavily influenced by the forces of the Enlightenment; though he may never have met Benjamin Franklin personally, Husbands seems to have been well acquainted with the *Pennsylvania Gazette, Poor Richard's Almanack,* and several political tracts dealing with local government in the colonies that Franklin had written and published during his middle years. The older man's example may very well have inspired Husbands to become something of a Franklin-style scientist, eclectic tradesman, and political and religious pamphleteer. Over the years Husbands acquired and developed skills in agriculture, flour milling, surveying, metallurgy, mining engineering, and local politics, but in his quick, impressionable, and erratic mind, the religion of George Whitefield and the political philosophy of Benjamin Franklin fused into a curious, volatile synthesis. He became convinced that the Old Testament Book of Ezekiel harbored a promise from God for a New Jerusalem on the western frontiers of America, in which small farmers and artisans would be able to obtain lands of their own and live in a pure political democratic republic.[11] Though this belief colored virtually all of Husbands's activities in the later years of his life, it impossible to determine exactly how far he had developed it by the first time he met Shubal Stearns. However, his own religious activities between 1740 and 1755, as well as the manner in which he executed his duties as land agent, clearly reveal that at least the embryonic form of the idea was crucial to his initiation of a relationship with the little party of Separate Baptists out in the northern Virginia wilderness.

Not too many years after he had joined the New Side Presbyterians, Husbands quarreled with the elders of his church, and by 1750 he had left the denomination altogether to join a congregation of the Society of Friends, or Quakers, in East Nottingham, Maryland. His conversion to Quaker belief was the subject of his first published pamphlet, *Some Remarks on Religion,* and although he may have begun to form his volatile Ezekiel theory while still a Presbyterian, he certainly would have nourished it and developed it more distinctly in the context of the Quaker ideal of individual revelation by an inner light. In 1750 his first wife, whose maiden name may have been Cox, died and left him with three young children, but instead of settling down to raise them on lands his parents had deeded to him in Cecil and Baltimore Counties, he seems to have left them in the care of others and made a sea voyage to Barbados. After his return from the tropics the next year, he paid his first visit to North Carolina, tarrying a brief while in the southern coastal county of Bladen and perhaps scouting potential land investments before returning to Maryland and once again becoming prominent in the affairs of the East Nottingham Quakers.[12]

His involvement with the aforementioned land company, which consisted of several Pennsylvania and Maryland farmers and artisans who themselves were probably Quakers and which may have been financed largely by Husbands with his own capital, began at about this point. Like so many other land companies being formed by speculators at that time, its chief concern was the purchase and settlement of property in the North Carolina backcountry Piedmont deeded by royal grants to North Carolina royal governor Arthur Dobbs and other wealthy colonial dignitaries, as well as property in the Granville Tract, a huge holding comprising nearly the whole northwestern quarter of the colony and owned by Lord Granville, heir of one of North Carolina's original Lords Proprietors who had refused to give up his holding when North Carolina changed from a proprietary to a royal colony. According to North Carolina historian Blackwell P. Robinson, royal grants were nearly always given with the provision that the grant's proprietor must settle one white person on every two hundred acres of the grant and that all unsettled lands in it should revert to the Crown after ten years had elapsed.[13] Dobbs had been involved in this venture even before he had been appointed North Carolina's royal governor, settling Irish Presbyterians from Ulster, Scottish Highlanders fleeing their country after Bonnie Prince Charlie's defeat at Culloden Moor, in addition to Pennsylvania German, English, and Welsh immigrants from all points, on his Carolina lands. Besides these there were already some mixed-blood white/eastern coastal Native American groups in the area, their gene pool perhaps further augmented with a little Afro-Portuguese blood from shipwrecked sailors. Like all the wealthy and ambitious British colonial landlords of his time, Governor Dobbs was willing to take virtually all comers on his lands to get the maximum return on his investment. So, of course, were the great lords' middlemen, the land companies, by buying immense tracts of granted property and then selling it in smaller plots at a profit.

To be fair, though, the central and western North Carolina lands thus being thrown into market were indeed an appealing place to settle and live. Sandwiched between the Cherokee territories in the Appalachian mountains on the west and a dense range of pine forest on the east that separated the area from the more developed and settled "low country" of the coastal flats, the Piedmont, or upland region of the colony, was a vast space of forest, grassy plain, and canebrake interspersed with gently rolling hills. It was contained mainly in three immense counties: Anson, Rowan, and Orange. Settlers there could expect a hard life but a good one, with all the opportunities a new land offered for the taking. Thus in the fall of 1754, at roughly the same time the Shubal Stearns party was arriving in northern Virginia, Herman Husbands formed his land company and set out alone for North Carolina again, this time establishing temporary residence on Nutbush Creek in the north central county of Granville and from there making an extensive reconnaissance both of Granville Tract lands and of the Rowan and Orange County backwoods.

Upon his arrival at Orange Court House (seat of government for the county, subsequently known as Corbinton and later as Hillsboro), Husbands threw himself into backcountry life and a whirlwind of activity not only in behalf of his Pennsylvania and Maryland Quaker clients but of other established settlers, among whom he undoubtedly sought to attain a position of leadership and influence, as well. It was here that he must have heard of the country's sore lack of religious establishments, if indeed he did hear such; in any case, it was only partially true. German settlers in the backwoods had already imported the Moravian Church, a denomination whose leadership was so utterly like the structure of the Anglican episcopacy that the Moravians enjoyed quasi-official status in the colony as an "ancient" branch of the Church of England. Moreover, although there were so few, if any, Lutheran or Reformed ministers in the backcountry that the German adherents of those faiths mostly employed schoolteachers as lay readers of their respective liturgies, there had been three German Baptist "Dunkard" or "Tunker" congregations established by Rev. Daniel Leatherman on the Yadkin, Uwharrie, and upper Pee Dee Rivers as early as 1742.[14] Incidentally, these Dunkards, who practiced trine immersion face foremost rather than single immersion back foremost as did most Baptists, were historically as well as ideologically closer to the old English General Baptists than either group ever acknowledged at the time.

Among settlers of British extraction, the report of religious dearth Husbands said he had received was closer to the truth, if only slightly. Presbyterians there were in plenty among Dobbs's Ulster and Scots Highland tenants, but at this early date most of them were isolated from their other neighbors for the same reason the Germans were—the language barrier. Many of the Scots and Irish, and especially the women, were fluent only in their respective Gaelic dialects. Even so, Presbyterian establishments elsewhere made what efforts they could to supply them with preaching, however sporadic the ministers' visits, and they enjoyed Governor Dobbs's blessing in so doing. In general, it cannot be said that the English and Welsh settlers were totally unchurched either, familiar as the whole settled portion of the continent was at this time with the periodic evangelistic crusades of George Whitefield, who was still active as ever in the New World as well as the Old. Even Husbands's and his patrons' own Quaker denomination had already organized two monthly meetings in the uplands, near Deep River, the first three years earlier and the second just that year. But the one fact that Husbands appeared not to emphasize, at least when he spoke to Shubal Stearns later, was that the Baptists, both General and Regular, had already made perhaps the most respectable showing of church organization in the backcountry.

Paul Palmer's early work along the eastern North Carolina seaboard has already been noted, though by this time most of his remaining followers had been converted to the Regular Baptist persuasion by Philadelphia missionaries who were even then laboring in that area; but the Palmer General (later Free Will) Baptists still maintained at least one unpastored church as far west as Grassy Creek, in Granville County near Husbands's temporary base at Nutbush Creek. Even further to the southwest, the newly formed Charleston Association in South Carolina was making inroads north at a praiseworthy rate. That year Charleston had already helped organize one Regular Baptist church at a settlement of transplanted New Jerseyites in the wilds of Rowan County and had even acquired the Philadelphia missionary Benjamin Miller to serve as their first pastor. Miller was a veteran of the church reorganization at Opequon who before that had labored with several others in the east among the Palmer churches. Only a little further off and still in Rowan County, about thirty miles from the Orange County border on a Yadkin tributary known as Abbott's Creek, lay exhorter James Younger had come up from South Carolina in 1753 with a few other Baptists from Charleston Association's Pee Dee Church and had established worship as a branch congregation or "arm" of the older church.[15] As far as the newcomer Herman Husbands was concerned, however, though he undoubtedly admired the antiestablishmentarian stance of both German and English Baptists, in all likelihood he hoped that his contacts with the Rowan and Orange County settlers might further his and his land company's patrons' Quaker presence as a major upland religious force—thus letting the Society of Friends take one more step closer to his envisioned New Jerusalem in the west.

Husbands thus looked over lands and prospects in the backcountry through the last months of 1754, concentrating his attentions partially on the availability of town lots in Hillsboro but most particularly on a budding settlement at the Rowan/Orange County border on a minor tributary of the Deep River. Sandy Creek, as it was known, was west of Haw River and northwest of its union with Deep River to form the Cape Fear River. In his conversations with Rowan and Orange County officials, however, Husbands seems to have received one bit of information extremely disturbing to him, in the context of his Ezekiel theory. The Provincial Assembly, meeting at Edenton on the east coast under the leadership of Governor Dobbs, was at its current session trying to legislate a Vestry Act to aid the missionary arm of the Church of England, the Society for the Propagation of the Gospel, in establishing and maintaining a Virginia-style system of Anglican parish churches throughout the settlements of North Carolina.[16] The measure had been attempted at one time or another by every royal governor the colony had had in office, but it had never passed for various reasons including the fact that there had always been a shortage of qualified Anglican parsons in the province; had there been as great a supply of these in North Carolina as there were in Virginia, neither Paul Palmer, the Quakers, nor the Regular Baptists could ever have enjoyed such an easy time in establishing toeholds as they did. This time, though, it looked as if the long-awaited Vestry Act would pass, conceivably bringing with it all manner of restrictions and regulations against dissenters in both east and west.

Because of persistent land-fraud rumors in the uplands, Husbands knew he had to make a trip to Edenton to examine records with Lord Granville's land agent there anyway, and so while at the unofficial provincial capital in December 1754 or January 1755, the speculator presented a petition to Governor Dobbs and the assembly in which he argued vociferously against the legislation.[17] To the assemblymen, at least two or three of whom had to have come as representatives of the upland counties and none of whom were aware of Husbands's radical religious notions, his frantic harangue to prevent the founding of Christian churches in an area that had so few must have seemed ridiculous. At any rate the Vestry Act was passed and sent to George II's Privy Council for approval, a necessary step before its becoming law, after Governor Dobbs adjourned the assembly on January 15, 1755.[18] Husbands, his hopes to keep the Established Faith out of the uplands dashed, returned to the backwoods to lick his wounds and plan once again.

Husbands needn't have worried all that much. Though the province seems to have been laid off in British- and Virginia-style parishes, there were still too few Anglican parsons to serve them all, especially in the upland backcountry, and the full provisions of the Vestry Act never could be implemented even right to the last, when the British lost control of North Carolina after the Battle of Moore's Creek Bridge in 1776. However, at the time, the threat of establishmentarianism ruining his picture of a backwoods New Jerusalem must have seemed very real to Husbands. In spite of his disappointment, though, he still undoubtedly hoped that he and his land company clients could thwart the danger by increasing and strengthening the position of the Quakers in the uplands, perhaps even making the Society of Friends the dominant religious presence before the effects of the Vestry Act materialized in the western counties. To add insult to injury, however, when he went back to Maryland in the spring of 1755 to meet with his patrons, he found that each and every one had decided against pulling up stakes and committing themselves to the Carolina backcountry, thus leaving Husbands with that mammoth investment of the land company all on his own shoulders. Husbands remained undaunted, for some reason—the New Jerusalem belief seems the only one that makes sense out of his next decision—and he stubbornly resolved to develop both his projected Sandy Creek settlement and his personal reputation as a backcountry civil, political, and religious leader all on his own. Before the end of summer, he returned to North Carolina and purchased, in addition to two town lots in Hillsboro, an extensive property tract on Sandy Creek that he augmented gradually to include over ten thousand acres in both Rowan and Orange Counties.[19]

And here, finally, was where Shubal Stearns and his ragged little group of New Englanders, stuck in Hampshire County, Virginia, thirty miles off the main road for settlers migrating from north to south and praying, singing, and shouting all to themselves in a virtual wilderness, entered the picture. As he passed through the Shenandoah basin near the start of his trail overland back to North Carolina, Husbands would have had several things on his mind: first, that his vision of a backwoods democratic New Jerusalem depended on a strong antiestablishmentarian presence in the uplands; second, that the Quaker support from his land company clients, on which he had counted to further this dream, had completely fallen through; third, that the strongest organized antiestablishmentarian religious presence already in the backcountry were the Baptists; and fourth that, if he couldn't have his first choice of denominations to help him found the New Jerusalem before the hated and feared Vestry Act were implemented he'd better make a second, workable choice and make it quickly. If he were in this frame of mind, it is easily conceivable that Husbands should have stopped off to talk to members and officers of one or more of the three Shenandoah basin Regular Baptist churches, perhaps trying to convince the entire congregations to join his Sandy Creek settlement, and it is just as conceivable that he could have been referred by them to the Stearns party across the hills on Cacapon River, whom all may have regarded as just a little too far off center to make good, respectable Regular Baptists. Of course the little company of Separate Baptists, having no real aim or ambition other than finding their great and extensive work somewhere in the west and chafing at the bit to leave their prospect-barren Hampshire County settlement, would have fit Husbands's bill perfectly, perhaps the very uniqueness of their style of worship and preaching appealing to his sensibilities as publicist and showman for New Jerusalem democracy, and any deal that he may have struck with Shubal Stearns on the matter would have been regarded by both parties as mutually beneficial. One or two church members may even have accompanied Husbands to North Carolina to verify the Marylander's claims, perhaps prompting Stearns's June 1755 letter to Noah Alden. Again at this point it must be stressed that the details of this Stearns/Husbands connection in Virginia are purely speculative, but the cold hard fact remains that Stearns and his followers did indeed leave Hampshire County in the summer of 1755, traveling in a beeline directly to Herman Husbands's temporary base on Nutbush Creek in Granville County, North Carolina, and then proceeding west in company with him to the Sandy Creek lands he had just purchased.[20]

Thus between Shubal Stearns and Herman Husbands was born an odd relationship, perhaps the oddest religious/secular mix of all in American history. Like the older Baptist historians' possibly rose-colored take on the little Separate Baptist group's move to North Carolina to begin with, at least one Stearns biographer actually claimed the connection to have been foreordained and inspired by God Himself. Writing in the heady days of Theodore Roosevelt's first term as President in an America with the victory against Spain fresh under its belt, just becoming a great world power, extremely proud and utterly convinced of its own greatness, rural Carolina Baptist minister A.J. Patterson boldly held forth that "God used Husbands as a political agitator and Elder Stearns as a Gospel instructor to enlighten the country and prepare the way for enduring homes for tender consciences."[21] The true scope of Husbands's political agitation over the next sixteen years, and its effect on Shubal Stearns, Governor Dobbs, and Dobbs's successor will be examined in due course, and the reader may judge whether Patterson was right. All seemed well on Sandy Creek in the fall of 1755, however. Husbands quickly built a gristmill and began to sell and survey land for other settlers including his Separate Baptist newcomers, to whom he may have rented or sold properties at reduced prices in recognition of their position and anticipated labors. The one missing Separate family from the Sandy Creek settlement was the ever-independent Daniel Marshall, who took his family further southwest to the Uwharrie valley in Rowan County and homesteaded there.[22] There is some disagreement between historians and historical records as to whether Shubal Stearns himself ever acquired any lands in North Carolina, but as the flock's leader he may have been given a cabin and small farm, cheaply or even gratis, on Husbands's properties or on those of his brothers or brothers-in-law. And not long after the New Englanders had cobbled themselves a little meetinghouse together, in a small grove of trees near a rock spur at the corner of Husbands's Sandy Creek tract, and constituted themselves formally into the Sandy Creek Separate Baptist church on November 22, 1755, none could harbor any more doubts whatsoever that God had ordered and inspired their call to a great and extensive work in the west.

For the religion and the preaching of Shubal Stearns exploded over the Piedmont like a hurricane, the enthusiasm it generated rivaling that of the original Whitefield Revivals and its success surpassing anything that either Stearns or Husbands could possibly have hoped for. Once the Carolina settlers—themselves strangers in a new land and only then being formed and molded by a combination of their heritage and their new environment into the American pioneer culture that would conquer Kentucky, Tennessee, and all points west—heard Stearns's loud, melodious preaching cant and the corresponding singing, laughing, shouting, and weeping of his small flock, the sights and the sounds held them spellbound, convincing them that through the New Birth in Christ they, too, could experience a happiness and a joy beyond anything their precarious frontier existence could fling at them. Isaac Backus's biographer Alvah Hovey considered Backus a remarkably successful evangelist for baptizing 62 persons in New England between 1756 and 1767, while taking missionary trips totaling 14,691 miles and preaching 2,412 sermons.[23] In comparison, Stearns, with assistance from Daniel Marshall and Joseph Breed, working only in the scattered settlements of the North Carolina backcountry between November 1755 and January 1758, led more than 900 souls rejoicing into the baptismal water, 590 of whom became members of his Sandy Creek Church itself and the others gathered in additional churches he organized.[24]

For the preservation of much of what we know about Shubal Stearns during this period we have to thank Morgan Edwards, a native Welshman and minister of Philadelphia Association who in 1772, recognizing the unifying and homogenizing effect his association was exerting among American Baptists of all types generally, set out to form a plan, with the Association's support, to unite all the groups at least loosely around the rite of immersion. His ambition never materialized, but at his plan's inception he did travel extensively among Baptist congregations, communities, and associations all over colonial America, gathering histories, tidbits of data, and even gossip of all with whom he came in contact. His *Materials Toward a History of the Baptists in America*, though unfortunately never fully published nor even in many instances edited or rewritten after he took his original, scrawled notes as he traveled, is a joy and a delight for the historian to read. Edwards was a classical scholar, trained at Britain's Bristol Baptist College, and a philosophical but extremely evangelistic Calvinist who took his association's 1742 Confession as law and gospel; but at the same time he was a very pithy, rural Welshman at heart who never sugar-coated anything for his potential readers' tastes (with one notable exception that will be noted in due course, and he even gave a frank explanation for that). His impressions are biased in many instances but always honest; where he found distinctions of local culture he appreciated them and gave them their due, where he found reason to praise he did so, and where he found occasion to criticize and ridicule he often laid it on with a trowel, amusingly, sometimes praising and condemning the same person, church, or association simultaneously. To Morgan Edwards a South Carolina nabob was a South Carolina nabob and a Virginia cracker was a Virginia cracker—to name just two of the descriptive terms he used so effectively, often against enemies of the Baptists.

Edwards visited Sandy Creek Church evidently within a year of Shubal Stearns's death. Consequently he was careful to note that all the data he gave concerning Stearns were not direct impressions but the recollections of Stearns's wife Sarah and his North Carolina friends, many of whom had known him from the first. Nonetheless he painted a vivid picture of Stearns and his everyday life. He noted, as he did for all the churches in his *Materials*, the Sandy Creek congregation's financial arrangements with its minister: like so many early Separate Baptists, and before them General Baptists, Stearns received no salary and probably would have turned one down if it were offered him, but he nonetheless had received "presents" including garden produce, grain, and assistance with farm labor amounting to a net value of about twenty British pounds per year. And for the rest of the description, on which much of the remainder of this chapter must needs be built, we had perhaps best let the pithy Edwards and his preacher informant Tidings (pronounced *"Tidin's"* and most often spelled *"Tidence"*) Lane speak for themselves:

> Mr. Stearns was but a little man, but of good natural parts, and sound judgement. Of learning he had but a small share, yet was pretty well acquainted with books. His voice was musical and strong, which he managed in such a manner, as one while to make soft impressions on the heart, and fetch tears from the eyes in a mechanical way; and anon to shake the nerves, and to throw the animal system into tumults and perturbations. *All the Separate ministers copy him in tones of voice and actions of body; and some few exceed him* [emphasis added]. His character was indisputably good, both as a man, a Christian and a preacher. In his eyes was something very penetrating, which seemed to have a meaning in every glance, of which I will give one example: and the rather because it was given me by a man of good sense, I mean Tidence Lane.
>
> "When the fame of Mr. Stearns' preaching (said Mr. Lane) had reached the Yadkin, where I lived, I felt a curiosity to go and see him. Upon my arrival, I saw a venerable old man sitting under a peach tree with a book in his hand, and the people gathering about him. He fixed his eyes on me immediately, which made me feel in such a manner as I had never felt before. I turned to quit the place, but could not proceed far. I went up to him, thinking that a salutation and shaking hands would relieve me; but it happened otherwise. I began to think that he had an evil eye, and ought to be shunned; but shunning I could no more effect, than a bird can shun the rattlesnake when he fixes his eyes upon it. When he began to preach my perturbations increased, so that nature could no longer support them, and I sunk to the ground."[25]

Before we examine this remarkable scrap of biography further we should look at one more anecdote of Shubal Stearns's preaching, this one given to Edwards by Elnathan Davis who, like "Tidence" Lane, was a young Separate minister raised up under Stearns's wing:

> Elnathan Davis had heard that one John Steward was to be

baptized such a day by Mr. Stearns. Now, this Mr. Steward being a very big man, and Stearns of small stature, he concluded that there would be some diversion if not drowning; therefore he gathered about eight or ten of his companions in wickedness and went to the spot. Shubal Stearns came and began to preach. Elnathan went to hear him, while his companions stood at a distance. He was no sooner among the crowd but that he perceived some of the people tremble, as if in a fit of the ague; he felt and examined them, in order to find out if it were not a dissimulation; meanwhile one man leaned on his shoulder, weeping bitterly; Elnathan, perceiving he had wet his new white coat, pushed him off and ran to his companions, who were sitting on a log in the distance. When he came, one said, "Well, Elnathan, what do you think now of these damned people?" He replied, "There is a trembling and crying spirit among them; but whether it be the Spirit of God or the devil, I don't know; if it be of the devil, the devil go with them, for I will never more venture myself among them." He stood a while in this resolution; but the enchantment of Stearns' voice drew him to the crowd once more. He had not been there long before the trembling seized him also; he attempted to withdraw; but his strength failing and his understanding confounded, he, with many others, sunk to the ground. When he came to himself, he found nothing in him but dread and anxiety, bordering on horror. He continued in this situation some days, and then found relief by faith in Christ. Immediately he began to preach conversion work, raw as he was, and scanty as his knowledge must have been.[26]

It will be remembered that no such remarkable tales of Stearns's preaching feats had ever been noted in his ministry elsewhere before, neither in Connecticut nor in Virginia. If these North Carolina experiences were typical, though—and there is every indication that they were—they present a picture of Shubal Stearns that is at once charming and unsettling. With Edwards we grin with wry amusement at the picture of Stearns, like a small Bantam rooster, baptizing the giant Cochin John Steward at the risk of drowning both himself and his candidate, and we raise our eyebrows at the extraordinary powers accorded his eyes by his rural backcountry listeners. We are tantalized by the statement that Edwards had heard several men, and maybe women as well, tell "like stories of impressions [Stearns's] presence made upon them for which they could not account," dismissing them all but the one given him by the level-headed Tidence Lane as backwoods superstition; if this is so it is a regrettable loss to historians and folklorists. Overall, though, we are given the likeness of a short, spare man who had large, bright, piercing eyes, which would have been exceptionally prominent in a small and narrow face. This unusual countenance may not even have been noticed by his family or the Connecticut neighbors with whom Stearns grew up and lived, but in a freshly settled territory where all were relative newcomers, he could have appeared either demonic or angelic depending on the mental state of the beholder—and in the case of his converts, perhaps with one perception following the other. As will be demonstrated in the next chapter, more than one Stearns convert experienced a terrifying sensation of physically meeting the Devil after hearing Stearns preach—and before experiencing the New Birth.

The author knows he is making a risky metaphor here, but it appears that Stearns's countenance made him a sort of Rasputin of his day and place. With this, though, Edwards's assessment of Stearns as "indisputably good, both as a man, a Christian and a preacher" needs to be stressed again; perhaps a more apt comparison could be made with Stearns to the late Lubavitcher Rebbe, Menachem Mendel Schneerson. Until his death in 1994, Schneerson, whose personal charisma was so overwhelming that his Hasidic followers actually proclaimed him as the Messiah, likewise was reputed to exert a terrifying power and sense of control with his eyes; so much power, in fact, that the famed author Chaim Potok once frankly confessed, on national television no less, to a completely irrational but very personal and real fear of being in the same room alone with the grizzled old *Rov.* If Stearns exuded this same aura of power, though, at least he never used it for his own personal gain and gratification, as did Rasputin; but sadly, as will be shown later in this work, like Rasputin, it failed him at the very hour when he needed it the most.

So much for Stearns's eyes, at least for the time being. The operative element of Stearns's power in Elnathan Davis's story is "the enchantment of [his] voice" rather than the particular effect of his eyes, and of course the enchantment, such as it was, lay in Stearns's use of the New England Holy Tone as it had come into use among the New Lights in the wake of the 1740s Whitefield Revivals. Using Edwards's own descriptions for a guide, we can picture the image and the sound of Shubal

Stearns in the pulpit. In what must have sounded something like an old-fashioned rural Maine accent, he seems to have given forth his variation of the New England Holy Tone in a musical voice, alternating soft and soothing tones and melodies with loud and harsh ones, moving back and forth across the preaching stand and perhaps making contact, by embraces and handshakes, with his shouting, weeping, mightily amazed, and awed listeners; a bit of evidence that will be introduced in the next chapter indicates that Stearns, like George Whitefield himself and the later Welsh practicioners of *hywl*, may have interspersed the lines of his preaching cadence with melodious, trilling outbursts of the interjection, "*Ohhhhh!*"

Modern Appalachian scholars would have us believe that the many variations of the traditional central Appalachian preaching cant, as described so completely and sympathetically by Howard Dorgan in his numerous studies of modern old-time central Appalachian Baptist groups and subgroups, all sprang from a supposed traditional *hywl* cadence brought to this country by immigrant Welsh ministers and that in later years may have been influenced by the New England Holy Tone. Since this theory lines up conveniently with the Old Landmarkers' claims of an ancient Baptist church surviving hidden in the Welsh hinterlands for fifteen hundred years, negating all other denominations' claims to legitimacy, they have generally endorsed it and helped propagate it, furthering the confusion. But Morgan Edwards's *Materials,* in both his expressions of his own views and in his accounts of early colonial ministers who were Welsh like himself, show that this is patently untrue. Edwards *never* employed a preaching cant or cadence himself and neither did other Welsh ministers of his pre-Whitefield generation who migrated to the American colonies; had he or they done so, Edwards was blunt, honest, and culturally conscious enough to have admitted it and to have made the obvious comparison between *hywl* and the New England Holy Tone himself. This circumstance by itself is enough for the author to venture the hypothesis that *hywl* did not precede the New England Holy Tone historically but that it, like the Tone in America, became a phenomenon of the aftermath of George Whitefield's revivals in Wales, and for the same causes. It was certainly employed in Wales later by post-Whitefield Baptist evangelists such as Christmas Evans, but no evidence exists that it was ever used before Whitefield or his Welsh partner, Howell Harris, began their ministries there. Additional Edwards data strengthening this hypothesis will be introduced in its due course. If this is the case, though, it becomes obvious that the father of traditional Appalachian preaching, the author of the *Ur*-version, so to speak, of all the Appalachian mountain pulpit tones that Dorgan describes so well, is none other than Shubal Stearns himself. Moreover, it cannot now be ascertained just how much direct influence the very dialect with which Stearns spoke exercised over the development of the distinctive speech of the American Southeast—but, given his position, it could have been enormous. A culture, a new synthesis of Old Country and New World influences, was being born on the North Carolina frontier, and whether Stearns's arrival in the colony was due to divine providence or the crafty machinations of Herman Husbands, he came at just the right time to make his own preaching style and perhaps even his own rural New England speech patterns a permanent part of that culture.

At any rate, Edwards's general conclusions on the preaching mode of Stearns and his successors in North Carolina ran thus in 1772, with no mention of Welsh antecedents whatsoever:

> As for the outcries, epilepsies and extacies [*sic*] attending their ministry they are not peculiar to them; the Newengland [*sic*] Presbyterians had them long before; and in Virginia, it is well known that the same effects attend the ministry of some clergymen of the Church of England, particularly Rev. Messrs. Deveraux Garret and Archibald McRoberts [both of whom had New Side Presbyterian backgrounds]. The enchantments of sounds, attended with corresponding actions, have produced greater effects than these; though I believe a preternatural and invisible hand works in the assemblies of the Separate-baptists bearing down the human mind, as was the case in primitive churches, I Cor. XIV.25.[27]

In the instances where Edwards appears critical of the Stearns style, he refers to it as "the tones, actions and violence which are the Shibboleths of the Separate Baptists," and "the outcries, extacies and epilepsies which are so much thought of among them." He casually dismisses Daniel Marshall, who must have used at least a mild version of the Holy Tone himself, and with whom Edwards certainly had a direct interview and may even have heard preach, as "a man of no bright parts nor eloquence nor learning. Piety, earnestness and honesty are all he can boast of."[28] Of the unordained Joseph Breed, whom he may have met as well, he says nothing except to list him and his wife as church members. It is not even known exactly what he would have thought of Shubal Stearns himself if he had enjoyed an opportunity to interview the little preacher directly and hear him in action in the pulpit; and yet, the warmth of the memories of Stearns's North Carolina friends and coworkers fairly glows from his pages, and his overall assessment of the Separate Baptists as a whole is actually positive and even friendly in spite of his numerous criticisms. By the dramatic and quick effect of his message, by his preaching tones, by his eyes, by the fact that he was simultaneously a religious leader and himself a rough, rustic settler utterly like his backcountry neighbors, Shubal Stearns truly did fit the bill of Ezra Pound's poem and Simon Zelotes' Goodly Fere. At the same time a father in the Gospel and a rough country man who understood rough country men, a leader as well as a shipmate or companion, for the next several years Stearns exerted a power and an influence for the New Birth in Christ in the uplands of North Carolina of which most ambitious evangelists can only dream. And too, even as Pound himself penned the poem rather than some anonymous bard of yore, so did Shubal Stearns himself establish so much that has endured in the religious culture of the land he made his home.

Until the last section of this chapter we have been compelled by necessity to examine the life of Shubal Stearns more by a study of the larger forces that influenced him than his own actions; though this study must continue to a certain extent, we may now, and indeed have already begun, to speak more and more of Stearns's own actions and the way they influenced others. The era of the Goodly Fere in North Carolina, the time of the birth of Appalachian religious culture, had begun and would continue for fourteen to sixteen years before larger events again forced a change. Still, the nagging question remains: if Herman Husbands was as instrumental as he seems to have been in bringing Shubal Stearns and his flock to North Carolina in the first place, is it also possible that he initially worked behind the scenes, without Stearns's knowledge, as promotions man and spin doctor for the Separates and their cause? It is known that, near the time Stearns's record of conversions and baptisms in the backcountry reached the nine hundred mark in 1758, a mob of at least seven hundred men had also collected at the Rowan County seat at Salisbury to protest the Vestry Act during a visit from Lord Granville's land agent.[29] Was Husbands responsible for this, too? And was it he, more than anyone or anything else, who kick-started the little preacher's ministry in the backcountry by spreading suggestions among the settlers of the power of Stearns's eyes and his preaching, all for his own upland political causes and the furtherance of his ambitions of a backwoods democratic New Jerusalem? The thought haunts, but we will never really know for sure.

5

CHAMOMILE

1755–1765

> These Baptists are like a bed of chamomile: the more one stamps upon them, the further they spread.
> —reputedly remarked by a Virginia country lawyer

Though we left the last chapter with an unanswered and unanswerable question, if indeed Herman Husbands's promotion of the Separate Baptists was a political gambit of his own design, it paid off well. As the uplands continued to fill up with settlers, Husbands himself may have realized that the Quakers could never have competed with the Separate Baptists in the backcountry, even under the best of circumstances. The two Quaker monthly meetings already established in the uplands at Husbands's arrival enjoyed a modest prosperity, and three more meetings appear to have been started at various locations by 1757. Their increase, however, came mostly gradually from northern immigrants, the Quakers making very few converts among those who had not had a background in the faith already. And some families of immigrant Friends eventually disowned their heritage and became Baptists. Squire and Sarah Boone, parents of Daniel Boone, and Edward Williams, father of Daniel Williams, pioneer Baptist preacher of eastern Kentucky, are but a few examples of Pennsylvania emigrant Quakers who became Separate Baptists after moving to North Carolina.

Husbands remained a Quaker, though, at least for the time being. He continued developing his properties on Sandy Creek and indeed kept purchasing acreage in the uplands until 1762, but in 1759 for some reason he abruptly left the province and returned to Maryland. Relocating in Frederick County, he made his living there by managing the Fountain Copper Works, part of which he or his parents may have owned. After three years at Fountain Copper Works, he moved back to North Carolina, resettled at Sandy Creek, and married for the second time. His bride was Mary Pugh, a member of the Cane Creek Quaker Monthly

Meeting, and during their brief marriage Husbands was active in local government in such minor positions as overseer of Sandy Creek and road juryman. In January 1764, though, the Quakers "disowned" Husbands over some matter of church discipline; Husbands himself wrote later that he had been turned out because he had played the Good Samaritan and come to the aid of another Quaker already under censure by his Monthly Meeting.[1] It may have been the truth. In those days the Quakers were vociferous excommunicators for reasons that seem hypocritical, Puritanical, and downright mean to modern readers. As a matter of fact, Squire Boone had been censured by his Quaker Meeting because he would not banish a young daughter who had gotten pregnant before marriage from his household. But then again, Husbands was later accused, albeit by a biased recorder, of being "churched" for immorality. At best, his own well-established propensity to put a positive spin on his own actions does make his claim perhaps a bit suspect. At any rate, after his second wife died around 1764 or 1765, he married the third time to Amy Allen, another Quaker, nineteen years younger than he. She was immediately barred from Quaker fellowship for "marrying out of unity."[2] Husbands and his new family, which eventually came to number eight children, still remained in the Quaker community, however, and apparently he lost no political face among his neighbors of either Quaker or Baptist persuasion.

The Quakers may actually have done him something of a political favor, because though he was no Deist, he was now able to present an image of himself even more like good old Ben Franklin: still in the church community and recognizing the need of the "ignorant and unenlightened" for the church, but aloof from involvement in it himself due to his own impression of the strength of his morals, his enlightened and liberal ideas, and his superior intelligence. It is a commonly held myth that America's Founding Fathers were evangelical Christians, thus making the United States a God-ordained and specially blessed nation; actually most of the principal players in the American Revolution were rationalists and liberals of the image the excluded Husbands now projected, who used and worked the church for all it was worth because they regarded it as the best vehicle through which to agitate the unenlightened and bring them to their views on government. Though only about a third of all American colonists actively supported the Revolution, another third being British sympathizers and the rest not caring either way, Husbands was truly in the coming American fashion now.

Still, if Husbands was as instrumental as we suspect in establishing Shubal Stearns and his family in his Sandy Creek settlement, as well as being influenced on his own so mightily by George Whitefield's preaching, we may wonder why he himself did not cast in his lot with the Separate Baptist cause, let the little bright-eyed preacher immerse him, and join in their work. There could have been several reasons. One of the main ones may have been his community position as outlined above, but two stand out over all the rest. For one, Shubal Stearns, finding no active legal persecution against his cause in his new backwoods home, was decidedly and stubbornly nonpolitical (at least in the secular sense). For the other, even if Stearns had been a secular political crusader, Husbands was extremely cagey, advocating and agitating whatever democratic and liberal causes caught his fancy but always playing his own hand close and safe and never *quite* committing himself to anything that might involve a risk to him personally. His agitation may have brought about the 1759 demonstration at Salisbury to Lord Granville's land agent against the Vestry Act, but we know with a good deal of certainty that he was neither leader nor member of the actual mob itself. But we digress. Our purpose in this chapter is to look at the actions of Shubal Stearns and his followers during this same time period, the decade from 1755 to 1765, and to examine the religious rites and institutions Stearns brought to and established in the North Carolina backcountry, the sum total of which was the primary foundation of the religious culture of the central and southern Appalachians. Most of Stearns's rites, their origins, and their antecedents have been discussed in an earlier chapter, so perhaps it is best simply to present the institutions by giving a factual account of events themselves, and the causes and effects that transpired from them.

It has already been noted that Stearns himself was a wild success from the very first, and that his little Sandy Creek Church did not stay small for long. It is possible that he, Daniel Marshall, and Joseph Breed intended to hold services there on a weekly basis, but they soon must have found that to be impracticable simply due to the demand for their services. As "Tidence" Lane's and Elnathan Davis's stories have already shown, a sermon and service by the little musical-voiced preacher might be required any day of the week, outside or in, and perhaps even several times on any given day and location. At the same time, Daniel and Martha Marshall, homesteading down in the Uwharrie valley, quickly met up with the little group of Regular Baptists already extant on Abbott's Creek and offered to hold services for them as well. James Younger and his Abbott's Creek neighbors were charmed by the Marshalls, and even the formally trained Regular minister over at the Jersey Settlement, Benjamin Miller, seems to have looked on them favorably, remarking that "if he had such warm-hearted Christians in his church he would not take gold for them"[3]. The duties of the one ordained and two unordained ministers (and perhaps Martha Marshall as well, as a prayer and song leader and even an exhorter) found them, from the first, stretched quite beyond concentration on a single meetinghouse every Sabbath. Thus the practice of having one weekend-per-month regular meetings at their churches was born out of simple necessity. The Abbott's Creek Baptists evidently joined Sandy Creek Church as members and then continued to hold meetings nearer their homes as a branch congregation or "arm." Soon Sandy Creek established other "arms" as well. Morgan Edwards notes that some early Separate Baptist churches including Sandy Creek held to the weekly administration of communion and probably foot washing as well, and other congregations did so four or more times during a year (one notation in the *Materials* states that Sandy Creek was observing the feast every other week in 1772). But it must be remembered that these frequent sacraments were most likely spread out between the various arms of a given congregation, first at one location and then another in a circuit that depended on how often the various flocks wanted to observe the rites. One weekend at Sandy Creek, one at Abbott's, the rest at other settlements, and both impromptu indoor and outdoor weekday services whenever and wherever one was called for: this was the best that Shubal Stearns could have done, given his circumstances. Only within the last forty years or so have some Appalachian rural Baptist congregations given Stearns's original necessity-based system any modification in their churches.

Nonetheless, at Abbott's Creek and perhaps other places as well, Stearns now had the assistance of another unordained exhorter in James Younger. It is difficult to assess how much either Younger or Joseph Breed may have helped the group, though, as neither Edwards nor the other writers mention anything about their actual preaching. Given Younger's background with the Regular Baptists, he may simply have never been able to pick up on the use of the New England Holy Tone, Stearns's exposition of which had quickly set the popular standard for upcountry Baptist preaching. It should be mentioned here, though, that James Younger, like Morgan Edwards, was a native Welshman,[4] and if he had had any background in the use of the Welsh *hywl* preaching cant he undoubtedly would have tried to employ it; this is yet one more indication that *hywl* had not come into general use among Welsh Baptists before 1745–1755. Joseph Breed's possible pre-Holy Tone background among the General Baptists at the old Groton Church may have left him in a situation similar to that of Younger.

Stearns did make use, at least partially, of one other preacher who had no background in the Holy Tone. This was one John Newton, a young middle-colony immigrant to the upcountry who may have been the first settler not directly a member of the Stearns party to join Sandy Creek Church. Newton was born in Pennsylvania on August 7, 1732, and converted and baptized there at Philadelphia Association's Southampton Church by Rev. Joshua Potts about 1752 (North Carolina Baptist historian G.W. Paschal makes the erroneous assumption that Newton moved to Southampton County, Virginia, and joined a General Baptist church there but Morgan Edwards's records of Newton, Potts, and Southampton Church prove it otherwise). Newton appears to have moved to the Orange/Rowan border country a little before Herman Husbands or the Stearns party arrived there. He stated that he had first been given a "calling" to preach, either by Sandy Creek Church or the impressions of his own conscience, on March 7, 1757,[5] but apparently he did some exhorting as a Stearns assistant some months even before that. He seems to have been a well-educated, thoughtful young man, and Edwards's records of his activities indicate that he was gifted in the leading of public prayer and much more inclined to use direct reading of the Scripture in his attempts to win souls than Stearns or the other preachers, whose impassioned sermons dealt more with the experience of the New Birth in Christ itself. Newton's preaching activities, and his relationships with Shubal Stearns and his other ministering brethren, will be examined in detail in due course.

Favorably though he might regard Daniel and Martha Marshall and their family, it seems that Benjamin Miller over at the Jersey Settlement never really got a chance to work with the couple or with Stearns. He appears to have gone back north some time soon after January 11, 1756,[6] leaving the church at the Jersey Settlement pastorless, and incidentally leaving Shubal Stearns as the only ordained English-speaking Baptist minister in that part of North Carolina. Despite their lack of a pastor now, though, the Jersey settlers seem to have held themselves tenaciously aloof from the ministrations of the Separates at this time. Benjamin

Miller and the Charleston Association had left them with a church organization, a government, and a doctrinal and practical outlook such as they had known in their northeastern coastal home, and they were evidently determined to keep it even if it meant remaining pastorless until the Charleston Association could find another formally trained Regular missionary to serve them. Subsequent evidence indicates that this difference in outlook between the Jersey settlers and the newly made Separate Baptist proselytes on Abbott's Creek provoked some hard feelings, certainly among the James Younger flock and perhaps on both sides. The Abbott's Creek Separates stuck to their guns just as obstinately as did the Jersey settlers, and before long they obtained permission to build a log meetinghouse on property purchased by Elijah and Alice Teague from Squire W.M. Buis about the same time Benjamin Miller returned north[7]. Soon they were petitioning Stearns's church at Sandy Creek for their own formal constitution and for the ordination of Daniel Marshall as their moderator, or pastor.

Here Stearns was faced with a problem. Apparently he had no qualms about gathering Abbott's Creek Church under a constitution and covenant; Wait Palmer had done as much for him and his family at Tolland in early 1751, and he had likewise set Sandy Creek Church "in order" with no other ministerial assistance. The preamble of the covenant he seems to have written for Abbott's Creek is that which is listed in the fourth chapter, showing his combination Six Principle and moderate Calvinist doctrinal outlook. However, he himself had been ordained to the Baptist ministry in a ceremony in which two ministers officiated, and nothing would do but that he should find another Baptist preacher, somewhere, to help him ordain Marshall. Cultural and linguistic differences being what they were on the Carolina frontier at this point, the question of seeking German Dunkard help for the ordination was probably never even considered by Stearns. However, it seems that Younger and the others figured that their old pastor down in South Carolina on the Pee Dee, Joshua Edwards,[8] would be willing to help them out in this matter, and so a party of men that probably included Younger, Stearns, and Marshall themselves set out from Rowan County down the Yadkin to its confluence with the Pee Dee and from thence on into South Carolina to request his officiation at the ordination. Governor Dobbs's papers mention a two-hundred-mile-long wagon road that connected the Rowan County seat, Salisbury, to Charleston,[9] and it was probably on the first section of this undoubtedly rough thoroughfare that the party traveled.

Like Morgan Edwards and James Younger himself, Joshua Edwards was a native Welshman born and raised, evidently in the Baptist faith, in Pembrokeshire in 1704 and migrating to Delaware as a teenager. He had joined the Welsh Tract Church there at age eighteen and had not resettled in South Carolina until 1749. He was himself not ordained as a minister until Pee Dee Church installed him as pastor in June 1752. Nonetheless it was under his pastorate—incidentally for which he was paid the salary of four hundred British pounds per year plus "perquisites which may [have been] worth fifty pounds more"[10]—that Pee Dee had dismissed or "given off the arm" of settlers up on Abbott's Creek in 1753. He even appears to have heard something of the new Separate Baptists to his north, though his source is unknown. Younger thus may have expected a happy reunion with his old pastor, and certainly if the modern Appalachian scholars are right about the Welsh *hywl* preaching cant as an ancient tradition, he would have had one. Possibly even more than Morgan Edwards, Joshua Edwards was steeped in Welsh Baptist customs, and he would have been appreciative of any *hywl*-like pulpit mannerisms he heard from Stearns or Marshall if the cant had been a part of his upbringing. Joshua Edwards found nothing in common whatsoever with the North Carolinans, though, and undoubtedly to Younger's rude awakening and chagrin, he harshly and deliberately rebuffed Stearns and Marshall as the leaders of "a disorderly set which permitted women to pray in public, allowed every ignorant man to preach that chose, and encouraged noise and confusion in their meetings."[11] So much for contemporary evidence on the true origins of traditional Appalachian preaching, but regardless of the question of pulpit cadences, the shock, hurt, and humiliation that the Abbott's Creek party received from Joshua Edwards, coupled with the snub they felt they had already gotten from the Jersey Settlement, was the start of much trouble and strained relations between the Regular and Separate Baptists in the South for years to come.

As luck or providence would have it, though, the party's trip to South Carolina was not a waste. The Pee Dee Church had, in time, given off more arms than just the one at Abbott's Creek; another existed as a church in its own right now, at Lynch's River several miles distant, and of which Younger must have been advised by some of his friends at Pee Dee. The Abbott's Creek party now applied to the minister here for assistance. Rev. Henry Ledbetter, a Virginian by birth, and baptized and ordained as a Palmerite General Baptist minister in eastern North Carolina before embracing Calvinistic principles during the Philadelphia missionaries' reform efforts there, had moved to South Carolina and had been called to the pastorate at Lynch's River with his General Baptist ordination apparently never even having been called into question. Though evidently of a somewhat cranky disposition himself—according to Edwards he was subsequently dismissed from the pastorate for "trying to purge the church of tares," and when he moved back to Tar River in eastern North Carolina, he appears to have taken some books, which were church property, with him[12]—his own background with both General and Regular Baptists was close enough to the patchwork of influences that were the Separate Baptist heritage to make him amenable to the Abbott's Creek group's request for assistance in ordaining their new pastor. He readily agreed to journey back up the Yadkin with the North Carolinans, and with his help, Daniel Marshall got ordained and Abbott's Creek Church installed its new pastor.

Interestingly, Benedict, Semple, and most subsequent historians identify Ledbetter as Marshall's brother-in-law as well as Shubal Stearns, but here again a careful examination of Edwards's *Materials* proves the oft-repeated statement to be erroneous. Ledbetter was married to one Edy Clark, of no family connection either to Stearns or Marshall, and the couple lived in Virginia and the Carolinas all their lives. Most likely the party responsible for the error was the typesetter who first prepared Abraham Marshall's biography of his father for publication;[13] this is the first recorded instance of the statement, and it leads us to wonder just how many such mistakes have been perpetuated through history due to similar flukes.

At any rate, now Shubal Stearns could depend on Daniel Marshall for help in ordinations and other matters that might require two full-fledged ministers rather than petitioning for outside aid. Although Marshall's time may have been taken up slightly more with duties at Abbott's Creek, there is every evidence that he still performed quite a bit of ministerial work for the Sandy Creek congregation as well. Marshall appears to have been something of a "primary" evangelist; Stearns was no less so, but he exhibited more pastoral and organizational skills. Marshall seems often to have taken one or more assistants such as Joseph Breed, John Newton, James Younger, or even his wife Martha with him, out to search the uplands for unpastored settlements in which he could spread the Gospel. When, as frequently was the case, he got some religious interest aroused at one of these locales, he reported the matter to Stearns who then accompanied him back or visited the place himself to hold further services. This two-pronged Marshall-and-Stearns attack, so to speak, appears to have been a common element of their labors at this time, and after this manner they influenced the pastorless little General Baptist church on Grassy Creek in Granville County to become yet another arm of the Sandy Creek congregation some time in 1756.[14] From this settlement Stearns soon got another preaching assistant, a young farmer named James Read who was completely illiterate at the time of his conversion and subsequent baptism. With his wife's tutoring, Read finally did learn enough at least to read the Scriptures.

It was to be John Newton, though, who provided Shubal Stearns with an introduction to the next Separate Baptist preacher at Sandy Creek who would receive full ordination. Like James Read and indeed most who would be ordained by Stearns's and Marshall's hands over the next few years, he was a young, unschooled, sensual, and extremely rough North Carolina backwoodsman, and his name was Philip Mulkey. Twenty-three or twenty-four years old at the time he first came into contact with the Separates, Mulkey had been a fiddle player and a typical good-natured frontier hell-raiser—"his character before his conversion had nothing in it that was singularly evil," as Morgan Edwards put it—and although Mulkey's essential shallowness shines like a silver teaspoon through the conversion experience he related to Edwards, his words blaze, in local color, with the joys, fears, superstitions, and the general rough-and-tumble existence of that time and place:

> One night (saith his narrative) as I was going home from the house where I had been playing the fiddle to dancers, a hideous specter presented itself before me just as I opened the door; the effect was, fainting, and continuing as dead for the space of about 10 minutes, as the people about me report the matter; when I recovered, I found an uncommon dread on my spirits, from an apprehension that the shocking figure, I had seen, was the Devil, and that he would have me. However, I mounted my horse and went homewards. My fears had so disordered my understanding that I fancied the first tree I came to bowed its head to strike at me, which made me start from it. Happening to look up, I fancied that the stars cast a frowning and malignant aspect upon me. When I came home I went to bed and endeavoured to conceal the matter from my wife; but it could not be, for thenceforth I could

neither eat, nor sleep nor rest for some days; but continued to roar out, "I am damned! I shall soon be in hell!" Her attempts to comfort me were vain; and my emaciated body and ghastly visage terrified her. All this while my heart was murmuring against God for making me for no other purpose than to burn me; amongst which murmurings this thought came, My burning in hell will be a display of God's justice and so far I shall be to his praise and glory. It is hardly credible that such a thought should relieve; but so it was, that I found myself much easier when I perceived that God had any use for me, or that I should be any way profitable to him; and that he made me for his glory. I strove to please him by reformation and obedience (for some spice of love came in with the fore-mentioned thought), but yet I was a wretched man. As I was reading these words (if ye have not been faithful in that which is another man's, who will give you that which is your own?) The following thought started in my mind, that God would not trust me until that I had proved that I was faithful to another master. Upon this I resolved to serve the devil faithfully.

Meanwhile a benighted stranger (John Newton) came to my house to read a chapter (53rd of Isaiah) and prayed; and thereby turned my thoughts to Christ, and salvation by him, for the first time. The novelty of this matter, and the possibility it introduced, that my sins had been laid on Christ and that God had stricken and smitten Christ for them (so that he could spare me without falsifying his threatenings or violate his justice) affected me in such a manner as exceeds description. I found an inclination to adore the stranger, and to question whether he was an angel or man? But made no discovery thereof (nor of my thoughts) to him. The next day he departed, and as he was going this thought came in my mind, There is Lot going out of Sodom! As soon as he disappears fire will come down and burn me and mine! I ran after him and kept my eye on him; but the wood presently intercepted the sight; upon which I threw myself to the ground expecting fire and brimstone. I continued in this posture some time almost dead with terror. Finding the fire did not come immediately I began to hope that it would not come at all; and thereupon prayed that God would spare me. I received comfort; and was running to tell my wife of it; but before I reached the house I lost all comfort and my distress come [*sic*] on again. In my agonies I said, many a time,

"O that John Newton had stayed! O that I were as good as John Newton!" Upon which this text crowded into my mind, the spirit of Elijah doth rest on Elisha. I could not discern how this text concerned me; or why it bore so on my mind? At last I said, who knows but it may mean, that the spirit of John Newton shall rest on Philip Mulkey? I persuaded myself that this was the signification; and blessed be God, my hope was not disappointed; the spirit of God came whom I found to be a spirit of liberty, of comfort and of adoption. My wife saw a surprising change in my countenance. I told her the whole matter, and began to preach up conversion to her. She understood me not, though I persuaded myself I was able to make everyone sensible what the newbirth means.

I took my Bible and hastened to my neighbour Campbell; when I came I opened at the 3rd ch. of John and, putting my finger on the 3rd verse, said, "See here, neighbour Campbell, what Jesus Christ saith; he saith we must be born again or not see the kingdom of God!" My neighbour swore at me most desperately, adding, "What devilish project are you now upon with the word of God in your hand?" Upon which he stripped, and sprang out of doors, challenging me to fight. I sat down in the house and began to weep. He sprang in and (skipping and bounding about the floor spitting on his hands and clenching his fists) dared me to fight. I replied, "You know, my dear neighbour, that I am unable to beat you; but now you may beat me if you will; I shall not hinder you!" Hearing this and seeing me all in tears made him look as a man astonished. He put on his shirt, and sat by me, and we both wept. But my talk of the new birth was not understood my him any more than my wife. Soon after I made myself known to Shubal Stearns and church, and was surprised to find that they understood the newbirth, and had knowledge of the tribulations attending it which I had fancied peculiar to my own case.[15]

Philip Mulkey was baptized at Sandy Creek by Shubal Stearns on Christmas Day, 1756, and very soon afterward began preaching himself. He apparently so impressed everyone with his abilities, especially those members of a large Sandy Creek branch congregation some distance up Deep River in Rowan County, that in October 1757, when they were ready to be constituted as a church in their own right, they petitioned

Stearns and Marshall for his ordination so he could be their pastor. This was a scant ten months after Mulkey had been first converted, but in spite of the Pauline injunction against the ordination of novices as bishops found in I Timothy 3, the two older ministers readily complied. Morgan Edwards listened to him preach fifteen years after this, by then Mulkey having relocated to western South Carolina, and was sufficiently impressed with the awe in which Mulkey's congregation regarded him and the style, if not the content, of the sermon he heard to pen this glowing, yet shrewd, analysis:

> Mr. Mulkey's acquirements entitled him to no higher degree than that of an English scholar, neither is there anything extraordinary in his natural endowments, except a very sweet voice, and a smiling aspect; that voice he manages in such a manner as to make soft impressions on the heart and fetch down tears from the eyes in a mechanical way. [Famous British actor David] Garrick is said to have learned a solemn pronunciation of the interjection "O!" from Dr. Fordice; but if I mistake not, both [Garrick and Fordyce] might learn from Mulkey to spin that sound and mix it with awe, distress, solicitude, or any other affection. His success has been such as to hazard being exalted above measure in his own esteem, and the esteem of his converts; but a thorn was put into his flesh about 4 years ago which will keep him humble while he lives, and teach his votaries that he is but a man.[16]

Exactly what this "thorn" was, Edwards never did say. But before we continue our study of this third Separate Baptist preacher to be ordained in the south, we must also look at a gloomy postscript that a tired, aging Edwards added to his notes, apparently in the last year of his life (1795): "Oh! Lamentable. This Philip Mulkey whose experiences are related above, who appeared so eminent as a Christian and minister has appeared to be the instrument of converting a number of souls; has been now for a course of years in the Practice of crimes and enormities at which humanity shudders."[17] As with the "thorn" comment, Edwards does not elaborate; but if these "crimes and enormities" were something that even the blunt old Welshman hesitated to pen, they must have been very shocking indeed. The reader is undoubtedly familiar enough with the antics of some modern television evangelists to venture a few plausible guesses about them. David Benedict adds the further dark com-

further dark comment that after Mulkey began to "stumble," he "soon fell into many heinous sins, and remained, when an old man, an outcast from the church, and a disgrace to that precious cause, of which he had been such an eminent champion."[18] At least the sins of the parent appear not to have been visited upon the children: G.W. Paschal (who, in the manner typical of the more modern Baptist historian dealing with unpleasant facts, tried to muddy the waters around the whole Stearns/Newton/Mulkey connection just enough to make things sound better than they actually were) informs us that Mulkey's son Jonathan became an honorable minister himself and pastored congregations of former Sandy Creek members in the extreme western North Carolina and eastern Tennessese mountains.[19] Jonathan's sons John and Philip, located in southern Kentucky, and the Kentucky Baptist historian J.H. Spencer confirms John's "unblemished moral character" as a minister despite a tendency to be "unstable and carried about by every wind of doctrine"; this statement will be explained in a later chapter. Philip was both a deacon and preacher who labored in conjunction with Jonathan, and this Philip had a son named for his rascally old great-grandfather's first benefactor among the Stearns party: John Newton Mulkey.[20]

An Arminian might say that Philip Mulkey backslid and fell from grace; a moderate Calvinist would judge him never to have been truly converted in the first place; a high Calvinist might remark that he was only fulfilling his predestined end; and a skeptic of any sort would use Mulkey's example to try to prove that Shubal Stearns's upcountry Separate Baptists and all other similar religious revival movements are so much hysteria-induced malarkey. Regardless of the opinion taken, though, the questions still nag: how could the Sandy Creek and Deep River Churches—and especially Shubal Stearns himself—have placed so much trust in Philip Mulkey, whose "smiling aspect" so painfully proved itself to be a vacant grin, to ordain him to the full function of the ministry less than a year after his profession of faith as a new convert at the church? And if Mulkey had been ordained so soon, why was not the faithful John Newton, whose "spirit" the erratic Mulkey coveted at the time of his supposed rebirth, ordained just as quickly or even sooner? Edwards could declare that Stearns, in spite of his small share of learning, was "pretty well acquainted with books"; he liked John Newton as well, and the man's very choice of text to read to Mulkey in 1756 is indicative of Newton's own careful Scripture-based method of evangelism. But all Edwards needed to report to reveal just how harebrained Mulkey had always been was Mulkey's own 1772 exegesis of the texts he had associated with his conversion some sixteen years before. There can be only one answer: within ten months of joining Sandy Creek Church and probably in less time than that, Philip Mulkey had "outstripped" John Newton in style by learning to mimic Shubal Stearns's pulpit address nearly perfectly. In so doing Mulkey simply became a convincing but cheap replica of Stearns himself. Cogent evidence for this is found in Edwards's own account of Mulkey's preaching in 1772, which he depicted using almost exactly the same descriptive terms he used to portray Stearns in the pulpit; the most graphic detail included was Mulkey's dramatic, musical interjection *"Ohhh!"* and this author ventures a guess that Mulkey picked that up from Stearns as well. Though Edwards complimented Newton's preaching highly, he never found anything so remarkable about the style of it and indeed nothing remarkable about either the style or content of Daniel Marshall's. Edwards and indeed most other early Baptist historians give credit to Shubal Stearns for both dramatic style and Scriptural content, and we hope that they are accurate; but unfortunately, among his early backcountry Carolina converts, Mulkey's style quickly and easily triumphed over Newton's substance, and it is one of Shubal Stearns's greatest failings that he allowed this to happen, much less endorsed it. The possible causes for his treatment of both Mulkey and Newton, however, will be discussed in due course.

Even so, there is no record of any animosity on the part of either Newton or Mulkey in these years; Newton even named one of his sons Philip, and until at least late 1767 or early 1768 they seem to have enjoyed a cordial working relationship. In addition, Stearns might be excused for overlooking a few things in the year after Newton and Mulkey met because by this time he was so utterly busy with preaching tours, one wonders how he even found leisure to sleep or to eat a meal, much less provide guidance to two younger ministers. At least by 1757 he and Daniel Marshall had both begun to leave the upcountry and go on itinerant tours through the lowland coastal flats and even the maritime counties of North Carolina. Though the Separate Baptists never quite established the hold here that they enjoyed in the hills, Stearns's and Marshall's preaching in this region was met with considerable success as well as a good deal of criticism, perhaps partially deserved, from the lowland Anglican parsons. "The strolling preachers from New England," fumed one irate divine on the coast at New Bern, were "preaching up the inexpediency of human learning and the practice of moral virtue, and the great expediency of dreams, visions and immediate revelations."[21] This particular parson mistook Stearns and Marshall for Whitefield- and Wesleyan-style Methodists and actually wrote the Society for the Propagation of the Gospel, apparently taking George Whitefield to task for their conduct. A few years later, when Whitefield visited New Bern on a tour of itinerancy, he asked the minister's parish clerk about the matter. The rector noted:

> In his conversation with the Parish Clerk he mentioned the particular number of small tracts that the Society had sent me, and seemed to intimate that in my letter to the Society, I had improperly called the enthusiastic sect in these parts by the name of Methodists, for that none were properly called by that name but the followers of himself and Mr. Wesley. Tho' with submission to Mr. Whitefield, granting that they were not his immediate disciples and followers, I do affirm that they sprung from the seed that he first planted in New England and the difference of soil may perhaps first caused such an alteration in the fruit that he may be ashamed of it. However, I think his discourse on the whole has been of some service here, for he particularly condemned the rebaptizing of Adults and the doctrine of the irresistible influence of the Spirit, for both which the late Methodists in these parts had strongly contended; and likewise recommended infant Baptism, and declared himself a minister of the Church of England.[22]

This is, as has been noted, the only time George Whitefield appears ever to have been advised of Shubal Stearns's work, and he more or less completely, if untruthfully, disowned the whole of it. It is odd, too, that none of the divines of the Established Church ever compared or contrasted Stearns's efforts to the earlier Palmer churches whose conference, through the efforts of the Philadelphia and Charleston missionaries, was now an auxiliary of the Charleston Association. Nonetheless, not all eastern North Carolina Anglican clergymen were quite so vituperative in their condemnation of Stearns. Witness Rev. Michael Smith, writing from Johnston County in 1758: "I find that these preachers have been of great service to me in my office, for many of the back settlers who were in a manner totally ignorant of the Christian religion and overrun with sensuality have been roused from their treacherous slumbers, brought to a more serious way of thinking, and from hearing ignorant enthusiastical harangues have been prepared for more solid discourses."[23] Faint praise indeed, but more charitable at least than Whitefield's repudiation of Stearns's work.

The records of Stearns's and Marshall's early labors in the east are extremely spotty—their detractors writing more about them than their supporters ever did or even could—but we do know that the two gathered at least five "arms" of Sandy Creek Church in the low country within a few years' time. These were on New River and Lockwood's Folly in Onslow County; Black River, near the mouth of Bull Tail Creek in New Hanover or Sampson County; Great Cohara Swamp in Sampson County; and on Trent River in Jones County. The young ministers either raised up in these congregations or perhaps in some cases moving east from Sandy Creek to serve them were Ezekiel Hunter, Charles Markland, and James Turner. Philip Mulkey also did some itinerant preaching and baptizing at these places after he was ordained, and the patient John Newton, still unordained in spite of his productive service, moved to Black River to preach to the church there and enjoyed much success for several years in spite of having to call on Stearns, Mulkey, or other ordained ministers for assistance in baptismal and communion services.

It is not known for how many years Shubal Stearns took these eastern trips regularly. It appears, though, that after Hunter, Newton, and the other younger ministers became successfully established in the low country, he cut back on them at least a bit, and perhaps more after Hunter and a few of the others had been ordained. His primary focus of concentration, and we may presume his heart as well, was always in the western backcountry. Perhaps with this in mind, or perhaps because he felt that God was telling him to do so, in late 1757 or early 1758 Stearns formulated a plan for a centralized organization for his Baptists, with its base to be in the uplands and near his own home: a new, and in fact the first, formal association of Separate Baptists. This is certainly not a step that any Regular Baptist organizers would have taken at this juncture. In keeping with their heritage as former Independent Puritans, the Regulars emphasized the power and the work of the local church over the power of an association or collection of churches. In every early case where a Regular Baptist association was established, it was done so only after a number of churches had been working and supporting one another in the same general area for several years, and even then it was set up as merely an advisory body that could not compel any of its component churches to accept its advice. The middle-colony coastal Regular churches had had a simple annual get-together for nineteen years before organizing the Philadelphia Association in 1707; though the first Regulars in South Carolina had come there from the Maine district of Massachusetts in 1682, the Charleston Association was not formed until 1751; Benjamin Miller and the other Regular missionaries on the northeastern North Carolina coast had already effectively supplanted the Paul Palmer movement, and its conference was now maintained simply as an auxiliary branch of the Charleston Association, but the Kehukee Association would not be organized from the churches there until 1769; and yet Shubal Stearns, with only three churches, Sandy Creek, Abbott's Creek, and Deep River, fully constituted in the backcountry and three fully ordained ministers, himself included, was actively encouraging his more than nine hundred communicants to form an association little more than two years after he first set foot in the uplands. Indeed, his proposal was for an association very little like the Regulars had, and it was certainly an institution that none of Stearns's erstwhile New Light brethren in New England, either of Separate Congregational or Separate Baptist persuasion, would have tolerated even for a moment. According to Morgan Edwards, Stearns's idea was to organize the association as an ecclesiastical council, with members chosen by its component churches, yet greater in power than the churches themselves and with authority to impose rule over them. And though he admired Shubal Stearns, or at least the impression that was given him of the little preacher by his contacts in the upcountry who had known him, Edwards heaped especial scorn on this idea:

> A mistake ... this association fell into, relative to their power and jurisdiction, [was] that they had carried matters so high as to leave hardly any power in particular churches, unfellowshipping ordinations, ministers and churches that acted independent of them; and pleading "That though compleat power be in every church yet every church can transfer it to an association"; which is as much to say that a man may take out his eyes, ears &c. and give them to another to see, hear &c. for him; for if power be fixed by christ in a particular church they can not transfer it; nay, should they formally give it away yet is it not gone away.[24]

Regarding this state of affairs, the Baptist historians besides Edwards have mainly been silent, probably, this author conjectures, because the principle on which Stearns's association was founded is so contrary to most modern Baptist denominational polity—written polity, at least. David Benedict simply made a reference to the Edwards statement above, and Semple ignored the matter altogether. More recent religious and denominational historians such as James Tull, Sydney Ahlstrom, and G.W. Paschal, however, do comment on the Stearns policy and most seem to think that he was inspired to adopt it from his background and his experiences with the Established Presbyterian Church in Connecticut. Paschal states that Stearns "had been schooled in his New England home into accepting just such arbitrary dealing by the church councils,"[25] and given the fact that his preaching had gained such a massive and enthusiastic following so quickly, Stearns truthfully might have considered a strong centralized extra-church government necessary to keep his people, scattered in settlements dozens of miles apart that now reached from the upcountry all the way to the southeastern coast of North Carolina, orthodox in faith and doctrine. On the other hand, it is plausible that the sudden rush of power had gone to his head, and he was acting arbitrarily as a self-established religious authority. Given his subsequent unblemished record—had he tried to set himself up as a new prophet of some sort, Edwards would have been all too willing to write a complete and critical account of it—the former possibility is by far the more likely one. Even so, it remains that the Connecticut state church and its legal status, under the Saybrook Platform, were the very entities against which Stearns and indeed all other New England New Lights had rebelled in the wake of the Whitefield Revival. Could it truly be that Stearns was now giving his Baptists elements of the very state church he and his family had condemned and withdrawn from more than a decade before, the church that had endorsed the Halfway Covenant and that would have barred him from the ministry due to his lack of formal schooling? Unless he was gone into megalomania by this time, and it must be stressed that there is no evidence whatsoever that this had happened or indeed ever would occur, the Established Church hypothesis just makes too little sense.

This author theorizes that Shubal Stearns did indeed adopt an associational polity based on his prior experience, from a source that, while obvious to anyone who has researched the origins of the Separate Baptists in New England, seems to have been overlooked by every one of the historians who have written accounts of his life and ministry. He must have gotten it from the only organized Baptists he had known in

New England during his three-year tenure there as a Baptist pastor, the same Baptists who had probably introduced him to so many of the beliefs and customs he introduced into Christian worship in the backcountry, including foot washing, imposition, anointing of the sick, and Abbott's Creek Church's Six Principle–based church covenant: the old General Baptists of either Wightman Jacobs's small Windham County Yearly Meeting in Connecticut, the older Rhode Island Yearly Meeting in which Valentine and Timothy Wightman, Daniel Fiske, and Joshua Morse had been raised up to the ministry, or, very probably, both groups. The Generals' own practice of maintaining associations with a tight central control, which they let supersede the power of individual churches, and the overlording power that a General Baptist association could exert, have already been amply demonstrated. The imbroglio regarding General Baptist work with the Separate Congregationalists, though it must have been building up for some time at least within the Rhode Island Yearly Meeting, did not become a completely public matter until June 1758, at least six months before Stearns came up with his associational plan for the backcountry. It must be repeated here that no direct connection between Stearns's Tolland church and either the Windham or Rhode Island Six Principle associations has ever been documented, except through Wait Palmer's relationship to the Wightmans and Joshua Morse's Rhode Island background, and the surviving records of the Rhode Island Yearly Meeting between 1750 and 1755 are so spotty that this question may never be satisfactorily answered. Still, this theory makes more sense and fits the subsequent facts better than any of the others. Shubal Stearns was a Baptist and proud of it, and he proposed to give his followers the only type of Baptist association with which he had ever been acquainted.

At any rate, not long after Philip Mulkey's ordination, Stearns rode a circuit between his three organized churches, explaining his idea and asking them to send delegates for the purpose of organizing the association at Sandy Creek Church in January 1758. The meeting was held accordingly and the Sandy Creek Association of Separate Baptists was born, evidently with no other covenant, constitution, or listing of articles of faith except the beloved New Light principle of "the Bible and it alone"—that is, unless the association adopted some brief nonspecific statement of faith such as the Abbott's Creek covenant. Unfortunately most of the early records of the Sandy Creek Association, which still exists as a Southern Baptist body, were destroyed in a fire in 1816. According to the group's clerk at that time they were scanty enough even if they had survived the blaze.[26] We do have one eyewitness report of this first Sandy Creek Association session from James Read, who was there evidently as a representative of Sandy Creek Church's arm on Grassy Creek in Granville County and who penned it probably many years later, after he had learned to write: "At our first association we continued together three or four days. Great crowds of people attended, mostly through curiosity. The great power of God was among us. The preaching every day seemed to be attended with God's blessing. We carried on our Association with sweet decorum and fellowship to the end. Then we took leave of one another, with many solemn charges from our reverend old father Shubal Stearns to stand fast unto the end."[27]

Though he couldn't have meant to do so, Read tantalizes us; he seems to tell us everything and nothing simultaneously. No word regarding an agenda or parliamentary procedure is found, and for that matter there are no details even of the association site's physical layout. Nonetheless there are a few things that can be inferred, with a fair degree of probability, about the initial session of this very first American frontier Baptist association meeting. The most obvious is that the preaching of the Gospel, apart from any other work the association might have done, was carried on continuously for three or four days. In addition, it is clear that the crowd that attended was composed not only of Stearns's Baptists from Sandy Creek, Abbott's Creek, and Deep River Churches and their various and scattered arms, but a great multitude of onlookers from other denominations and even the unchurched, making the affair, in spite of the January weather, not only a religious but a social event. It is thus probable that the Sandy Creek Association set the prototype for all such later American rural Baptist gatherings: the "business" of the association being transacted in the meetinghouse by messengers appointed by their churches, but by far the greater number of attendees remaining outside, perhaps in a grove of trees or a brush arbor, listening to and participating in an almost continuous outdoor worship service of preaching, praying, singing, and exhorting, with the quasi-liturgical evangelistic hymns of Watts, Newton, Toplady, and Charles Wesley being "lined" to the crowds from the few hymnbooks in Old World modal melodies between sermons. The Sandy Creek Association might even have followed what became the common schedule not only for later Baptist association meetings but also for late-eighteenth- and early-nineteenth-century Methodist and Presbyterian camp meetings: beginning the worship services on a Friday night, continuing with morning and evening meetings on both Saturday and Sunday, and finally closing the services and dismissing the assembly at about noon the following Monday. George Whitefield himself may have employed this schedule at least at times in his outdoor gatherings. Although Deborah McCauley makes a convincing argument for its antecedents in the Presbyterian "sacramental revival" gatherings in late-sixteenth- and early-seventeenth-century Scotland and Ireland, it could have had as many or more roots in the old community covenant-owning rite of Puritan New England. One wonders who was the catalyst for its initiation in the southern highlands. Shubal Stearns, with his combination New England Presbyterian–New Light Baptist heritage, is as good a candidate as any so far named by the historians and a better one than most.

Perhaps the most important, and telling, comment that James Read makes, though, is the title he gives to Stearns, mentioned in the introduction of this book as being in direct disobedience to Matthew 23:9: our Reverend Old Father. According to Paschal, G.W. Purefoy, David Benedict, and most other sources, the Sandy Creek Association did not even elect a moderator to preside over its business sessions during most of its early history, the reason being that "it was thought unfit that the permission of a man should be got by one who was speaking for God and His kingdom."[28] If this was the case, though, how could the enthusiastic and noisy Separate Baptists have had an assembly with anything approaching the "sweet decorum" of which Read spoke, let alone avoiding the Babel of everyone negating all others' voices by speaking at the same time? Again there can be only one obvious answer. Shubal Stearns, though perhaps not called by the title of moderator, at least just yet, served in that function and more besides. Not only would he have maintained order during the business sessions, but he undoubtedly formulated both church and associational policy, answered queries from congregations, and adjudicated disputes practically all by himself, with the approbation of Daniel Marshall, Philip Mulkey, and other messengers appointed as delegates by the churches, who served as his councilors—or, more likely, merely as his advisors. Though the old General Baptists both in Old England and New had governed by this same conciliar rule, there is no record of any one individual General Baptist minister ever having exerted such power and influence over an association, and perhaps it is no wonder that Paschal and other historians were blinded to Shubal Stearns's General Baptist influences. After all, the Sandy Creek

Association made Stearns as powerful among his Separate Baptists as Solomon Stoddard had been, under his own Halfway Covenant, back in western Massachusetts and Connecticut in the days of Stearns's youth.

This brings us back to the matter of megalomania. If Shubal Stearns so far had not let all the adulation he had received in the backcountry, and the power and influence he now wielded, go to his head, was he showing signs of "the big head" now? We cannot know exactly what went on in Stearns's mind, and thus the question could be argued either way; however, in light of both the preacher's prior and subsequent history, an alternative, simpler theory, and indeed one whose details have already been noted and demonstrated, reveals itself. From his birth, Shubal Stearns had occupied the position of oldest son in a large rural New England—and for that matter a northeastern Appalachian—family, and since he had reached his majority he had, in a very real sense, been a clan leader in secular, and later in religious, terms. His whole life so far had been shaped in this context, and he knew no other. His brothers and sisters and even his parents, who had followed him south, had honored his position in the family probably since the late 1720s or early 1730s and his role as minister and pastor at least since 1745, possibly even three to five years before that. Even without any assumed pride he could have accepted this as his lot in life quite unconsciously. His family's regard for him would only have furthered the wild adulation with which his musical, emotive New England Holy Tone preaching had been accepted on the backcountry frontier, and all of his converts, who would already have been in awe of him as something of a father figure spiritually, were taught, by example, to hold him in the same regard his family gave him simply by observing the actions of Sandy Creek Church's charter members. Assuming that such was the case, his almost complete control over the Sandy Creek Association and all its churches was, therefore, undoubtedly by the full consent and approbation of most, if not all, of the backcountry Separate Baptists involved. Strangely but truly, the blinders of his own experience may even have made Stearns unaware that he controlled such power, even without the influence of the General Baptists from which he drew his inspiration or the imposing figure and reputation of Solomon Stoddard from his youthful memories. He was such a kindly, fatherly, patriarchal figure to his congregants that even his blindnesses may have been lovable.

Still, Shubal Stearns must not be thought of as a bishop or priest, at least in the sense that his backwoods followers would have pictured such a figure in the Old World or even the New England context. If he had tried to portray himself as such, his listeners probably would have regarded him with the same suspicion they would have given any outsider trying to assume power over them—and, as will be demonstrated in the next chapter, of these there were all too many already. However, his status in the new Sandy Creek Association still fit perfectly with the picture of the regard given the Goodly Fere by Simon Zelotes in the poetry of Ezra Pound. In a secular and economic sense, Stearns was the simple rural farmer he had always been, even in New England; any neighbor passing by his property at certain times of the year might see him outside hoeing corn or digging potatoes when he had leisure from traveling and preaching to do so. Many of the "presents" he received for his preaching were probably in the curt commands so many Sandy Creek adolescents would have heard from their fathers: "Go and help old Brother Stearns get his field work done." And yet, when it came to religion, these same neighbors regarded the words of Shubal Stearns as *the* definitive counsel on Scriptural interpretation, church government, dispute settlement, or any other matter. He was at the same time their good old neighbor *and* their leader. Although his name has been largely forgotten among Appalachian old-time Baptists, the positions he and his junior advisors assumed and exemplified were soon institutionalized in the offices of the association moderator and his "Committee on the Bill of Arrangements," and both are still extremely strong forces within the hill-country Baptist subgroups and the culture that has grown around them. From henceforth native Appalachian rural Baptists would maintain the same live-and-die stance on "the Bible and it alone" that Shubal Stearns himself had given them; but before committing themselves to anything remotely novel from the association's way of doing things, they'd see what the moderator and his committee had to say about it first. And so the attitude still remains.

Unfortunately, though, of course no human can live up to the image of the Goodly Fere of Pound's verse. To Christian believers, there has been only one in the entire scope of mankind's history who ever fulfilled the qualifications and to them He is the object of worship. There was no way Shubal Stearns could have met, at all times, the expectations of the image of him embraced by his North Carolina followers, and his very human limits, rather than any pride, deceit, or dishonesty on his part, were the cause of most of his later problems. As an example, we can here speculate further on the John Newton/Philip Mulkey issue. There are few, if any, records of Stearns's agreeing to ordain another minister unless a newly constituted church needed a pastor or moderator; Daniel Marshall was thus called to this office by Abbott's Creek Church when they "armed off and organized," and likewise Philip Mulkey was ordained so he could care for the new Deep River Church. Mulkey's ability to mimic Stearns explains the rustic Deep River congregation's interest in him as pastor rather than the more methodical, less flashy John Newton, but why should the fatherly Stearns have acquiesced and ordained a green-as-a-gourd young preacher simply because the Deep River members demanded it? It has long been a maxim that imitation is the sincerest form of flattery, and one wonders how much Philip Mulkey, with his "very sweet voice" and "smiling aspect," simply used his imitation of Stearns's pulpit cadences to play up to the little preacher, thus advancing his own standing politically within the Stearns following once he discovered the possibilities of advancement among them. On the other hand, John Newton, who had already proven his commitment to the Separate Baptist cause, remained unordained even after the Black River Church, to which he moved at least by 1760, was ready for a fully ordained pastor. Was Regular Baptist–trained Newton perhaps a little hesitant about accepting the Stearns idea of the association's authority superseding that of the church? Was his wife not a Baptist, perchance? Was he a tad too fond of the Regulars' Philadelphia Confession over the idealistic New Light concept of "the Bible and it alone" to suit Stearns? Was he not quite as skilled in the pulpit cadences of the New England Holy Tone as Stearns perceived that a God-called minister should have been? Or was he simply perhaps just a bit aloof, as committed to and ready to labor for the Baptist cause in the uplands as Shubal Stearns was, but insisting somewhat on standing upon his own two feet in so doing? We will never know for sure, but in the political patronage system that inevitably springs up within a following such as Stearns had, all of the above guesses are plausible and any of them would have been crucial in determining Newton's standing in the Sandy Creek Association. For whatever reason, John Newton remained unordained even at Black River and though, as it has already been noted, he had taken the matter cheerfully in stride so far, the circumstance would ultimately bring both him and Shubal Stearns to great grief. The true tragedy was that Stearns, tenaciously plowing his life's furrow, up in the yoke as a good ox should be but wearing the blinders of his experience, didn't even recognize the coming snag until it was too late to prevent the plow from striking it. But this will be explained more fully later.

After the new association was organized, though, in spite of the hard feelings and acrimony that Stearns and his followers had encountered when they had come into contact with the South Carolina Regular Baptist churches, the Sandy Creek moderator may even have hesitantly explored the idea of a closer union or "correspondence" relationship with the Charleston Association to the south. The chain of events that led to this began probably with the new missionary that the Charleston Association finally found for the Regular Baptist church at the Jersey Settlement in Rowan County, a young Hopewell, New Jersey, native named John Gano. Gano had been at Opequon Church with Benjamin Miller and other Regular missionaries when they had reorganized the church there in 1751, though he had not been ordained at the time nor actually participated to a great extent in the work. He had taken some theological training, though, under Isaac Eaton at Hopewell Academy near his home, and after his ordination as a Regular Baptist minister, he had done some valuable missionary work of his own, again with Benjamin Miller and others, among the Paul Palmer churches on the northeastern North Carolina seacoast. In fact, Morgan Edwards, who knew the missionary well for many years, considered Gano's preaching of tantamount importance to the coastal effort, writing in his usual blunt style that "Gano clenched it"[29] for Calvinistic doctrine and Regular Baptist usages among the former Palmer churches. After his eastern triumph, as it were, Gano lived a long, full, and adventurous life that included experiences as pastor in both New Jersey and New York, military chaplain in the American Revolution, and pioneer preacher in the Kentucky Bluegrass.

But the fall of 1758 found Gano again in the south in response to the Charleston Association's and the Jersey Settlement's request for a missionary. At the settlement he reorganized the church, and in urban style appointed a board of trustees composed of members of all denominations represented there to oversee the use of the meetinghouse. Meanwhile, preaching and baptizing on his own, he seems to have taken the time to observe his Separate Baptist neighbors at Abbott's Creek and perhaps in other Rowan County settlements as well. Thus it happened that Gano attended Sandy Creek Association's 1759 association meeting. This appears to have been the third session of the association, as a second session was held some time in the summer of 1758. G.W. Paschal, drawing from the accounts of earlier historians, relates what transpired:

Mr. Gano was received by Stearns with great affection; but as there was at that time an unhappy shyness and jealousy between the Regulars and Separates, by the others he was treated with coldness and suspicion; and they even refused to invite him into their Association. But Mr. Gano had too much knowledge of mankind, humility and good nature, to be offended by this treatment. He continued awhile as spectator of their proceedings, and then retired with a view of returning home. Stearns was very much hurt and mortified with the shyness and incivility of his brethren, and in the absence of Mr. Gano expostulated with them on the matter, and made a proposition to invite him to preach to them. All were forward to invite him to preach, although they could not invite him to a seat in their Assembly. With their invitation he cheerfully complied, and his preaching, though not with the New Light tones and gestures, was in demonstration of the Spirit and of power. He continued with them to the close of their session, and preached frequently, much to their astonishment as well as edification. Their hearts were soon opened towards him, and their cold indifference and languid charity were before he left them enlarged into a warm attachment and cordial affection. And so superior did his preaching talents appear to them that the young and illiterate preachers said that they felt as if they could never attempt to preach again.[30]

Part, or perhaps even most, of this account must be true. Joshua Edwards's insults to Stearns, Daniel Marshall, and James Younger down on the Pee Dee in South Carolina in 1756, as well as the Jersey Settlement's entire attitude toward their Separate Baptist neighbors at Abbott's Creek, would explain the 1759 Sandy Creek assembly's cold and suspicious treatment of Gano. However, by the same token, if Stearns himself suddenly decided to extend friendship and courtesy to Gano, which appears to have been the case, his doting followers would have taken the diplomatic shift completely in stride, and the end results would have been much like Paschal describes. As for the question of their reception of Regular-style prepared sermons unseasoned by the Holy Tone, though, in light of John Newton's status the Paschal account hardly adds up. Evidence will be shown subsequently that, if indeed John Gano had warmed the Separates,' or even only Shubal Stearns's, hearts toward the Regular Baptists, it was only a temporary thaw. In response to Gano's

1759 excursion, Philip Mulkey did indeed visit the Charleston Association in 1762, bringing with him to the meeting some queries evidently sent to the body by Stearns and the Sandy Creek Association. Of their nature nothing is known, but minister Oliver Hart of Charleston Church was appointed to answer the questions, and he and Evan Pugh, now a minister at Pee Dee but formerly a member of the same Opequon Church in northern Virginia that the Marshalls and the Breeds had joined prior to 1754, were designated as delegates to make a return visit to the Sandy Creek Association to try to establish fellowship and union. Unfortunately, nothing else is known beyond the fact that this attempt at dialogue ultimately failed.[31]

In the meantime, much more had occurred in the North Carolina backcountry. In fact, the Sandy Creek Association was now growing at such an amazing rate that, even if we had complete records of all that transpired, the direct sequence of events would be hard to follow. First, after the October 1757 ordination of Philip Mulkey came the ordinations of others such as James Read and the constitution of more churches from the arms spreading in all directions from Stearns's Sandy Creek Church. The Grassy Creek fellowship where Read labored must have been one of those "armed off and organized" in 1758, and at least a few of the arms in the eastern lowlands under the care of Ezekiel Hunter seem to have achieved this status in 1758 as well. Joseph Breed preached for a time to a new arm of the Deep River Church on Little River in Anson County, but his work there was soon supplanted by that of two brothers named Joseph and William Murphy. Both were converted at Deep River, Joseph having been "wicked to a proverb"[32] before this according to Edwards, baptized in 1757 by Shubal Stearns, and brought up in the ministry under his fatherly wing. Although they were actually about Philip Mulkey's age, they were so youthful in appearance that for years they were jokingly referred to as "Murphy's Boys." Despite this, as Shubal Stearns began to work more and more at new arms of Sandy Creek Church on Caraway Creek and Haw River in the Piedmont, it would be the Murphys who would take the New England Holy Tone and the Separate Baptist gospel up into the southeastern Appalachian mountains proper.

A hot border war with the Cherokee broke up the Jersey Settlement, its church, and other Rowan County pioneer outposts early in the year 1760. Many settlers not only at the Jersey outpost but all over Rowan County fled back north—John Gano and his family all the way back to

New Jersey, and even several of the Boones up the Yadkin as well. Those that were left pretty much had to acclimatize themselves to their new homes and accept the ministerial services of Daniel (and Martha) Marshall, James Younger, and the Murphys, the only Baptist ministers left in the region. Joseph Murphy was ordained in 1760 and William in 1761. Joseph, in addition to his pastoral duties at Little River, traveled extensively up the Yadkin over the next several years to preach in the new settlements as they were formed. For reasons that will be discussed in the next chapter, he finally moved to the upper Yadkin frontier in 1769 or 1770, remaining a citizen of what was to become Surry County, North Carolina, for the rest of his life. A charming description of one of Murphy's old "arm" congregations in that area, at the Mulberry Fields near present Wilkesboro,[33] is found in the memoirs of Revolutionary War general William Lenoir, for whom both a county and city in North Carolina are named. As Lenoir, who as a young man certainly seems to have had an eye for the ladies, relates, evidently the settlers' necessity of making do with what they had made Murphy either unable or unwilling to enforce the strict dress and hair-length code of Stearns and the other Separates further to the south and east:

> Surry was frontier country in 1775, including Wilkes, Ashe and Burke and extending to the Mississippi River [Tennessee did not yet exist]. It was thinly inhabited being an entire desert.
>
> Then the Mulberry Fields Meeting House was the only place of worship in said county. It was built by the Baptists and very large congregations of different persuasions of people attended their meetings. The gentlemen generally dressed in hunting shirts, short breeches, leggins and moccasins. The ladies in linsy (flax) petticoats and bed gowns and often without shoes in the summer. Some had bonnets and bed gowns of calico, but generally of linsy, and some of them had on men's hats. Their hair was commonly clubbed.
>
> Men generally had long hair and wore it either in a cue or clubbed. Once at a large meeting I noticed that there were but two ladies who had on long gowns. One of them was laced genteelly and the body of the other was open and the tail thereof drawn up and tucked in her apron or coat string. They appeared very orderly and devout at meetings, and going to their homes you would find them living well and they would treat you with great hospitality,

giving you plenty of pork, beef, bear meat and venison; also milk, butter, cheese and honey. The buffaloes and elk were then chiefly destroyed. And when you left them, as there were no public roads and few plain paths, the men would go with you to show you the way until you could be accommodated by some other person. You might travel hundreds of miles and not meet with any person who would receive any pay.[34]

Some of these church members were described by Edwards as being "the remains of Mr. Gano's church in the Jersey-settlement,"[35] and he tells us that Murphy's flock as a whole was a little divided over the practice of foot washing after communion services; it was probably these former Regular Baptists, unused to the custom, to whom Edwards referred. Other members apparently included the churchgoing component of the Boone family. It is not known exactly where Squire Boone and his family attended the Baptist church after his exclusion by the Quakers, though initially they lived not far from either the Jersey Settlement or Abbott's Creek. After the aforementioned Cherokee war, though, they did move further up the Yadkin, from whence Boone's sons Daniel and Squire Jr. first visited Kentucky at the behest of North Carolina superior court judge and land speculator Richard Henderson in 1769. During this period, Joseph Murphy's name is connected with that of George Boone and several men of the Bryan or Bryant family, Daniel Boone's in-laws, at the Shallow Fords or Timber Ridge Church that was the first that Murphy had gathered on the upper Yadkin.[36] Although Morgan Edwards fails to mention his name in connection with any church in the region, Squire Boone Jr. is known to have been an "occasional," if not an ordained, Baptist preacher, and if this is so it must have been under Joseph Murphy's guidance that he got his start in the ministry.

William Murphy pushed forward into the Appalachian mountains even further than his brother had done, and by the time of his ordination in 1761, he was settled and preaching in southwestern Virginia near the headwaters of the Roanoke River. Even before he arrived there, though, the Separate Baptist fire had already come to the area, and in a characteristically unusual way. In the summer of 1758, Tidence Lane's younger brother Dutton Lane, on a visit to North Carolina from their parents' home in Pittsylvania County on the Virginia/North Carolina border, accompanied Tidence and his family to a few of Shubal Stearns's spirited meetings on Caraway Creek in Orange County and evidently had as rude an awakening to his soul's status as Philip Mulkey had claimed two years earlier. Morgan Edwards writes a droll, tongue-in-cheek account of what transpired afterward, evidently near Tidence and Esther Lane's cabin:

> As [Dutton] was returning from hunting with the game and his rifle in his hands he fancied that he saw the devil, standing in the way before him; upon which he stopped, meditating what to do; to go on (he thought) was daring; and to fly, cowardly; firing at him, he judged, would be vain; therefore he turned on one side and took another path; when he came between him and home he fancied the devil was pursuing him, but dared not to look back; he quickened his pace, till he came near the house; then bolted the door, and fell down with rifle and game and all, on the floor. After continuing in this situation for a while he came to himself, but never got rid of the fear till he was plucked as a brand out of the burning. How true is it, that some are saved with fear?[37]

Dutton Lane found his peace in the New Birth in Christ and baptism by Shubal Stearns in Caraway Creek in September 1758, and shortly thereafter he felt a divine inspiration to preach. He invited Stearns, Marshall, Philip Mulkey, and the Murphys to come help him spread the gospel to his neighbors in the isolated settlements and forts of Pittsylvania County, Virginia. Although Richard Lane, Tidence's and Dutton's father, was greatly dismayed to have two of his sons involved in what he perceived as a radical religious movement—before he himself was converted under Dutton's preaching, that is—Stearns and his children in the faith were almost as successful here as they had been back on the Rowan/Orange County border in North Carolina.

One of their most notable converts was a colonel in the local militia and the quartermaster of an isolated outpost known as Mayo's Fort, Samuel Harris. Unlike most of Stearns's followers, he had been brought up as a landed gentleman, in his case in that early Samuel Morris "Lutheran" enclave of Hanover County, Virginia. Harris had remained a Churchman, however, and according to Edwards, he had been "educated in a manner suitable to his station." Before moving southwest as well as afterward he had served as an Anglican churchwarden, sheriff, justice of the peace, and in other lucrative local offices at that time open only to the Virginia gentry or their sycophants. When the Separate Bap-

BEGINNINGS OF THE STEARNS MOVEMENT, 1755-1762

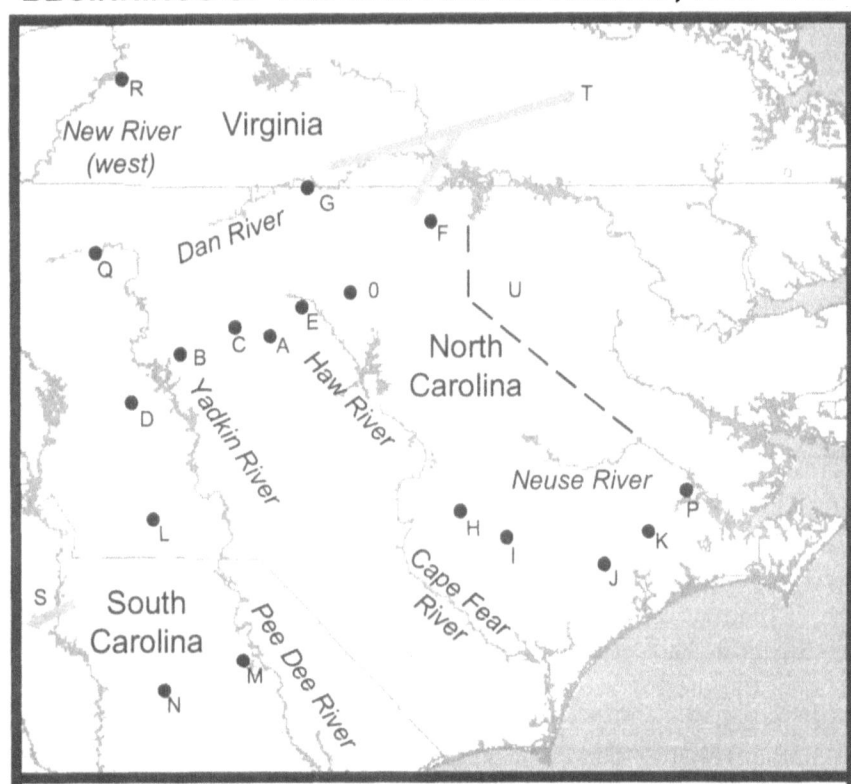

A - Sandy Creek Church (1755)
B - Abbott's Creek Church (1756)
C - Deep River Church (1757)
D - Jersey Church (Regular Baptist)
E - Haw River Church (1764)
F - Grassy Creek Church (1758)
G - Dan River Church (1759)
H - Great Cohara Church (1757-1760)
I - Black River Church (1757-1760)
J - New River Church (east)
K - Trent River Church (1757-1760)
L - Little River Church (1761)
M - Pee Dee Church (Regular Baptist)
N - Lynches River Church (Regular Baptist)
O - Hillsboro (county seat, Orange County)
P - New Bern (provincial capital of NC after 1765)
Q - Shallow Fords Church (1768-1769)
R - Holston-Staunton or Blackwater Church (1768-1769)
S - Later Separate Baptist settlements (after 1762) between present Spartanburg, SC, and Augusta, GA
T - Evangelistic tours of Samuel Harris, James Read, et al. into the Virginia Tidewater region, 1765-1771
U - Territory of Paul Palmer General Baptists (Regular Baptists after 1753-1754)

tists came to Pittsylvania, though, his whole outlook on life changed. Witness Morgan Edwards's account of his conversion, which will bring a smile, and perhaps a fond tear, to anyone who has ever attended a backcountry Appalachian Baptist church during a successful revival meeting:

> [Harris's] conversion (like most of the Separate ministers) was brought to pass in an unusual manner; it began with a deep seriousness without his knowing why or wherefore; conversation, and reading, directed his attention to the cause; pressed with this conviction he ventured to attend the ministry of the Baptists; his distress increased; and his heart (as he used to express it) was ready to burst. Once as the people rose from prayers, the Colonel was observed to continue on his knees, with his head and his hands hanging down the other side of the bench; some of the people went to his relief, and found he was senseless as in a fit; when he came to himself he smiled, and brake out in an ecstacy of joy, crying, "Glory! Glory! Glory!" &c.[38]

Perhaps another smile can be gleaned from Harris's next visit to Mayo's Fort after his New Birth and his baptism:

> When Mr. Harris got relief in soul-affairs, he returned to Mayo with provision for the garrison; but he had not long been in the fort before he went to the corps of officers and began to preach to them the necessity of the new birth; in the course of his harangue one officer interrupted him saying, "Colonel! You have sucked much eloquence from the rum-cask today! Pray let us taste, that we may declaim as well, when it comes our turn!" Mr. Harris said, "I am not drunk!"; and resumed his discourse. He had not gone far, before another in a serious manner looked him in the face and said, "Sam! What the devil ails you?" Mr. Harris replied in the words of the man of Tarsus, "I am not mad, most noble Festus," &c. and otherwise talked so well that the officer became seriously affected, and is now a humble Christian.[39]

The end results of these dramatic Pittsylvania County meetings were the constitution of Dan River Church in the south of the county, over which Dutton Lane was ordained as a minister and where Samuel Harris, though at Mayo's Fort having already proven to be a very successful evangelist himself, at first was ordained in the quaint old Stearns office of "ruling elder"; and the Blackwater or Holston-Staunton Church to the north, with meetinghouses both at the head of the Staunton branch of Roanoke River and on the Blackwater tributary of New River, where William Murphy was ordained. Dan River Church likewise rapidly branched out to include several arms, one being further up New River from Blackwater, that the family of another Kentucky pioneer Separate Baptist preacher, Robert Elkin, appears to have attended; others were on Buffalo and Irvine Rivers and on Fall Creek, and still another was located on Hogan's Creek over the border in North Carolina. It might be mentioned here also that William Murphy's Blackwater Church appears to have been the spiritual home of yet another western pioneer preacher, Robert Stockton, who later moved to Kentucky, as well as several other ministers who later settled in Tennessee.

If things were not hectic enough for Shubal Stearns, though, shortly after the beginning of the Pittsylvania County, Virginia, meetings most of his original charter members at Sandy Creek Church seem to have begun something of another Appalachian tradition—outmigration. Joseph and Priscilla Breed, Daniel and Martha Marshall, Enos and Elizabeth Stinson, Jonathan and Rebecca Polk, and Peter and Ebenezer Stearns and their wives all joined Philip Mulkey and nearly the whole memberships of Abbott's Creek and Deep River Churches in a mass migration to western South Carolina. The reasons for this great mass move, occurring about 1761 or 1762 (although Philip Mulkey is believed to have first visited the South Carolina colony and made at least preliminary arrangements for it in 1759) are not quite clear. Perhaps the heated Cherokee border war in Rowan County, which had caused John Gano to quit the frontier and return with his family to New Jersey, had much to do with it; another possible cause, that of reduced property taxes in the southern colony, will be discussed extensively in the next chapter. For the Stearns family personally, the deaths of their parents, old Shubael and Rebecca, might have been a contributing factor as well. No record of the couple's death dates has survived, but by this time both would have been in their late seventies, a remarkably advanced age for the frontier. Regardless of the reasons, though, as in the case of their 1755 move to North Carolina there was the prospect of fresh land just thrown into market and ready for development. In the case of the South Carolina western backcountry, some settlements were in areas so remote as to be outside the jurisdiction of county courts. Horse thieves and other outlaws prowled the area, and a rough justice was exercised and executed against them by self-appointed groups of backwoodsmen who styled themselves as "Regulators" and who provided the only police force the settlers had until the establishment of county courts in the South Carolina backcountry.

For whatever reason, Philip Mulkey and his followers, including Joseph and Priscilla Breed and their family, settled on Fairforest River, a tributary of the Tyger River in what was then Craven County, South Carolina, and Deep River Church in North Carolina became Fairforest Church in South Carolina. The remaining members at Deep River, under the care of an unordained preacher named Nathaniel Powell, moved their memberships back to Sandy Creek Church and worshiped again as an arm congregation, finally entering into the constitution of Haw River Church in 1764. Likewise Daniel Marshall settled on Beaver Creek, about ten miles from South Carolina's border with Georgia, not far from Augusta, and Abbott's Creek Church became the Stephens' Creek Church in that region. It is not known whether James Younger was still alive at this time, but there were a few families remaining up at Abbott's Creek; these, like their brethren at Deep River, simply became members of the old Sandy Creek Church again and kept their meetinghouse as an arm under Stearns's care and that of one of his young assistants, James Billingsley. In this status the Abbott's Creek arm remained until it was armed off once again as a church in 1783 under the care of pastor George Whitefield Pope. Meanwhile, Mulkey and Marshall continued working as hard as ever in their new homes, preaching, baptizing converts, and establishing arms of their respective churches quickly. Within a few years, one of these, at a branch of the Santee River known as the Congaree, was ripe for constitution, but before it was even organized Philip Mulkey's old benefactor John Newton, still unordained despite his years of success at Sandy Creek, Deep River, and Black River, moved south to live and to preach to the congregation there about 1765—very probably at Mulkey's request.

Meanwhile, back at Shubal Stearns's old home, in 1762 the congregation at Sandy Creek Church moved into a brand-new meetinghouse, described by Morgan Edwards as thirty by twenty-six feet—the building could never have accommodated the immense crowd that regularly attended there without stairs or a ladder and a second-story gallery, and even then it was probably jam-packed at most services—and built on

(Above) The old Sandy Creek Church, in present Randolph County, North Carolina. This log meetinghouse, undoubtedly nearly identical to the second meetinghouse (1762) built on the same property during Shubal Stearns's lifetime, was constructed around 1801. Courtesy Randolph County Public Library, Asheboro, North Carolina. *(Below)* The interior of the old Sandy Creek Church facing the pulpit, much as it must have looked during Shubal Stearns's lifetime. Courtesy Randolph County Public Library, Asheboro, North Carolina.

land donated by Seamore York, one of Stearns's close neighbors and who probably was a deacon or ruling elder at the church. Elnathan Davis, with assistance from Nathaniel Powell and other younger men, began to preach for Stearns at Haw River, and Tidence Lane started to give Stearns pulpit assistance at Sandy Creek itself. Together with James Billingsley over at the Abbott's Creek arm, Tidence Lane and Davis appear to have been the younger preachers most closely associated directly with Stearns in the latter years of his life and ministry. Of Stearns's direct family very few remained in the Sandy Creek community now, possibly only the patient, faithful Sarah, but perhaps Isaac and his daughter Hephzibah as well. One wonders whether the childless, aging preacher became lonesome in his last years for his sisters Martha, Rebecca, and Elizabeth and brothers Peter and Ebenezer, with whom he had labored so hard and experienced so much joy at Tolland, Opequon, Cacapon, and Sandy Creek, and whose growing families were now scattered through the western South Carolina frontier. It does not seem all that likely, however; for within a decade of his arrival at Sandy Creek, Shubal Stearns, with the musical, hypnotic power of his own preaching, the support of his family, the organization of the Sandy Creek Association, and the quiet, insistent force of his own personality as eldest brother and Goodly Fere to all who followed him, had made much of the entire English population of the western backwoods of three separate colonies his extended family, and he ruled over it like the genial old New England community patriarch that must have been his unconscious ideal. Morgan Edwards, Robert B. Semple, and David Benedict all tell us that in the first fourteen years of the Sandy Creek Association's existence, its annual sessions were always held directly at the old Sandy Creek Church or a meetinghouse near it such as Haw River or Little River. They consistently drew great crowds of Stearns disciples from as far away as the Separate Baptists had scattered. From the North Carolina lowlands where Charles Markland, Ezekiel Hunter, James Turner, and their associates labored ceaselessly in spite of the criticisms of Anglican parsons; from the South Carolina backcountry, beset with outlaws and policed by Regulators and that Daniel and Martha Marshall, Joseph and Priscilla Breed, Philip Mulkey, John Newton, and so many of the Stearns family now called home; from the headwaters of the Yadkin, where tough Joseph Murphy and his younger, new-converted colleagues risked all manner of frontier dangers to carry out their commission; and from even the wildness of southwestern Virginia, where Dutton Lane, William Murphy, and Samuel Harris challenged soldiers, hunters, and farmers alike with the preaching of the New Birth in the New England Holy Tone; from all these places joyful pilgrims came streaming back once a year to the Sandy Creek Association, their spiritual home and base, to worship with, recount happy news to, and show their love for their Reverend Old Father and Goodly Fere. G.W. Paschal, quoting Semple on the subject, notes that "The sessions were all held in the vicinity of Stearns, and the elder preachers. The younger ones, from Virginia and both the Carolinas, attended constantly, and derived much knowledge and consolation from the conversation of the more experienced. From such accounts as can be had, it appears that these associations were conducted with peace and harmony, and were productive of extensive usefulness."[40]

The tendency, noted so sympathetically by nearly all Appalachian scholars, of displaced, outmigrated Appalachian people to return "back home" for such gatherings, is thus no new phenomenon appearing only in the modern age; its historical antecedent is more than two hundred years old, and it was in connection with good old Shubal Stearns and his Sandy Creek Association that it first appeared.

We may therefore perhaps best close out this chapter, and what was undoubtedly the happiest period in Shubal Stearns's life, with his own words, from a letter to his old friend and Tolland colleague Noah Alden dated October 16, 1765. The Sandy Creek Association's annual meetings were now held regularly on the second weekend of that month, probably for the convenience of the backcountry farmers who would have had most of their crops gathered in by then, and the six-day revival of which he writes may have been a preliminary gathering for the 1765 sessions: "The Lord carries on his work gloriously in sundry places in this province, and in Virginia and South Carolina. There has been no addition of churches since I wrote last year but many members have been added in many places. Not long since I attended a meeting in Hoy [Haw] river, about thirty miles from hence. About seven hundred souls attended the meeting, which held six days. We received twenty-four persons by a satisfactory declaration of grace, and eighteen of them were baptized. The power of the Lord was wonderful."[41]

6
MESHECH
1765–1771

> Woe is me, that I sojourn in Meshech, that I dwell in the tents of Kedar; my soul hath long dwelt with him that hateth peace. I am for peace; but when I speak, they are for war.
> —Psalm 120:5–7, King James version

Considering the thousands of sermons that Shubal Stearns must have preached in North Carolina, it is odd that we know little or nothing of the actual texts he took for his discourses. It has already been shown, though, from the writings of Stearns detractors as well as supporters, that he emphasized personal revelations from God such as the one he believed he had received in 1754 as a call to his great work in the west, and he must have remarked on these quite a bit while in the pulpit. If this is so, certainly the most poignant text the old preacher ever took, and one to which he must have referred again and again in the last year of his life, was of another, perhaps last, claimed direct revelation to him from God that took place right after a terrific thunderstorm on September 7, 1769. Stearns was away from Sandy Creek at the time of the storm, probably on a preaching appointment, and he began to wend his way homeward, evidently on foot, as soon as he could after the storm subsided. Morgan Edwards, who probably heard the tale from Tidence Lane and Elnathan Davis, recounts what happened next:

> As he was ascending a hill in his way home he observed in the horizon a white heap like snow; upon his drawing near he perceived the heap to stand suspended in the air fifteen or twenty feet above ground. Presently it fell to the ground and divided itself into three parts; the greatest part moved northward; a less towards the south; and the third, which was less than either but much brighter, remained on the spot where the whole fell; as his eyes followed that which went northward, it vanished; he turned to look at the

other, and found that they also had disappeared. While the old man pondered what phantom the division, and motions of it, meant, the thought struck him: "The bright heap is our religious interest; which will divide and spread north and south, but chiefly northward; while a small part remains at Sandy Creek."[1]

As certainly as Stearns's revelation about the great work in the west came true in 1755, so did this prophecy fulfill itself within two years, and in both cases there is no way either to prove or disprove Stearns's claims of having received divine messages. Sadly, though, the hand of man is as demonstrable in the second instance as it is in the first. Even if Shubal Stearns did immediately and correctly interpret the parting of the clouds as a revelation, by September 1769 he should have, and very probably already had, come to an identical conclusion about the future of his flock simply using plain old horse sense. By this time dark thunderclouds of another sort were already ominous on his horizon, and it was beyond his ability to stop the coming storm. Even so, he tried; though one would think he should be fatalistic and complacent about the matter after this supposed 1769 revelation direct from the hand of God, he broke his heart trying.

The power and influence Shubal Stearns held over the English population of the North and South Carolina and southwestern Virginia backcountry by the time of his 1765 letter to Noah Alden were unprecedented for any pastor, and, with the exception of George Whitefield himself, for any religious leader in America. His and his younger colleagues' continued wild successes, however, bore with them the seeds of destruction for the very organization that he had chosen and used so effectively as the vehicle of his power. Stearns's very leadership style shows us that he visualized the Sandy Creek Association in the limited terms of the context of his own life, and that he intended to try to maintain it as a stable, prosperous little New England-style patriarch-led community concerned only with the cause of Christ and the Separate Baptists. But it was now behemoth-sized, spread over the western and large portions of the southern territories of three separate colonies, and in the violent clash of cultures and ideas that occurred all over North America in the late 1760s that would lead to the American Revolution, there was simply no way that Shubal Stearns or any other man could have maintained the Separate Baptist organization in the tight, small community-style stability he visualized. Though he might claim to experience divine revelations, Stearns literally could not see beyond his own limitations, and even as the group prospered something was bound to break somewhere. As it happened, tragically for Stearns, three separate difficulties united a little more than a month after the revelation he claimed to have received to produce not just a break but a disastrous explosion.

Though all that is written in this chapter has been taken directly from established historical sources, none of the historians quoted seem to have been willing to recount the entire story. Like good Baptists both before and since, when they came to the essential unpleasantness that surrounds so many of the details of the Sandy Creek Association's actions between 1768 and 1770, they either ignored them entirely or in part, depending on the individual cases they were trying to make in favor of the Baptists—or at least those parts of the denomination with which they agreed. As a prime example, not one writer but Edwards has ever dealt with Stearns's claim to a divine vision in 1769, and nearly all—Semple, Benedict, even Spencer and Paschal—drew on his *Materials* as a primary source for their own works. Their historical accounts thus turn into opinions of how things should have gone, and later historians who use most of the older chroniclers as their own sources have perhaps remained ignorant of a crucial aspect not only of Appalachian religious history but American religious history as well. Although this author knows he runs the same risk of editorializing himself he hopes at least that he is giving a complete presentation of all the pertinent facts and a fair view of a picture that has lain ignored for more than two hundred years.

Though the three difficulties mentioned occurred almost simultaneously, they must be examined separately for the sake of clarity. Perhaps the best place to start is in South Carolina with the one whose beginnings have already been noted: the status of Shubal Stearns's faithful ox over so many years and at so many different locations, John Newton. As has already been noted, Newton, still unordained in 1765, had moved from Black River to South Carolina to provide preaching services for the soon-to-be-organized Congaree Church in the backcountry, very probably at the direct request of the man whom he had befriended more than ten years before at Sandy Creek, Philip Mulkey. Newton proved as effective at Congaree as he had in North Carolina, and approximately twenty-eight new converts were added after his arrival, though of course they were baptized not by the unordained Newton but by Daniel Marshall. One of these converts, Joseph Reese, soon began to assist Newton in the pulpit, and evidently Fairforest Church, from whence the Congaree flock was an arm, petitioned the Sandy Creek Association in 1766 for Congaree's formal constitution as a church in its own right and probably, as was customary, for the ordination of Newton, their senior minister, as pastor. Stearns sent Joseph Murphy south to assist Marshall and Mulkey in Congaree's official organization, and Murphy, Marshall, and Mulkey duly gathered the church in formal constitution a little more than a month after Sandy Creek's 1766 session, but neither Newton nor Reese was ordained. It was the same old story of Newton's previous decade of work: successful, spiritual, dedicated, and biblically oriented though he might be, something, some aspect about Newton's preaching, or maybe simply about the man himself prejudiced Shubal Stearns against John Newton, and he would permit no presbytery sent by Sandy Creek to ordain him to the full function of the ministry. And when the Goodly Fere spoke, Daniel Marshall, Philip Mulkey, Joseph Murphy, and for that matter every minister and church in the Sandy Creek Association listened and obeyed without question.

G.W. Paschal is the only historian besides Edwards this author has been able to find who examines this case in much detail, and although similar accounts may be found in other regional Baptist histories, all must draw on Edwards, who knew and personally liked both John Newton and Joseph Reese, as their main source. Paschal does his dead-level best to present Shubal Stearns as a proper modern Southern Baptist in his dealings with Newton, all concerned with Newton's supposed lack of education as the probable primary hindrance to his ordination, but if the author may speak frankly here, Paschal was either as blind as a bat to all religious considerations other than those of his own denomination or he was blatantly and consciously covering up the facts. In one instance he even attempted to present a hypothesis that Newton had been ordained already in North Carolina, without introducing a shred of confirmatory evidence and even though it negated his other claim about Newton's supposed lack of education. As has been noted, this is typical not only of Paschal but most writers of his ilk, and a historian concerned with the truth must often search through much similar chaff to find it. But Morgan Edwards knew literacy and illiteracy both when he saw them, and he spoke without prejudice about the illiterate when he could observe their piety, honesty, and success at preaching. John Newton, as he noted from his own observations, was a literate, intelligent man who was as committed to the cause of the Baptists as was Shubal Stearns himself.

The possible axes Stearns had to grind with Newton, and their conceivable causes, have already been noted in the previous chapter, and though any and all may have played a part in the older preacher's prejudice, this author's hypothesis, for what it's worth, is that Newton simply stood a little more aloof from Stearns than the old man or his other children in the ministry would have liked, whether on the Philadelphia Confession, the concept of church independency, or just his own personality. Regardless of the cause, though, Congaree Church remained without an ordained minister for over a year, sending over to Fairforest and Stephens' Creek for assistance when the fellowship had converts to be baptized. As most of the charter members of the new church were South Carolinians unacquainted directly with Stearns, unlike the transplanted flocks that were the basis of the Fairforest and Stephens' Creek congregations, they may have done a good deal of stewing and meditating on the whole matter, undoubtedly wondering how one little preacher up in the backcountry to the north could exert so much influence on their congregation as to deny them an ordained minister. Had Stearns himself attended the presbytery instead of sending Joseph Murphy, things might have turned out better, or perhaps not; certainly, though, if Congaree Church's messengers to the 1767 session of the Sandy Creek Association resubmitted their petition for Newton's ordination, they received no notice, although in that year the association sent a presbytery more than two hundred miles into eastern Virginia to organize another new church. Bur after thinking the matter over during the winter of 1767— and admittedly, possibly at Newton's own suggestion—Congaree Church simply took matters into its own hands. The members sent to the old church on Pee Dee for the services of Evan Pugh, and to Charleston for Oliver Hart, and in keeping with the Regular Baptist independent-church tradition, these two ministers visited Congaree in February 1768 and ordained both John Newton and Joseph Reese to the ministry.

As modern Appalachian old-time Baptists are wont to state, or rather grossly understate in similar situations, Newton's and Reese's ordination by the two Regular Baptist preachers caused trouble in the association. In fact, it was probably the biggest slap in the face Shubal Stearns had ever so far received since coming to the southeast. Up to this point, it can be imagined that one sorrowful look from those large, bright, and expressive eyes could have cowed most of the headstrong bucks among his young ministers into submission, and very probably inspired tearful apologies. In the interval between the February ordinations and the October 1768 association sessions, one wonders how Daniel Marshall and Philip Mulkey responded to Congaree's action. Though Daniel Marshall probably could be expected to empathize with his wife's brother and consequently treat Congaree and its newly ordained ministers coldly, it is certain that Mulkey genuinely liked Newton personally and regarded him as instrumental in his own conversion; given his character, perhaps his sweet voice and smiling aspect got a lot of practice for eight months while he tried to play both sides of the conflict at the same time. Regardless, though, there is no record of Mulkey supporting either Congaree or his old friend when the association convened back in North Carolina in October. Morgan Edwards records that Newton and Reese were both present at Sandy Creek for this meeting, and the end result was that the two were censured for acting independently of the association, which is as much as to say they were condemned for acting independently of the Goodly Fere. Daniel Marshall probably introduced the legislation onto the assembly floor at Stearns's behest, but if Stearns was determined that the association should act upon it, it is extremely doubtful that Philip Mulkey, or anyone else, would have opposed.

All was not lost for Newton and Reese, though. A censure was merely a rebuke, and, like many an old time Baptist minister and association delegate in Appalachia in years to come, Joseph Reese took the politically prudent course of action simply by caving in, "making satisfaction"—apologizing for the fact that he had "offended the brethren"—and submitting himself to the will of the association. This pacified Stearns and the group, and it is a clear indication of the old preacher's essentially loving, big-brotherly nature that Reese was immediately forgiven and that his ordination by Pugh and Hart was then actually confirmed by Sandy Creek Association. But for John Newton, this was too much. He had labored with Shubal Stearns in North Carolina back when the Separate Baptists had only begun their ministry at Sandy Creek; he had itinerated right along with Stearns and Daniel Marshall and his preaching had met with success; he had served both Black River and Congaree Churches in all the duties of a pastor, though his lack of ordination prevented him from performing baptisms and perhaps officiating at communion as well; and he had stood by for years watching his converts such as the flamboyant Philip Mulkey and younger men such as the Murphys, Dutton Lane, and James Read become fully ordained ministers while he himself was denied the office probably on the flimsiest of excuses. According to Edwards, he forthrightly told Stearns and the association that "he thought he had done what was right, and would make no acknowledgements." The association—of course, through its moderator, Stearns—responded by issuing an order for Congaree Church to silence John Newton from preaching. Joseph Reese, now confirmed in his ordination and evidently under the temporary spell of the Stearns personality cult that must have manifested itself so strongly at the association meeting, agreed to do this, and the Congaree delegates returned home at the meeting's close.

Edwards tells us that Congaree Church obeyed the order of their association and forbade Newton from preaching, "while he was in the midst of a useful and successful work." Does this mean that he and Reese had been engaged in a revival or protracted meeting at the church, breaking off in the midst of it to attend the Sandy Creek Association in North Carolina and then returning? Or was it simply a revival of the type so many rural southeastern communities enjoyed a century and even two centuries ago, with enough grassroots interest among the congregation to prompt them to hold prayer meetings at various homes two and three times a week, souls being converted all the while? We will never know, but regardless of the nature of this useful and successful work, it was undoubtedly quenched by the church's obedience to the association order. And after a brief while, the whole matter began to bear on the consciences of the Congaree members, Reese included. It is yet one more testimony to the power of Shubal Stearns's personality that Joseph Reese should have been so suddenly swept up in his spell as to agree, at the 1768 association session, to see that his colleague was silenced, but as Edwards writes, "Both Mr. Reese and the church were afterwards convinced that they were wrong in obeying the mandate of the association, and restored Mr. Newton." This restoration may have taken place as early as the fall or winter of 1768–1769 or as late as the fall of 1770, but after all Newton had been through over so many years, his observation of Joseph Reese under the Stearns spell at the 1768 association had probably been just the icing on the cake of his hurt and humiliation. Although he remained a church member and kept his ministerial credentials, even in 1772, when Edwards met him, he had not fully reassumed his ministerial work.[2] To return to Shubal Stearns, though, as he ascended that hill near his home back in North Carolina in September 1769 he probably didn't even quite realize he had played the tyrant eleven months before; and even as he saw his supposed divine revelation, one problem undoubtedly already on his mind was what to do at the forthcoming 1769 association meeting about Joseph Reese and the Congaree Church, who were undoubtedly agitating for Newton's ministerial restoration if indeed they had not already carried it out on their own.

Stearns's second concern would have been something of a contradiction in terms, since it involved the most dramatic of all his association's successes so far. It will be remembered that the 1760s were the beginning of civil unrest against British rule in the American colonies with the passage of the Stamp and Declaratory Acts and the consequent colonial protests and product boycotts. In the settled Tidewater of lowland eastern Virginia, an emerging and steadily growing middle class was just beginning to feel its strength and tentatively test the boundaries of the British-based caste system established in the Old Dominion by Governor Berkeley and his cronies more than a century earlier. As historians and sociologists have often noted, religion can be a powerful catalyst for such groups to assert themselves, and if the times had been right in the early 1740s, such might have been the case for the Whitefield-based "Lutheran" movement in the central counties of the colony noted earlier. As it was, the "Lutherans" had become New Side Presbyterians, and they had been an accepted sect and part of the norm in that section of Virginia until Samuel Davies, their pastor, left; but as noted in Edwards's comments, a couple of young ministers raised up among the New Sides, Devereux Jarratt and Archibald McRoberts, had taken Anglican orders and were bringing some of the same style of evangelism to their parish congregations. Likewise accepted and tolerated were the small group of Regular Baptists in the northern part of the colony, which now consisted of Opequon, Ketocton, Smith and Lynville's Creek, and Broad Run churches, all belonging to the Philadelphia Association. These four congregations and their ministers, John Garrett or Garrard, John Alderson Sr. and John Jr., John Marks, and David Thomas (Samuel Heaton, former pastor at Opequon, was gone by this time), were dismissed from Philadelphia and organized themselves into the Ketocton Association in 1766, their ministers protected by certificates from Philadelphia that allowed them to be recognized by the county courts as sanctioned dissenters. The year before Ketocton was organized, though, one Allen Wyley, a Culpeper County native who himself had only recently left the Church of England and been baptized by David Thomas at Broad Run Church, set in motion a chain of events that made the earlier "Lutheran" movement look tame. The end result was a social shakeup throughout the whole Virginia colony from which the old aristocratic class structure would never quite recover.

Wyley, the new Broad Run convert, had proven himself to be a good Regular Baptist, inviting his pastor, David Thomas, to his home to hold services and establishing interest in the Baptist cause in Culpeper County in spite of some opposition and protest he encountered from his former parish rector, churchwardens, and members. But he had also heard tales of the preaching of the Separate Baptists to the southwest, perhaps partly from the recollections of John Alderson Senior and John Garrard who had met the Marshall, Breed, and Stearns families at Opequon more than a decade before, and possibly from simple community gossip about Colonel Harris, the Hanover County gentleman who had moved to the Pittsylvania County wilds, forsaken his roots and his class, as it were, and joined the group there. Simply put, whether from a religious or class concern or likely, whether he would have admitted it or not, both, Wyley decided to take a trip to the southwest to visit Samuel Harris and to hear him preach. He did so some time in the year 1765 and was so impressed with what he heard that he invited Harris back to the Tidewater to preach for the Culpeper congregation started by him and Thomas that met in his house. Harris agreed, and after taking three days to prepare for the journey, he accompanied Wyley to Culpeper. In his meetings at Wyley's house, he so overwhelmed the entire neighborhood that a riot actually broke out between Wyley and his supporters on one side and the parish parson and his followers on the other. Fleeing by night into neighboring Orange County, Harris held additional services in the tobacco barn of a young farmer and friend of Wyley's, Elijah Craig, and here he stirred up as much excitement and interest, as well as controversy, as he had in Culpeper. Though Harris could have been arrested for violation of the colony's ecclesiastical laws during this trip, he was not, and after a few days he bade farewell to his new friends in the Tidewater, encouraging them to hold meetings among themselves, and returned home to Pittsylvania. He undoubtedly expected that Wyley's pastor, David Thomas, could pick up where he had left off, baptize the converts, and organize churches in Culpeper and Orange Counties when the time was ripe. He may have felt that it was only right for Thomas to do so; there were no Separate Baptist churches within nearly two hundred miles, and Thomas and his Regular Baptist brethren were a lot closer.

If Harris indeed supposed his work in the Tidewater was over, though, he was wrong. Not too many weeks passed before a knock sounded on his door again. This time it was not Wyley but Elijah Craig and two others, perhaps his brothers Lewis and Joseph, and they had made the long journey to the southwest settlements to beg Harris to come back and baptize them. When David Thomas had come to visit and to preach to them, one of the first things he had done was to complain about the preaching of such "weak and illiterate persons" by whom they had been so stirred up;[3] and although ten years before they might have taken such a haughty statement from an educated, paid minister with his dissenter's license in his pocket quite meekly, they were not inclined to do so now, and their dander was up. They didn't want to be Regular Baptists, they wanted to be Separates just like Harris, and it was only at this time that they learned, to their amazement, that Harris was not even ordained as a minister but only as a ruling elder. Nonetheless Harris agreed to take them and their neighbors up in the Tidewater under his wing, and he accompanied them some sixty miles on into North Carolina to see James Read at Grassy Creek and ask him to come along with them to perform baptisms.

According to Read, he had been experiencing spiritual impressions about preaching in Virginia himself for some time before and was just then preparing to travel northward with a neighbor and fellow church member named Graves. He and Graves immediately agreed to go with Harris and the Craig party back to the Tidewater, though, and one of the Craigs went ahead as a sort of advance scout, so to speak, to arrange preaching appointments for Harris and Read in Orange, Spotsylvania, Hanover, Caroline, and Goochland Counties. After filling a few local appointments, the two Separate preachers, the two Craigs, and Graves followed the scout on into eastern Virginia. When they came near Elijah Craig's barn in Orange County on a Friday they saw an enormous congregation of people already assembled and anxious to hear them. They girded up their loins with prayer and meditation and set to work holding services; Read baptized nineteen on the first day and more in the days afterward. On Saturday David Thomas and John Garrard of the Regular Baptists showed up, and after Harris and Read had conferred with them both parties desired to unite in the work, but the Virginia small farmers would have none of it. Many of Allen Wyley's friends, perhaps a little more complacent about social convention, sided with Thomas, Garrard, and the Regulars, but the greater majority of the Virginia small farm families there, including the Craigs, felt more rebellious and clung to the Separates. The two groups wound up holding Sunday services a small distance apart from one another, with Read and the Regulars both officiating at baptisms.[4] With Harris and Read's triumphant continuation and completion of their eastern tour, the stage was set for the Separate Baptist brushfire to spread over the Virginia Tidewater with a vehemence unheard of even in Shubal Stearns's earliest days in North Carolina.

It was mentioned in the last chapter that the progress of the Sandy Creek Association in North and South Carolina between 1759 and 1765 is difficult to pen simply because so many souls were being converted and baptized and so many churches were being organized and arms formed simultaneously in the two provinces. But this is even more the case in eastern Virginia between 1766 and 1769, when the young Tidewater farm families inured to a culture of respecting their "betters" in a carefully maintained caste system began to hear the Gospel for the first time, not from educated divines whose social rank they were coerced to honor, but from men whom they knew to be their own social equals. Samuel Harris returned time after time to the Tidewater, sometimes with James Read, others with Dutton Lane or William Murphy, and later on with other young and unordained Virginia and North Carolina preachers being raised up to the ministry at Dan River and Grassy Creek like Jeremiah Walker, William Mash, John Weatherford, and Thomas Mullen. Their success grew exponentially as young eastern Virginians such as the Craig brothers, John Waller, Andrew Tribble, and James Childs joined the preaching ranks. By 1768 all were feeling the heavy hand of legal persecution for preaching the Gospel and holding meetings without dissenters' licenses and for disturbing the peace, as well as being subjected to sporadic attacks from Anglican rector-inspired mobs in various locations. At different times Harris was attacked and dragged about by his hair or his limbs, his young converts often returning the violence blow for blow and provoking free-for-alls, and both he and many of his young ministerial disciples were frequently arrested and hauled into county courts where, if they were not given terms of imprisonment outright, they were charged not to preach at that location any more. But nothing could now stop either Harris or the movement that had exploded around his labors. The works of Semple and Spencer in particular are full of these exploits and they make a provocative, compelling read.

We might do well to take a momentary digression here, to examine the exact nature of the Tidewater meetings held by the Separates. As noted above, at their first meeting at Elijah Craig's barn, Harris and Read commenced on a Friday, and they conducted services through the weekend and at least one day beyond. If this was their standard of practice, they had undoubtedly gotten it from Shubal Stearns at association sessions and perhaps other "big" meetings down in North Carolina, but the service schedule has been associated to a greater extent by historians with the American Methodists and Presbyterians in their later camp meetings than with the Baptists. In fact, some claim that the nineteenth-century version of the camp meeting was not born until 1799 or 1800 at the beginning of the so-called Great Revival in Kentucky, with the ministry of the evangelical Presbyterian James McGready. Deborah McCauley, in her *Appalachian Mountain Religion: A History*, postulates that McGready drew on the "sacramental revival" gatherings of his Scotch-Irish Presbyterian heritage for his preaching success at this time as well as earlier, and that this Scots Presbyterian tradition gradually intermingled with "Baptist revival culture."[5] However, at least one Methodist historian, Charles A. Johnson, frankly admits that the closest historical antecedents to the great nineteenth-century camp meetings were the pre-Revolutionary Virginia meetings of Samuel Harris, James Read, their younger Spotsylvania County, Virginia, disciple John Waller, "and many other evangelists from the generating center of Guilford County [formed from Orange and Rowan Counties in 1771 around the territory of Sandy Creek], North Carolina."[6] These were actually referred to at the time as camp meetings, though the crowds were fed by neighboring farmers rather than bringing all their own provisions as in later Methodist/Presbyterian tradition; one other notable difference and its probable cause must be mentioned later. And in McGready's case, though he undoubtedly did draw much on his Old Country heritage in his Presbyterianism and in his ministry, he grew up not far from Sandy Creek Church in the Orange/Rowan border area. Moreover after receiving his ministerial credentials in Pennsylvania, he was sent back to North Carolina to labor among the churches of the Orange Presbytery that had been formed by that time. One of his congregations was even located on Haw River, another pre-Revolutionary Separate Baptist stronghold where Shubal Stearns and Elnathan Davis had labored years before him.[7] One of his converts and subsequent ministerial colleagues in the Piedmont was Barton W. Stone, and both men were responsible for the formation of recognized Appalachian denominations after the Presbyterian hierarchy disowned their revivalistic work: in Stone's case the Springfield Presbytery, later known as the Christian Church, and among McGready's followers, though he himself returned to the mainline fold, the Cumberland Presbyterians. The question may be asked bluntly: just who influenced who in the establishment of these dramatic outdoor meetings on the frontier? The forgotten Shubal Stearns emerges once more as a prime candidate for the catalyst of the entire camp meeting culture.

Be that as it may, though, between 1766 and 1769 Harris, Read, and the others labored away at their "big" meetings. The atmosphere is described most vividly by David Benedict:

> Read and Harris continued to visit these parts for about three years with wonderful effect. In one of their visits they baptized seventy-five at one time, and in the course of one of their journeys, which generally lasted several weeks, they baptized upwards of two hundred. It was not uncommon at their great meetings for many hundreds of men to encamp on the ground in order to be present the next day. The night meetings, through the great work of God, continued very late; the ministers would scarce have an opportunity to sleep. Sometimes the floors would be covered with persons struck down under the conviction of sin. It frequently happened that when they would return to rest at a late hour they would be under the necessity of arising again through the earnest cries of the penitent. There were instances of men traveling more than one hundred miles to one of these meetings; to go forty or fifty was not uncommon.[8]

In the meantime Harris and the other preachers dodged the officers of the law as best they could. Some Virginia counties appear to have been more zealous about enforcing ecclesiastical laws than others, and either Harris or various ones of his followers would be taken to court to be sentenced to jail terms, after which they simply picked up the work where they had been forced to leave it off. The author has not been able to find any record of James Read being captured or serving any jail time, though, and some of the younger ministers—especially Elijah Craig's brother Joseph—had an endearing streak of earthy mischief in them that helped them evade capture and undoubtedly made many a Tidewater constable wish he was in some other line of work. Witness this account from Semple:

I do not recollect, though a zealous preacher, that [Joseph Craig's] persecutors ever got him into prison. He had a method to baffle them. He was once preaching at a place, and the officers came after him. Stepping out at a back door he ran into a swamp, supposing he was safe, but they took his track with a gang of dogs. To evade the dogs he betook himself to a tree, from which his pursuers shook him down as if he were a wild beast, and demanded his going with them to court. After reasoning with them a while he refused to go. But they forced him on a horse, and perhaps tied his hands. On the way he reasoned thus: "Good men ought not to go to prison, and if you will put so good a man as Joe Craig in prison I will have no hand in it," and threw himself off the horse, and would neither ride nor walk, behaving perhaps as David did, before Achish, king of Gath (I Samuel 21:10). They let him go.[9]

On another occasion at Fredericksburg, when his brother Lewis along with John Waller and James Childs were sentenced to a term of imprisonment and a great crowd of curious onlookers were following the preachers and deputies to the jail house, Joseph sneaked in behind the mob. Waller and the others were singing the mournful old Isaac Watts hymn "Broad Is the Road That Leads to Death" as they were being marched in shackles to jail, and, observing that some of the onlookers were getting mightily disturbed at the hymn's message, Joseph saw the opportunity for a prank that he just couldn't pass up. He roared out in a mighty voice, "ARISE, YE DEAD, AND COME TO JUDGEMENT!," and many in the crowd, thinking that Judgement Day had come and they were unprepared, fainted dead away.[10]

So perhaps until 1767 Shubal Stearns could only have been glad for every bit of news he got from Tidewater Virginia. Had he not been nearly sixty years of age by 1765, he might even have tried to make the grueling trip northeast himself occasionally, though it would have involved a much longer distance than even Harris and Read had to travel. As it was, though, the Craig brothers, John Waller, James Childs, and other young Virginia proselytes started, probably as early as 1766 and technically as members of the Dan River Church, to come by droves to the Sandy Creek Association's annual sessions to meet the Goodly Fere themselves and to witness and participate both in their elders' worship at the place they regarded as their spiritual home and in their adulation of the old man. The journeys to Sandy Creek, the "generating center" as Charles Johnson termed it, not only of their faith but of their newfound consciousness of the power the common man could exert in a changing America, must have assumed something near epic proportions in the young eastern lowlanders' minds. However, the eastern Virginians, their very New Birth and choice of the Separate Baptists as a faith originating in the beginnings of a class struggle, brought an element of bellicosity to the association that Shubal Stearns could hardly have welcomed entirely at the time. Some of the reasons for this must wait to be explained, but for now suffice it to repeat that Stearns himself had heretofore never had to stand in the breach in North Carolina for his cause and for his young converts the way the still-unordained Samuel Harris had been forced to, both against mobs and in court in Virginia. The only similar experience with legal persecution that any North Carolina Baptists had had, either the Regularized easterners or the Sandy Creek Association in the west, occurred about 1767 according to Edwards, when approximately seventy-two people were summoned into one or more county courts to answer complaints of blasphemy, riots, and heresy. We do not even know if Stearns was one of those charged, but the North Carolina courts were so liberal and open-minded that they accepted the Baptists' defense entirely regarding blasphemy and heresy and determined that the only riots raised were by those who disturbed the Baptists' assemblies.[11] One reason for this leniency may have been the fact that the chief justice of the North Carolina Superior Court during this period, Martin Howard, was reared in a family of General Baptists in Rhode Island and did not join the Church of England until five years after he came to North Carolina. We may still wonder why, though, in a colony whose judicial system had pretty much left the Baptists alone heretofore, even in spite of the sporadic complaints of the eastern Anglican rectors such as the ones discussed in the previous chapter, the Baptists were objects of legal concern now. That is, unless the prosecutions attempted were in response to disturbing news the North Carolina government may have received of the activities of Read, Harris, and the other younger Sandy Creek Association preachers in eastern and central Virginia from the colonial or county authorities in that region.

Even so, in his days as a Separate Congregationalist, Stearns himself had signed petitions to the Connecticut government in behalf of his denomination, and from his New England background he would have understood what the Tidewater Virginians were going through. His main concern would have been that he was, figuratively speaking, a grandfather rather than a father to these new converts, and Samuel Harris was exhibiting some different ideas about raising them than he had. This does not necessarily mean that he viewed Harris as a rival, though he ultimately could have, or that Harris ever tried to set himself up as another Goodly Fere, though all too many men in Harris's position would have been willing to do so. Venerated as he was by the Virginia Baptists until his death in 1799, Harris's actions spoke louder than words that he discouraged his followers from thinking of him too highly. In this he may have learned something from his mentor Stearns's subsequent failings, but even at the start of his Tidewater ministry he was more willing to let his converts act upon their own thought and initiative than Stearns ever was, particularly in regard to the Regular Baptists.

It has been shown that Harris probably fully expected David Thomas and his colleagues to pick up the work where he had left off after his initial meetings in Culpeper, and that in spite of Thomas's calling him "weak and illiterate," he would have taken the Regular minister on as a preaching partner at Elijah Craig's barn had the congregation permitted it. As the Regular Baptists in northern Virginia experienced a revival of their own between 1766 and 1769, small scale compared to the Separate Baptist movement but dramatic nonetheless, Harris probably quickly realized and accepted the fact that, in spite of the hard feelings generated initially, his converts would ultimately come to some mutually beneficial working relationship with the Regulars. If he did not encourage this to happen, he did not stand in its way, either. As the Regular Baptists moved further in-country to the borders of Separate territory, they became somewhat "Separatized" and more loudly evangelical, as Morgan Edwards's copy of this excerpt from the journal of Daniel Fristoe, a young Virginian ordained to the ministry in the Ketocton Association not many years after it was organized, aptly reveals:

> Sat., June 15, 1771. This day I began to act as an ordained minister, and never before saw such manifest appearances of God's working and devil's raging at one time and in one place . . . The next day (being Sunday) about 2000 people came together. Many more offered for baptism, 13 of which were judged worthy.
>
> As we stood by the water the people were weeping and crying in a most extraordinary manner; and others cursing and swearing and acting like men possessed. In the midst of this, a tree tumbled

down, being overloaded with people who (Zacheus like) had climbed up to see baptism administered; the coming down of that tree occasioned the adjacent trees to fall also being loaded in the same manner; but none were hurt.

When the ordinance was administered and I had laid hands on the parties baptized, we sang those charming words of Dr. Watts, "Come we that fear the Lord." The multitude sang and wept and smiled in tears, holding up their hands and countenances toward heaven in such a manner as I had not seen before.

In going home I turned to look at the people who remained by the water side and saw some screaming on the ground, some wringing their hands, and some in extacies [sic] of joy, some praying; others cursing and swearing and exceedingly outrageous. We have seen strange things today.[12]

Strange as the service might have seemed to Fristoe, Edwards knew that such meetings as this one had been taking place among Shubal Stearns's followers for a decade and a half already, and that it was already a growing tendency among the Ketocton Regulars. As such, and as time passed, some of the best young Virginia Separate preachers became attracted to the Regular Baptists, began to endorse a partial or even a total acceptance of the Philadelphia Confession, and joined the Ketocton Association. James Ireland, a young schoolmaster converted to the Separate Baptists in 1768, and even the redoubtable Elijah Craig were among this group, and the former young dirt farmer Craig was even chosen to bear Ketocton's letter of correspondence to the Philadelphia Association one year.[13] Despite this, all his life Craig remained bitterly opposed to the idea of a minister receiving a salary for his preaching;[14] he must have had some good, heated discussions over this with his new Regular Baptist brethren over the years.

Another example of Ketocton's influence over the burgeoning Separates in the north of Virginia was discovered by Morgan Edwards in Jeremiah Walker, a member at James Read's Grassy Creek Church and one of the first young North Carolina preachers to come forward and assist Harris and Read in Virginia. Edwards found that

> Mr. Walker is remarkable for a strong memory, good understanding, joined with an insurmountable modesty. His preaching is very acceptable to all though he has renounced the tones, actions and

violence that are the Shibboleths of the Separate Baptists. Nay, he hath discouraged the outcries, extacies [*sic*] and epilepsies which are so much thought of among them. These things made disagreeable impressions on his brethren of the Separate order so much that they talked of breaking fellowship with him; but others knowing his turn and capacity for public business opposed the motion; this, with a sermon . . . (from the words "I am Joseph, your brother whom ye sold into Egypt") reconciled matters pretty well, though, I believe, his tastes and inclination would rather lead him to associate with the Regular Baptists; but the other can not yet spare him.[15]

Paradoxically, though Walker's example and perhaps others made Edwards hypothesize that all Separate Baptists were by 1772 as much in agreement with the Calvinistic precepts of the Philadelphia Confession as were the Regular Baptists, declining to endorse the Confession merely because they had a scruple about man-made creeds, in truth Walker, and for that matter Samuel Harris, John Waller, Joseph Craig, and others as well, were still committed Arminians who preached a salvation available to all throughout the entire course of their ministries.[16] There were other cases, though, that are also perhaps typical of the Separates' country hardheadedness in matters of doctrine, in which former evangelistic Separate Baptists wound up out-Regularing the Regulars in terms of Calvinism. Witness one more account of a very successful young Separate preacher of the late 1760s and early 1770s, William Marshall, who actually was an uncle of the later Chief Justice John Marshall and who let a close study of Calvinistic precepts get to him. Quoted by J.H. Spencer, this passage was written by another minister, John Taylor, who was converted under Marshall's preaching in the days of his evangelism:

> In the days of his success, he preached after the apostolic mode, strongly urging repentance toward God and faith in Christ Jesus, and with longing, heart-melting invitations, exhorting every sinner in his congregation to seek the salvation of his soul . . . He now studied consistency, beginning with God's decrees. There he found eternal justification couched in the doctrine of election; and so on with the several links of his chain, till he was led to find out that the gospel address was only to certain characters, which, when explained, were already righteous, though they well deserved

the name of sinners. But as for *mere* sinners, the law of Moses only was their portion ... He found that a number of his Baptist Christians could not eat what they called his strong meat. This led him to doubt their Christianity, or at least, the soundness of their faith.[17]

The reader must keep in mind here that the Separate Baptists were still gaining followers at a breakneck speed, even more in Virginia than in the Carolinas, and we cannot know exactly how far these various doctrinal trends had progressed by 1769. It's a fair bet that at least Jeremiah Walker's adoption of the Regular preaching mode had begun to cause some confusion by this time, although we are not able to ascertain whether the move to break fellowship with him came from James Read and Grassy Creek, Walker's new congregation in Amelia County, Virginia, or even from Shubal Stearns himself. It is almost certain that Samuel Harris wouldn't have participated in any such action. Like Elijah Craig, for many years he was violently opposed to any preacher taking pay for his services,[18] but although he is said to have had a pulpit manner more like Daniel Marshall's than any other of the senior Separate ministers,[19] he had no quarrel with the pulpit address of the Regulars. We can say this much for certain: the Sandy Creek Association sent a presbytery north in 1767 to formally organize one church in the Tidewater, known as Upper Spotsylvania, as has already been noted in connection with John Newton's case, and four or five more were similarly constituted in 1768 at Elijah Craig's and other places, but not one single minister was ordained to serve as pastor to any of them—not even Samuel Harris.

In retrospect this seems ludicrous. Samuel Harris had turned out to be Stearns's most successful younger evangelist, but for three and a half of the most wildly productive years of his ministry, the Sandy Creek Association did not deem him fit to baptize a convert. He had always had to take James Read, Dutton Lane, or occasionally William Murphy along to officiate at baptismal rites.

We do know this further for certain: despite the fact that no Separate ministers had yet been ordained in the Tidewater, the Ketocton Association at its August 1769 session had prepared a letter to Shubal Stearns and the Sandy Creek Association seeking correspondence and fellowship and were sending delegates, Richard Major, a man named Saunders, and Stearns's old acquaintance John Garrard or Garret, to Sandy Creek's 1769 session on the second weekend in October.[20] We do not know whether Stearns had, by September, been advised that the Ketocton letter was coming, though it is entirely likely, as association leader, that he had. Regardless, this vantage point allows us to look at Stearns's 1768 actions regarding John Newton from another angle. Harsh though Stearns might have been with Newton in spite of their longstanding acquaintance, the possibility exists that the "order of 1768" may have been as much to send a not-so-subtle message to Harris and the Virginians to distance themselves from the Ketocton Association as to punish Newton for permitting two Charleston Association ministers to ordain him. If this was the case, it meant that Stearns was now acting more like a rural political leader than a Goodly Fere, but he may have felt he was being forced to use political techniques to maintain the power he had heretofore exercised simply by the force of his personality and his followers' respect for him.

The Virginia Separates had further complicated the matter, though. Busy as Harris had been in the Tidewater, he, with assistance from some more young exhorters at Dan River Church, had found time to build the congregation's Fall Creek arm up until it was almost ready to be constituted as a church on its own; the Fall Creek flock was even meeting on Harris's own property, and he was donating beef and other staples from his own supply for their "feasts of charity."[21] Under the circumstances, if Dan River Church petitioned the Sandy Creek Association's 1769 session for Fall Creek's constitution, and asked for Samuel Harris to be ordained to serve as its pastor, the request would be much more difficult politically to turn down than Congaree's had been for Newton. By now, whether Stearns realized it or not, any small disagreement he could have chosen to pick with Harris had the potential of throwing the Sandy Creek Association's entire Virginia contingent into distress and confusion. So, as Shubal Stearns ascended that hill near his home after the thunderstorm on September 7 of that year to claim his revelation, the actions of Samuel Harris, the Virginians, and the Regular Baptists in Ketocton, Charleston, and the newly formed eastern North Carolina Kehukee Associations must already have been as much on his mind as the actions of Joseph Reese and John Newton during the previous eleven months. It is doubtful that he had been as distressed by the terrible thunderstorm on that date as he was by the tornado of his thoughts as he tried to determine what to do next.

Thus far, though, Stearns's concerns in 1769 seem rather petty in retrospect. If he was by this time resorting to machine politics to maintain his power, they were undoubtedly very real to him, but both the South Carolina and Virginia difficulties could be solved with ease if he only proved willing to loosen up a bit and not treat his congregants as if they were his little brothers and sisters always in need of his counsel and direction. However, a third difficulty was brewing and was by this time ready to boil over right in Stearns's home province, and if the tensions in the South Carolina and Virginia contingents of Sandy Creek Association could be compared to a flame and a fuse, this third North Carolina conflict would prove to be the powder keg. It has come down to us in history by the name of the North Carolina Regulators' War, and while its aftermath was crucial to the development and continuance of the movement that Shubal Stearns had begun in the backcountry, more than anything else it made Stearns one of Appalachian history's truly tragic figures.

The Regulators' War was an almost inevitable by-product of the weaknesses of North Carolina's colonial government, given the tensions generated over North America in general during the late 1760s and early 1770s. The executive branch of the colony's rule was vested in the office of royal governor, a direct Crown appointee who was also commander in chief of the colonial militia and whose approval was necessary for any bill to be passed into law. The legislature was divided into an upper house or council, also royal appointees but whose selection was generally on the governor's recommendation, and a lower house or assembly, made up of representatives elected by the freeholders of the boroughs and counties of the province. Finally, the judicial branch was composed of the six-circuit North Carolina Superior Court with its chief justice, another royal appointment, and two associate justices who were gubernatorial appointees; and the inferior or county courts with their own justices and officers, likewise gubernatorial appointments and who were responsible for nearly all the functions of local government. The weakness of the system lay in the fact that its royal appointees were given no salaries by the Crown for their services but rather were utterly dependent financially on the assembly. The collection of revenues for the Assembly's appropriations in turn depended all too much on the personal honesty of the individual governor-appointed county sheriffs, who were responsible for the collection of taxes and the supervision of elections as well as law enforcement. Though the sheriffs in the eastern lowland counties could be watched closely by the royal governor, in the western counties of the province they and their handpicked followers, who almost always included local lawyers, court registrars, and other petty officials, were likely to have complete control of local affairs, with plenty of opportunities for tax and fee embezzlement, extortion, and election rigging, and many ways to cover their tracks out of the governor's sight. The colonial government often turned a blind eye to the actions of the western sheriffs for the simple reason that their guilt was frequently too hard to establish legally, given the cadre of lawyers in the sheriffs' local machines, and in investigating and prosecuting accusations against them both governor and assembly ran the risk of losing further revenue to them, monies that were difficult or impossible to trace. As might be expected, the principal victims were the small farmers of the Orange, Rowan, and Anson County Piedmont backcountry, mostly because of the sheer scarcity of hard cash. When trading among themselves, the uplanders generally used the old barter system, though some were prepared to act as small-scale moneylenders to their neighbors. They were often land-rich, however, and a common dodge of sheriffs who wanted to pick up prime developed acreage easily and cheaply for themselves or their cronies seems to have been to show up at a farmer's door unexpectedly and demand cash payment for taxes. The sheriff would then refuse to be delayed while the property owner hurried off to a neighbor's to try to borrow money; sometimes an extra fee was charged for the delay and often the sheriff would confiscate the title to the land before the owner could gather enough cash and reach the county seat to pay. And more often than not, the luckless tax delinquent would find his property in the possession of one or more of the sheriff's friends or political allies, sold for much less than its assessed value.[22]

Legal and other courthouse fees were another matter, and perhaps one of equal or greater concern to the upland farmers. Their rates were fixed by statute, but often a service for which one fee should be charged was divided up by court officials so two or more fees could be demanded, and even under the best of circumstances in the extant political and legal system, enforcement of the fee statutes was difficult if not impossible. There was a widespread perception that lawyers and court officials worked hand in hand with the sheriffs to postpone legal cases so larger fees might be collected. To make a long story short, the good-ol'-boy system was alive and well in North Carolina even before the birth of the United States, and the principle of commensal (perhaps more accurately, parasitic) patronage thus established and entrenched was a catch-22 that has never totally been broken in the American Southeast to this day, even with the change from colonial to home rule and the fact that the descendants of the system's first victims are now as often as not local officeholders themselves.

The primordial good ol' boys of western North Carolina came, like the great majority of settlers, from the northeast and in a few instances the Old Country, and for a time the most successful of them all—though, as a native New Yorker, a Yale graduate, an Anglophile, and an aspirant and sycophant to the upper crust, he would have been furious to have been given the modern Southern slang title—was a young lawyer named Edmund Fanning. Of a family that itself had been based first in Groton and New London, Connecticut, Fanning is thought to have migrated south simply to seek his fortune. His brother William was, interestingly, an Anglican clergyman in Tidewater Virginia during this same period, and one historian indicates that it may have been under William's influence that Edmund tried his luck in the Carolina backcountry.[23] William Fanning's position in Virginia may also have been crucial to certain events that followed for Shubal Stearns and the Sandy Creek Association, as will be evidenced shortly. At any rate, Edmund Fanning was admitted to the bar at the Orange County seat of Hillsboro, and his first political appointment, that of town commissioner, occurred in 1760. The next year he was appointed prosecutor for the Crown for the inferior, or county, court, and in the meantime he formed a couple of business partnerships with both Virginians and North Carolinians, probably in land companies. In 1763 he was appointed as public registrar for Orange County and given a commission in the county's militia, both prime jobs for an up-and-coming good ol' boy, but Fanning's ambitions still grew and he became a frequent visitor to the provincial capital at New Bern on the coast. The source of his most important later political appointments was a young British military officer named William Tryon, who had been sent to the province by the Crown in late 1764 to act as lieutenant to the ailing royal governor Arthur Dobbs. Fanning seems to have cultivated Tryon's friendship from the first, and when Dobbs died in 1765 and Tryon became royal governor in his stead, the patronage began to come thick and fast. During the last period of the Stamp Act controversy in 1766, when one of the associate justices of the Superior Court, Maurice Moore, published an inflammatory pamphlet condemning the Act, Tryon revoked his judgeship and appointed Fanning as Superior Court justice for the Salisbury district; Fanning was elected to a seat in the Assembly the same year. He was next elevated to the rank of colonel in the Orange

County militia, and appointed as a trustee to, and then president of, Queen's College, a new academic institution in the town of Charlotte. In the meantime he had purchased so many town lots in Hillsboro as well as property tracts surrounding it, perhaps with Orange County sheriff Tyree Harris's strong-arm assistance in property confiscation, that one of his friends jokingly dubbed Hillsboro with a new name in recognition of its new, powerful good ol' boy's various offices and estates: "Fanningsburg."[24]

Fanning of course had his admirers in the backcountry, at least initially, and in truth the extortions he perpetrated in his office as court registrar were petty compared to those of Tyree Harris himself. Still, if he benefited from Harris's crookedness, he was hardly less guilty. The only charge ever proven against him, though the possibility that the tracks of more of his crimes were covered up by collusion with other governmental officers, was that his usual fee for registering a deed was six shillings, almost three times the price set by statute. With his acquisition of power, he did become extremely arrogant towards those he regarded as his inferiors, however, and this tendency, combined with an apparent streak of cruelty, was undoubtedly felt by almost every small farmer in Orange County who had to do business with Fanning's office. Thus, though perhaps at least in part unfairly, Edmund Fanning and his connections to William Tryon came to epitomize everything that was wrong with local government to the great majority of Orange County's residents.

When the uplanders first discovered the flaws within the political system under which they lived, they responded to them in various ways. There were, of course, the usual outbursts of individual bad temper, which often resulted in a farmer's being charged with libel and jailed for a time, along with yet another fine to drain his small portion of hard cash. Some simply moved further southwest to the South Carolina frontier where, as has been mentioned, no county courts as of yet existed and where self-appointed bands of residents styling themselves as Regulators provided their own law enforcement. It has been noted already that tax and fee difficulties may have been one of the primary reasons for the migration of the Marshall, Breed, Stinson, Polk, and Mulkey families as well as those of Peter and Ebenezer Stearns, and for all we know Shubal and Sarah Stearns might have joined them had Shubal not felt committed, in his role as the Goodly Fere of the backcountry, to remain on post at his old Sandy Creek home base. Even those settlers who stayed in North

Carolina increased their trade with South Carolina over the eastern lowland markets of their own province. Still, their lot was hard when time came for tax assessment and property registration. As early as 1764, grievances had begun to be aired in public increasingly and jointly, and riots and other disturbances had broken out at the courthouses of Rowan, Anson, and Granville Counties as well as at the Orange County seat of Hillsboro. Governor Dobbs had responded by issuing a proclamation forbidding officials to take illegal fees, but as has already been made obvious, there was no way that the proclamation could be enforced. Thus the tempers of the upland farmers kept brewing and brewing, and the 1765 passage of the Stamp Act, coming hard on the heels of Dobbs's death and William Tryon's accession to the royal governor's chair, inflamed the farmers finally to consider organizing and amassing a concerted response to the government.

In all fairness it must be said that Governor Tryon opposed the Stamp Act personally because he knew it would drain North Carolina and indeed all other American colonies of money. However, it was the law, and he was determined to enforce it while it was in effect even though loud protests came not only from the western portions of the province but even the farmers and merchants of the eastern lowlands. His demotion of Maurice Moore from his Superior Court associate judgeship has already been mentioned, and this occurred even though he agreed with Moore on the one issue personally. But while Tryon was attempting to deal with North Carolina's own Sons of Liberty club that had sprung up in the east in imitation of the northeastern organizations of the same name, protests of the unrelated western good-ol'-boy issue became increasingly louder and more articulate as well. A month after the Stamp Act had become public news, George Sims, a Granville County schoolmaster, drew up *The Nutbush Address*, a pamphlet that vividly described courthouse ring injustices and embezzlements in his home county, and he was promptly charged in the Granville County court with libel, found guilty, and jailed. Sims's pamphlet was widely read locally, but when other Granville County residents encouraged by it sent a petition to the Assembly for a redress of the grievances the *Address* outlined, their court officers just as promptly sued the petition's signers themselves for libel. Still the influence of *The Nutbush Address* continued to spread, and shortly after the Stamp Act's repeal by Parliament in the spring of 1766, a group of irate yeoman farmers assembled at Maddock's Mill near Shubal Stearns's home on Sandy Creek; taking a cue from the rough self-appointed law enforcement their neighbors enjoyed in backcountry South Carolina, the men at this meeting banded together to determine "whether the free men of this county labor under any abuses of power or not," styled themselves as Regulators, and issued a document called "Regulator Advertisement Number 1" calling for "all the people of the province to put an end to local oppression."[25]

Why Sandy Creek, of all places? There is one immediately obvious answer: Herman Husbands. Given his known beliefs, combined with his already-proven eloquence and skill at persuasion and agitation in spite of his reluctance to commit his own person to the causes he espoused, he was as much a natural catalyst to his increasingly irate neighbors in their protests of the abuses of the courthouse rings as he possibly had been for persuading them to hear and join Shubal Stearns's Separate Baptists a decade before. Still on Sandy Creek as an excluded Quaker and self-styled enlightened disciple of Benjamin Franklin, Husbands was as ecstatic as might be expected over the success of the various colonial Sons of Liberty organizations' application of financial pressure on Parliament in the Stamp Act controversy. When the Stamp Act was repealed, like most of his countrymen Husbands temporarily forgot or chose to ignore that its replacement, the Declaratory Act, asserted Parliament's absolute right to tax the colonies as it saw fit. It would be the Declaratory Act that would finally bring about the American Revolution a few years down the road, but obviously in Husbands's eyes, with the Stamp Act repeal the American people had already struck a blow for liberty—as well as for his prophecy that a democratic New Jerusalem was forthcoming on the western frontier. He thus took the lead in his neighbors' complaints about a local problem that needed to be addressed with a local solution, and over time managed to inflate them, both literally and figuratively, to revolutionary proportions.

In the context of subsequent history, the Regulators' War has thus often been viewed retrospectively as a set of actions of simple and honest grassroots American patriotism, sort of a prelude to the Revolution, with the liberty-loving North Carolina backwoodsmen fighting their cruel British lords and suffering and dying to maintain their rights. G.W. Paschal especially wanted to paint the backcountry's residents, particularly the Baptists, in this light. But in reality the situation was much different. Though led by a man with a hidden belief and an agenda of his own, in the minds of most of its participants the Regulator movement was at first simply a protest both in word and action of unfairnesses in local government. The royal and parliamentary government that served as a backdrop was accepted without question by nearly all those involved. Most of their later excesses were merely the product of Husbands's attempts to exploit them for the sake of his own plans. Martin Howard, the Rhode Island Baptist-reared Superior Court Chief Justice, came out in favor of the Stamp Act, but he was trusted by most Regulators, even at the peak of their activities, because he was a royal appointee; Maurice Moore, who was restored to his associate judgeship after the Stamp Act repeal, and Richard Henderson, likewise an associate justice after the Regulator movement got underway and who like Moore opposed the Stamp Act, to say nothing of his close friendship and working relationship in Kentucky land speculation with Daniel Boone, were suspect in the minds of the Regulators because they were gubernatorial appointees.[26] Moreover, many of the known Regulators turned out to be either Loyalists or inactive in the Revolution, and most of the eastern lowlanders who opposed them in the Regulators' War proved themselves to be ardent patriots. One of the Regulators' particular targets besides Edmund Fanning, William Hooper, later was a signer of the Declaration of Independence, and one of their bitterest lowlander enemies, Samuel Johnston, was a delegate to the Continental Congress and later one of the first senators from the state of North Carolina. But we digress once more. Though our story does involve the governmental loyalties, local versus Crown, that Herman Husbands managed to blur during his tenure as Regulator leader, it primarily concerns one expressive-eyed little preacher who, even as he began to witness the fragmentation of his control of his Virginia and South Carolina churches, all of a sudden found his North Carolina congregations ablaze in Regulator agitation—gratis from the man who had helped him get his start in the backcountry in the first place.

    We will never know for sure just how closely the ministers and members of the Sandy Creek Association as a whole were involved in the Regulator movement at its inception and the first two years of its existence. The only historians who discuss the Baptist connection with the movement are Morgan Edwards and G.W. Paschal, and both of these had their own reasons to slant the story. Edwards was frank about his: by his own admission he tried to de-emphasize Sandy Creek's participation in the North Carolina conflict lest the whole mess ultimately become another Munster tragedy.[27] References to this bizarre 1534 German Anabaptist bloodbath were already being thrown in the faces of the Virginia Separates by both parish rectors and newspaper editors in efforts to compare the Separates to the "madmen of Munster" and thus slow or halt their progress, and the Baptists, who were no Old Landmarkers at this period by any stretch of the imagination, were just as stoutly denying any Anabaptist connection with the simple claim that the Bible was their only criterion and by it they were willing to stand or fall.[28] But Edwards's comment about Munster in and of itself implies two things. One, that he knew his history well enough to recognize that the Separates were causing a dramatic class shakeup in Virginia that, before the Revolution and with effective agitation, could easily have escalated into the outright war the Anabaptist movement in Germany ultimately became; and the other, that even though the North Carolina Separates were probably merely concerned with courthouse reform and would have scorned or ignored Herman Husbands's own bizarre New Jerusalem idea had he tried to stress it to them, Husbands's belief actually was so dangerously close to that of the Munsterites' that the Separates' very association with the ex-Quaker could have had tragic and bloody repercussions in both colonies. This may now seem to have been an extreme position for Edwards to have taken, but even in 1772, with the Regulators' War ended, the subject of the Baptists' involvement in the movement was still too ticklish to discuss frankly and openly.

Paschal took nearly the opposite tack. He served up good old American apple pie tempered to the digestion of the late 1920s if not the early 1930s, equating the Regulators' War with the Revolution at every chance he got, making Governor Tryon into a devil straight out of hell and sent to persecute the poor liberty-loving Baptists, frequently taking Edwards (who did in fact remain a Loyalist throughout the Revolution in spite of considerable criticism and persecution) to task for not concurring with his hindsight opinions and ignoring the older writer completely on the occasions it was possible to do so. When comparing his and Edwards's histories, one is tempted to offer a pithy comment much like the old Welshman himself might have penned: it is indeed a shame that Paschal was not around in the late 1760s and early 1770s so he could have set both Edwards and Shubal Stearns straight about a few things. Nonetheless Paschal did have access to numerous North Carolina historical documents that do in fact link individual Separate Baptists more closely to the Regulators than Edwards would have felt safe in stating in 1772, even if Paschal's interpretation of them is consistently blurred by the Revolution. These include at least four petitions signed by Shubal Stearns himself in behalf of various men in trouble with the law due to Regulator activity as well as some of the "Advertisements" signed by Regulators themselves who were known Separate Baptists; these names included even those of the preachers James Billingsley, Francis Dorsett, and Nathaniel Powell. Shubal Stearns's close friend Seamore York has also been identified by some as a Regulator for a time, but Paschal tried to de-emphasize this because York turned out to be a Loyalist at the start of the Revolution, actually gathering a company of thirty-four men to fight against the patriots at Moore's Creek Bridge in 1776.[29] Evidence exists in the writings of both Edwards and Paschal that, although Joseph Murphy was probably not a Regulator himself, his Little River Church was stocked full of Regulator sympathizers if not outright participants, and at least two known Regulator leaders, Benjamin Merrill who later fell extremely four of the law, and the preacher James Stewart, were admitted Baptists. Stewart was a Separate, but Merrill appears to have belonged initially to the Regular church at the Jersey Settlement until it had been broken up by the Cherokee war.[30]

This is not to say that Merrill and Stewart were *the* Regulator chieftains. Herman Husbands was the closest thing to a leader that the group had, but as has been noted, true to Husbands's character, it was a leadership merely of agitation and incitement in which he craftily wove his own agenda into the simpler complaints of his followers. There was no one man who ever actually provided any other definitive direction to the organization, and perhaps that was the way Husbands, with his garbled mix of extreme social democratic politics and esoteric theology, thought proper. James Hunter was known as "the General of the Regulation," though the fighting record he left at the end of the Regulators' War certainly didn't merit it; Rednap Howell was "the Poet," Thomas Person of Granville County was for some reason known as "the Brains," and there probably existed some additional nicknames among the backcountry farmers for other prominent Regulators such as William Butler, Peter Craven, Ninian Bell Hamilton, and Jeremiah Fields. Nicknames and reputations notwithstanding, we may now relate a brief account of their activities up to the fall of 1769; at least at first they were pacific enough.

The letter calling the men of Orange County together at Maddock's Mill in the spring of 1766 had been a public and peaceful invitation and was actually read in open court. Several court officers, in spite of their bad reputation as a group, deemed the call reasonable and agreed to attend the meeting themselves. The haughty Edmund Fanning, however, declared the meeting an "insurrectionary step" and refused to attend. Given his already-close relationship with Governor Tryon, most of the other officials pragmatically changed their minds about attending as well. The Maddock's Mill gathering therefore accomplished very little other than a few resolutions to keep an eye on the officeholders from henceforth; according to Edwards and Paschal, many at the meeting, most of whom would have to have been Separate Baptists, were opposed to any further actions at the time because "it was too hot and rash, and in some things not legal."[31] The group thus faded to the background temporarily, as did Herman Husbands from all appearances, during the next year and a half or so merely publishing some more "Regulator Advertisements" and, according to North Carolina historian William S. Powell, engaging in only a few "minor clashes" with the authorities though Powell does not specify their nature.[32] The anger of the uplanders was on a slow burn at the excesses of the good ol' boys, though, and with agitators like Husbands, as well as James Hunter, William Butler, and the rest, it was bound to flare up brightly again.

The flare-up came in the spring of 1768, with almost simultaneous announcements from both local and provincial authorities: Governor Tryon announced the levy of a new tax on imported wines and two new poll taxes to raise ten thousand pounds to finish building his new executive palace at New Bern on the coast, and Orange County sheriff Tyree Harris gave notice that he would receive county tax payments at only five specified places, with an additional two shilling, eight pence fine on every delinquent payment. The Regulators began to assemble again, with Herman Husbands in his favorite place a little further in the background, and soon sent a delegation to Sheriff Harris to request a list of their taxables, a statement of the disbursement of public money, and a copy of the law establishing fees for deeds and other official papers. Though this action implied no argument from the Regulators concerning their tax obligation itself, Harris refused to comply with the request, and Edmund Fanning harshly, imperiously, and gratuitously denounced the delegation for "daring to suggest questioning them before the bar of their shallow understanding and attempting to set themselves up as sovereign arbiters of right and wrong."[33]

Fanning's attitude only made bad tempers worse among the Regulators, and to cap it all off Sheriff Harris picked this, of the worst possible times, to confiscate a Regulator's horse, bridle, and saddle for delinquent taxes. When Fanning, in his office as justice, left Hillsboro to attend a court session at Halifax, a posse led by Peter Craven, William Butler, and Ninian Bell Hamilton returned to town, stole the horse back, and for good measure took their long rifles and fired a volley of shots into the porch and roof of Fanning's house. When Fanning got wind of the disturbance, he immediately ordered the arrests of Craven, Butler, and Hamilton, called out seven companies of local militia, and made preparation to retake the town, as it were. But this time he and the other Orange County leaders had acted so blatantly high-handedly and botched things so badly that the citizens of Orange County were supporting the Regulators solidly, and most of the militia members refused to rise.

Politically, the situation was as bad as it could be for Harris and his cronies. With the people backing the Regulators on one side and Governor Tryon's pet Edmund Fanning, still in Halifax and itching to ride back to Hillsboro in triumph, expecting them to restore the status quo on the other, the sheriff made it appear that they were taking steps toward establishing a peaceful dialogue with the Regulators but wrote to Fanning that they were merely playing for time. Meanwhile the Regulators asked Herman Husbands and a few others to act as their representatives in the meeting with the officers. But before negotiations could be opened, Fanning returned to town in a rage, evidently bringing the secretary to the governor with him as added authority. He and Sheriff Harris arrested William Butler and Husbands for "inciting the people to rebellion" and Craven and Hamilton for their part in the horse theft. After a brief trial before a lower court justice they were jailed at Hillsboro, but Fanning's intention was to convey Husbands to New Bern as soon as possible. The news spread like wildfire through Orange County and so much further incensed the people that by dawn the next morning, seven hundred men, from all appearances including James Billingsley, perhaps Nathaniel Powell, and undoubtedly many other Separate Baptists, gathered near Hillsboro to break Butler, Husbands, and the others out of jail. For the time being, the farmers and hunters of the backcountry had called the good ol' boys' bluff; nowhere near that number had responded to Fanning's militia call-up, and the frightened officials released the prisoners to meet with and pacify the mob. Tryon's secretary further quelled the mob's bellicose spirit by promising that the royal governor himself would receive their petition to investigate conditions in Orange County, and see that they received justice to boot, if they would only disperse and return to their homes.

Here William Tryon finally entered the picture on his own. Whether he realized it or not, his secretary had acted expediently, and if he had simply said nothing and made good the secretary's promises, things might have turned out differently. He knew he could have; once he even admitted in a letter he was well aware of the fact that "the sheriffs [of the western counties] have embezzled more than one-half of the public money ordered to be raised and collected by them ... [about £40,000] ... not 500 of which will possibly ever come into the Treasury."[34] But fear of upsetting the rickety status quo and possibly losing further revenue must have overrode all other concerns. Tryon claimed that the secretary had exceeded his authority; he did release the amount of taxes due for the previous year, issued another proclamation requiring all court officials to post their fees, and promised to have the attorney general prosecute all officers duly charged with extortion, but he refused to treat the Regulators as a legitimate organization. In turn the upland mob threatened to disrupt all court activity and county governmental functions until they received satisfaction, and after being personally presented with "Regulator Advertisement Number 8" at New Bern by James Hunter and Rednap Howell, who assured him that the group meant no disrespect to King George but only sought redress for the abuses of the backcountry's corrupt officials, Tryon promised to visit Hillsboro personally in July for the Superior Court session where Butler and Husbands were to be tried, and to see that Edmund Fanning answered the charges against him as well. As events proved, though, like many a southern politician since, Tryon was talking out of both sides of his mouth, but at least his intentions were nonviolent so far.

On his arrival at Hillsboro, Tryon attempted to call out the militia again to protect the court, but the general population was still so strongly in sympathy with the Regulators that the Governor found himself in the same fix Edmund Fanning had been in a few months earlier. Hardly anyone in Orange County was willing to respond to the call out of respect for the Regulators' cause, and Tryon was forced to canvass Rowan, Mecklenburg, and Granville Counties as well as Orange to assemble a force of 1,461 militiamen. The makeup of the force thus assembled was curious. More than a fifth of them were commissioned officers including eight generals and seven colonels including Edmund Fanning; six were actually members of the upper legislative house, eighteen were in the lower house, and numerous others held petty governmental offices. The connection between the civil and military forces made evident here is proof enough of the control the courthouse rings and the good ol' boys exerted throughout the province, especially in the west.[35] For filling out the rest of the militia body, though, Tryon seems to have employed some hyperbole to stir the wrath of the Presbyterians in the backcountry, especially the Scottish Highlanders who, in spite of the fact that most had come to America in the wake of Bonnie Prince Charlie's defeat at Culloden, were among the most fiercely loyal British subjects in the region. According to Herman Husbands, as quoted by both Morgan Edwards and G.W. Paschal, Tryon told the Presbyterians that the Regulators were a "faction of Quakers and Baptists who aimed at oversetting the Church of England."[36] The few Presbyterian ministers promised loyalty from their congregations and the Highlanders certainly responded in kind, proof positive for Paschal that Tryon was out to persecute the poor Separate Baptists, but what he ignored or seemed not to realize was that Chief Justice Howard's General Baptist background and the activities of Samuel Harris, James Read, and the other North Carolina Separates in Tidewater Virginia both had to be figured into Tryon's accusation, which was mere propaganda made to raise the militia anyway. Both Martin Howard's background and his status as a royal appointee were a measure of safety for the Separates, and given the trust that they showed in his judgement they knew it. Likewise, it must be remembered that Edmund Fanning's brother William was an Anglican clergyman in the Tidewater, and given the bellicose, militant stance the young Virginia Separates were taking there, Tryon's accusation against the Baptists actually may have been a direct quote from a letter written by William Fanning to his brother Edmund and passed on to the governor. But here it becomes evident that Shubal Stearns's flock was beginning to be caught up in an extremely vicious circle. They may have been getting the reputation of lawbreakers and rebels in North Carolina less from their Regulator involvement than from news of their actions in Virginia, and in the Tidewater their reputation was only being made worse by news of their participation in the 1768 flare-up at Hillsboro. It may be significant that June 1768 marked the formal commencement of concentrated legal persecution against the Separates by the Virginia county courts. Until then they had suffered more at the hands of mobs to which the county officers turned a blind eye,[37] but now with the showdown at Hillsboro in full swing so did the Virginia Separates' legal status worsen. Moreover, one small aspect of Samuel Harris's ministerial career that occurred about this time seems to have been ignored by virtually all the historians except Morgan Edwards: "in Hillsborough [sic] he went to preach to the prisoners, and was locked up in gaol for some time."³⁸ When exactly did this occur, what, of all things, was Samuel Harris doing in North Carolina at this time or afterward, who were the prisoners he preached to, and why, since no North Carolina Separate had ever fallen foul of the law yet, was he jailed as well? And did Shubal Stearns support him in this venture or not, and if not, was it because he was frightened or simply overwhelmed by the completely confused loyalties festering within the whole mess? We may speculate but never know the answers; however, we must perk our ears up at this one shadowy reference to a link between the activities at Hillsboro and those in Tidewater Virginia, one whose full explanation may very well be lost to time and obscurity.

But to return to the Hillsboro difficulty, Tryon finally got his overbrassed militia gathered and proceeded to try to restore order at the Orange County seat. He enforced his command for all public officials to post their legal fees, demanded the collection of taxes for the previous year, and had Chief Justice Howard call the Superior Court to order for the trials of Butler, Husbands, and the others and even Edmund Fanning. In response to the Butler-Husbands trials some 3,700 Regulators gradually collected near the banks of the Eno River near the town, and in spite of Tryon's pacifying political promises to Hunter and Howell and the fact that Fanning was going to be tried himself, for a while it looked as if an out-and-out battle would erupt. It never really materialized, however; in spite of their numerical superiority, the Regulators really were rather cowed by the trained militia under officers' command: not even "General" James Hunter was willing to assume field command of their own forces, let alone Herman Husbands. Moreover, a rumor actually started that Tryon would attempt to incite the Cherokee against them, though as he and their representatives met to parley he assured them that this was not so. Anyway, he promised them that he would ensure that Butler, Husbands, and Fanning alike received fair trials and that all other Regulators involved would be granted a pardon on condition that they deliver nine named leaders up for trial, surrender their arms, pay their taxes, and go home. The Regulators made no promise, delivered up no leaders, and only thirty gave up their arms, but they did go home and everyone breathed a sigh of relief. The threatened "Battle of the Eno" was over.

Tryon then proceeded to business in Superior Court, and though Paschal would have us believe his first motive was the destruction of the poor Baptists, he actually appears to have used some canny politics in an attempt to make the whole wretched Regulator conflict go away so that he and all involved could return to their well-loved status quo. Herman Husbands was actually acquitted, according to his own tale on the condition that he should "in the future overlook extortion and seek to pacify the public mind";[39] William Butler, Peter Craven, and Ninian Hamilton were found guilty of starting the spring 1768 riot in which the horse was stolen back and the shots fired into Fanning's house, fined fifty pounds apiece, and sentenced to six months imprisonment, but Tryon immediately granted executive clemency and pardoned them. Fanning was convicted on five counts of extortion for his six-shilling registry fees, fined one penny for each offense plus court costs, and perhaps at Tryon's urging promptly resigned his office as registrar.[40] The whole business had required Tryon's presence in Hillsboro nearly three months, and sometime after the twenty-fifth of September he returned to his capital at New Bern on the coast. So far, so good in terms of pragmatic southern political theory both then and now, but Herman Husbands, though unwilling to fight himself, had no intention of either overlooking extortion or pacifying the public mind, and after the backcountry farmers heard of Fanning's one-penny fines, not to mention the five thousand pounds that must now come out of their pockets for both Fanning's and Tryon's militia calls in relation to the 1768 riot, he could make sure their anger stayed festered.

Most historians agree that the Regulator leaders used most of late 1768 and nearly the whole of 1769 to try to press their case legally through the provincial assembly. This was indeed so, in part; after the 1768 fiasco, Fanning lost his own seat in the assembly as representative from Orange County and none other than Herman Husbands was elected to fill it, along with Thomas Person as the assemblyman from Granville County. But good ol' boys would be good ol' boys, and Governor Tryon contrived, perhaps under the advice of a few of Fanning's other cronies, to elevate Hillsboro to official borough status so its citizens could send their own representative to the assembly, and of course Fanning won this new seat easily. This particular assembly was scheduled to convene at New Bern on October 23, 1769, but before we return to Husbands's, Person's, and Fanning's actions therein we need to examine the twelvemonth between Tryon's exit from the backcountry in September 1768, to Shubal Stearns's alleged vision in September 1769, in more detail. During this period, the Regulator spirit had expanded from its original base in Orange, Rowan, and to a lesser extent Granville County, and similar though smaller disturbances were raised in Anson, Johnston, and Edgecombe Counties as well. And when all the facts are considered, it becomes obvious that even the Regulators in Orange County were by no means completely peaceful during this time. William Powell recounts that they actually degenerated more or less into a gang of bullies, possibly from their own frustrations but equally likely from the inspiration of Husbands, who could use tales of their violence as a political tool at New Bern. They broke into petty courts, drove judges from the bench, and set up mock courts of their own. Armed with large cudgels and cowhide and cow's-tail whips, which in most cases they appear to have preferred over firearms, they dragged attorneys through the streets and publicly beat and humiliated them, and were not above assaulting peaceful citizens who refused to endorse their actions.[41] Even Sheriff Harris appears not to have been able to enforce basic law and order, undoubtedly for fear of being lynched himself. Besides this, though not much has been said about it, there seems to have been a lot of hot-blooded, idle boasting going on back and forth between some of the Regulators in 1769 about renewing their quarrel with Tryon, taking up arms again, and warring on the unfair provincial government; a cause from which, though Herman Husbands seems to have so far characteristically safely distanced his own person, he did little or nothing to calm or dissuade, and probably quietly encouraged. After all, he was an enlightened soul with superior intelligence, or so he thought, and they rough country men, and true to the actual practical spirit of the Enlightenment in the American colonies, he could exploit their mob anger politically to advance his own causes at the assembly in New Bern while remaining above it himself. As a side thought, and this is pure speculation on this author's part, the Regulators' actions during this period, and the lowlanders' growing antipathy to them, may very well have been the first recorded group conflict of rural hill people versus more settled and cultured flatlanders in American history. The present reputation given to Appalachian natives as being rustic, backward, impulsive, ignorant, and violent hillbillies possibly had its beginnings in the Regulator conflict during this very time.

Be that as it may, though, in this year—the fall of 1768 to the fall of 1769—Shubal Stearns had seen the Regulators evolve from a political action group ostensibly intent on obtaining the redress of their grievances by peaceful and legal means to a hot-tempered mob bent on responding to a faulty government with the disruption of *all* law and order and whose members were now taking their frustrations out on any obstacle they imagined they had. Herman Husbands no doubt took the political stance that he couldn't calm his followers and therefore their grievances must be satisfied, while privately defending both them and his theology by a line of reasoning close to the famous later revolutionary maxims: the end always justifies the means, and one cannot make an omelet without breaking a few eggs. Stearns, of course, could make no such rationalizations, and moreover, when the actions of Samuel Harris and the Virginia Separates are considered in light of all that had befallen the North Carolina uplanders in 1768, and what his Separates had been accused of in both provinces, his position, not to mention that of the Sandy Creek Association, looked doubly ominous. If indeed Samuel Harris made his trip to Hillsboro in this year, Stearns's own confusion and fear, combined with his disgust at the fools his neighbors had become through Husbands's agitation, may have been the primary reason that he did not accompany his younger colleague. But to put things into proper perspective we must remember that the October 1768 session of the Sandy Creek Association, in which John Newton was censured and to which Samuel Harris and his Tidewater converts brought such horrific tales of imprisonments and persecutions in Virginia, was held only about two weeks after Governor Tryon had departed Hillsboro following the Eno threat and the Regulator trials. Besides the group's already obvious internal difficulties, what kind of fears and misgivings must have been generated in Stearns's mind that summer simply over the idea of hosting the gathering so soon after, and so close to the site of, the spring riot? Had not Governor Tryon departed when he did, given his propaganda statement to the Presbyterians that summer, what might he have thought that the association was up to, especially with all those young men present from Tidewater Virginia? Of course Stearns did host his association despite whatever misgivings he may have entertained, and if there was any statement made or action taken by the group regarding the Regulator movement in 1768, the historians are silent on it. But again, after the long, hard year of political electioneering, Regulator bullying and general anarchy in the uplands in 1769, when Shubal Stearns climbed up that hill after the thunderstorm on September 7, he must have already known that his association was going to have to come up with some policy statement on the Regulators to guide his members. His other two concerns would have been small potatoes compared to this third one. The local thunderstorm that he had just seen was similarly a spring freshet compared to the torrent of violence that the uplands had endured for a year and yet would endure for nearly the next two. Divine vision or no, Stearns would indeed have been a fool not to have at least considered dividing up the association into provincial groups by this point simply to isolate the mounting troubles within and without the body and give himself peace of mind from at least a few of them. If indeed the cloud he saw gave him a revelation, it was nothing that common horse sense shouldn't have told him already.

But when it came to his beloved church members, Shubal Stearns, the Goodly Fere, was paternal rather than practical, and though the difficulties facing him in the 1769 association session seemed monumental, from all evidence he appeared to be willing to tough out whatever troubles came. One would think that, if he had really believed he had been given another revelation from God and had interpreted it correctly on September 7, the vision and his—and his little brothers and sisters in the faith's—obedience to it would have been the first item of business on the Sandy Creek Association's 1769 roster. But it was not so. The association evidently opened in the usual way. Undoubtedly, as always, it was a social gathering as much as a religious function for the backcountry men and women, and among the crowd of worshipers, Ketocton Association visitors, and neighbors assembled to observe the proceedings and exchange greetings, there were probably peddlers and horse traders out to make a profit from the crowd as well, and maybe even a "jockey ground" some distance from Sandy Creek Church where the youngbloods of the settlements could try out and match their horses. This was certainly the common setting, during many years, for countless Appalachian Baptist gatherings for which the Sandy Creek Association served as the prototype. The author must repeat that it is regrettable that none of the minutes of these early Sandy Creek gatherings survive, but we do have one very good and perceptive record of a Separate Baptist association that occurred only about a year and a half after this one from the pen of one John Williams, a young Tidewater Virginia preacher. The first day of the 1769 Sandy Creek gathering must have been very much like this example, with some of the principal ministers and exhorters named herein undoubtedly serving at that time as well and even acting in the same manner:

> Got to the Association about one o'clock. Brother [Thomas] Hargitt was then about to preach to about 1,200 souls, from 40th

Chapter Isa., 11th verse ... Brother [John] Burruss got up immediately after and preached from Isa., 55, 3d verse ... [This would have been the introduction and then the introductory sermon, followed by handshaking and prayer] with a good deal of liberty, set the Christians all afire with the love of God; Assembly praising God with a loud voice; Brother [John] Waller exhorting till he got spent; then Brethren [William] Marshall and [Elijah] Craig both broke loose together, the Christians shouting and they speaking for the space of half an hour or more; then ceased. Intermission for about one hour, then the delegates associated themselves together; a moderator chosen ... a clerk nominated ... Then the letters from several churches were read. Then concluded for that night.[42]

Williams goes on to record the events of the Sunday services and the two days' church business afterwards, during which many of the ministers, including himself, were sent outside to conduct services for the worshippers and visitors while the affairs of the association were being settled. For the sake of brevity they will not be recounted here, but suffice it to say on that first day of the 1769 session at Sandy Creek, the delegates from the churches of all three provinces undoubtedly hid the growing tensions within the body under a mask of joy and fellowship such as Williams described. This proved to be the case as well for the association about which Williams wrote, and the author has seen the same phenomenon many times even in his own short lifetime. There is something illusory about the first day's service of an association with a character like Sandy Creek's. The joy of meeting friends one has not seen in perhaps a year, the chance to get together for visiting, singing, and preaching while renewing those friendships, or perhaps just the cherishing of tradition once it has been established, can make everything seem all right even in the instances when it is not. When all goes well through an entire session, it is indeed heavenly, and thus must most of the Sandy Creek sessions prior to 1768 have proceeded under Shubal Stearns's benevolent autocracy and his congregants' trusting acceptance of it. But there are times when the sweetest prayer or sermon of the first day may be offered by the man who exhibits the worst display of temper or the most insidious tendency toward backstabbing on the second or third, and although Stearns had not suffered this particular problem as of yet, his own interaction with both members and visitors was about to make the slightly hurt feelings and ruffled feathers of the year before seem like nothing.

To determine exactly what happened at this October 1769 Sandy Creek session we must use what sources we have, and they are only two, the writings of Robert B. Semple and Morgan Edwards. All other historians draw from them, but Semple treats only of what was important to the Virginia Separates and though Edwards gives detail that is a little more frank, one must occasionally read between the lines and pay as much attention to what is *not* written as to what *is* written. But still, John Williams's account of the later association seems to have rung true for this one: "*Monday Morning:* Monday fast-day among us. The brethren delegates met at the meeting-house by three hours b'sun [about 9:00 AM]. Brother Lewis Craig opened Association by divine service. Brother Harris gave the delegates a very warm and melting exhortation. Then proceeded to business. We went on very well about an hour and a half, then a dark cloud seemed to overshadow us...."[43]

We know that Shubal Stearns was present and presiding at this session as always, but it must be admitted that there is no record of how the difficulty concerning John Newton and Congaree Church was handled this year if indeed Newton's restoration had already taken place. Had this already occurred, the church may have been censured again or even barred from seating its delegates. On the other hand, it is equally plausible that Congaree's threatened reversed stance in support of John Newton was quietly and prudently overlooked in light of the two other tense problems that Stearns was trying to guide the assembly through. But we do know that the presence of the Ketocton Association's delegates, with their conciliatory, diplomatically worded letter, did prompt a lengthy debate in a body that had long been used to rubber-stamping Shubal Stearns's advice and his decisions. According to Semple, the principal objections to fellowship with Ketocton voiced by the majority of Separates and thus most probably by Stearns himself were that they held too tightly to some objectionable articles of the Philadelphia Confession and that they were not scrupulous enough about their manner of dress, which may have included considerations of the men's hair length. Judging from later evidence, it is probable that the western North Carolina and the two southwestern Virginia churches, with the exception of Samuel Harris, backed Stearns solidly, the eastern North Carolinans perhaps less so in consideration of the fact that the Kehukee Association had been organized two months before in part of their territory and they might already have entertained some ideas of eventually establishing a similar relation with the new body. The South Carolinans may have been likewise split on the issue among the diehard pro-Stearns stance of Daniel Marshall, the opposition opinion of Joseph Reese and John Newton, and the vacillation of Philip Mulkey. There was evidently a division of opinion among the young Tidewater Virginia firebrands as well. Semple states that after this lengthy debate, the Ketocton offer was rejected by a "small majority," though paradoxically he immediately quotes Elijah Craig reiterating that Sandy Creek had been accustomed *never* to doing anything except by unanimous vote, patiently and humbly praying and fasting until the delegates were all of one mind and one accord[44]—which, in light of Stearns's and the body's 1768 action against John Newton, seems hardly believable at least at this period. By the time Semple wrote Craig for his historical recollections, about 1807 or 1808, Craig was living in central Kentucky near his brothers Lewis and Joseph and had become a very successful farmer, businessman, and even a whiskey distiller (this was an age when "taking a dram" while not drinking to excess was not considered a sin among Baptists), and he may have viewed his memories through rose-colored glasses. One would hope at least that, while answering Semple's letter, he had not imbibed too much of the bourbon whiskey that he invented and developed, Craig's other claim to fame.

Still, the Goodly Fere must have effectively managed to smooth things over at least partially by agreeing to the organization of Samuel Harris's new Fall Creek Church along with some more freshly gathered Tidewater bodies, and acquiescing to the ordination of both Samuel Harris and Jeremiah Walker. Edwards's *Materials* state that Harris was ordained on October 11, 1769. The ceremony thus must have taken place not in the church where the candidate was to be installed as pastor or moderator as was customary but right there at the association meeting itself probably with Stearns officiating in the ordaining presbytery. Walker, on the other hand, was ordained a month or so later at the Amelia County, Virginia, meetinghouse where he preached regularly.[45] Being able to witness the joyous rite of Harris's ordination, which they had desired for so long, probably took much of the bad taste of the debate out of the Tidewater Separates' mouths, as Stearns undoubtedly knew it would; and so for a time, all was ostensibly peace and harmony again.

But of course there was yet one matter to be dealt with, the Regulator issue, and in the environment of the association setting, this could prove to be as dangerous as a cocked gun. The context of the community social function of the Sandy Creek Association again must be repeated and stressed here. In the crowd outside along with the visitors, peddlers, horsetraders, and worshipers there were undoubtedly many high-spirited Regulators as well, not a few of whom were, in addition, Separate Baptists themselves. Husbands himself was very probably a visitor on the grounds as the assembly to which he had been elected was not scheduled to convene in New Bern for two more weeks, and at least three other Regulator chiefs besides Benjamin Merrill were known to have been present also. Some may even have been drunk at this time, as there were likely as many whiskey and brandy sellers on the grounds or at a short distance from them as other peddlers. In years to come, the associations that descended from Sandy Creek would begin to elect "committees on order" to work with county peace officers to quell such goings-on at their yearly meetings, but given the Separates' legal status at this time even in North Carolina, especially since James Billingsley's, Nathaniel Powell's, James Stewart's, and others' participation in the 1768 Hillsboro fracas, they could depend on no help from Sheriff Harris or any of the magistrates. At any rate, drunk or sober now, most of the Regulators were undoubtedly in the same surly, bullying mood in which they had festered for a year and were spoiling for another fight wherever they could find one.

And find one they did, as soon as Shubal Stearns and the Sandy Creek delegates addressed the Regulator issue in the meetinghouse. Considering the Regulators' increasingly unpredictably violent actions the matter was probably not all that difficult to take up, though we have no way of knowing which church or churches submitted queries about it. No criticism was made of the fact that Separates had joined in the general protests of the crookedness of the actions of the courthouse rings and of the sheriffs' high-handed tax collection methods, for undoubtedly most if not all of the western North Carolinians present had suffered more or less because of them. No one was censured even for participating in the 1768 riot and its aftermath. However, one resolution, probably worded by Shubal Stearns himself, was passed in connection with all future possible Regulator activity within the association; unfortunately, true to Stearns's character, he seems to have presented it in the same big-brotherly way he had always handled his members' church affairs and transacted their association business, and at first reading it comes off sounding rather harsh. According to Edwards, the "order" read as follows: "If any of our members shall take up arms against the legal authority and abbet [*sic*] them that do he shall be excommunicated."⁴⁶ In all likelihood Benjamin Merrill was not in the meetinghouse when the order was passed, although James Billingsley, Nathaniel Powell, and James Stewart undoubtedly were unless one or more had been sent out to preach at the "stand" to the worshipers and visitors. In light of all the changes to the bad within the Regulator organization since the 1768 riot, the three preachers, as well as all others in the house, could see that their Goodly Fere was at least taking a stance that was based on the Pauline and Petrine doctrines of subjection to the civil government for the sake of the cause of Christ. So it is highly likely that, as it had been in all the good, peaceful, joyous association sessions of a few years before, they deferentially acquiesced to his and Sandy Creek's authority over the matter. Even the Virginians probably joined the North Carolinians in acquiescence; though many of them had been involved in fistfights and had been arrested and jailed for preaching, this was not their quarrel. At this time in the Old Dominion, they merely sought legal recognition of their worship under the 1689 British Toleration Act and, whether they realized it or not, a simple recognition by the Virginia government and society at large of the power of their social class.

But in associations of Sandy Creek's combination social/religious setting, news can travel from the quiet—or noise, as the case may be—of the meetinghouse to the general public on the grounds quite fast, and this 1769 session was no exception to the rule. It soon began to be whispered, and then noised more loudly, among the crowd that Shubal Stearns and the association were threatening to "church" the Regulators, and this was all the excuse the surly, hot-tempered farmers involved in the movement needed to start a ruckus. Undoubtedly before anyone in the church house quite knew what was happening, four Regulator chiefs had burst through the meetinghouse doors, strode angrily and threateningly to the pulpit, and loudly asked if what they had heard was true.⁴⁷

The author must beg leave here to do a little more speculation, given the brevity of the Edwards account, but he feels that he has attended enough rural association meetings of this type to understand why Edwards was so brief in this instance. The four Regulator chiefs who had burst in were very likely Herman Husbands, James Hunter, Rednap Howell, and William Butler, although Benjamin Merrill himself could have been one of them. The first four mentioned led the next major Regulator riot together in Hillsboro after this, and it is probable

pared to lead one now. And they weren't asking the whole association for an answer either, but one man, the one who stood in the stand presiding over the business: the Goodly Fere, Shubal Stearns, whom they had to have known as the true power within the Sandy Creek Association ever since it had been organized. The moment thus came to a showdown between the little preacher and the man who had brought him to North Carolina in the first place, and even for the same reason Husbands had cultivated Stearns's and his family's friendship: his own oddly mixed religious/political agenda, in Husbands's mind moving right along into place as he watched over and discreetly supervised the actions of the Regulator mob. If Husbands was in true Enlightened patriot character now he was probably trying to play good cop to Hunter's, Howell's, Butler's, and maybe even Merrill's roles as bad cops, acting to a packed house of association delegates and preachers as well as, undoubtedly, a multitude of furious Regulator foot soldiers crowding into the doorway behind them, and an even larger mixed crowd of church members and mere onlookers who had left some poor bewildered young Separate preacher exhorting to himself at the stand so they could come gawk at this new excitement. Pressing their noses to the windows like they were staring at two fighting cocks in a pit, some were rooting, as it were, for one rooster, some the other, and many must have cared little for the outcome so long as they could see one get his craw spurred open and die. And taking the whole scene in from the best visual vantage point in the house, the pulpit, was the main character, the Bantam up against four tall Cochins, an utterly shocked, horrified, and bewildered Shubal Stearns.

What must have gone through Stearns's mind in that few seconds between the question and his answer? He'd been warned in the Gospels that he could expect to have to bear witness of his faith even though he might have to give up his life in so doing, but these angry men were questioning not his faith but his position on their actions. Was it the same thing or not? Should he maintain his stance as if it were his faith rather than only a secondary belief based on it? And what would happen now if he reiterated his opinion of the Regulators' actions during the past year? The Regulators had already proven themselves capable of and willing to assault and brutalize anyone whom they perceived as a threat, and Stearns was now not only a little man but an old one. Could he withstand an assault on his person the way dissenters had done in the New England of his youth? Even if he were not attacked now out of respect to his ministerial office, would the Regulators sneak onto his small property some night and burn his house and barn, perhaps killing Sarah, his brother Isaac, and niece Hephzibah in the process? And perhaps worse yet, what if his little brothers in the faith, watching tensely from their seats all over the meetinghouse, decided to "take up his part" in the immediate attack that threatened? The young Tidewater Virginians had already proven willing to defend Samuel Harris with their fists against rowdy mobs. There is no doubt that the North Carolinans and even many of the South Carolinans were even now ready to do the same thing for Stearns, but they were all unarmed and the Regulators evidently carried their trademark clubs and whips, if not their firearms, with them wherever they went. How many lives would be lost if this association turned into a riot? Even if there were no fatalities, would news of the fight send Governor Tryon storming back upcountry with several companies of lowland militia to restore order—and if he did return to restore order, whom would he blame? He'd already accused the Regulators of being a faction of Quakers and Baptists out to overthrow the Church of England, in order to get Presbyterian troops to rise in the uplands; what ungodly conclusions would he draw now? If there was ever a no-win situation, this was it, and Shubal Stearns was more painfully aware of that fact now than anyone else. That is, of course, unless the providence that he trusted had brought him to the backcountry now provided a timely miracle.

Thus if Stearns had ever truly possessed the supernatural power in his eyes with which he was credited by so many of his Separates, he needed that power now more than any time in his life. Had he been able to use his eyes according to the reputation given him, and them, he could have simply stared down the Regulator chiefs, as well as their followers crowding one another in the church doorways smelling blood and ready for war, into guilt and submission to the authority of God, and they would have turned away and left him and his association in peace. Both his power and that of his cause would only have been strengthened in a manner that Edwards, Semple, Paschal, and the other historians could have trumpeted to the high heavens. If Stearns had had sufficient coolheadedness and presence of mind to respond to the fury of the Regulators with even a simple diversionary tactic, he had a chance of at least forestalling the threatened battle, and if he brought the gambit off his wonderful eyes probably still would have gotten the credit. But now the power both of his mind and that of his eyes—if indeed he had ever possessed any except in the minds and consciences of his hearers—failed him utterly. Shubal Stearns stood in the pulpit before the angry Regulator chiefs glaring up at him, an aging, confused, shocked, and frightened little man who, in his prime and with the facilitation of Herman Husbands, had by chance or divine design given the North Carolina backwoods its own native religion and religious culture. But the good days were over now, and in perplexity Stearns looked about him as his original connection and relationship with Husbands stood ready to blossom fully into a malevolent fruit. "The Kingdom of Heaven suffereth violence, and the violent take it by force," the Lord had said; Herman Husbands was now showing his interpretation of that cryptic Scripture passage, and was a scene like this truly to which it referred? But the moment, the eternity, was over, and Shubal Stearns finally answered the question put to him with the best resources he had. We do not know exactly how he replied, only that "the answer was evasive; for they [sic] were in bodily fear. This checked the design much...."[48]

The tempers of the Regulator chiefs were pacified and they stalked back outside, perhaps to hear a few shaken young preachers try to resume the violated worship service at the stand. All must have been quiet in the house and business probably was taken up where it had been left off before the fervid interruption. But though there had been no blood shed or even fists thrown during the affray in the church, there was one casualty who would now suffer through a lingering illness from which there would be no recovery: Shubal Stearns, who had fatally wounded himself with his own words. For perhaps the first time his Separates had witnessed such behavior from him, and maybe even the first time in his adult life, he had replied to a demand with a mealymouthed, uncertain answer that every delegate and visitor in the house could see had been based on bodily fear more than any other consideration. No matter now that he had undoubtedly been acting under duress in the best manner his shocked and astonished mind could muster, or that he may have answered hesitatingly and fearfully, and maybe even untruthfully, as much for their safety's sake as his own. For nearly fourteen years now his backcountry converts had looked up to him almost as a demigod standing away from and above all his younger colleagues, capable of paralyzing sinners with his expressive eyes and the enchantment of his loud, musical pulpit cant, preaching them a Gospel they accepted implicitly as the truth and making most of their religious decisions for them like a concerned and loving big brother. Under the moderatorial image he had projected, his association had spread over much of the settled territory of the American Southeast. And now the South Carolinians, most of whom had stood by his decisions even when he had unjustly rejected the work and the credentials of one of their best preachers and they couldn't see the reason for his so doing; the Tidewater Virginians, who had preached right on in spite of mob attacks and terms of imprisonment and who were inured to physical violence against themselves as a matter of course; and his own especially beloved North Carolinians and western Virginians, who were children of the Reverend Old Father in a relationship closer than any of the others had ever known; all in the packed church now saw Shubal Stearns, their big brother in the faith, their Goodly Fere, revealed for what he was: a man just like themselves. And though the delegates would have been too shaken at the spectacle of Stearns's fearful reaction to pronounce any judgements yet and though the aging preacher still had his staunch supporters in men like Tidence Lane, Elnathan Davis, the Murphys, Seamore York, and even the ex-Regulator James Billingsley, for most of his followers Stearns's humanization was the unforgivable sin. There is only one other recorded action that the 1769 Sandy Creek Association took before the delegates departed, undoubtedly dazed, for their homes, that of appointing the association meeting for 1770 at James Read's Grassy Creek Church in Granville County.[49] Grassy Creek was an unusually long distance from Sandy Creek considering that most of the association's meetings had traditionally been appointed at or near Stearns's home on the Rowan/Orange border; the decision to hold the 1770 meeting at a location closer to the Old Dominion was probably prompted out of consideration to the Virginians. One wonders, though, whether Shubal Stearns might also have encouraged the selection of Grassy Creek in the pathetic and forlorn hope that church moderator James Read, who himself had baptized so many of the young Tidewater converts and in fact was still active in the "big" outdoor meetings in Virginia that he and Samuel Harris had begun, could possibly help his Reverend Old Father restore some of his lost prestige. We will never know.

The provincial assembly convened in New Bern a little less than two weeks later, as has already been noted, with Thomas Person now serving as representative from Granville County, Herman Husbands from Orange, and Edmund Fanning from the newly reclassified Hillsboro town. According to William Powell, both houses of this particular assembly actually were inclined to hear petitions from and address the problems voiced by the Regulators, but instead Person, Husbands, and the other lower-house assemblymen, who were becoming ever more and more outspoken about Revolutionary ideals, wanted to put the cart before the horse and introduce issues between the colony as a whole and King George's government instead. They drew up a petition to the Crown listing several of these disputes, and on receiving it a highly angered Governor Tryon promptly dissolved the Assembly before it could enact further legislation.[50] Thus the Regulators' hopes for justice from the 1769 Assembly were dashed. In fairness it must be said that if their representatives had not overreached themselves at the session, things would have gone better for them.

Meanwhile, back in the upcountry things were still bad and getting worse. The Regulator organization was gaining more power than ever, but there is a good deal of evidence that now, rather than trying to win the uplanders' voluntary support, though they yet enjoyed a good deal of it, the Regulators had become so confident of the rightness of their actions that they were increasingly using the same terrorist techniques they had employed at Sandy Creek at the fall association session to silence their critics and to draft soldiers into their ranks. Only worsening this reign of terror was the widespread confusion that now existed within the backcountry's religious base due to Shubal Stearns's evasive, halting reply to the Regulator leaders' demands for an answer from him at the session. By far the majority of Stearns's people had been used to obeying "the order of the association" without question as simply the right thing to do, without even needing to think about matters themselves, and an iffy, uncertain answer from Stearns was completely out of their frame of reference. They thus began to interpret the 1769 Regulator ruling from two different viewpoints probably without considering the essential rightness or wrongness of the question, only the moderator's and association's ruling: one, that it was forbidden to join or support the Regulators, because Stearns had said so initially when the matter had been taken up in the business meeting; and the other, that the Association would permit it, because the Goodly Fere had at least hinted at that idea in order to pacify the Regulator chiefs once they had stormed in. Chaos reigned. Tough young Elnathan Davis tried to enforce the first viewpoint at Haw River, probably more than any other reason because of the closeness of his relationship to the old preacher at Sandy Creek, and he very nearly succeeded in spite of the facts that everyone recognized the essential unfairness and corruption of courthouse-ring government and that the ex-Regulator Nathaniel Powell was one of his ministerial assistants. At their monthly business meeting the last Saturday in November 1769, the church voted to reaffirm Stearns's original "order" that "if any of their members should join the Regulators, or take up arms against lawful authority he should therefore be excommunicated."[51]

The Regulators swiftly responded, according to Edwards, by commandeering the members' rifles, evidently breaking into their homes like the gang of bullies and thieves to which they had degenerated, to accomplish their purpose. They severely beat one prominent Haw River member, Robert Mash or Marsh, and then threatened him with thirty lashes a month until he got in the right frame of mind and joined their organization. Though Edwards does not record it, other members may have received the same treatment, and we have no way of knowing how many men from Haw River, or for that matter other places, became Regulators by bowing down to this kind of coercion.

For G.W. Paschal this must have been exceptionally hard to read about, so badly did he want the Separate Baptists to be Regulators and the Regulators to be patriots, and in his own writings he often delicately sidesteps issues or splits hairs over the wording of church documents to try to prove that the Regulators had not really become as bad as they were. Still, though he probably never intended it to be so, his writings do prove that, even through harsh persecution, the Haw River Separates held on stubbornly to their pacifistic stance until the first days of the Revolution. James Childs, who had been one of the first Tidewater Virginia Separates ever to go to jail for preaching without a license, moved south to the Haw River area in 1770 to become the pastor or moderator of Rocky River Church when it was "armed off" from Haw River. He became so heavily influenced by this position of pacifism, as well as, perhaps, by the personality of the old Goodly Fere a few miles to the north and Elnathan Davis's respect for him, that as late as 1776 he was still preaching that it was wrong for a Christian to bear arms, and he was quickly rewarded by the local Revolutionary "Committee of Safety" with a jail term and possibly exile to South Carolina for his beliefs. In this connection it is interesting to note that one other lesser-known preacher in the Haw River region, James Perry, whom Paschal accused of being a follower of Childs, was likewise jailed at the time for taking a stance on nonresistance,[52] but of course to Paschal, Childs and Perry were cranks who got just what they deserved, and Davis must have been temporarily misguided. The concept of conscientious objection evidently was recognized little or none in the Revolution, and perhaps Paschal felt that it never should have been; but the whole issue goes to show exactly how far a few words from old Shubal Stearns could go within his Baptist family circle.

A short distance away at Little River, Joseph Murphy may have tried to take the same stance as Elnathan Davis at Haw River out of respect to Stearns, but at this church he didn't get very far with it. The Little River Separates were much more committed to the Regulator cause than Elnathan Davis's flock had been in spite of the anarchy the Regulators had created, and they undoubtedly justified their actions by quoting the Goodly Fere's uncertain statement to the Regulator chiefs after their takeover of the 1769 session. Of course Murphy couldn't, or didn't know how to, argue with this, and he just seems to have quietly stepped out of the picture. Though he was still the titular pastor or moderator at Little River, he moved up the Yadkin and took his church membership to the Shallow Fords or Timber Ridge where he pastored also, and he left Little River's flock mainly in the hands of two unordained exhorters named John Bullen or Bowling and Edmund Lilly, whose preaching was evidently more pro-Regulator and therefore acceptable to the congregation. Timber Ridge Church, being in the sparsely settled western frontier of the province, had a congregation more inclined at least to be neutral to the Regulator controversy further southeast, though it is known that one company of backwoodsmen from this region did participate in Regulator activity in 1771. Even here, however, there is evidence that Murphy's insistence on honoring Stearns's original "order" may have caused one other young preacher at Timber Ridge's Mulberry Fields arm, William Cook, to advocate nonresistance himself at the outset of the Revolution. Cook was never jailed for his beliefs, but he was given a thorough grilling by both the Rowan County Committee of Safety and his church, and he finally dropped the stance.[53] Again Paschal excoriates the treasonable act of not being a through-and-through supporter of the Revolution, but it is remarkable that the only three "nonpatriotic" Baptist ministers he could find in the entire state of North Carolina during the war were all located in this one backcountry area, where the words of Shubal Stearns had always been given such deferential respect.

Though the aging Stearns still leaned on Tidence Lane and James Billingsley heavily for support at Sandy Creek and Abbott's Creek and they seem to have provided it willingly, later evidence indicates that even the Goodly Fere's home church experienced severe perplexity over their moderator's show of fear and his two varying statements, which perhaps the old man's pride prevented him from acknowledging or explaining. None of his members here had been conditioned to think for themselves, and thus no one really knew what to do. Evidently Shubal Stearns was not elucidating the matter for them. The western Virginia churches under the care of Dutton Lane and William Murphy were from all appearances in the same quandary, but to the northeast in the Tidewater, Samuel Harris's and the young Virginians' actions seem to have been quick and decisive. Themselves inured to mob hostility, they would have regarded Stearns's response to the Regulators as an inexcusable sign of weakness, and as such after December 1769 they simply began to organize churches and ordain ministers on their own, without bothering to follow the traditional practice of consulting Stearns and the association. Lewis Craig, John Waller, John Burruss, and many others including even James Childs were ordained around this time and in this fashion, probably with Samuel Harris and Jeremiah Walker officiating as presbyters. William Murphy and Dutton Lane may have provided at least some assistance in these chores as well, but it is less likely, as there is some indication in Semple's writings that the western Virginia churches were less than pleased with the easterners' disregard of Stearns.

The oddest emotional casualty of all, however, may have been James Read. Shubal Stearns had been his Reverend Old Father ever since he had been a Christian. Read had based his life and his ministry in the context of Stearns's leadership ever since he had been converted; but he was undoubtedly a witness to all that had happened in the meetinghouse on that fateful day when the Regulator chiefs had stormed in, and the sight simply may have shattered him. The author begs the reader's pardon here for appearing to try to excuse the inexcusable, but the fact is that Read was still attempting to hold his "big" meetings in the Tidewater during this time, and at some point in the summer of 1770 in Spotsylvania County, with Samuel Harris absent on a brief visit to South Carolina, Read seems to have done some deed that rocked the entire Tidewater Separate community with scandal and embarrassment. Of the nature of his scandalous behavior we know nothing, as both Tidewater Separates at the time and later Baptist historians were extremely hush-hush and fretful about the matter; but it is at least certain that Read did something more than get in a fight, which the Tidewater Separates were used to, or get drunk, which of course was considered a sin but with nowhere near the opprobrium that was attached to it after the temperance movement came into style in the nineteenth century.

That leaves only a limited range of possibilities for Read's sin, and the author wonders if some evidence of its nature might be inferred from a rule that John Waller, who was ordained in Spotsylvania on June 2, 1770,[54] not long before Read's downfall occurred, started to enforce for his own camp meetings at this time. In Waller's meetings, women were not permitted to enter or remain on the campgrounds from one hour before sundown until one hour after sunlight.[55] The author knows that it is entirely possible that Read simply could have fallen prey to his own popularity and let the flesh get willing and the spirit get weak, as so many evangelists both big and small have done since as well as probably before, without tying the scandal into the general chaos into which the Goodly Fere's flock was steadily descending after the 1769 association. But still, he cannot help but wonder if Read's shaken mental status after seeing his Reverend Old Father put to shame had something to do with his behavior.

At least of Read it can be said that he came to himself, realized the gravity of his misdeed, acknowledged his fault, and attempted to make things right. He was quickly barred from preaching and taking communion in all the Tidewater churches, and rather than cause further ruckus there he simply trudged home to Grassy Creek, never again to return to eastern Virginia as the evangelist he had been, and presented himself for the judgement and discipline of his church. This added one last tragicomic act to Shubal Stearns's predicament as association leader, for if he had ever put any trust in either Grassy Creek Church or James Read to help him mollify his position with the Tidewater Separates at the 1770 association meeting, his hopes were now dashed in the rudest manner possible. He must have known there was no way he could even rebuke Harris and the Virginians for their independent actions since October without Read's help. In addition, it must be remembered that Grassy Creek, like all the churches Stearns had raised up and cared for, was not inclined to deal with weighty matters like this on its own; it brought such cases forward to the association and let Stearns judge them and deal with them himself. Thus Stearns may have spent the tense late summer of 1770 riding back and forth between Orange County and Granville County, wearily trying to take care of the lapsed-but-repentant Read's church work possibly with help from Dutton Lane over the line in Virginia, and preparing the flock for what everyone knew was going to be the most embarrassing situation any church could ever encounter at an association—the public censure and very probably the full excommunication of its own pastor for a sin he frankly admitted. With the prospect of the eastern Virginians coming to the association more independent of Stearns's influence than ever and now having a basis for that independence in Read's folly, out for Read's hide and looking for someone to blame for their embarrassment over the summer, thoughts of the upcoming association must have been equally unpleasant to Stearns. Read had disappointed him so badly both politically and personally that it is certain he never trusted the younger man again. One wonders if, now, Stearns might have wished that he had simply gone outside with the Regulator chiefs in October 1769 and let their soldiers beat him to death with their clubs—certainly the physical pain involved would have been brief compared to the seemingly unending heartache he had brought on himself by his one fateful moment of hesitation and indecision. To him the entire world must have appeared to have gone insane, and if he had heard the news two weeks before the setting of the association that the preacher under whom he had been converted originally, and who years later had spurned his work, George Whitefield, had died and been buried in Newburyport, Massachusetts, he probably would have taken it as just one more omen of misfortune and death.

At about the same time as Whitefield's death, though, Stearns would have had even more stress closer to home. Regulator violence again exploded in Hillsboro at the September term of Superior Court and this time against Daniel Boone's land-speculation mentor, Associate Justice Richard Henderson. The Regulators' bellicose attitude had accomplished them nothing in the 1769 Assembly, even with pro-Regulator delegations from the upland counties, except to make the deliberative body as a whole more concerned with the suppression of anarchy than the satisfaction of their grievances. Now the backcountry group seemed determined to bring matters to their very worst. The riot began innocently enough, with Jeremiah Fields asking to read a Regulator "advertisement" in court that added accusations of jury rigging to their much-voiced complaint of courthouse-ring extortion. Almost before he had finished speaking, though, a mob of 150 Regulators led by Husbands, Hunter, Butler, and Howell and armed with cudgels, whips, and large switches forced its way into the courtroom, as they had been doing in petty courts across the uplands for two years now, and tried to make the governor-appointed Henderson leave the bench. On hearing an angry protest from attorney John Williams, they went wild, demolishing the courtroom and seizing Williams, Edmund Fanning, and assistant attorney general William Hooper, who as has been noted was later to sign the Declaration of Independence. Hooper was "dragged and paraded through town and treated with every mark of contempt and insult,"[56] and Williams was given a severe thrashing in spite of his advanced age, but the Regulators reserved their particular spleen for Edmund Fanning. They pulled him from the courthouse and dragged him through the mud street by his heels, gave him a brutal whipping and then broke into his house, destroyed his furniture and papers, and leveled the building to its foundations. Strangely enough Fanning's law office right across the street was not even touched, but many of the other town dwellers cowered in fear while more citizens were assaulted and rocks were thrown through windows as the Regulators ran up and down the streets like packs of wild dogs. They seized control of the town and a terrified Richard Henderson promised that the court would acquiesce to their demands the next day, but he slipped away on horseback that night to his home on Nutbush Creek in Granville County—not far, in fact, either from Grassy Creek Church or from the old temporary base Herman Husbands had used to establish his and the Stearns family's homesteads on Sandy Creek. A little more than a month later Henderson's barn and stables burned to the ground, and though it was never proven legally, it was widely assumed that the Regulators had torched them in revenge for his broken promise and his relationship to Governor Tryon.

Sandy Creek Association thus met for its October 1770 session at Grassy Creek Church right in the middle of the terrible interim between the Regulators' seizure of power in Hillsboro and the burning of Judge Henderson's buildings. One can only imagine what tension everyone at the setting must have felt, given the happenings of the previous year as well as those at Hillsboro a month beforehand, but we have no concise account of the proceedings other than that of Semple's from the already-quoted manuscript of Elijah Craig, who was present on the grounds and at the business:

> At this session they split in their first business. Nothing could be done on the first day. They appointed the next for fasting and prayer. They met and labored the whole day until an hour by sun in the afternoon, and could do nothing, not even appoint a Moderator. The third day was appointed for the same purpose, and to be observed in the same way. They met early and continued together until 3 o'clock in the afternoon without having accom-

plished anything. A proposal was then made that the Association should be divided into three districts, that is, one in each State [*sic*]. To this there was an unanimous consent at once.[57]

We will never know whether Semple edited and abridged Craig's account or not. Elijah Craig was not in the habit of pulling punches. At about the same time he was corresponding with Semple over historical matters, he published a tract criticizing one of his fellow Kentucky immigrant ministers, a Nova Scotian named Jacob Creath, that undoubtedly would have earned him a lawsuit for slander and defamation of character in modern times. Even with Semple's possible expurgation of Craig's style and meaning, though, we can see that, his supposed September 1769 revelation notwithstanding, Shubal Stearns kept his children in the faith there at Grassy Creek for three whole business days, not counting Sunday services, hoping against hope that they could all be of one mind—that is, of *his* mind—as they had been in the happy and innocent days of yesteryear. No matter how many fasts or prayers he appointed, though, the support just wasn't coming. The North Carolina historians' claim that the Sandy Creek Association somehow transacted its business in its early years without the supervision of a moderator rings hollow here, even though Stearns himself might not have been called by that title; however, from the Semple/Craig account we can also see that the "split in the first business," as it was called, very likely took place without so much as a harsh word, let alone a heated argument. All the Virginians and South Carolinians would have had to do was to gather sufficient support within their own ranks to sustain a motion to *elect* a moderator rather than letting one man, Stearns, have the office by acclamation. Even if the motion was met with opposition, as it almost certainly was from at least the majority of North Carolinians as well as Dutton Lane's and William Murphy's southwest Virginians, the strength of its supporters could keep it on the floor indefinitely while effectively hindering all of the association's other business until it was voted on and decided. The Tidewater Virginians even appear to have been prepared to forego dealing with James Read's downfall for the sake of this move, perhaps now thinking, in Regular rather than Stearns's General-based Separate Baptist terms, that his censure or exclusion could and should be a matter for Grassy Creek Church itself to deal with, rather than the whole association. Even the Regulator troubles at Haw and Little Rivers, as well as other places, could not be brought up and discussed.

Shubal Stearns had lost enough face before the association in the previous year to haunt him for the rest of his life. His hope that he could once again return to the influence and power he had once enjoyed was that the association delegates should forget his failings of the year before, which of course were indeed understandable within the circumstances. But with James Read's heedless and hasty destruction of his political influence in the Virginia Tidewater crowning the already-extant dissatisfaction there, as well as in South Carolina, that wasn't going to happen. It was only human that Stearns should dread losing face with his beloved association for the second year in a row, and he knew if he allowed the motion to pass and a vote to occur there was a better-than-average chance he'd lose his position, perhaps to Samuel Harris, and even if he did manage to keep the moderator's chair by a small majority, the unanimity of the association was forever broken. In fact Harris would have no easier time living up to the image of the Goodly Fere than Stearns himself had, and there is no doubt that the younger man knew it. Hence Stearns held up the motion by calling for the praying and fasting, fasting and praying, over two long days. By three in the afternoon on the third day he must have realized that it was all over. If the association divided, Stearns may have thought he could perhaps at least keep his North Carolinians within the self-sufficient little New England-style community that seems to have been the limits of his vision, if only these Regulator troubles would just blow away and time could turn back a few years. It is tempting to speculate that he began to interpret his "revelation" of September 1769 thirteen months after the fact rather than with the immediacy that is indicated in Tidence Lane's and Elnathan Davis's accounts to Morgan Edwards. Of course this heartbreaking split must happen; that big cloud he'd seen after that terrible storm back September a year ago, dividing into three and separating, must have been God's way of telling him it was foreordained. When one's world crashes down, one attempts to make sense and perceive an order among the shattered pieces in the best way one can, and this could have been the aging, tired, and disappointed Goodly Fere's way. He may even have made the suggestion to divide the association along provincial lines himself, ironically, the very last of his "orders" that all of his beloved converts would have agreed to with a hollow echo of the unanimity they used to share with him.

At any rate, the Sandy Creek Association's 1771 session was then appointed to be held at Haw River. The proposed new Virginia group, which would be named the Rapidan Association after the Tidewater's Rapidan River but which would come down to us in the pages of Semple's history simply as the Virginia Association, was scheduled to hold its first session at Thompson's Meetinghouse in Louisa County, Virginia, the last weekend of September 1771. The new South Carolina association, with additional irony named Congaree after John Newton's home church, was appointed to meet at Saluda at about the same time. Shubal Stearns dismissed his flock without transacting any other business,[58] perhaps trusting in the brightness of the little center cloud in his 1769 revelation, which he thought represented North Carolina, for comfort and sustenance in dealing with the shock and hurt of his rejection in a world he could no longer comprehend.

But even this was to be denied him. As it turned out, Harris's Virginia delegates already had their agenda thought out, and six churches of their number actually staged a brief business meeting of their own right on Grassy Creek's grounds immediately after Stearns had dismissed Sandy Creek. Two of the participating delegations, Dutton Lane's from Dan River and William Murphy's from Blackwater, would have been pro-Stearns and mightily displeased about what had just happened, but the others agreed to stage another association meeting with all the Virginia Separate congregations at Elijah Craig's the following May for the purpose of organization. But at the same time a number of North Carolina delegates also seem to have asked Harris to go on a tour through their churches that fall, through the winter, and on into the spring to preach, baptize, ordain, and generally fulfill the functions for which they had been accustomed to depend on Stearns alone. It was as if now they wanted to acknowledge Harris as Stearns's successor to power and begin following him as the next Goodly Fere, and if Harris had really been power hungry, he could have exploited this situation to no end. To his credit he entertained no ambitions along this line, but still he must have known when people are accustomed to following a charismatic leader, they must be eased out of their mind-set gently and slowly. He agreed to make the tour, worked all that winter and spring at it, and even made a report of it to the new Rapidan Association when it convened at Elijah Craig's Blue Run Church in Virginia the following May.[59] Semple gives no details of this tour other than the fact that it was made, but Morgan Edwards does list a few ordinations Harris assisted in during its course as well as one very curious anecdote: at Haw River, "a rude fellow came up to Mr. Harris and knocked him down as he was preaching."[60] How this act of persecution could have occurred at a place where neither Shubal Stearns nor Elnathan Davis had ever faced any difficulties along that line, to say nothing of the church's outspoken stance on pacifism since the year before, is anybody's guess, but one wonders if the rude fellow was pro-Stearns rather than anti-Baptist. If this is so, it shows that the Goodly Fere still enjoyed affection and support for his position—and probably a lot of it at that—among the common people in the backcountry, but this is hardly the way the old preacher would have liked for it to be exhibited. The whole incident, added to the very fact of the Harris tour itself, was just one more humiliation in a life that now seemed to hold nothing but disappointments and humiliations for Shubal Stearns. As an afterthought, at least we know that this tour could not have been the occasion when Harris was clapped in the Hillsboro jail, as the Regulators were still in control of the town during this time, and law enforcement was virtually nonexistent unless they themselves saw fit to carry it out vigilante-style.

Despite the position the North Carolinians were trying to put him in, however, it is entirely probable that Harris visited Stearns several times during his fall and winter visit. One can fairly picture their forced, uneasy politeness to each other as they tried to salvage a remnant of their former rapport, the Goodly Fere still in his old mindset, Harris in a new one but sympathetic to the limitations of the older man's understanding of events and his poignant interpretation of his 1769 "vision," and both apprehensive in their own ways about what the future might hold. One wonders whether Stearns may have recalled similar forced conversations between himself and old Stephen Steel in Tolland in his own younger days as a New Light exhorter full of the rhetoric of George Whitefield. In addition, it is almost certain that Stearns and Harris got together over one unpleasant job, that of James Read's discipline at Grassy Creek. The association had never gotten to the point where it could deal with the matter in October, so Read applied directly to the church on November 21, very close to the time of Richard Henderson's barn burning nearby, with a confession of guilt and a profession of repentance. A majority of the church members themselves were willing to excuse him, but "doing everything by unanimity they called for helps." These helps, which certainly would have included Stearns and Harris both, advised the church simply to exclude him and take his ministerial credentials, and this is what the congregation did. Though they had liked Read personally, he had caused a great deal of shame to both Harris and Stearns from two different perspectives, and although Harris would come to trust Read again, there is no evidence that Stearns ever did. In July 1771, probably the one-year anniversary of the exposure of his sin, Read requested that Grassy Creek take up his case again for restoration to fellowship, but the members still refused, perhaps quoting Stearns in their reply that they did not think his repentance was "evangelical."[61] This repeated experience of being rejected by his Reverend Old Father must have been particularly crushing to Read, but then again, Stearns was only human—a difficult idea for the North Carolinians to be forced to comprehend now—and as prone to hard feelings as any of the rest of us. Moreover, if Read was hurt by this consequence of his actions, he got over it; Shubal Stearns never did reconcile himself with Read's folly, and perhaps not for lack of trying, either.

During the Harris tour and afterward the Regulator troubles just got worse, if that is conceivable. It will be remembered that Herman Husbands was still an assemblyman, in spite of the fact that he had taken such a prominent part in the September riot; but then again so was Edmund Fanning who, having recovered from his bumps and bruises at the hands of the Regulators, responded to the attack, and to Judge Henderson's barn-burning, by leading a party of his own followers at night guerilla-style to Husbands's own large farm on Sandy Creek and laying it waste.[62] Husbands fled to New Garden near the old Quaker settlement, evidently expecting protection from his pacifistic former brethren and crying foul over the fact that Fanning had turned the Regulators' tactics back on him. He was finally expelled from the assembly and jailed again, though, on December 20 for publishing a seditious letter in the *North Carolina Gazette* to Maurice Moore, which he claimed was a reply to a letter from Moore in which the Associate Justice had blamed all the Regulator troubles on Husbands and James Hunter. The existence of the letter from Moore was never proven, but the grand jury at New Bern nonetheless failed to indict him, probably out of fear of an upcountry reprisal, and he was released once again in February. As soon as Husbands had been jailed in New Bern violence flared again in the western counties,[63] and while the assembly was still in session, its members got word that the Regulators were gathering in force to march down the Neuse River to New Bern, release Husbands, and effectively start a provincial civil war. This was merely a rumor and perhaps instigated by Husbands's cronies themselves—it was just their style—but it did scare Governor Tryon and the upper and lower houses of the assembly sufficiently to make them put their noses to the grindstone and enact some good and beneficial pieces of legislation quickly. Among other things, they reformed the method by which sheriffs were appointed, passed new laws fixing attorney's fees, enacted a measure to provide for the more effective collection of small debts, and most importantly, reduced the power of the western county officeholders by reducing the size of the enormous backcountry counties themselves, carving out the new Wake, Guilford, Chatham, and Surry Counties all in the regions where the Regulators were most numerous. The Regulators themselves had asked for every one of these measures, and for the moment it appeared that they had won the day.[64] In the new arrangement, Sandy Creek, both church and community, and all the former Rowan/Orange border country wound up in the territory that would comprise Guilford County, and thus that name is given as the primary site of Shubal Stearns's labors by most historians even though it was formed so late in his ministry.

If the rumormongers had hoped to improve the situation by their wagging tongues, however, they soon learned better because they took their craft just a hairsbreadth too far. Just as the assembly was finishing the legislation that might have cooled the tempers of the participants on both sides of the controversy for good, word came again that the Regulators had already assembled in Cumberland County and were at that moment preparing to start their march on New Bern. Though the legislative reforms remained on the books, the royal governor and assemblymen panicked again, this time with fury rather than out-and-out fear. Later Continental congressman and United States senator Samuel Johnston introduced a drastic Riot Act to be in force for one year, giving Governor Tryon the right to put any county in the province under martial law as needed and the attorney general the power to prosecute charges of riot in any Superior Court. In the case of a riot, all who failed to answer a Superior Court summons within sixty days were to be declared outlaws by the old British definition, placing them literally outside the protection of the law and subject to be harmed or killed on sight by anyone with impunity. Armed with the Johnston Riot Act, William Tryon readied his lowland militia for whatever the Regulators might throw at them.

It was probably about this time that Herman Husbands finally realized he had overreached his hand, but still the Regulators acted defiantly. Still in the uplands and having never made ready for the Cumberland County march at all, they now sent messengers closer to the lowlands in Bute, Edgecombe, and Northampton Counties seeking recruits. At Salisbury in Rowan County, Benjamin Merrill's neighbors swore that they would neither pay their taxes nor allow any judge or Crown attorney to hold court there, retaliating to the Johnston Act by themselves declaring Edmund Fanning an outlaw whom any Regulator might kill on sight.[65] At Hillsboro, however, the Regulators professed willingness to allow their cases to be tried by Chief Justice Martin Howard, but invoked similar threats of assault or murder against both Maurice Moore and Richard Henderson as well as Fanning.[66] Likewise they sent word to Tryon again that if he brought a lowland militia into the backcountry, "every man would take his horse from his plow" and meet the force—that is, "unless he came to punish according to their deserts the original offenders in government," in which case they would join forces with him.[67]

Actually, if William Tryon had wanted to at this point, he could have washed his hands of the whole Regulator controversy and still come out looking as clean as a hound's tooth in the eyes of his superiors. At this very season he received word from London that he had been promoted to the royal governorship of New York to replace John Murray, Lord Dunmore, who himself was assuming the governorship of Virginia. Had he been so inclined, all he had to do was leave for New York and let his appointed successor in North Carolina, Josiah Martin, assume the reins and take over the situation as he thought best. But Tryon, whether to his credit or not, was made of sterner stuff, and he was determined to hold his position in North Carolina until the Regulator issue was resolved. As it turned out he didn't have long to wait. The ever-growing thunderhead finally broke loose in March, when Governor Tryon ordered that the regularly scheduled spring sessions of Superior Court be held at Hillsboro and Salisbury according to plan. The justices of course filed a formal protest with the Council for the sake of their own safety, and the Council responded likewise formally by advising Tryon to call out the militia and march on the backcountry to restore order. Tryon ordered General Hugh Waddell to take 284 men, including their officers, up the Cape Fear River to Salisbury to try to restore control there. He himself assembled a larger militia force in Johnston County, 1,068 strong and many bought with the forty-shilling bounty he offered, and after drill they finally broke camp on May 3 to march west to Hillsboro. They arrived there May 9 with no difficulty and Waddell, who was already in Salisbury, set out with his force to meet Tryon. But as soon as they crossed the Yadkin they met up with a large force of

Regulators under the command of Benjamin Merrill. The idea of firing on their own countrymen was more difficult for the militiamen than Waddell had ever expected, and though no casualties were recorded, Waddell's force was definitely put to the worse, especially since a few men in Merrill's force had intercepted a shipment of gunpowder on the way up from South Carolina for the troops' use. Rather than saving it for Merrill's men, however, the nine young Regulators who had beaten off the troop convoy and captured the shipment foolishly burned it.

Waddell called a hurried council of his officers and decided the best thing to do, at least until their men got their nerve up to fight fellow North Carolinans, was to fall back to Salisbury. This they began, but Tryon, who within two days had gotten word of Waddell's plight, set his force out immediately from Hillsboro to march west to Waddell's rescue, issuing strict orders to his soldiers against foraging along the way. They expected the march to take them right through the heart of Regulator country, but as they stopped to rest on the banks of Big Alamance Creek, a little less than twenty miles east of Sandy Creek, on May 15 or 16, they were met by a body of Regulators two thousand strong. The historians are a little vague on exactly when, where, and how this Regulator army was assembled to march and meet Tryon's militia. None was above the rank of captain and many had even come to the field unarmed, as if they were simply there to support their neighbors or perhaps, if Paschal was right in his narrowly legalistic interpretation of the Sandy Creek Association's initial 1769 directive regarding the taking up of arms against the Government, there were a lot of Separate Baptists present who were trying to help the Regulator cause and obey "the order of the association" at the same time. According to Powell, Herman Husbands, James Hunter, and the other leaders must have expected that the sheer size of their force would simply overawe and frighten the Governor into granting their demands, and Husbands undoubtedly envisioned himself again as the good cop who could effect the reform by playing Enlightened Soul while standing on the backs of his unruly followers.

But the situation had now spun completely out of Husbands's control. A few young hotheads went on the scout and captured two militia officers on a similar expedition, Colonel John Ashe and Captain John Walker, and handled them in classic Regulator fashion, nearly beating the hide off them with whips after taking them behind their lines as prisoners. The main body of the two thousand assembled Regulator soldiers raised a mighty howl at this, not against the militia or the captured officers, but in opposition to the men who had beaten the prisoners, and they threatened to give up the cause entirely if such acts were repeated.[68] This is one more slight, and admittedly tenuous, bit of evidence that there were many Separate Baptists in the field that day on the Regulators' side; one would like to think that the sight of the captives' flayed, bloody backs might have awakened in them a memory of what had almost befallen their Goodly Fere a year and a half earlier, and with it the spark of realization of the state to which they had let themselves descend since beginning to listen to Herman Husbands's agitation. And now, there across the field from them were the Governor and his militia, and there was no turning back.

Husbands himself now was in a decidedly intriguing situation. His words more than anyone else's had brought all these men to the banks of Big Alamance, and now his control over them, such as he had, was falling apart before his eyes. Those who hadn't been disaffected by the whipping of Walker and Ashe, especially the younger ones so easily influenced and already inured to Regulator violence as a matter of course, were now so careless that they were staging wrestling matches with one another, frolicking and capering on the creek bank as if this whole scenario were some monstrous rural county fair put on for no other purpose than their entertainment. The New Jerusalem of the backcountry seemed far off now, and when Tryon began to use the services of a parson, Rev. David Caldwell, to act as an intermediary to communicate with the Regulators and encourage their submission, Husbands seems to have suddenly remembered he'd been a Quaker and that Quakers were supposed to be pacifists. At any rate he evidently changed his stance quickly, and he frantically began to advocate peace and compromise along with Rev. Caldwell. Tryon's terms were inflexible, but not impossible to comply with: the Regulators would be required to submit to the government and disperse, and if they obeyed he would take no further punitive action. But now not even Husbands's new expressions of pacifism could alter the attitude he had built into the Regulators over the last three to five years, and most stood fast on the banks of Big Alamance in spite of both his and Caldwell's exhortations. Powell tells us that Husbands, then "realizing the hopelessness of the situation, mounted his horse and quietly rode away"[69]—from all appearances, still on the high moral ground of a Son of the Enlightenment, once again rising above the conflict by his superior force of reason. His departure from the battlefield marked the end of his involvement with the Regulators. Somehow, in western

North Carolina lore and historical tradition, this action has never been viewed in anything less than a positive light, and Husbands's reputation as a backwoods patriotic hero remains unsullied. But we shall hear more of him, even though North Carolina historians, as a rule, would prefer to have him left in that supposedly high moral stance he took on the banks of Big Alamance that fateful morning in May 1771.

Husbands was now gone, and Tryon sent one last message to the Regulators: return peacefully to their homes or be fired upon, with one hour's grace in which to decide their course of action. He put his troops into battle formation, and after the hour was up he sent an officer to bring back the Regulators' reply, which turned out to be typical rural bluster: "Fire and be damned." In Tryon's mind that settled it. He shouted the command to shoot, but found that his militia was as hesitant about firing on their own countrymen as General Waddell's had been. Whether he is to be praised or condemned for it, the man had courage: when he saw the irresolution of his troops he stood up on his stirrups in front of them and roared once more, "FIRE! FIRE ON THEM OR ON ME!"[70] The battle was joined.

The fight at Big Alamance lasted for two hours, and it was a fight to the finish. The Regulators were organized into companies, but, either from having imbibed too much social democratic theory from Herman Husbands or from the instinct of countless generations of wild Scottish, Irish, and Welsh warriors who had been similarly beaten by the armies of the English kings, each company of men operated independently of the others and there was no way they could offer any concerted resistance to the trained militia. The best showing was made by the tough mountain men who had come from the upper Yadkin; firing from behind rocks and trees Indian-style at the artillery gunners, they succeeded in driving them off and even advanced so far into Tryon's held position that they captured one of his cannon. But of course no one thought to reinforce them, and even as they made this small success, most of the once proud and defiant Regulators were running from the battlefield like so many scared rabbits. Tryon could have had his men pursue them and cut them to pieces had he wished, but as it turned out, they surrendered quickly enough and he could afford to be magnanimous, even if in the heavy-handed style of the British colonial officer. Tryon took fifteen prisoners and had one executed on the spot after a summary court-martial as a show of force, but it was an unnecessarily cruel act; the Regulators were beaten for good, and they knew it. The other prisoners were bound for trial at Superior Court in Hillsboro, and Tryon had his own surgeons tend the wounded Regulators left on the battlefield. Advancing the twenty miles to Sandy Creek the next day to meet Waddell's militia coming from the west and to place Benjamin Merrill, James Stewart, and some of the other Yadkin leaders under arrest, he proclaimed a general pardon for all who would submit to the government and take an oath of allegiance, with a few of the leaders excepted.[71]

The question of whether Tryon's mop-up operation in the backcountry after the Battle of Alamance proves that he was a bloody tyrant or simply a determined colonial officer with limited circumstances trying to restore order as best he could after two years of anarchy is too big for the scope of this book. When he arrived at Sandy Creek, he began to receive the loyalty oath from all comers, and he had his men destroy the farms of most of the Regulator leaders. He sent twelve captives to Hillsboro for trial, and when a death sentence was passed on them all, he pardoned six including the Separate minister James Stewart. Unfortunately, the mere layman Benjamin Merrill was hanged with five others at Hillsboro on May 30. Tryon's greatest failing may have been to let his toady Edmund Fanning, still a colonel in the militia and a participant at Alamance, act as if the victory had been an official endorsement of Fanning's conduct. Fanning took a company of troops through the upcountry that spring and relentlessly pursued those he perceived to be influential Regulator supporters, in essence forcing them into outlawry under the provisions of the Riot Act. One of his particular targets was the unfortunate Joseph Murphy, probably because he was the moderator or pastor of the intensely pro-Regulator Little River Church even though he himself had tried to discourage the members' Regulator activities. Morgan Edwards describes these events directly from Murphy's family's own recollections and even adds a bit of invective against Fanning on his own: "The vile Col. Fannin accused him of aiding and abetting the Regulation whereof he was as clear as any man whatsoever. Yet a party of horse was sent to seize him but could not find him . . . a detachment of dragoons entered his house, stole his papers, and a new pair of stockings, which were the most valuable things they saw in his little cot."[72] Though it is possible that Murphy fled to Blackwater in Virginia to stay with his brother William until the terms of the Riot Act expired, Paschal believed that he found refuge on the upper Yadkin not far from Shallow Fords or Timber Ridge Church, in a cave on the Boone family's property.[73] Murphy himself never told Edwards, and we will never know for sure.

One thing was certain, however: when Governor Tryon finally departed the backcountry for his new appointment in New York, taking with him Edmund Fanning as his personal secretary and leaving the province in the hands of his less rigid and more sympathetic successor, Josiah Martin, he did so having never gotten his hands on the one man whom he undoubtedly desired to punish the most. Even as the Battle of Big Alamance was raging, Herman Husbands had sped west in fear for his life, gathered his family, hurriedly packed together what belongings he could and fled to western Pennsylvania before either Tryon's or Waddell's troops could ever reach the Rowan/Orange border, using the droll alias of "Toscape Death." He was found guilty of treason in North Carolina *in absentia;* all his property was confiscated, and he was the only Regulator leader not finally pardoned by Governor Martin. But from the relative safety of western Pennsylvania that, like most of the colonies, had no extradition procedures, he had a chance to let his vitriol spew forth again in three pamphlets defending his actions during the Regulators' War, the last of which he entitled *A Fan For Fanning*. As has been noted, in some circles his reputation remains unblemished. To give the man credit where credit is due, some of the more moderate ideas he voiced during the Regulators' War were indeed quietly incorporated into North Carolina's first state constitution, but he never did realize how far events would outpace him and how much grief he himself had brought to the men and women who had taken his rhetoric too seriously. But lest the reader should think that this book has judged Herman Husbands too harshly or perhaps that the author is a Loyalist, an Anglophile, or just too much a disciple of Diogenes, the remainder of Husbands's life and activities will be examined briefly in the next chapter. The events in question will speak all too cogently for themselves.

For now, though, we must return to the life of Shubal Stearns, and sadly, there is not much more to tell. We left him hurt and dazed by the events at the 1769 and 1770 Sandy Creek Association meetings, his reputation in Virginia, South Carolina, perhaps the lowland Separate churches in eastern North Carolina, and even to a certain extent in the western uplands, slain by nothing more than his own humanity. The very fact that Morgan Edwards's contacts in the backcountry recounted the story of his claim to the vision he saw after the storm in September 1769 is indicative that the old man probably preached about it frequently, perhaps even continuously, in the last portion of his life, for more than anything else as a desperate attempt to convince his own spirit that the world around him still made sense and that his work had not been in vain. The aftermath of the Regulators' War had to have been a veritable nightmare for him, testing the faith he had in providence to the utmost. Tryon had his base camp on Herman Husbands's property, now held by the government under attainder, and Stearns must have had a firsthand view of the rough justice the royal governor was dispensing. Though Sterns would have been gladdened by the reprieve of the preacher James Stewart, the worst part of the nightmare had to have been Benjamin Merrill's hanging. According to Paschal, Merrill was originally sentenced to the old barbaric British punishment for treason, that is, drawing and quartering, but if it was so it is almost certain that the hanging was the only portion of the sentence carried out. Be that as it may, though, Merrill's wife and ten children were present at the execution, and whatever Jemima Merrill saw at the scaffold that day left her with mental problems the rest of her life. As has been noted before, Shubal Stearns's name appears on at least four petitions for clemency for condemned Regulators including Merrill; though Merrill had opposed him consistently since the 1769 association, there is no doubt he tried to help the Regulator captain as best he could, especially since he knew Merrill was taking the punishment Herman Husbands had led him to, and indeed was dying in Husbands's place. Since Joseph Murphy was in hiding from Edmund Fanning, Stearns may even have had to help with Merrill's burial obsequies himself.

And as a final grief, he saw that he had deceived himself totally; the one little joyful spark within his vision, the small, bright cloud that he perceived to represent his North Carolina churches, proved to be just as ephemeral as the others. For once the Regulators' War was over, the tired and disillusioned families of the North Carolina Piedmont, Regulator and non-Regulator alike, their prosperity and their lives violated by the good ol' boys, the Governor, and the Regulator leaders all, simply began packing up and leaving in droves. Morgan Edwards recounted that within one year of the Battle of Alamance and in spite of the new counties created in the uplands by the assembly, at least fifteen hundred Piedmont families had gone away like dust in the wind, and many more were simply waiting to dispose of their lands before joining them. According to the statistics Edwards provides, Little River Church, which had had a membership of five hundred communicants in five meetinghouses in its heyday, sank to a congregation of forty-eight, stretched between four meetinghouses, in no time flat. Joseph Murphy's new church up the Yadkin at Shallow Fords or Timber Ridge held its own, and so did Elnathan Davis's flock at Haw River, in Shallow Fords' case probably due to its distance from the seat of the Regulator troubles and at Haw River undoubtedly due to the strong consistency if not the deep thought of moderator Davis. The eastern churches were largely unaffected by the Regulators' War to the extent the western churches were, with the exception of the church at Great Cohara Swamp in present Sampson County that was reduced to a membership of eight souls,[74] but by and large they seem to have been so disillusioned with their shattered image of Stearns that every one of them joined the new Quehuky or Kehukee Regular Baptist Association within a few years. In fact, the church at Great Cohara seems to have been the first to do so. In the uplands, though, the pattern was almost uniform and in fact Stearns's own beloved Sandy Creek Church, mother of them all, was one of the very hardest hit. Boasting a membership of six hundred six at its prime and a consistently huge congregation over sixteen years, within the briefest of spaces it had shrunk to one less than it had had at its constitution: fifteen members including Tidence and Esther Lane, James Billingsley and Seamore York and their wives, James Younger's daughter and son-in-law James and Anna Evans, and Shubal and Sarah Stearns themselves, spread between the two meetinghouses at Sandy Creek and Abbott's Creek. Had Stearns been a younger and more adventuresome man, he might even have pulled up stakes and gone with his members; but he was sixty-five years old now, worn out and sick at heart if not in body, and he just watched helplessly as his children in the faith set their faces and departed, perhaps forlornly hoping for just a few to change their minds and stay by him, the desolation of the Piedmont community they left behind matching the desolation of his own soul.

The historians recount that these refugees from the Regulators' War settled in several locations. Some moved further into the western North Carolina mountains, up past the head of the Yadkin into the headwaters of the New and Watauga River valleys and into the foothills of the Smoky Mountains; others joined the growing settlements of the western South Carolina and northeastern Georgia hills. Still more pioneered the Clinch and Holston River valleys of the panhandle of extreme southwestern Virginia, and from all accounts, the greatest number moved as far away from the Piedmont as they safely could, into the wild lands of what would become eastern Tennessee. The east Tennessee refugees' 1784 secession from North Carolina to organize the state of Franklin and the resultant five-year civil war between the "Franklinites" and the North

PRINCIPAL MIGRATORY ROUTES OF NORTH CAROLINA UPLANDERS AFTER THE REGULATORS' WAR, 1771-1772

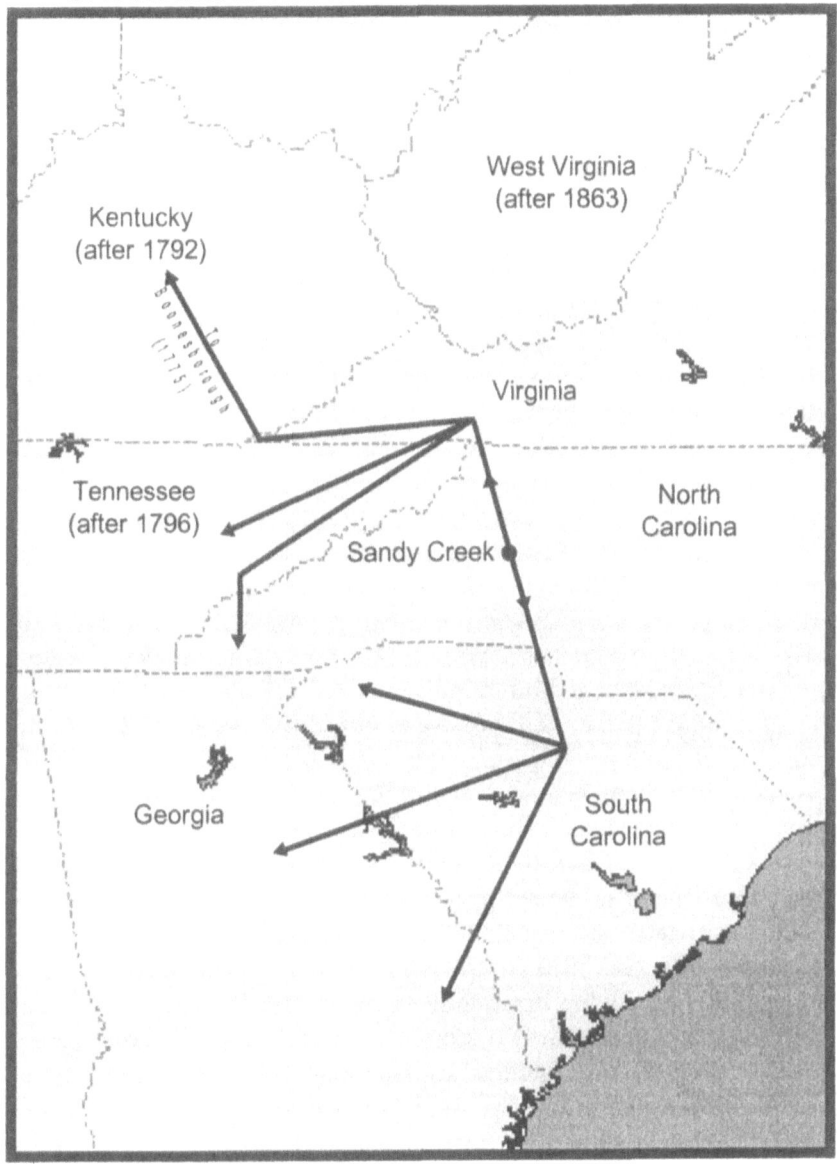

Carolinians aptly evidenced their still-smoldering dislike of the good ol' boys of the Tarheel State; most of their courthouse-ring and eastern lowland enemies had, in fact, found comfortable livings within the new North Carolina state government. And according to William Powell, some of the remainder of the ex-Regulators, perhaps those Edwards described in 1772 as waiting to dispose of their properties, either forgot or tried to forget that they had hated Judge Richard Henderson so intensely and they joined the Boone brothers in migrating to Kentucky in the spring of 1775 and building Henderson's new settlement for his proposed "Transylvania colony" at Boonesborough.[75] In short, the refugees of the Regulators' War formed a significant portion of the earliest settlers both in the Kentucky Bluegrass and in central Appalachia proper, and the accounts so common in high school history books and local-color love stories and novels of the intrepid pioneers of this region, moving in simply because they were of virile and independent stock and valuing the idealistic concept of the freedom of the frontier above all else, are in large part a pleasant and romantic deception. The Regulators' War refugees resettled because they felt they had been driven out of the North Carolina Piedmont by forces both without and within, and given the hard choice of attacks by the Cherokee and Shawnee versus their exploitation by the good ol' boys in their former home, they were willing to take their chances with the Indians.

But Shubal Stearns did not live to see his children in the faith tame the central portion of the mountain range in which he had spent his boyhood and young manhood, so long ago and so far away to the northeast. The last actions of church management that can be traced to him with any degree of probability are the rejection of James Read's appeal for reinstatement at Grassy Creek Church in July 1771, and his presence as moderator at the setting of the Sandy Creek Association at Haw River Church in October of that same year. Though Haw River was, at the time, undoubtedly the largest and strongest church in the association and could have provided a fair-sized congregation just of its own members, with all the outmigration that had occurred and was still continuing in the uplands and with Joseph Murphy still hiding as an outlaw under the terms of the Riot Act, the session must have been a sad, hollow exercise, a mere ghost of the happy times Stearns had known with his children in the faith only a few short years before. Less than three weeks after the 1771 session, Stearns wrote his will. Even though it was probably dictated to a backcountry justice of the peace who added the legalese at Stearns's bedside, rather than written directly by him, his words and his character come through nonetheless, and so perhaps we should let the document, given here in its entirety, speak for itself:

> In the name of God, Amen. This 24th day of October, 1771 I, Shubal Stearns of North Carolina and County of Guilford, being very sick and weak in body, but of perfect mind and memory, thanks be given unto God; therefore calling unto mind the mortality of my body, and knowing that it is appointed of all men once to die, I do make and ordain this my last will and testament; that is to say, principally and first of all I give and recommend my soul into the hands of Almighty God that gave it, and my body I recommend to the earth, to be buried in decent Christian burial, at the discretion of my Executors; nothing doubting but at the General Resurrection I shall receive the same again by the mighty Power of God. And as touching such worldly estate wherewith it has pleased God to bless me in this life with, I give, devise, and dispose of the same in the following manner and form.
> First I give and bequeath to Isaac Stearns, my Dearly beloved brother, all my wearing cloaths of all sorts both inside and outside cloaths of all sorts of every kind. Also, I give to my well and Dearly beloved wife, Sarah Stearns, all and singular my lands messages and tennements together with all my household goods together with all my estate to be for her use while she liveth, for her support, in this life, and after her death to be sold by my Executors, Semore York and Tidence Lane, whom I likewise constitute, make, and ordain my sole Executors of this my Last Will and Testament and all the money arising from such sale to be equally divided between my dearly beloved brethren and sisters as followeth (viz) Peter Starns [sic], Isaac Starns, and Ebenezer Starns, Rebacah Polk, Elizabeth Stimson and Martha Marshall and I do hereby utterly disallow, revoke and disannul all and every other former Testaments, wills, legacies, and bequests and Executors, by me in any ways before named, willed and bequeathed, ratifying and confirming this and no other, to be my Last Will and Testament. In witness whereof, I have here unto signed, sealed, published, pronounced and declared by the said Shubal Starns as his Last Will and Testament, in the presents of:

Thomas Swift
Shubal Stearns
Jermiah York, Jurat
Sarah Starns (her mark)
Sarah Cunerad (her mark)[76]

Stearns lingered twenty-seven days after making his will and died on November 20, 1771, two days short of the sixteenth anniversary of the constitution of Sandy Creek Church. He was buried not far from the meetinghouse where his melodious preaching cant had resounded so often, his burial services probably conducted by Tidence Lane and undoubtedly attended by the few souls left there at the time. The church, in more than one faction, and the community are in the territory now comprising the northeastern corner of Randolph County, and his grave there may be visited to this day. Whatever disease had made him weak and sick in body, as he described in his will, there can be no doubt that he simply worried himself to death over the state of the Sandy Creek Association, the hanging of Benjamin Merrill, and the exodus of his children in the faith, and he perished finally with, if not of, a broken heart.

Though in 1772, Morgan Edwards noted the expressed intention of Tidence Lane and the other remaining Sandy Creek members to erect an appropriate monument over their fallen leader's grave, they all seem to have neglected it in their eagerness to dispose of their lands and get out of North Carolina. Until the early part of the twentieth century, the grave of Shubal Stearns, the Goodly Fere, the Man who Baptised the South, was marked only by a simple field sandstone with the stark inscription crudely carved theron:

S.S.
1771

7
REQUIEM
1772–1801

Perhaps in this neglected spot is laid/Some heart once pregnant with celestial fire;/Hands, that the rod of empire might have swayed,/Or waked to ecstasy the living lyre.
—Thomas Gray,
"Elegy Written in a Country Churchyard"

History often seems to exhibit the keenest sense of irony to be found anywhere.

As any serious student of the American Revolution knows, that great conflict was no more a common man's crusade than any other war has been. The high ideals of life, liberty, and the pursuit of happiness expressed so eloquently in the Declaration of Independence became the holy creed of America only when enough influential planters, merchants, and businessmen in the colonies found the Declaratory Act bad for their finances and were persuaded that they could do better economically by rebelling and establishing home rule. Their positions allowed them to take the high moral stance on liberty, however, as did that of the ministers and churches they patronized, which were mainly Congregational or Presbyterian and often with a New Light background. And in addition to their own rhetoric, they gleefully used the pro-Revolutionary preaching their tithes and subscriptions paid for to make patriots out of the common herd, those who could tar and feather the remaining Loyalists for them and drive them out of the country while they remained on their high moral ground, and who would serve as foot soldiers in the Continental Army that they trusted to protect their interests. Neither did America win the war easily; it would have been virtually impossible without the support of the French, in whose interests it was to throw a stumbling block in Great Britain's way whenever and wherever they could, and even then there is no way that the war would have ended after the battles of Yorktown, which we won, and Blue Licks, which we lost, if the

British had found it fiscally and politically advisable to continue its prosecution. In essence, we simply wore them down, the same way the Irish did under Michael Collins and Eamon DeValera, and Ho Chi Minh and his followers did, first to the French and later to us, in Viet Nam.

There was no way, though, that the great mass of American citizens could have realized this at the time of the Peace of Paris in 1783. To them, the merchant-backed Congregational and Presbyterian preachers' pro-Revolutionary sermons simply meant that God was on their side and their cause must be just, and the end of the war meant that God had declared His judgement in the matter. Herman Husbands, exiled from North Carolina, still with a price on his head and living in Bedford County, Pennsylvania, throughout the Revolutionary years, was no exception. Given his millennial loose screw, the war was bread and butter to him. In September 1776 the Pennsylvania State Convention, recognizing his abilities, appointed him to the Bedford County Board of Commissioners and Assessors, and in the two years afterward he represented Bedford County in the state legislature. Besides publishing a paper money scheme and urging his former religious brethren, the Quakers, to support the new state constitution, he again brought out his skills at mining and metallurgy and successfully prospected lead deposits for ammunition for the Continental Army. Though he was too old to volunteer for the army himself now, a fact that must have been extremely convenient for him, the Revolution thus gave his sorry showing in North Carolina a few years before a veneer of respectability.

During all this, he never quite lost sight of his backwoods New Jerusalem as God's plan to provide small farmers and artisans with land and political democracy, and he now believed it would be founded across the Alleghenies. Beginning in 1779 until his death, he actually drew maps of the Holy City based on texts from the Book of Ezekiel and data he gathered on trips through the mountains, and he frequently wrote of the coming millennium both in his own pamphlets and under the pen name of "Allegheny Philosopher" for Andrew Ellicott's *Maryland and Virginia Almanack* between 1781 and 1792.[1] However, in the meantime, fate or the devil had thrown another stumbling block in the pathway of his vision with the creation and ratification of the United States Constitution that he believed was nowhere nearly democratic enough, even with its Bill of Rights attached, for Christians in the millennium. Accordingly he looked to the French Revolution as the true herald of the New Jerusalem rather than the now-disappointing American one. To be charitable, he may never have heard of all the atrocities of the Reign of Terror. Or then again, he might have; the actions of the Regulators in the last two years of their existence under his leadership certainly leaves the question of his limits open.

As such, it was predictable that Husbands should have gotten himself involved in another rebellion sooner or later, and when the new federal government levied an excise tax on the whiskey his western Pennsylvania neighbors distilled and marketed as a primary source of their income, he got his chance. Though he had now reached his threescore and ten, Husbands's behavior during the Whiskey Rebellion of 1793–1794 was hauntingly, ominously similar to that of the Regulator leader he had been a quarter century before. In his writings he declared himself a moderate, eschewing violence and advocating a petition campaign to President Washington and Treasury secretary Hamilton for repeal of the excise law and further supposedly democratizing amendments to the Constitution, but in his speeches to the Whiskey Rebels, his millenarian, antigovernment rhetoric was so vitriolic that Congressman Albert Gallatin, who was part of a government delegation that tried to negotiate a settlement with the rebels in September 1794 and who heard him speak, dubbed him "The Pennsylvania Madman."[2] It was the North Carolina upcountry all over again: Husbands talking out of both sides of his mouth, spewing an ostensibly moderate course of action to protect himself while his listeners beat up federal tax collectors and shot up and smashed the stills of those farmers trying to comply with the excise law and pay their taxes.

The Whiskey Rebellion ended virtually the same way as did the Regulators' War, with the appearance of a governmental army, this time led by no William Tryon, Hugh Waddell, or Edmund Fanning, but by General Henry Lee (father of Robert E. Lee, incidentally), Treasury secretary Hamilton, and President Washington himself—with the exception of James Madison's frantic actions when the British were burning the capital during the War of 1812, the only incidence in American history in which a sitting President has directly taken the field of battle as commander in chief of his own troops. For Husbands, though, events took an additional, and appropriate, downturn this time. As Benjamin Merrill and the other North Carolina Regulator leaders had watched him do in 1771, now Husbands saw the most violent of the Whiskey Rebel chieftains, David Bradford, escape down the Ohio River to French territory on the Mississippi to evade capture, and Husbands himself was among the first arrests made in Bedford County in October 1794. He was taken to Philadelphia, tried in U.S. Circuit Court, found guilty of treason, and sentenced to hang.[3] However, the senators from the state where he was still regarded by many as a hero, Alexander Martin and Timothy Bloodworth of North Carolina, as well as Drs. Benjamin Rush and David Caldwell of Philadelphia, interceded for him with President Washington and he escaped the noose. But perhaps in and of itself Washington's clemency was not for any virtue of Husbands's; to Alexander Hamilton's dismay, the President pardoned all the Whiskey Rebels eventually anyway. As it was, Husbands spent his last several months in jail, died in total ignominy at a tavern on his way home to Bedford County about the middle of the year 1795, and was buried in an unmarked grave. He was survived by his third wife, Amy, and eight children.

Had Shubal Stearns still been alive to hear of Husbands's fate, he might have responded with a wry Scripture quotation: "Whatsoever a man soweth, that shall he also reap." But though the circumstances of Husbands's final downfall and death are ironic enough within themselves, the greatest irony lies in the fact that the very government that sentenced Husbands to death for treason, which itself had been founded upon the principle that the long-cherished British belief in the Divine Rights of the Crown was so much hogwash, came to sustain and encourage a part of Husbands's creed as a matter of its own policy—not the idea that God was miraculously going to create a New Jerusalem of democracy across the Appalachians but that the government itself, acting as the special agent of God, had *already* created the New Jerusalem and it was there for the taking as the divinely given inheritance of the United States. It has been noted earlier that perhaps a third of the American population held patriotic sentiments during the course of the war, with another third Loyalist and the remainder neutral. After the struggle was over, however, all were virtually unanimously patriotic, egged on by the pro-Revolutionary preaching paid for by the merchants, businessmen, and planters who had underwritten the War, and now imbued with the notion of a God-ordained manifest destiny to claim all the land as their own and the assurance that the Creator of Heaven and Earth had already stamped His blessing upon any means that would accomplish that end.

The attitude was only reinforced as time went along, and it goes a long way in explaining why so many young American men, especially Kentuckians, would march lemming-like behind their leaders to be butchered in a fruitless, idiotic attempt to conquer southern Canada in the War of 1812, the nation afterward hysterically and pathetically clinging to the idea that America had again been victorious; it provides a patent justification for the atrocities inflicted upon Native Americans who, though they themselves were guilty of their own savageries, were only trying to fight for their native land against hostile invaders and treaty-breakers, a concept the white settlers did not recognize except within their own terms; and it was even the foundation for both Union and Confederate beliefs and attitudes before and during the Civil War, in the Southerners' case with all the attendant indignities and cruelties inflicted upon those whom God's Own White Men had enslaved. The doctrine of divine recognition of American superiority went international when the United States finally succeeded in seizing Florida from the Spanish and Texas from the Mexicans, perhaps in the eyes of some erasing the blot on the nation's escutcheon made with the botched attempt on Canada in 1812–1814, and later at the time of the Spanish-American War with the acquisition of Guam and Puerto Rico. It was questioned at first only by the Lost Generation and its related writers and thinkers after World War I, and until Viet Nam blew a bit of the arrogance out of us, very few Americans seriously doubted it. It was even resurrected for the benefit of Ronald Reagan in the 1980s, with appropriate hymns of praise by Lee Greenwood and Charlie Daniels to boot. The great theologian Karl Barth was never so wise as when he penned the simple statement that men are not good, they have never been good, and they will never be good, and there is no doubt that Shubal Stearns would have agreed with him entirely. But was Reagan also correct, at least perhaps in part, in stating that the Nicaraguan contras of the late 1970s and early 1980s were the moral equivalent of our founding fathers? Though the question will never be taken up at a national DAR meeting, when considering Herman Husbands and the mind-set his beliefs exemplified and helped to initiate, one wonders, and we must only hope and pray that Timothy McVeigh will not be considered by some war-torn future generation as a true American patriot, and Christian Identity as the One Holy Apostolic Church.

But enough. The author fears that he has rivaled Herman Melville for digressions from his point already, but the fact is, the rose-coloring that authors have given American history in general have also supplied the written, as well as oral, histories of the Baptists in this country with their own stained-glass windows. For this reason the life and the work of

Shubal Stearns, when they have been remembered at all, have often been grossly misinterpreted. Had he lived until the Revolution broke out, would he have been a patriot, or—shudder—like his close friend Seamore York or his first biographer and chronicler Morgan Edwards, a Loyalist? The question is not even relevant. After he had made Sandy Creek his home in late 1755, he adopted the backcountry settlers of the upland North Carolina Piedmont as a family of little brothers and sisters in Christ. Whatever might or might not have happened they and their welfare would always have been the true object of his loyalty, let time and chance happen as it would and kings and kingdoms rise and fall as they may. Governmental loyalty would have been only a secondary concern to him in any case. Like any big brother, he sometimes ordered his spiritual siblings about in ways that were subjective, shortsighted, and on occasion downright bad for them, but there can be no doubt that he did it all with a genuine love and affection that for many years were heartily reciprocated by his multitude of converts to the Baptist faith. Only when events too big for him to control tore his community apart did he lose this reciprocation, and the loss killed him. But the Baptists, Regular and Separate both, were quite as pro-Revolutionary at least by the end of the war as were the more respectable Congregational and Presbyterian ministers who agitated Republican principles for the benefit of their financiers, even if Baptist preachers were seldom, or in the case of the rural Separates never, compensated with handsome salaries. In fact, the idea that the new government would allow for freedom of worship and their own long-held principle of separation of church and state made them feel as if they were, in a sense, America's own special faith.

While there can be no doubt that, had it not been for Shubal Stearns and his work, the enormous southern branch of the denomination would never have established itself and prospered as it did, when early-nineteenth-century American historians such as Robert Semple and David Benedict came to read Morgan Edwards's pre-Revolutionary accounts of Stearns's running his association with a strict central control in the manner of the old British and New England General Baptists, his disapproval of the actions of the Regulators in North Carolina, and especially his 1769 order forbidding the taking up of arms against the standing government, they simply couldn't find a way to put the information in the post-Revolutionary context then expected, equating Christianity and patriotism, and make either Stearns or the supposedly patriotic Regulators look good. Thus they hedged, left out some details, modified others, modified others, and left much data they collected on historical relationships maddeningly vague in an apparent effort to keep their readers from the temptation of correlating it, in essence keeping what they considered politically correct and casting the bad away. For years, Stearns was portrayed only as a rustic cousin to the mainline Regular Baptists who absorbed his followers. In the 1930s George W. Paschal cast him and his career in a better light and has since been echoed by other Baptist historians, but this polemical redemption has produced its own side effects: at least one modern "scholarly" paper, whose title and author are not listed here for charity's sake, now claims that Stearns was the pioneer exemplar of modern streamlined Southern Baptist revival techniques.

To be honest, though, many former Sandy Creek Association churches made it easier for the historians to want to fudge simply by their own actions. This was the case with the Congaree Association in South Carolina. Daniel Marshall, though still a tireless evangelist in spite of his advancing years, never developed the leadership and organizational capabilities of his wife's oldest brother. For all we know, when Marshall pastored churches, and he did serve in that office in several instances, he may have depended on his redoubtable Martha not only for testifying, exhorting, singing, and leading in prayer, but for private counsel as well. Thus it devolved to the charismatic but unstable Philip Mulkey to assume the mantle of association leadership in the province, and though originally the South Carolina Separates stood for a legitimate gripe in the matter of John Newton's mistreatment by Shubal Stearns and Sandy Creek, under Mulkey's erratic hand the group kept the quarrel of the prerogatives of the association versus the rights of the church alive throughout its short existence. Daniel Marshall distanced himself from the center of the controversy early by moving to Kiokee Creek in northern Georgia in 1771, where he organized a few churches in spite of Virginia-style ecclesiastical laws and won the admiration of Baptist critics and supporters alike by staying in north Georgia and giving hope to his neighbors in the darkest days of the southern campaigns of the Revolution. John Newton joined him here, in spite of their differences of opinion, and resumed the ministry Shubal Stearns had tried to take from him. Old Joseph Breed reached his threescore and ten and passed away in the year 1778.[4] But the Congaree Association, beset as it was by infighting over the power of the association and its moderator versus the local churches; the shift of the Revolution's principal theater of operations southward to King's Mountain, Cowpens, and the Ninety-Six in the early 1780s; and the public scandal of Philip Mulkey's exposure for vice and hypocrisy; simply tore its own organization apart, and it ceased to exist about the time the Revolution ended. The Congaree churches Daniel Marshall had gathered in Georgia organized the Georgia Association not long before Marshall's death on November 2, 1784, with both John Newton and Daniel's and Martha's oldest son Abraham as two of its principal ministers, and the Separate remnants in South Carolina founded Bethel Association about five years later.[5] Neither of the new organizations retained the name of Separate Baptist, and both united in fellowship with the Charleston Association on modified evangelical Calvinistic terms—possibly because Charleston was using its own confession of faith by then, independent of the Philadelphia document to which the Goodly Fere had shown such a strong aversion.

Northward in Virginia, the changeover was a bit more stable but somewhat more complex. It was noted in the previous chapter that the older Separate churches in southwestern Virginia supported Stearns much more outspokenly than did their young Tidewater brethren, and in fact neither Dutton Lane, William Murphy, nor any representatives from Dan River or Blackwater churches even bothered to attend the Rapidan Association's organizational meeting at Elijah Craig's in May 1771, causing their fiery young colleagues to accuse them of being "in distress."[6] Nonetheless they did finally get their ruffled feathers smoothed and entered the provincial organization probably that fall, and the next year the Rapidan Association even picked up James Read's church at Grassy Creek in North Carolina as well. Undoubtedly with help from Samuel Harris, a full two years after Read's exclusion he finally got his church membership and preaching credentials back. Read never did try bigtime evangelism again, needless to say, but he did serve as a reputable pastor at Grassy Creek as well as several other newer backcountry Virginia and North Carolina congregations as they were gathered, and he stuck close to his old partner Samuel Harris until his death in 1798.[7]

The new Kehukee Regular Baptist Association in North Carolina attempted to form a union with the Separate Baptists as early as 1772, not with the Regulation-decimated Sandy Creek group, some of whose churches were already coming into it, but rather with the younger and bolder group of Tidewater Virginians. The overture was rejected, however, mainly because of Kehukee's heritage with Paul Palmer; at this time many of the old members baptized by the overzealous, ultra-Arminian Palmer before they had been converted were still alive, and the Rapidan Association insisted on the principle of immersion only as a testimony post-conversion. Many of the Kehukee churches were not willing to put these old members through the shame of a re-baptism, preferring to wait and let the problem settle itself with time, while others, which must have included some of the Separate congregations taken in by Kehukee, were inclined to agree with Rapidan. In 1775 the body split into two. One side gathered the mixed Separate and reformed Regular congregations and organized in 1777 under a newly coined name, United Baptist, and gained a relationship with the large Virginia Rapidan Association. The other group, which retained the name of Regular Baptist, kept to its relationship with the Charleston Association and stood aloof from the Virginians for some time.

In the meantime, though, the Rapidan Association was going through considerable infighting on its own. The group tried an experiment in ordaining "Apostles"—Samuel Harris, John Waller, and Elijah Craig— that fell flat after about a year; immediately after that they got into a major dispute over Calvinism versus Arminianism, with Harris, Waller, and Jeremiah Walker leading the general-atonement party and Elijah and Lewis Craig, William Murphy, and John Williams as spokesmen for limited atonement. In 1776 Waller evidently got sort of caught up in the spirit of the times, causing several of the Arminian-inclined churches in Rapidan to pull away on their own as the so-called Independent Baptists. The division was healed in a year or two, however, and Waller and his churches were welcomed back into the Rapidan fold even though the issue that had created the breach had never quite been solved to everyone's satisfaction.

Eventually, although there did remain some Arminian as well as Calvinistic extremists in the body, most were content to settle down on the formula of John Leland, himself a New England Separate Baptist who had settled in Virginia and in the Rapidan Association around the time of the Revolution and who probably, whether he knew it or not, very nearly echoed Shubal Stearns's own sentiments. As he described it, the most successful, spiritual preaching that could be done was "the Sovereign Grace of God, mixed with a little of what is called Arminianism."[8] The difference now was that the years of the Revolution and its victorious conclusion had brought a similar settling effect to the Tidewater Separates' worship traditions. No longer needed as a class protest statement, the preaching cadence the eastern Virginians had picked up from Samuel Harris, James Read, Dutton Lane, and William Murphy and thus indirectly from Shubal Stearns, faded quickly into the background in many areas. The "warm and pathetic address, marked by strong gestures and a singular tone of voice" described by Semple in his discussion of the New England Holy Tone was now thought of as "odd tones, disgusting whoops and awkward gestures" smacking of "enthusiasm" rather than rational piety,[9] perhaps good for humorous memories but not for an acceptable pulpit address in a newly Republican Virginia with the old caste system supposedly gone forever. This is not to say that the New England Holy Tone, or for that matter the foot washing rite or shouting during worship, disappeared from the Tidewater altogether, at least for a few years yet. But by the time the Separates in that region formed a General Committee with smaller district associations in 1783, as a whole they were calling the Philadelphia Confession the best composition of the kind then extant, and their practical differences with the Ketocton Association and the Regular Baptists had become so blurred as to be almost invisible—even to their similar use of the old Puritan divine John Cotton's catechism *Milk for Babes* as the forerunner of Sunday school for their young. Elijah Craig's and James Ireland's defections to the Ketocton Association have already been noted, and in the growing Bluegrass settlements in the Kentucky territory, a multitude of transplanted eastern Virginians who had been Calvinistic Separates united with the few Regular Baptists there to adopt the Philadelphia Confession to form the Elkhorn and Salem Regular Baptist Associations in 1785.[10]

Thus in 1787, when the Separates' General Committee finally established formal relations with the Ketocton Association and both sides dropped their respective titles and became United Baptists, it was merely a formalization of events that had been evolving ever since the Virginia Separates had broken away from the Sandy Creek Association and struck out on their own, as well as a reflection of national support for a federal union at the time. The General Committee, now united with the Ketocton Association, was in fact put together almost like the new federal government: the organization was composed of delegates from the individual district associations, and it provided checks and balances to insure stable interactions between the district bodies while keeping them united as a whole, much as the Constitution did for the individual states. As such the Separates' creation was more the ancestor of the modern Southern, and other Baptist, state conventions and associations than anything that the Regular Baptists themselves had devised before it, and its similarities to the new government of the United States in a sense hallowed the

Virginia—as well as all other American—Baptists' perceptions of themselves as America's Denomination. That in turn, of course, gave rise to many later apocryphal stories such as the one in which Thomas Jefferson got his ideas for a republican form of government by watching Elder Andrew Tribble transact business at a small Baptist church near Monticello (would that the claim could be proven by DNA testing!) and that John Gano, as an Army chaplain, had baptized George Washington.

Given the warp and woof of history, one wonders what, if anything, would have happened differently if Samuel Harris had tried to step in Shubal Stearns's shoes as Goodly Fere of the Separate Baptists. We will never know, but the fact is that Harris neither desired nor sought the adulation Stearns had received prior to 1769, even though a large number of Separate Baptists in North and South Carolina and even Georgia and Virginia were at first willing to give it to him. His election to the ill-fated office of "Apostle" proves the nearly unanimous confidence shown in him. As it happened, though, the southwestern Virginia Separates including Dutton Lane, William Murphy, and their churches organized the Strawberry Association in 1776 simply for the sake of their convenience and in recognition of the spread of their work. Although Harris remained very much the grand old man of Virginia Baptists up until his death in 1799, he kept his church membership at Fall Creek, and when Strawberry was formed he bowed out quietly and gracefully from the leadership of the larger Rapidan body to assume the smaller association's moderatorship. Even then, however, a large number of western North Carolina Separate churches—in fact all but one of the congregations west of Rowan County—left the now-decimated Sandy Creek Association to join Harris's and Lane's new organization, almost as if they all were still trying to lay Stearns's mantle of leadership on Harris's shoulders. (The small congregation that remained a member of Sandy Creek was the one on Deep Creek in Surry County that had been gathered and was pastored by Joseph Murphy.) Harris still refused even this honor, assisting Strawberry's western Carolina churches in organizing a conference of their own rather than trying to assume any direct Stearns-style leadership over them. When the Rapidan Separates organized the General Conference in 1783, Strawberry participated only as a member district association and not as a leader. The union between Separate and Regular Baptists and the name United Baptist was adopted by Strawberry and its Yadkin conference at the same time in 1787. After Harris went into the organization of the association in which he spent the last portion of his life, Roanoke, in 1788, the Yadkin Baptists seem to have given up on making him another Goodly Fere and formed their own association, Yadkin, in 1790. At about the same time the factions of the Kehukee Association, along with the former Separate churches they had picked up, reunited, the Virginia churches in the body then forming the Portsmouth Association.

In the meantime, in the territory that would become eastern Tennessee, the former Regulator refugees who had settled there had organized churches of their own. Part of their first ministerial aid seems to have come from that branch of Dan River Church on the extreme upper New River at the Virginia/North Carolina border in the person of Robert Elkin, who began preaching at age twenty-six in 1771 and who was probably the son of Richard Elkin, a longtime member and an exhorter himself at Dan River.[11] The first two congregations said to have been gathered there, one on Clinch River and the other on the Holston, are reputed to have been scattered by a war with the Indians occurring about 1774. Elkin persevered in the work, though, and appears even to have gone up into Tidewater Virginia in 1779 to help one Captain William Bush bring a new group of settlers to a Holston valley location called Wolf Hills, later known as Abingdon, Virginia, the following year. He organized a church among the Bush settlers in 1781 at Wolf Hills with the help of Lewis Craig, who at that time was leading his famous "Traveling Church" from Spotsylvania County through Cumberland Gap and northward to the Kentucky Bluegrass. Within another year Elkin and his Wolf Hills Church followed them and established their own meetinghouse on Howard's Creek not far from Boonesborough.[12]

Though Elkin had left the Tennessee/Virginia border country behind, his shoes were filled by a number of capable, and older, ministers who were moving in. These included Tidence Lane, who had finally pulled up stakes from Sandy Creek about 1779, possibly after the death of Sarah Stearns, and William Murphy, who along with several of his members had left Blackwater Church and the headwaters of the Roanoke to start anew in the east Tennessee country. Others such as Virginian James Keel and South Carolinans Jonathan Mulkey and his brother Philip followed, and the churches that they gathered and pastored sought to keep their connection with the old Sandy Creek Association even though most of the Baptists across the mountains in western North Carolina had abandoned it to affiliate with Strawberry Association in Virginia.

For a while the churches on the Tennessee frontier united in a small conference auxiliary to Sandy Creek, much like the Yadkin conference of Strawberry Association, but in 1786 Lane and Murphy took the lead in "arming off" Holston Association from Sandy Creek. As successor to Shubal Stearns as pastor at Sandy Creek Church, Lane was elected the new group's first moderator and Murphy was chosen as its first clerk. However, in spite of Sandy Creek's and their old mentor's opposition to the Philadelphia Confession, the new group adopted it. Perhaps one reason was that they felt they needed to distinguish themselves from the Methodists who themselves had established a conference on the Holston as early as 1783, a year before the group formally broke with the Church of England—now known in America as the Protestant Episcopal Church—and organized themselves as a denomination in the United States. Another reason may have been that the formerly Separate-majority Elkhorn and Salem Associations in the Kentucky territory had already adopted the Confession a year before Holston was formed, and the Holston Separates thereby felt safe in following suit.

Regardless of the causes, Tidence Lane remained "not so hard in doctrine as some of his brethren, his doctrinal belief being a modified Calvanism [sic]." When asked about the circumstances of Holston's organization a few years later, William Murphy categorically declared that Holston had endorsed the Confession only as "a general statement of principles" and that no one in the association had ever been bound to a strict observance of the precepts of the document.[13] In fact, some old Separates in Holston may never have accepted any portion of the Confession, and it is certain that Robert Elkin never did. Although he had an opportunity to bring his Howard's Creek Church into Elkhorn Association just like Lewis Craig did with his "Traveling Church," now settled on Gilbert's Creek in the Bluegrass, he and a number of other churches and ministers living south of the Kentucky River including the Virginians Andrew Tribble, James Quesenberry, Thomas Ammen, and Joseph Bledsoe, as well as North Carolina's Squire Boone and many others, abstained from the union and organized their own South Kentucky Association of Separate Baptists in 1787. South Kentucky rejected the Philadelphia Confession, like their old Goodly Fere claiming that their creed was "the Bible and it alone," and held to a belief in the "general provision" of the atonement,[14] yet Confession-owning Holston Association maintained a warm fellowship with the body in the first few years of their mutual existence, with many Holston members and ministers such as James Keel and the Mulkey brothers migrating northward to join it as well.[15] Although South Kentucky lost a few members and churches to a breakaway body, Tate's Creek Association, which endorsed a partial acceptance of the Philadelphia Confession on the order of the Virginia Baptists' 1787 union, it gained other members with more Tennessee, North Carolina, and Virginia Baptists moving northward who organized another association on Green River about 1799 or 1800. The Regular-Separate union that had taken place in Virginia in 1787 was not duplicated in Kentucky until 1801 in the wake of the so-called Great Revival (already mentioned as the phenomenon that also gave the Cumberland Presbyterians and Barton Stone's Christian Church their start) and even then not by the use of the Philadelphia Confession but rather with a homemade document called "The Terms of General Union" that guaranteed that "the preaching Christ tasted death for every man shall be no bar to communion."[16]

With the formation of the Kentucky General Union of Baptists in 1801, the South Kentucky Association divided itself into North and South District Associations to join other Kentucky United Baptist associations in correspondence and fellowship, and with this division the final remnant of Shubal Stearns's New Light Separate Baptists was assimilated into the greater Baptist "family"—or so the historians would have us believe. It has been demonstrated that, although at least in Kentucky that final remnant held onto the old Separate Baptist positions for what seems like an extraordinary number of years in this national atmosphere of Baptist union, most of the former Separates went into the fold without a whimper, much less a forceful statement of their own principles as opposed to those of the Regular Baptists. Sandy Creek, Strawberry, the component groups of old Rapidan, Yadkin, Holston, the Bethel and Georgia survivors of the Congaree group, Elkhorn, and Salem—all these associations, and their oldest members who could recall what had brought them into existence, were so diffident about their real background that they seem simply to have cast their collective memories away and moved on. In fact all those organizations named above are presently affiliated with the Southern Baptist Convention, which holds with its historians that the entire Separate movement was some sort of aberration; perhaps benign, perhaps malignant, but one that good orthodox mainline American Baptists were able, thank God, to control and to rectify. This tendency of Southern Baptists to disdain Baptist groups that have broken ranks with them or perhaps never joined their organization in the first place for whatever reason, as somehow similarly aberrant, is by no means uniform but it is not uncommon either.

But this also does not quite fit the historical picture. In the brief and rather slanted account of the Cumberland Presbyterian Church given in his *History of Kentucky Baptists,* J.H. Spencer, himself an implicit believer in the ideals and the organization of the Southern Baptist monolith, postulated in 1885 that the Cumberland Presbyterians were and are a Presbyterian-Methodist hybrid and that the group could not possibly survive much longer simply because of the "tendency of the universal law of hybrids, *to return to the original stock* [Spencer's emphasis]."[17] Strange as it may sound, his explanation was actually halfway accurate. The denomination did indeed split in 1906, with about half its churches returning to the mainline Presbyterian fold and the other half surviving to maintain the Cumberland subsect, which still exists. But here is another keen irony. Had Spencer only been able, or willing, to admit that his own denomination was itself the hybrid that objective historical research has proven it to be, rather than the one unerring true faith through history that perhaps both mainline Southern Baptists and Old Landmarkers would like for it to be, then he could have found a far better example of his odd "stock" hypothesis among the Baptists of central and southern Appalachia and the region's "daughter" associations of those named above. For here in this original Regulator refuge, a large group of Baptist churches and associations still exist that descended directly from the work of Shubal Stearns, which the mainline denomination conveniently classifies as aberrant offshoots; and here, among them as well as newer subsects and faiths sprung from them, the beliefs, practices, and modes of worship Stearns brought to the first settlers in upland North Carolina still remain not only as *a* major foundation but *the* major foundation of Appalachian religious culture. *"I ha' seen him eat o' the honey-comb / Sin' they nailed him to the tree,"* Ezra Pound had Simon Zelotes say in the rough Scots border burr that is a foundation of our own Appalachian dialect. Not only did Shubal Stearns first enunciate that for us in our own language, he gave us the power to enunciate it to others as a distinct expression of our faith.

The above claim should not be construed to dispute Deborah McCauley's hypotheses and conclusions about the fundamental factors of Appalachian mountain religion, the blend of "Scots-Irish sacramental revivalism," "Baptist revival culture," and "plain-folk camp-meeting religion," with its dash of Old World Pietism thrown in, that she so capably maintains to have been welded together in the southeastern mountains to form a distinctive, Appalachian concept of God and Christianity. The author does wish, however, to remind the reader and to stress the fact that nearly the identical amalgam of influences formed the total religious experience of Shubal Stearns and his family— the original Old Brethren of Appalachian legend—before they left New England for North Carolina. These influences included the Presbyterian Puritan State Church of Connecticut, the evangelical Methodism of George Whitefield's revivals with their structural similarities to the sacramental gatherings of Scotland and northern Ireland, and the small, nearly pietistic community of Rhode Island's and eastern Connecticut's original General Baptists. Under Stearns's patriarchal leadership, they presented this entire melting pot of their own religious lives as a unified whole to the settlers of the upland backcountry no sooner than they had arrived there in late 1755. The likelihood that Presbyterian "Great Revival" preacher James McGready was as much influenced by the Stearns traditions he must have observed in his boyhood home of what was to become Guilford County, North Carolina, as by the sacramental-revival Presbyterianism of his ancestors, has already been noted and discussed. And of course the Methodists who manned the next great wave of revival to cross the American Southeast and into the Appalachians were, in the days before the denomination institutionalized itself to accommodate a progressive world, simply another expression of one element of the same Stearns amalgam. At any rate, it is no wonder that so many Carolina Piedmont and later Appalachian settlers of Presbyterian and Anglican stock joined the Sandy Creek Association and subsequently the rural Stearns-based Baptist churches they found in their new Appalachian homeland; if the "McCauley mix" of religious influences that represented the best New World fusion of their own collective Old World traditions was not already securely in place under the direct influence of Shubal Stearns and the Old Brethren at least by the mid-1760s, the Goodly Fere certainly provided the ideal foundation on which it could build and the catalyst by which it developed. While the post-Revolution American denominations institutionalized, Appalachian mountain religion remained in essence the pre-Revolutionary, personality-based, and in many instances patriarch-led entity it had been under Shubal Stearns. The point could even be argued that the work of Stearns played its own part in unifying the entire Appalachian culture, secular as well as religious, into an entity as distinct as itself.

The author is neither a theologian nor a sociologist, but he suspects that, whatever else may be said within either academic discipline concerning the supposed "anti-missionary" attitudes of the Appalachians in general, their rejection of the American institutional concept of a missionary is based more on the images of coldness, remoteness, aloofness, and impersonality that the idea conjures up than anything else. Whatever faults Shubal Stearns had—and it has been shown that there were more than a few—coldness, remoteness, and impersonality, and for that matter a superior attitude other than that of a bossy but loving and concerned older brother, were not among them.

Of course, though, culture and religion are never static entities but dynamic processes, and if the children of Shubal Stearns and the Old Brethren maintain the strengths of their ancestors in the faith, they have also inherited their weaknesses. The history of Appalachia's native Baptists and the newer regional denominations that have sprung from them has been, from the very first, a tale of splits and divisions, partial reunions, and then more splits, almost exactly like the Sandy Creek Association in the last three years of Stearns's life and essentially for the same reasons. The Sandy Creek Association broke apart due to forces of social change that were, and are, impossible for any one man, even a leader much wiser and more farsighted than Shubal Stearns was, to control; the details of the John Newton difficulty, the amazingly rapid growth of the Separate movement under Samuel Harris in Virginia, and even the Regulators' War were not diseases to the body as much as they were symptoms of the larger state of affairs. As such, the splits within the Stearns Appalachian Baptist "family" have in nearly every case been, at rock bottom, the result of a given portion of the "family's" attempt to respond to one or another aspect of social change in an effort to incorporate the change into its tradition for the benefit of the "family" and its ministry. Another group or groups oppose the selected response, battle lines are drawn, and eventually the positions taken by both sides of the issue are as often as not more reactionary than either side had held beforehand. And in such a case both factions are usually led by charismatic patriarchal figures who are regarded by their respective followers as true exponents of the ways of the Old Brethren, each side maintaining its own perspective of what those ways really were and agreeing only in their mutual lament that they cannot enjoy the fellowship and love of yore, in the days of the Old Brethren when all was peace and joy and there were no splits and divisions. Thus herein may lie the biggest irony of all Appalachian history: the name of Shubal Stearns has been virtually forgotten in the mountains ever since the second generation of Separate Baptist ministers such as Tidence Lane and William Murphy went to their rewards. Yet in their production of this gaggle of little mini-Stearnses, whose pictures are so often hung on mountain church walls right next to artists' representations of Jesus Christ himself, the native Christians of Appalachia aptly reveal that they have been looking for the Goodly Fere ever since his death in 1771—without even knowing who the little bright-eyed, melodious-voiced preacher really was.

8

THE LEGACY OF THE GOODLY FERE

1801–2001

> ... But the mountain shall be thine, for it is a wood, and thou shalt cut it down; and the outgoings of it shall be thine; for thou shalt drive out the Canaanites, though they have iron chariots, and though they be strong.
> —Joshua 17:18, King James version

If the author were to examine the history of each of the various divisions of Shubal Stearns's children in the faith in detail, he'd need to add a second, and possibly third, volume to this work, but the accounts would be so drearily repetitive that the effort would be of little value. Nonetheless, for the sake of clarity and continuity this final chapter will attempt to give a brief overview at least of the major groups of Shubal Stearns's Appalachian descendants in the Gospel, and something of who they are historically and what they represent ideologically.

The relationships of the groups are, to say the least, as interesting and as warmly and at the same time maddeningly human as the little preacher who begat them however many begats back, and the author has attempted a partial and admittedly somewhat arbitrary classification of them based as much as possible on history and chronology. As such, the reader should bear in mind that some churches and groups have belonged in more than one classification at different periods in their history:

1. The Separate Baptists in Christ

However much J.H. Spencer wanted to treat the 1801 Kentucky General Union of Regular and Separate Baptists as an historical milestone, in terms of unification it was actually one of the saddest, most complicated failures in American Baptist history. As has been noted, the Elkhorn and Salem Regular Baptist Associations, composed originally of a few born-and-bred Regular Baptists but mainly of Virginia Separates who had adopted the Philadelphia Confession and Regular Baptist church forms, united with the noncreedal Separate Baptists of South Kentucky Association, made up of a mixed bag of North and South Carolinians, Tennesseeans, and Virginians, on the so-called "Terms of General Union" guaranteeing that "the preaching Christ tasted death for every man shall be no bar to communion." The document also declared that "a free correspondence and communion should be kept up among the churches thus united," but this provision rapidly proved to be completely ineffectual under the political system that rapidly developed within the loose structure of the Kentucky United Baptists' General Union.

When the Virginia United Baptists had organized in 1787, they had done so under the auspices of their own General Committee, which acted in behalf and over the individual district associations there as a stabilizing and strengthening influence much as the federal government bound the individual U.S. states together. Although the idea was bandied about among them at least as early as 1813, the newly united Kentucky Regulars and Separates formed no such body until 1832. In the meantime, the Kentucky General Union of United Baptists was a cluster of individual associations bound together loosely by yearly exchanges of letters of correspondence. Humans being the creatures they are and the Union itself being only a newly spotwelded collection of Regular, Regularized, and Separate Baptist churches, it was even more unstable than the United States had been under the Articles of Confederation before the framing of the Constitution. Both North and South District halves of the old South Kentucky Association had adopted Regular Baptist-style constitutions for their respective organizations in 1802 that ostensibly guaranteed the freedoms of the local churches and prevented associations from lording it over their members in the old autocratic Stearns style, but with the instability inherent in the state network, this provision was frequently flung down and danced upon. Within a quarter century of the ratification of the terms of General Union, the Kentucky Baptists had split into at least six different factions. A small Unitarian group under the leadership of Governor James Garrard, himself an Elkhorn Baptist minister, and Secretary of State Harry Toulmin, an English Unitarian preacher who was also president of Transylvania University in Lexington, was disfellowshipped by the Elkhorn Association the next summer after the terms of General Union took effect; the author wonders, admittedly with a bit of wry amusement, what modern Baptist church or association, Southern or otherwise, would dare to "church" a serving state or federal executive nowadays even if he built an altar to a pagan god—Eros, for example, who always has been popular among politicos in general—on the steps of his executive mansion.

The Licking Association of Particular Baptists, a hyper-Calvinistic group, broke away from Elkhorn seventeen years before the rejection of Baptist domestic and foreign missions by North Carolina's Kehukee Association, thus preceding the event generally regarded by historians as the birth of the "Primitive" Baptist movement in the South. A small southern Kentucky group made up primarily of Holston Association expatriates joined forces with Barton Stone's Christian Church, its own worship forms at the time very similar to those of the Separate Baptists, and because of certain obscure questions raised by Stone over the nature of the Trinity, they were promptly labeled "Arians" by the ministers of the General Union; they will be discussed further in connection with the next section of this chapter. David Barrow, who had been a protégé of Jeremiah Walker in the heady first days of the Separate movement in Virginia and later a member of the Kehukee and Portsmouth Associations before relocating to Montgomery County, Kentucky, in 1798, was kicked out of North District Association due to pressure from Elkhorn, its daughter association Bracken, and others in 1806 for advocating the gradual emancipation of all slaves and eventual abolition of slavery. The North District rather embarrassedly recanted its work in the affair a couple of years later and invited Barrow and his church at Mount Sterling back into the association. But Barrow refused, and he and a few other ministers and churches from North District and Elkhorn founded the "Baptized Licking-Locust Association, Friends to Humanity" and were sometimes called Emancipation Baptists. The fifth faction, though actually second in chronological sequence of formation, is the subject of our present study and will be discussed in its proper place, but first we need to examine the sixth and largest: the silent majority of United Baptists in the Kentucky General Union, who for thirty years made their homes on a virtual powder keg always ready to explode under them.

It must be understood that, generally speaking, the Kentucky United Baptists as a whole had tried to avoid each and every one of the above named splits for the sake of the state's denominational unity, and they actually did scotch several other breaches that would have split the General Union even further. It appears that most of these efforts involved attempts to appease the hyper-Calvinistic faction of the Elkhorn Association that broke away and organized the Licking Association over one difficulty or another they managed to stir up from time to time. The faction included several old respected Virginia preachers including Ambrose Dudley, John Price, Elijah Craig before his death about 1808, and even the old Philadelphia missionary John Gano before his death in 1804. Though in the long run the General Union gained absolutely nothing for its appeasement efforts, its leaders seem to have considered it politically advisable to continue making them, even as late as the middle 1830s after the first Kentucky Baptist Convention was formed. In 1829, one Licking Association minister, Ryland T. Dillard, and another prominent Licking leader, Jeptha Dudley, were even asked to sit on the board of trustees of the Kentucky Baptists' new college at Georgetown.[1] In the process of their efforts to control the divisions, though, the Regular, Regularized, and Separate portions of the General Union rapidly developed a political ethic in which "not giving any offense to the brethren" became the highest of Christian virtues, and strong opinions on any subject, unless an individual or group were assured of sufficient political backing to make an opinion safe to hold, were frowned upon as the most heinous of sins. Careful and astute political leaders who knew how to work the system to serve their own ends—in so doing often employing mob agitation techniques not unlike old Herman Husbands used back in North Carolina—quickly rose to the positions of "the brethren" one had to be careful not to offend, and of course these were the first of the mini-Stearnses whose word ultimately became law in the General Union. Kentucky Baptist government thus descended to a cheap cardboard copy of the Pope and his *Curia* (without, of course, the *Romanita* elegance), and to his regret the author must admit that this system remains the primary political power in a great many of the contemporary Old-Time Baptist Associations in the American Southeast.

Within the North and South District Associations, this political system was particularly insidious and devastating since the two had remained Separate Baptist the longest and, as has been noted, the Separates from the first had been conditioned to let their association leaders and councils do their thinking for them. Actions of association leaders and "orders" passed by an association for what its leaders considered to be temporary political necessities were hallowed in their minds: neither the "brethren" nor the "orders" were quite on a par with the Apostles or with Holy Writ, but the men and actions were both worthy of placement on some undefined pedestal above the mundane schemings of man. The condemnation of David Barrow by North District Association due to pressure from the Elkhorn and Bracken Associations, whose Bluegrass planter members found the idea of emancipation so horrifying, is but one example of the political system acting at its worst. Perhaps a better illustration of the machinations involved in the maintenance of "order" as well as what a preacher had to go through to stay in the good graces of "the brethren" can be found in North District's early minutes, and it involves the man widely regarded as the pioneer Baptist minister in eastern Kentucky, Daniel Williams.

Daniel Williams came to Kentucky with his father Edward from North Carolina in the first settlement at Boonesborough in 1775, later settling in Madison County where he was raised up to the ministry, probably under Andrew Tribble and Squire Boone at the old Tate's Creek Separate Baptist church there. When he moved to the territory of Montgomery County in the early 1790s, he had been instrumental in organizing two Separate Baptist churches, the first on Lulbegrud Creek and the second on Sycamore Creek where his church membership was at the time of the Regular-Separate union. When the North District Association was organized in October 1802, he seems to have enjoyed a good deal of popularity both with his congregants and in the association; he was picked by moderator Robert Elkin to serve on the body's first-ever arrangements committee as well as to bear North District's letter of correspondence to the Elkhorn Association in August 1803.[2] Soon after North District's 1802 session, however, two prominent Elkhorn members, James French and state legislator Jilson Payne, both transferred their memberships to Lulbegrud where, evidently, they immediately politicked and legislated the church's adoption of the Philadelphia Confession.[3] It is something of a suspicious circumstance that both prominent men should have chosen to "letter" to one rural Montgomery County church at the same time, and it is quite plausible that their move was encouraged and even engineered by General Union politicians, including North District moderator Robert Elkin himself. Although from all appearances Elkin remained pretty much an old-style Separate Baptist, he was determined to hold North District's position in the General Union at any cost. While being unable personally to advocate either the Confession or an extremely strong Calvinism, he may have regarded French's and Payne's presence in North District, and their advocacy of the Confession he himself personally could not stand, as a good buffering tactic for his association's continued cordial relations with Elkhorn. It is a fact that James French was elected as assistant clerk of North District that year and clerk in the year following, a position he kept for nearly the remainder of his life. The legislator Payne was almost always picked to serve on the moderator's arrangements committee, and in one or two extremely ticklish situations served as moderator himself although he was not an ordained minister. French's and Payne's positions of respect within the General Union, and for that matter within central Kentucky as a whole, enabled them to enforce their will over Williams's compliant Lulbegrud Separate congregation. However, there is evidence that Williams was far from satisfied with the situation, and although both Elkhorn clerk John Price and North District clerk and assistant clerk Moses Bledsoe and James French tried to smooth things over as much as possible in their minutes, it is obvious that tempers came to a head at Elkhorn's August 1803 association meeting, a few weeks before North District was scheduled to convene.

Elkhorn's meeting that year was hosted by Town Fork Church at Lexington, Kentucky, pastored by the old Philadelphia missionary John Gano who had moved to "the west country" with one or two of his sons, and it was very much the Lexington First Baptist Church of its day and time. One anecdote, which the author cannot verify with certainty, states that the church held its monthly meetings in the chapel of Transylvania University at least for a period, and it is possible that downtown Lexington and the Transylvania chapel were the locations of what transpired. However much Gano might have liked Shubal Stearns years before, evidently his kindnesses did not extend to Stearns's children in the faith in the former South Kentucky Association, and during the latter part of 1801 and most of 1802, Town Fork evidently made some strong complaints about Elkhorn's union with the noisy, rustic, and unrefined "Baptists who were denominated Separate." At its 1802 session, Elkhorn appointed a committee to visit the church several times over the next year to explain the union and pacify Gano's and the church's Calvinistic sensibilities, but at the same time Town Fork was appointed to host the 1803 association.[4] By that time Daniel Williams had seen two powerful former Elkhorn members "take their letters" to his Lulbegrud Church and then fob the Philadelphia Confession off on his congregation, and he was to bring North District's letter to the association to affirm the correspondence with Elkhorn for that year.

We do not know exactly what was said or done at that 1803 Elkhorn meeting in Lexington other than that which clerk John Price chose to reveal in his meeting minutes: Town Fork, as host church, introduced a resolution that "the union with the Baptists south of Kentucky does not in the least remove [the Elkhorn Association] from their constitutional principles," and the measure was passed by Elkhorn unanimously.[5] It is intriguing, though, to picture the rustic former Separate preacher, farmer, and hunter Daniel Williams there with his association's letter at the elegant Transylvania chapel, undoubtedly extremely discomfited at first by the urbane setting and fine clothing he saw, his discomfiture perhaps slowly changing to rage as he heard snide, and perhaps even openly derogatory, comments about his beloved Separate Baptists from John Gano and the church and association members as the resolution was discussed before the vote was taken. At any rate it is certain that Williams said something that got under Gano's and the Town Fork members' skins, although it may have been only in the form of irritated retorts to their complaints with perhaps a few additional angry references to Payne's and French's work of the past few months—and maybe a pithy observation that many of the association delegates there had *themselves* been Separate Baptists once upon a time. Elkhorn clerk John Price did not record one element of the circumstances in the association's minutes. However he and Town Fork member and association delegate Henry Payne (Jilson Payne's brother, incidentally) were present at North District's own meeting in October, where one of moderator Robert Elkin's actions was to appoint a committee consisting of himself, Price, Payne, and Tate's Creek Association ministers Peter and Archibald Woods and William Tharp "to examine the difficulty occurring at Sycamore Church"—Williams's home church—"and report at our next association."[6]

As has been demonstrated to be so often the case with Baptist records, so little is recorded, and we are left to wonder over so many nagging questions. Sycamore Church had a "difficulty"; did the body request help from the association, or was the committee foisted upon it? If there were a problem within the church itself, wouldn't Williams and his flock have been better served by a committee composed of men from neighboring congregations who knew the Sycamore members? Why should John Price and Henry Payne, or for that matter the Tate's Creek Association ministers, have been involved at all, unless the "difficulty" involved a complaint from Price and Payne regarding Williams's vocal Separate Baptist stance at the Elkhorn meeting, and Robert Elkin got the Tate's Creek men involved in the hope that their middle-of-the-road stance on the Philadelphia Confession would provide a buffer between Price and Payne on one side and he and Williams on the other? Whatever the case may have been, we can be sure of the one operative principle of General Union politics: strong opinions were not tolerated unless they had secure political backing. Williams was thus probably guilty of nothing more than speaking his mind, and the committee's visit to Sycamore was for no other purpose than to gratify the Elkhorn Association's and Town Fork Church's pride and to shut Williams up.

Soon after the 1803 session, Lulbegrud Church picked David Barrow for its pastor or moderator, and at the 1804 North District association meeting the committee reported back that the Sycamore difficulty had been "amicably settled."[7] Williams himself was absent from the association meeting that year, Sycamore Church being represented by his longtime eastern Kentucky partner Ambrose Jones and only one other delegate, but he did come back for the 1805 association session, just in time to see Bracken and Elkhorn Associations railroad David Barrow for advocating the emancipation of slaves. The state legislator Jilson Payne, now himself under Barrow's pastorship at Lulbegrud, was elected moderator for the year, very possibly at Robert Elkin's own suggestion, and he and clerk James French supervised the entire business. The matter took up the entire second business session of the association meeting. As a neat sideshow during the extra fourth day, after many of the delegates had already left for home, they even let a church on Bald Eagle Creek in present Bath County slip in a measure advocating the preaching of infant damnation (the church had taken on an extreme hyper-Calvinist from the Elkhorn Association named Richard Thomas as its moderator, and he later led them from the North District to join the Licking Association).[8] More will be said about this later, as the association and the French-Payne political team both paid dearly for those two items of legislation.

As might be expected, Daniel Williams was never again entrusted with a committee membership or any other position of responsibility in the North District Association, and from all appearances he never wanted one. He moved to the upper Licking valley of eastern Kentucky soon after the 1805 association meeting was over, and although he did organize two churches there that were admitted to the North District before being dismissed to go into the formation of eastern Kentucky's Burning Springs Association in 1813, he himself never returned to a North District meeting except on two occasions when he evidently thought he could not avoid it. Local eastern Kentucky legend, taking its cue from Williams's and his father's friendship with the Boone family both in North Carolina and at Boonesborough, holds that Williams came to the eastern mountains simply because he loved hunting and the solitude of the frontier, but this author cannot help but think that the pioneer eastern Kentucky Baptist preacher left Montgomery County for reasons considerably less romantic. There is every evidence that his departure from the Bluegrass was to escape the political hell into which he had watched the North District Association descend.

Williams's Burning Springs Association maintained a correspondence for several years with the North District in spite of his obvious aversion to the body, but the denomination now known as the Separate Baptists in Christ broke away from the South District Association and the General Union entirely and early on, unfortunately due to the same kind of politicking that drove Williams from the Bluegrass. J.H. Spencer relates two differing accounts of what happened, though both were probably partly true. It is safe to say, though, that the General Union took exception to the fact that a South District Association minister, John Bailey, held Universalist sentiments. Bailey believed that the entire human race would ultimately be saved in heaven whether they repented or not, and in his case the doctrine centered around a belief in "redemption from hell"—that is to say, hell was only a temporary state, much like the Roman Catholic concept of Purgatory. He had actually been expelled for a time from the old South Kentucky Separate Baptist Association for this belief, although another minister who may have held similar Universalist sentiments albeit without a belief in hell redemption, James Smith, was retained in fellowship but left the body to join the Tate's Creek Association when it broke away from South Kentucky.[9] Spencer quotes witnesses who aver that Bailey never did preach the doctrine from the pulpit but held it only as a private sentiment and others who say that if he did, he managed it in such a manner as to cause no offense to anyone who believed differently.

In any case, there was bad blood between the South District and Tate's Creek Associations at the inception of the General Union, due partially to the fact that the latter body had broken ranks with the Separate Baptists earlier but possibly from the difference made between James Smith and John Bailey as well. Tate's Creek's letter of correspondence to South District in 1802 was very nearly rejected—that is, until some of the visiting preachers from the other General Union associations illegally joined in the vote and the clerk counted them right along with South District's own church delegates. Despite the irregularity, the vote was upheld and the correspondence established, but the South District delegates made sure that the same circumstance didn't happen again. At the 1803 session, John Bailey was elected moderator and the Tate's Creek correspondence was rejected by a large majority. The South District's minority faction in favor of correspondence with Tate's Creek, led by Jeremiah Vardeman and John Rice, withdrew from the body to establish their own rump session after their leaders made some heated comments about Bailey's unusual beliefs, and the next year this rump faction of the South District was recognized by the other General Union associations as being the "legitimate" South District Association while the majority faction under John Bailey's leadership was universally rejected.[10] Jeremiah Vardeman thus established his reputation as a solid General Union man and went on to gain several lucrative Bluegrass pastorates including Lulbegrud and Grassy Lick in the North District after French and Payne disposed of David Barrow. His engaging personality even appears to have captivated Daniel Williams who, after meeting Vardeman in 1810 at one of his two returns to the North District, named his youngest son Jeremiah Vardeman Williams. By the early nineteenth century, the naming of sons for preachers whom parents admired had become a common practice; the names "Dow" and "Linzie," so common in Appalachia in the nineteenth and early twentieth centuries, originated with the Methodist circuit riders Lorenzo Dow and Marcus Lindsay. Even William Faulkner graced one of his more famous Yoknapatawpha County characters with Vardeman's name, perhaps without knowing where the unusual moniker had come from.

But with this South District split, the General Union made its first reinterpretation of the old Baptist doctrine of "close" or restricted communion. Until this time, from all appearances both Regular and Separate Baptists had simply restricted the ordinance to those who had been baptized by immersion, and in fact this was one of the Terms of General Union to which both Kentucky Regulars and Separates had agreed.[11] The presence of the supposedly "disorderly" faction of the South District led by Bailey in south central Kentucky, however, made the associations of the General Union forbid their members to take communion with the Bailey faction or allow the faction's members to take communion in their churches,[12] and thus was born the idea that letters of correspondence between associations were necessary for the members of one association to take communion with a church in another. The Bailey faction of the South District, cut off from the Kentucky Baptist community at large due more to the politicking of the General Union than any wrongdoing of which they had been accused, simply took back the old name of the South Kentucky Association of Separate Baptists and remained independent. They were criticized as "anti-missionary" from a Southern Baptist point of view because the association refused to get involved in the state and national Baptists' missionary societies as early as 1816, eleven years before the Kehukee Association's decision to do the same thing and in spite of the fact that the reorganized South Kentucky Association had the same modified Calvinistic, nearly Arminian theology as its North Carolina forebears and upheld "the Bible alone" as its confession of faith after the old Separate Baptist custom.[13] And in spite of additional criticism by J.H. Spencer for its refusal to play ball with the General Union politicians, the group prospered, John Bailey's Universalist beliefs apparently not affecting its doctrinal outlook in any way before their complete disappearance upon his death. At first the Separate Baptists in Christ kept close communion, accompanied in Stearns tradition by foot washing, only within their own brotherhood. But by 1873, most of the ministers recognized that the sheer number of splits over piddling questions within the Kentucky Baptists had so distorted their outlook on the ordinance that they declared that "no person has the right to debar one of God's children from his table."[14]

In years to come, the Separate Baptists in Christ expanded into other associations organized from the old South Kentucky group, including Nolynn, East Kentucky (apparently defunct or no longer connected to the other Separate Baptist bodies), Christian Unity, Mount Olive, and Southwest West Virginia Associations. These finally came to mimic the Virginia United Baptists in one particular by forming a General Association of Separate Baptists in Christ over the individual groups, and at one point they even initiated a denominational magazine, *The Watchman*, based in Kokomo, Indiana. Though sometimes not recognized as such the group is very much a native Appalachian denomination, still holding many of the traditions given to the Carolina uplanders by Shubal Stearns. Appalachian scholar Howard Dorgan, who wrote of the group after a 1991 visit to its General Association meeting at Russell Springs, Kentucky, remarked with some surprise on the participation level of the "sisters" he observed and the number of their vocal testimonies during the meeting.[15] But this is a tradition established among the Separate Baptists from the first, with its inception in the close relationship Shubal Stearns enjoyed with his baby sister Martha. The area around Russell Springs, in south central Kentucky not far from the ARC-defined boundary of Appalachia, is the group's geographical and ideological home base, and it has expanded northward, westward, and even eastward into central Appalachia proper by the same means as other Appalachian Baptist subgroups—outmigration, an intense desire on the part of the emigrants to maintain the faith of their homeland, and the enthusiastic, evangelistic preaching Shubal Stearns brought south to the hills so many years ago.

2. The Reformers, now called Churches of Christ

Though Deborah McCauley's *Appalachian Mountain Religion* recognizes this group of churches as an Appalachian denomination, McCauley notes it only in passing and with virtually no examination of its history or how it came to be established in Appalachia. Many of its rituals are almost exactly alike in form to those of most other mountain churches, but the tone of its usual expressions of worship seem markedly dissimilar to those she upholds as characteristics of true Appalachian mountain religion. This author assumes that, in addition, McCauley encountered many of the same difficulties he has found in researching this group, for it is well-nigh impossible to obtain any information that is even remotely objective concerning it or its claims to be a complete restoration of Christianity as it existed in the days of the Apostles. The sources are almost always either enthusiastically supportive or violently antagonistic, and none, Baptist or otherwise, seem to mind stretching the truth in varying degrees. The vituperative rhetoric heard from many of the group's members and preachers extends even to its main descendant denomination, the Christian Church (Disciples of Christ) with its national headquarters in Indianapolis, Indiana, and there is infighting among the various splinter factions outside the Disciple fold as well. Outside that organization there is considerable disagreement among congregations calling themselves Churches of Christ over exactly what attributes qualify a congregation's claim to be a "true" Church of Christ. Both the mainline organization and its conservative opponents classify those a shade outside the scope of their agreement as "Independent Christian Churches" rather than bona fide "Churches of Christ."[16] And all the above classifications are still referred to, somewhat unfairly and occasionally mean-spiritedly, by other rural Christians as "Campbellites" (in the southern mountains the name more frequently than not slurred to *"Cam'elites"*), which only serves to hurt and anger the adherents of the faith. Perhaps the author had better simply advise the reader to establish his own objectivity by consulting this work's sources or any others he might find. That disclaimer having been made, the fact, admitted even by the group's own historians, is that although the faith has expanded far beyond the hills of Virginia, Kentucky, and eastern Ohio where it was first established, many of its initial adherents, in Appalachia as well as the eastern Bluegrass, were Baptists of Separate descent who were rebelling against the Calvinism of the Philadelphia Confession and/or the General Union scheme of denominational government into which they had been propelled by their union with the Regular Baptists. Thus the Reformers—for that *was* what they called themselves initially—have their own unique place among the descendants in the faith of Shubal Stearns.

Details of the early life of Alexander Campbell, the exponent of the "Ancient Order" or "Ancient Gospel" as he and his readers chose to term it, have been the subject of a multitude of works before now and for the most part need not be repeated here save only to say that he was, like his father Thomas, a formally trained minister in the Old Light Antiburgher division of the Seceder Presbyterian Church—a mouthful of a sectarian name if there ever was one—who had become a Baptist a few years after he emigrated from northern Ireland to the Pennsylvania/Ohio border country. He settled in the northern panhandle of what is now West Virginia and gained his first fame in western Pennsylvania's Redstone Association as a debater for Baptist principles against ministers of other denominations. Perhaps his most famous debate was conducted at Maysville, in northeastern Kentucky on the Ohio River, against Presbyterian W.L. MacCalla in 1823. However, both Alexander and his father had just as much of a dislike for written creeds and confessions as did Shubal Stearns more than half a century before them, and both men dreamed of a union of all Christians simply on the precepts of the New Testament alone. Accordingly, later in the same year of the Kentucky debate, Alexander began to publish a newspaper, *The Christian Baptist*, to provide a voice for that which he termed "no other religious sect, excepting that ancient sect, called Christians first at Antioch."[17] More than anything else, this newspaper and its successor, *The Millennial Harbinger*, established Alexander Campbell's name and fame.

Of course, religious periodicals were within themselves no new thing.

Many denominational newspapers, serving as mouthpieces for their respective organizations, already existed in early-nineteenth-century America, and the Baptists in central Kentucky and eastern Virginia already had authored their share and more. Most were as partisan as the denominations they spoke for, and their editorials were written in the same bombastic, sarcastic, and well-nigh libelous style that passed for American frontier journalism in those days; the only reason most of the editors of these papers were not challenged to duels at one time or another is because they were Christians of one denomination attacking Christians of others, and neither of the parties wanted the notoriety of a duel—though it can be imagined that a good many editorial victims secretly wished they could afford it. Even then, though, dueling wasn't supposed to be Christian. But *The Christian Baptist* was no denominational mouthpiece, being edited, published, and to a great extent written by Campbell himself. The only positions it advocated were those which he considered based on New Testament Scripture. The only reason that any opinion contrary to his own, Baptist or not, appeared in the paper was for the purpose of his refutation of it in the same bombastic, sarcastic manner to which rural American readers were accustomed. But all things considered, Campbell was a reasonably good journalist as the breed went in those days and his paper was widely read—at first mainly by the younger, more literate generation of Baptists then springing up after the old fathers who had wrangled over the Philadelphia Confession and the Terms of General Union to produce the Virginia and Kentucky Baptist unions. Campbell's public readership as well as his private correspondence ultimately grew so large that the government had to found a post office for his use alone.

The real difference between Campbell's paper and others (which perhaps no one quite realized at the time, including possibly Campbell himself) was that it was a *religious* newspaper as opposed to a *denominational* newspaper, and in this sense it was very much the first of its kind in America and, unless one equates it with Martin Luther's printed tracts in sixteenth-century Germany, perhaps the first of its kind in the world. And that difference was very important indeed. All Protestant denominations held, as a fundamental article of their creeds, that they took the Old and New Testaments to be the inspired written word of God. So proclaimed Campbell's paper, clarifying its editorial position to a stance on the New Testament and it alone. But in its actual editorial pronouncements and the newspaper articles supporting them, summarizing and explaining the exact doctrines that would constitute this position, it assumed the role and function of a creed to many of its readers even though they believed *The Christian Baptist* to be completely noncreedal. Campbell became very much the "Editor Bishop," a term coined not by his critics but, surprisingly, by his followers. For this work the author wishes to voice neither a position of approval or disapproval of Campbell's beliefs and thus his specific doctrines will receive as little discussion or argument as is possible for the author to give; many Christians in Appalachia as well as elsewhere still do believe that these pronouncements are the pure, unadulterated, and correct interpretations of Scripture, and far more agree with all but a few of them. But the fact remains that *The Christian Baptist* began the first mass-media religion in American history, paving the way for later publications like *The Watchtower* and *The Plain Truth* that also claim to voice their own true interpretations of Scripture devoid of denominational or sectarian corruption and that, just like Campbell's papers, evolved into denominational periodicals in their own right.

Alexander Campbell never set out to organize even an association, much less another denomination, in his life, but *The Christian Baptist* was the means of communication and the cohesive, unifying, and driving force behind his followers as long as they remained a Baptist reform movement. *The Millennial Harbinger*, which succeeded it in 1829, provided the same channel of communication and strength for the collection of independent congregations the Reformers became after their break with the Baptists and their subsequent union—as related by historians, in an atmosphere hauntingly similar to the Kentucky Baptist union of 1801—with Barton W. Stone's Christian Churches in Kentucky. As the movement grew, the number of newspapers and editors serving as its mouthpieces began to multiply; if the movement's own historians are to be believed, its evangelists' desires and efforts to gain subscriptions for their preferred religious periodicals were second only to their efforts to baptize converts.[18] Ultimately congregations of readers could choose from multiplying divergent editorial slants; later "Editor Bishops" used the by-then traditional and accepted Campbell sarcasm to wage war with one another and magnify the differences of opinion, and this is how the great Campbell movement split into its various factions. Campbell himself saw the divisions coming not too many years after his readers had broken ranks with the Baptists. He wrote of the "unlicensed press" as the greatest danger to his followers' unity, fuming that many spinoff

Reform newspapers had "Editors just out of the shell of conversion; a youth converted this year, the next a preacher; the next a scribe, then an editor!"[19] He proceeded to call not for a creed to which his readers must subscribe but for essentially the Campbell equivalent: the limitation of Reform periodicals to three, one weekly, one monthly, and one quarterly, each dealing with separate journalistic topics. In a nation whose very Bill of Rights guaranteed the freedom of the press, however, this decree proved to be impossible for him to enforce without building the denominational structure he so roundly criticized "sectarian" faiths for possessing. Thus besides the mainline Disciple denomination, which did ultimately structure itself just that way, there now exist "Independent Christian Churches" and "Churches of Christ" in a multitude of more conservative forms, with their own newspapers and tract publishers serving the same purpose as *The Christian Baptist* and *The Millennial Harbinger* of so many years ago and providing the groups with their own loose equivalent of associations. The author classifies these conservative subgroups of the Reform movement, which refer to themselves mostly as Churches of Christ, as having an identification with the Stearns heritage in Appalachia greater than that of the mainline Disciple denomination for four reasons. First, their already-mentioned connection to the Separate Baptists at the beginning of their identification as a religious entity; second, the fact that although some mainline Disciple churches do exist in rural Appalachia, and old ones at that, the conservative subgroup Churches of Christ have by far the stronger rural base; third, that the Churches of Christ's relative simplicity of organization and insistence on traditional worship forms make their worship practices more like the original Baptists-turned-Reformers of the days when the movement first got underway; and fourth, the fact that, in fights both without and within, they can be every bit as endearingly and infuriatingly hardheaded (and divisive) as the backcountry Baptists from whence they sprung.

Be that as it may, the children of the Stearns legacy in general have Campbell's and his followers' Reform press to thank for the first historical recasting of Stearns's work. To Baptists both before Campbell and since, the Separates were rude country cousins whose rough edges had to be polished off by the educating and ennobling influences of the Regular Baptists. But to Campbell the Separates were the good guys, bravely maintaining their doctrinal stance on "the Bible and it alone" and upholding the "general provision" atonement of Christ in spite of the influences of the creed-bound Regulars, and, like Apollos, needing only a little more instruction for a full knowledge of true biblical faith, doctrine, and practice. Though this recasting of the image of the Separate Baptists is as skewed in its own way as that of the mainline Baptist position, it does reflect them in a more positive light, and the man who was undoubtedly the most popular early Reform preacher in the eastern half of Kentucky, "Raccoon" John Smith, was largely responsible for its introduction. Smith's first biography, or hagiography rather, was written by John Augustus Williams, and much of the information therein was taken down directly by Williams from Smith's own personal recollections. It was published in 1870 by R.W. Carroll and Co. of Cincinnati, also the publishers of Isaac Errett's *Christian Standard* that has been castigated by Smith's latest biographer, conservative Church of Christ elder Everett Donaldson, as being in his opinion one of the periodicals that led a large portion of the Campbell movement away from its original heritage.[20] Donaldson nonetheless drew on the volume heavily for his own series of books on Smith, but he did his own research as well and his references to court and church records and other independent sources provide a few, but certainly not enough, corrections to the Williams account. Chronologically in between the writings and research of Williams and Donaldson, yet poles apart from them in terms of historical accuracy, is Louis Cochran's historical novel *Raccoon John Smith*, published originally by Duell, Sloane, and Pearce in 1963 and reprinted since by the Disciples of Christ Historical Society in Nashville. Drawing on the writings of both John Augustus Williams and Landmark-thinking Southern Baptist minister Thomas M. Vaughan, whose father William, also a minister, was simultaneously one of Raccoon John's best friends and greatest doctrinal adversaries, Cochran presents something of a black-and-white melodrama rather than an accurate rendering of history, arbitrarily ascribing personalities, weaknesses, and strengths to his fictionalized characters in an obvious effort to prove his own points rather than draw the characters from life, and in the process he makes not a few unrelated historical blunders as well. Yet Cochran's book evidently has become accepted as accurate history in many, if not most, of the various branches of the movement that Alexander Campbell began. Raccoon John Smith historical and genealogical Web pages quoting Cochran dot the Internet, and even respected historians such as Donaldson and Leroy Garrett have drawn on the volume for their works.

To be fair to Cochran, though, he couldn't have made his historical romance quite so melodramatic if John Augustus Williams and Thomas M. Vaughan hadn't put their own slants, with each one trying to prove the veracity of his own faith, in their respective books. When historical records are examined closely, we find that even old Raccoon John put a slight recast on his own life as he gave his recollections to Williams—as each and every one of us might do quite unconsciously in the same situation. To prove this point completely, using the few but significant historical sources available including some of Smith's own recollections to Williams that do not quite line up with the rest of the story, this author could easily add another volume to a work already grown lengthy. Smith was every bit as confusing, interesting, and warmly human as was Shubal Stearns himself, and his biography certainly does merit further research. To understand the establishment of the Reform movement in this, the first section of Appalachia into which it was introduced, though, perhaps it will suffice to say that at least two of Smith's inferences to Williams are patently untrue. He claimed that he had known no other doctrine than a strict hyper-Calvinism in his youth and that he had never worked with Baptists of Stearns's influence before moving from Wayne County in south central Kentucky to Montgomery County and assuming the pastorates of the North District Association's Lulbegrud, Spencer Creek, Bethel, and Grassy Lick Churches. Born and raised on the Holston River in Sullivan County, Tennessee, in the days of the "State of Franklin" troubles with North Carolina, Raccoon John grew up under the preaching of Tidence Lane and William Murphy themselves, and in fact at his birth in 1784, the church to which his parents belonged was still a member of the Sandy Creek Association. Neither was Smith ordained to the ministry in Stockton's Valley Association, an early south central Kentucky offspring of the Holston Association, as he claimed later to Williams. If he had been, this would have been further Stearns influence: Stockton's Valley's first moderator was none other than old Philip Mulkey's son Jonathan. Not long after Smith was ordained Mulkey led a few Stockton's Valley congregations away from the association and into Barton W. Stone's newly organized group of Christian Churches—probably having been influenced by early "Republican Methodist" and later Stone adherent Rice Haggard, who had moved to the Stockton's Valley area at about that time.[21] This explains Spencer's disparaging comment about Jonathan Mulkey noted earlier, but in fact at the time Stone's group as well as Haggard's following worshipped after an order extremely similar to that of the Separate Baptists themselves.[22] However, although there were two Stockton's Valley churches in Wayne County not far from where Smith lived at the time he was ordained, he himself left Stockton's Valley altogether to join a church in the Tate's Creek Association. He was ordained here in 1808 by two ministers of this more Calvinistic group that had already involved itself deeply in the politics of the other major General Union associations, especially the North District. Nonetheless, for a time Raccoon John did keep one and perhaps two vestiges of his early life with the ex-Separates of Holston and Stockton's Valley Associations. He "loved melody" and used a "finely modulated" preaching cant that could be heard from two miles away, at least until his desire for acceptance among his more cultured brethren downstate prompted him to drop it.[23] But he never did quite get out of the habit of taking a chew of tobacco after he had finished one of his sermons, which were often two to three hours long.[24]

Other inaccuracies are introduced, or allowed to stand, because Williams had the habit of arranging his events not in historical sequence but as he thought they would emphasize his points best. This is especially true of his accounts of Raccoon John's early tenure as pastor at Lulbegrud, Grassy Lick, Spencer Creek, and Bethel: he skips from 1823 to 1827 and then back to 1823, then on to 1825 and so forth. In one instance, he relates an event in connection with the late 1820s that could not have happened before 1846, and he offhandedly notes that Raccoon John was elected moderator of the North District Association for the years 1824 and 1825 (as if hoping his readers wouldn't catch the fact that Smith had served in the office) in order to attribute an association "circular letter" to him that was actually written by James French. Even so, it must be admitted by all but the most diehard Landmark Baptists that Williams's work, when supplemented by Donaldson's additional research, is probably the most accurate historical rendering of the Kentucky Baptists' politics of the period yet written. John Smith assumed the pastorates of Lulbegrud and Grassy Lick Churches from Jeremiah Vardeman because the latter had found himself caught in an extremely embarrassing political tangle at Lulbegrud with Jilson Payne, recounted with flavor by Everett Donaldson as the story of "The Log That Split the Church," just as he was also beginning to advocate foreign missionary contributions in the North District. In a tragicomedy that might have come from the pen of Mark Twain, Lulbegrud split into two factions that insisted on holding their worship services on opposite ends of their meetinghouse. They were declared to be in disorder and barred from seating their delegates at North District's 1816 and 1817 sessions even though in at least one of those years the church was hosting the association meeting itself.[25] In a manner that would prove to be entirely characteristic of him in the future, Vardeman quickly backpedaled his way out of involvement with North District politics and tried to pretend that nothing had ever gone wrong, and Raccoon John pulled Vardeman's chestnuts out of the fire.

It is also quite likely true that Raccoon John found that he had to preach the Philadelphia Confession—albeit perhaps tempered by the then-popular theology of British Baptist Andrew Fuller—at Lulbegrud for the sake of Jilson Payne and James French, while simultaneously preaching Separate Baptist doctrine at backcountry Spencer Creek and Bethel and a sort of compromise between the two beliefs at Grassy Lick. Although he kept his membership at Grassy Lick, his undoubted favorite among the four churches under his care was Separate-oriented Spencer Creek. Here the historical recast of the Separates truly begins, as Williams paints a picture of the nobility of their creed of "the Bible and it alone" standing apart and away from the Confession-bound Regular belief in which Raccoon John was supposed to have grown up. But Smith's true previous experience with the Baptists, as opposed to that which he related to Williams and indeed most other of his acquaintances later, makes much of what he says in connection with this time period ring hollow. In truth he probably disliked the Separates as much as the Regulars, and with some justification considering the facts that they were tied to following charismatic leaders such as Robert Elkin who tried to put themselves up on Shubal Stearns's old pedestal and they still regarded the "associational orders" enacted by these mini-Stearnses as if they had been written in gold leaf and tacked on to the last page of the Bible as a supplement. It particularly infuriated Smith that the North District Association had caved in so easily to the politicking of old hyper-Calvinistic Richard Thomas at Bald Eagle Church in 1805, the result being the infamous, aforementioned "order" forbidding the ministers of the association to speak a kind word in behalf of a deceased baby. Smith, as was typical, placed the entire blame on the Philadelphia Confession and the Regular Baptists rather than the Separates for following their association leadership like so many dogs. Smith himself had lost two of his four children from his first marriage in a house fire, and his first wife had grieved herself to death afterwards; some evidence indicates that his second wife suffered from tuberculosis[26] and many of his children by her were sickly, with a high rate of infant mortality, and this 1805 travesty of an associational decision certainly would have been a tender point with him.

Be that as it may, it is certain that Bald Eagle Church, which had gone into the Licking Association within two years of the "hardshell" body's organization, was the target of his particular ire. Smith's brother Jonathan, now a preacher also, had moved to the Montgomery/Bath County area not long after Raccoon John himself did, and Smith seems to have made a concentrated effort to persuade the church to get rid of old Richard Thomas and install Jonathan as pastor. The church apparently staged some sort of public debate between Richard Thomas and Jonathan Smith, each man having prepared proposals of articles of faith for the congregation with Thomas's of course being strongly Calvinistic and Jonathan Smith's much milder in tone, and Raccoon John was present perhaps as moderator *pro tem*. After listening to their arguments back and forth, he laid a Bible on the table between the written copies of Richard Thomas's and Jonathan Smith's articles and proposed, "Since, brethren, neither will accept the creed of the other, let both come together on this Bible as the only Word of God, and the only bond of union."

"It will never do! It will not do at all!," spluttered Thomas. "Such a course would let in Arians, Arminians and every other kind of errorists! It will never do!"

Raccoon John replied smoothly, characteristically carrying his point as a concealed deadly weapon in a velvet glove of humor and camaraderie, "I cannot agree with my brother. In my judgement, the Word of God excludes all sectarians. But if the Bible, as he says, would admit them, how dare he form a creed to reject them?"[27]

As it turned out, Bald Eagle Church finally did oust Thomas, but Raccoon John's efforts to aid his brother were unsuccessful as well. The congregation installed a young man from among their own number, Samuel Jones, who maintained the position evidently as a "moderate" for nearly fifty years,[28] and unfortunately, young Jonathan Smith contracted an illness and died not long after the Bald Eagle confrontation.[29] Raccoon John did successfully bring David Barrow's Mount Sterling Church back into the North District about four years after the courageous old abolitionist's death. In the interim it may have joined the Licking Association as well to avoid returning to the General Union, as some of its records mention its connection with the "Particular" Baptists, whose name Licking also claimed.[30]

As a side note, it is interesting to compare the varying interpretations given to the entire scope of the North District Association's dealings with David Barrow by different religious historians each intent on proving their own points. John Augustus Williams felt safe in making the members of the Association out to be the pack of cowards that they were for railroading the old man out of their fellowship and gave Raccoon John Smith a close friendship with Barrow; J.H. Spencer embarrassedly admits that Barrow was a wise and brave man who sacrificed his own popularity to embrace a principle that was ahead of its time. Everett Donaldson, however, castigates Barrow for agitating an issue so volatile in antebellum Kentucky regardless of the motive, the reasons evidently being for "alienating his brethren" and "stirring up problems"[31] over an institution to which the Apostles were apparently resigned in the so-called primitive church. Odd indeed it is that the North District Association should find its sole historical support from an historian of a denomination hesitant to admit even that Baptists can be true Christians, especially since with this slant he shows his Old-Time Baptist heritage perhaps more than he even realizes. Alexander Campbell himself wouldn't touch the question with a ten-foot pole, even though he caused his popularity in the British Isles and Europe to suffer in so doing, but at the same time Raccoon John Smith's close North District co-worker, Buckner H. Payne, wrote the most chillingly extreme white supremacist pamphlet that this author has ever read. This author must make one more digression for an apology here. Feeling he does not have the expertise to address the matter even remotely adequately, he has not attempted to examine how much of the African-American Baptist, Methodist, Pentecostal, and even Reformer-based worship traditions now extant can be traced to the North and South Carolina, Georgia, and Virginia legacy of Shubal Stearns via slaves and slaveowners attending church together, though he believes there is much unreckoned evidence that the Stearns influence was considerable.

To return to the story, though, Raccoon John was popular at Mount Sterling Church, and even resigned Lulbegrud to the care of Daniel Boone's great-nephew Thomas in order to assume its pastorate. Smith owned slaves himself later in life[32] though evidently not at this time, and perhaps Williams was correct in stating that Raccoon John had enjoyed the friendship and confidence of David Barrow during the last years of the old man's life. However, Smith may have sought the church for himself just as he later campaigned for Jonathan at Bald Eagle in an effort, this time successful, to draw it out of the Licking Association and back into the General Union. His assumption of the Mount Sterling pastorate occurred only a little before he had begun to read Alexander Campbell's *Christian Baptist* newspaper; he seems to have volunteered to act as a subscription agent for *The Christian Baptist* in his locality, and he met Campbell personally not long afterward. From that time at least until the fall of 1827, he was an advocate, though perhaps somewhat reserved, of Campbell's interpretations of the "Ancient Order." For the first few years of its existence, the periodical was more inclined to criticize what Campbell considered wrong than to set forth a policy of what he thought was right, and Campbell spent much of his time criticizing the American Presbyterian, Congregational, and Baptist systems of domestic and foreign missions as being without Scriptural warrant. Though he later turned a complete about-face on this view of missions and was president of his own denomination's national Missionary Society for more than a decade and a half, for the time being his editorial influence wellnigh stopped support for Baptist missions in the state of Kentucky, and the arguments against organized missionary efforts still raised by Primitive, Old Regular, and other Separate-descended Baptist subgroups were actually originally articulated by Alexander Campbell himself—whatever the groups' gut instincts for so believing might be, and whether or not they know where their statements originally came from.

Campbell did not begin to advocate strongly one of his most controversial doctrines, that of the physical act of immersion itself for remission of sins to a penitent believer, until early 1827 when one of his associates, Walter Scott, made a successful evangelistic tour preaching it. This was also the same year in which Smith was finally censured by the North District Association for having begun to employ some practices Campbell advocated: changing the traditional baptismal formulary to include the phrase "I immerse you into the name of," reading from a new translation of the New Testament published by Campbell (which, incidentally, never came into widespread use even when Campbell was at the zenith of his popularity) during worship services, and employing a small change in the old Separate Baptist communion ritual in which communicants themselves broke bits of the unleavened bread from the loaves to take the sacrament rather than having it broken up by the preachers officiating at the service and then carried to the communicants by the deacons. The charges were brought against Smith primarily by James French at Lulbegrud, Jilson Payne having finally passed away in the fall of 1825. They were not an indictment of Campbell belief itself so much as nitpicky questions involving externals. However, it put Raccoon John Smith in the same predicament in which Daniel Williams, David Barrow, and even Jeremiah Vardeman had been before the association meetings of so many years past, and given the general state of Kentucky Baptist politics then still extant, Smith must have been aware during a good part of the year 1827 that unless he had someone with real political strength to "take up his part" at the association, his future as a minister in the North District was in jeopardy. From both the Williams account and the *Minutes* of the North District from that year, Smith evidently found such support, perhaps from his friend Vardeman over in Elkhorn who was likewise interested in Campbell reforms at the time or perhaps because he was simply so well loved by the members of the association in general.[33] Tragically, though, he had just buried an infant son, Joshua Carroll Smith, only a day or so before the association began; he was so heartbroken he asked his wife to make the trip to the association meeting at Cane Springs in Madison County with him for support, and in spite of her own heartrending grief she left their other children in the care of her brother and went.[34] As Smith stood before moderator David Chenault and clerk James French at the assembly and watched them try to incite the other delegates into a mob against him, though, he must have thought a lot about what his predecessors in the Lulbegrud pulpit, Williams and Barrow, must have gone through when they occupied that same space and had tried to stand on their own two feet under those same politics. Added to this must have been grief-dazed thoughts of his dead child back home in Montgomery County, just buried a few days before, and it is terrible to think of his meditations turning, as they must have, to that worthless, weak-kneed, political 1805 association order forbidding North District ministers to give a baby any hope in the afterlife other than an arbitrary election by an arbitrary God. Smith was let off the hook, so to speak, on the final day of business, with only a warning not to use the Campbell translation of the New Testament in church any more; but his thoughts of the dirty way with which he had been dealt, combined with grief over his child and the general spinelessness, brainlessness, and willingness to submit to the jacklegged political authority of his Baptist brethren must have kindled within him a burning fury that did not fully explode until the next spring.

For just as soon as winter broke in early 1828, Raccoon John Smith began to preach Campbell reform in earnest and with a vengeance. His goal was nothing less than the conversion of every congregation in the North District Association to Campbell belief, and after three years of virtually nonstop preaching all over the territory of the association, he very nearly reached it. Preaching Campbell's signature baptism doctrine now wholeheartedly, he immersed so many new believers and his influence grew so mighty that neither David Chenault nor James French quite knew what to do with him. He even converted Chenault's own Cane Springs Church right under the association moderator's nose. In these three years he baptized nearly nine hundred persons, matching Shubal Stearns's record in North Carolina between 1755–1758 although Smith was working in a much smaller and more densely populated area. This does not mean he converted all those to whom he preached entirely to his and Campbell's ideas, at least at first. Williams's work is of course full of banal accounts of Smith and his poor afflicted Reformer followers, succeeding in establishing the "Ancient Gospel" in spite of insurmountable odds and harsh persecutions, but there are a few more things that stick out of the whitewash. These were ex-Separate Baptists that Smith was dealing with, and they exchanged their old esteem for and belief in the metaphysical, emotional, joyous New Birth in Christ for Campbell's early-nineteenth-century rationalistic interpretations of the reception of faith with difficulty.

Smith thus worked like a demon to accomplish two things simultaneously in these few years: he gathered and organized several new churches simply on Campbell's interpretations of the New Testament, which had no love for the Baptists but whom he persuaded to "letter up to" the North District Association because he wanted the new congregations' political aid to overthrow the body and the governmental system it represented; and he played the part of the Goodly Fere, or at least a mini-Stearns, in the already-established North District churches for all the role was worth, stressing the goodness of the Separate Baptists' unwillingness to accept any creed other than the Bible itself, slowly and deliberately persuading them that *The Christian Baptist* offered the full and complete articulation of that belief, damning their neighboring Regular Baptists for the Philadelphia Confession and easing them away by degrees from their Separate Baptist outlook.[35] In the meantime he—and for that matter, his associates in the faith that were now increasing in number in nearly every one of the larger Baptist associations in Kentucky—employed every dirty political trick their older brethren had ever taught them and sanctified for them to swing Baptist association government into the hands of Campbell supporters. The Campbell-opposing Baptists responded in kind. As was inevitable under the weak Kentucky Baptist government even without such pressure as the Campbell Reform brought upon it in the late 1820s, churches and associations began to divide from one another once again. The following letter, written by Grassy Lick Church clerk James Mason to Alexander Campbell for publication in *The Millennial Harbinger* in May 1830 and reprinted in the Williams volume, gives a most perceptive view of the situation as it existed then between Smith and his Reformers and the North District Association. It should be kept in mind that Mason had been an unequivocal supporter of Raccoon John's reform efforts almost from the first:

> The happiness I once enjoyed in society has been destroyed by the schism that has taken place in the church at Grassy Lick, on account of an old written creed, as old as the church itself, called the "Church Covenant," which held forth, in eleven or twelve articles, the old system of John Calvin, and which a majority of the church, with Brother John Smith at their head, were determined no longer to put up with. After voting it out, they asked for letters, and constituted in less than two miles, where they meet to themselves, and have as little to do with those they left as Jews and Samaritans.
>
> I pled with these *Campbellite* brethren [Williams's emphasis], as they are called, to be patient, and let the old Covenant alone. I disbelieved it as much as any of them; but rather than cause a division of the church, I was willing to let it die a more lingering death; for I had no doubt that Brother Smith's preaching the Ancient Gospel, as he was constantly doing, would kill it without any other aid. I thought it would be better to take the fort by siege than to risk the lives of our men; but I could not prevail, and things are as above stated. I am yet in the old camp, viewed with a jealous eye by both parties, and not very popular with either; and though my views as respects the Gospel of Christ are pretty much in accordance with these reformers of yours, I am afraid to venture myself on board their boat, lest they run foul of a sawyer.
>
> I spent an evening with Brother Smith lately. I told him *it was vain to profess and preach Reformation, unless the world could see it in practice; for, if those who profess to have got out of Babylon do not*

manifest more of that love and humility, and more of the spirit of meekness and forbearance which dwelt in the divine Savior, than do those they left behind, they will make but little progress in doing good [again, Williams's emphasis]. This temper and spirit, I am afraid, are much needed among them. The war seems at present to be waxing very hot; and I think that, during the summer, the great battle will be fought, which will drive every one to his proper standard. The North District Association has already had a swarm out of her hive. An old man who has long been clerk of that body [James French] and has had possession of her papers and records, has lately taken it into his head to call a Council of such churches as he thought would favor his designs; seven only attended by their letters and messengers. These have, according to his designs, advised him to keep possession of the records of North District. They have appointed an Association to meet on the fourth Saturday in next month [June 1830, at Goshen Church] and have invited all the churches, or parts of churches that favor their designs, to meet with them; they will consider themselves the North District Association. I was instrumental in stopping the church at Grassy Lick from sending delegates to their first council [which occurred at Lulbegrud], but I am of opinion that I shall not succeed in stopping them again, as a majority of those whom your Reformers left behind [at Grassy Lick] are of the old Calvinistic stamp; so that no doubt remains that when the North District Association meets [at Spencer Creek], at the time appointed, their records and papers, with eight or ten churches, will be missing.[36]

Considering the overall tone that Williams tried to give his biography of Smith it is very surprising that he included this much of Mason's letter in his work. Other Campbell historians have used the letter as a historical reference as well, but they were generally always scrupulous to edit out the parts that cast Campbell and/or Smith in a bad light. In this letter, though, Mason's hurt, anger, and frustration at both sides of the controversy fairly leap off the page, and there is little wonder. When Smith and his faction left Grassy Lick, Raccoon John knew he couldn't risk appearing at the North District's association meeting as a member of a new church that could conceivably be rejected and denied representation. Instead he "took his letter" to Mount Sterling, and even though at the time they had already elected their representatives to North District, he talked them into holding another election, voting out one of their messengers, and sending him instead.[37] During this meeting, which occurred in the late summer of 1829, he effectively blocked questions about Alexander Campbell on the technicality that, since Campbell was himself not a member of the North District, the association had no right either to approve of or condemn him.[38] This blatant, underhanded politicking is given a good whitewash by Williams, and examples of it are to be found during this time among many, if not most, Kentucky Baptist preachers intent on bringing their denomination under the standard of *The Christian Baptist* and *The Millennial Harbinger*[39]—as well as among those who represented the opposition.

By 1830 nearly all of the major Baptist associations in the United States had lost members and churches to the Campbell movement as the group's members left or were forced out of the Baptist ranks. Preachers separated to both sides of the controversy, most remaining consistent in one or the other opinions but some, like Jeremiah Vardeman, playing both sides at different times; Vardeman caused so much embarrassment both to himself and his supporters by these tactics that he finally felt behooved to sneak off to Missouri with his family at about the time the whole mess exploded beyond repair in Kentucky. Only a few associations contained majorities embracing Campbell doctrine strongly enough to force Baptist minorities from them, and the North District was one of these few. Not that it remained in the form of an association for long, though. At least by 1832 this Campbell majority faction had essentially dissolved the body, and though its churches apparently did have annual gatherings simply for worship and fellowship for a while, they maintained their principal connection with one another in the same manner as Reform churches in the rest of the country: the subscription list of *The Millennial Harbinger*. The small minority faction of the North District referred to by Mason in his letter to Campbell, headed by James French and David Chenault, did continue as a Baptist association. Williams makes much of the persecution this group gave to the majority Reform faction and the apparent danger it posed to the Reform cause, but this is a sad, sick joke. The small minority North District United Baptist body had only ten churches in it, many of them very small, and a grand total of three ordained ministers, Chenault, James Edmondson, and Thomas Boone, to serve them all. Unless Raccoon John was obsessed with the idea of stamping out his opposition entirely and was willing to resort to hyperbole in order to try to accomplish that, they posed no more danger to him or his followers than a few mosquitoes.

Thus came the Disciples of Christ and later the "Independent Christian Churches" and "Churches of Christ" as heirs to the Separate Baptist movement in the foothills of Appalachia, and Raccoon John Smith enjoyed the reputation of a Goodly Fere among them until his death many years later. He was even called "Father Smith" in his later years,[40] as odd a moniker as old James Read had given Shubal Stearns considering the facts that both Separate Baptists and Reformers claimed to stand on a strict interpretation of the Bible alone as their creed and that the words of Jesus in the twenty-third chapter of Matthew's Gospel forbid all such titles. Raccoon John's intelligence and leadership abilities are unquestioned, and there is no doubt that he really believed in Campbell's cause. One wonders, though, if he ever allowed himself enough objectivity to admit, even in private meditation, that he had just jumped from one frying pan to another. By the middle 1830s, Smith was as involved as any other major Reform preacher countrywide with the petty quibbling over points of doctrine and practice engaged in by *The Millennial Harbinger* after the Reformers no longer had the Baptists to use for a sounding board. If, as Everett Donaldson suggests, he was opposed to the Disciples' extrachurch national Missionary Society, he had the sixteen years of Alexander Campbell's presidency of that institution to let his mentor know exactly how he felt, in no uncertain terms, about Campbell's complete about-face on the issue since the days he heaped such vituperative rhetoric on the Baptists for similar organizations. He must have read the related articles in *The Millennial Harbinger* with a good deal of bemusement as the Reform movement let go its first offshoot before it was a decade old and only a year or so after Campbell had separated from the Baptists, when Disciple preachers Sidney Rigdon (Campbell's secretary at the 1823 MacCalla debate) and Parley P. Pratt got so imbued with the idea of Ancient Order Restorationism that they linked up with a self-proclaimed prophet named Joseph Smith, who had only a handful of followers before Rigdon turned his Kirtland, Ohio, congregation over to him, and went on to found the Mormon movement. Most distressing of all to Raccoon John, though, would have been the sixteen year-long verbal sparring in *The Millennial Harbinger* between Campbell and Dr. John Thomas, Campbell's first rival editor and founder of the second Reform offshoot, since known as the Christadelphians. For in addition to insisting upon the reimmersion of all Baptists who joined the Reform movement because they had not known the clear meaning of the ordinance at the time of their Baptist immersions, an idea that Campbell loathed but that has since been adopted by many, if not most, of the conservative "Church of Christ" Reform splinter groups, Dr. Thomas preached infant damnation in a more severe form than even the most hyper-Calvinistic of Baptists ever would have dared. Thomas did not allow for the presence in Heaven of even *one* soul not mature enough to make a conscious, rational decision for Christ and immersion for the remission of sins.[41] Grieve and rant over the tragic deaths of poor little Eliza Baize (not "Eliza Blaze" as Louis Cochran named her for local frontier color), William Pinckney, Joshua Carroll, Richard Menifee, John Duke, Eli and Elvira Smith as Raccoon John might, there was no more North District Association to destroy in their memory. All he could do now was complain in letters to the editor, and from all evidence, he never even bothered.

3. The Appalachian United Baptists

Like the term "Churches of Christ," the title of "United Baptists" is nowadays a misnomer. Historically speaking, the great majority of the churches that used to be known as United Baptist went into the organizations of their respective Baptist state conventions and associations, which even the Kentucky Baptists formed in 1832 and reorganized in 1837 as a reaction to the Campbell movement. The term "United" was dropped by degrees and "Southern" took its place after the multistate Southern Baptist Convention was organized from these institutions in 1845, although according to Howard Dorgan a few of the individual southeastern associations in the Convention still retain the "United" name.[42] According to the latest published statistics, however, in the Appalachian Regional Commission areas of Kentucky, West Virginia, and Tennessee, there remain at least 176 churches known as United Baptist, in an unknown number of associations, which have either never been affiliated with the SBC or dropped out of it early in its existence.[43] Besides these, the large Bethel Association based in Missouri, organized in the early nineteenth century mostly from Kentucky immigrants, western Kentucky's old Green River Association and its affiliates, and a few other groups as far away as Maine perpetuate the United Baptist name. But these United Baptists are nowhere near being a united denomination. Perhaps they may be most accurately defined as a scattered collection of churches and associations mostly of Separate Baptist heritage that individually elected to remain aloof from both the mainline Southern Baptist denomination and the reactionary Primitive Baptist movement that followed in its wake. There are various reasons for this, mostly having to do with the maintaining of Separate Baptist doctrine and religious tradition, and preservation of the old title reflects their past history more than their present status. The "Duck River and Kindred" Associations of the "Baptist Church of Christ" of southeast and middle Tennessee, northern Alabama, and Georgia have the nearly identical doctrinal and practical outlook without the name, no doubt because the title of United Baptist was seldom used in those regions in the first place, and there are a few other associations known simply as Baptist who share the doctrinal/practical perspective as well. Other churches and associations that were once known as United Baptist have since become Primitive and/or Old Regular Baptists, and these groups will be discussed in more detail shortly.

For one example of the birth, or maybe more accurately the reinforcement, of this United Baptist position that occurred in the late 1820s and early 1830s, we may turn again to the small minority faction that was all that remained of Kentucky's North District Association after the Campbell Reform. Outpoliticked and outargued on every hand by the aggressiveness of Raccoon John Smith and his followers by the fall of 1829, David Chenault, James Edmondson, Thomas Boone (one more old North District minister, James Quesenberry, was probably in his dotage by this time and he died in the year following), and their hearers at ten North District churches simply gave up trying to keep the body together as it had been. As has been noted in the previous section, they, along with clerk James French, appointed two meetings of their own for 1830, the first at Lulbegrud and the second at Goshen Church, rather than joining the Reformers at their scheduled North District sessions at Raccoon John's Spencer Creek Church that year. In these two council meetings they hammered out their own position: from now on among the churches of their fellowship and correspondence, orthodoxy would be determined by the practices of the Elkhorn and South Kentucky Associations at the time of the Kentucky Baptist Union of 1801, with no other criterion, and all those who deviated therefrom would be judged as disorderly.[44] The minutes of the next year's follow-up association meeting, held at Howard's Upper Creek Church in Clark County, reassert the declarations of the Lulbegrud and Goshen councils along with a brief history of the Kentucky Baptists and their ancestors as French, Chenault, Edmondson, and Boone understood the subject. This document, long ignored by historians, is of extreme significance because it is untainted by the later influences of Old Landmarkism and is perhaps the only early Baptist historical statement that gives Shubal Stearns and the early New England Baptists from which he drew his own influences the credit they deserved in the growth and development of the Baptist denomination as a whole.[45]

The Red Bird Association, which had been organized by North District Elders George Baker, John Gilbert, and a few others in present Clay, Perry, and Breathitt Counties in Kentucky in late 1823, immediately adopted its parent association's stance. A correspondence was opened up on the same terms between the Laurel River Association in present Laurel and Clay Counties and the North District soon afterward.[46] Daniel Williams's Burning Springs Association in present Magoffin, Morgan, Johnson, and Lawrence Counties, under the leadership of Elder William Coffee since Williams's death in 1820, was more hesitant in following the North District's lead, probably because of Williams's own negative experiences with the body. In 1830 Coffee and his brother Jesse elected to attend Raccoon John Smith's larger meeting at Spencer Creek as Burning Springs Association delegates rather than the French/Chenault councils,[47] and from all evidence the Burning Springs Association desperately tried to maintain friendship with both sides of the controversy at least until 1835. This proved to be fruitless, however. As early as 1832, Raccoon John traveled east and organized one Reformer congregation at White Oak in Morgan County from former Burning Springs members, soon afterward gathered two others at Grassy and Lick Creeks, and in 1835 persuaded one entire Burning Springs congregation at the head of Red River in present Wolfe County to dissolve its constitution and adopt the principles of *The Millenial Harbinger*. Further toward the east on the Levisa Fork of Big Sandy River in present Johnson County, Samuel Hanna Jr., nephew and namesake of one of Daniel Williams's principal assistants in the organization of the Burning Springs Association, began to advocate Campbell-style reforms. The Concord Church across from the mouth of Miller's Creek, which had been gathered by his uncle before the older man and his family had moved to Illinois, was won over almost entirely. A similar event appears to have occurred within the New Salem Association of present Floyd, Pike, and Knott Counties, which had been organized from Burning Springs in 1825, at Mud Creek

Church in upper Floyd County, although it is unknown just how much either Hanna or Raccoon John Smith were responsible. But the end result was essentially the same as in the North District. A comparison of the 1834 and 1836 Minutes of the Burning Springs Association, along with other pertinent historical documents, leads us to only one conclusion. Tensions between Reformers and United Baptists must have finally escalated to a breach at the 1835 session, which had been slated to be held at Burning Springs Church in present Magoffin County. The Campbell party left in high dudgeon with Reformer clerk Caleb Kash actually confiscating all the body's records, some of which did not resurface until more than a century had passed, and the remaining United Baptists became more firmly fixed than ever on the policies the North District had reasserted five years before.[48]

Even so, the North District minority's 1830 decisions gave the body a reactionary dynamic that remained active long after the Campbell breach, and the group itself did not long remain associated with the United Baptists. Between 1837 and 1842, the body dropped correspondence with all its former affiliates except Burning Springs, losing many of its churches back to the mainline Kentucky Baptists in the process. Both the North District and Burning Springs eventually assumed a hyper-Calvinistic outlook and traded the old Terms of General Union for articles of faith in common with the Primitive Baptists. For many years the North District styled itself as an "Old" Baptist association;[49] in an ironic 1867 move that probably would have left old Daniel Williams turning in his grave, Burning Springs titled itself as a "Regular" Baptist association, finally assuming the name of Primitive Baptist in 1923. It remained for another "daughter" association of Burning Springs known as Paint Union, organized in 1838 from Burning Springs churches in present Johnson, Martin, Lawrence, and Magoffin Counties, Kentucky, and Wayne County, West Virginia, to assume the place of the most prominent United Baptist association in the eastern Kentucky/West Virginia border country. Paint Union's articles of faith, prepared in 1837 or 1838 by Elder Cornwallis ("Wallace") Bailey, moderator of the Burning Springs Church that eventually left its namesake association to join the newer organization, categorically stated the general-atonement position of the old Separate Baptists[50] and thus brought the body and its daughter associations (Zion, Mount Zion, Bethlehem, Blaine Union, Iron Hill, Olive, and New Hope) more stability from hyper-Calvinistic doctrinal changes than the Terms of General Union could ever offer. In a similar action in 1856, the North District gave off another "daughter," the Mountain Association of Old Regular Baptists in present Breathitt, Owsley, Wolfe, and Perry Counties, Kentucky, which has maintained its "Old" version of the Separate Baptist tradition without assuming the hyper-Calvinism its parent body developed.[51] Though the Old Regular Baptists will be discussed in more detail later in the chapter, it might be noted here that Mountain Association was probably the second Baptist association ever to adopt this name, the first being Twin Creek Association, a hyper-Calvinistic central Kentucky body that existed between 1850 and 1868 before it merged with North District.[52]

Though these names of "Regular" and "Old Regular" Baptist merit further discussion later, it might be mentioned that their peculiar adoption by these groups of almost no true Regular Baptist heritage whatsoever reflects one more bit of seasoning added to the mix of Baptist traditionalism: the already-cussed-and-discussed Old Landmark movement, which during the middle years of the nineteenth century was steadily gaining ground among both Southern and United Baptists. The movement was in part a frantic, bombastic attempt to negate the influence of Campbell's "Ancient Order" journalistic hyperbole by claiming to trace the Baptist Church, as it existed in America in the mid-1800s, in an unbroken line all the way back to John the Baptist via the British Particulars and the American Regulars. The writings and sermons of Landmark originators James Robinson Graves and James Madison Pendleton were roundly criticized from their first publication by more thoughtful Baptist evangelists and writers such as Virginia's J.B. Jeter, who also penned some of the most thoughtful critical essays on Alexander Campbell and his Reform movement. Graves's and Pendleton's claims are indeed preposterous and easily disproven in the face of objective historical research. They are based almost solely on their own idealistic speculations and an obscure pseudo-historical volume written in the early nineteenth century by British Baptist G.H. Orchard, who tried to identify every group in history that ever dissented from the Roman Catholic Church as Baptists, including the bizarre Cathars or Albigenses of Languedoc. However, the idea of a royal pedigree, however spurious, is of course appealing and will be believed by anyone who really wants one, and the movement has survived among such aspirants—of whom there are still many among rural Southern Baptists as well as their later offshoots. Even the respected David Benedict, in later editions of his *History*, saw fit to prostitute himself to Orchard's wild claims.

When Old Landmarkism came to Appalachia, though, the movement took its own special mountain twist. Graves, Pendleton, and their followers were definitely missionary in outlook, and as good Regular Baptists they were fierce advocates of the rights of the local congregation. In fact they traced their pseudo-genealogy through individual churches rather than larger groups, and their reasoning was so subjective that they claimed any Baptist church orthodox on their terms *had* to be part of the legitimate Apostolic Baptist succession whether its ancestry could be proven historically or not.[53] Of course these concepts of church independency and missions were completely alien to most Appalachian Baptists, who had their entire religious lives shaped within the old Stearns association-as-family context, so they simply swallowed what Graves and Pendleton claimed insofar as they could relate to it, emphasized the genealogies of their associations rather than their churches, and pretty much ignored the missionary angle altogether. In the process they began to try to trace their group ancestries back to the Philadelphia Association rather than to their actual origins, their memories of the Goodly Fere faded even further into oblivion as they swallowed Graves's and Pendleton's exciting new interpretation of the identities of the Old Brethren, and the name of "Regular Baptist" came into great vogue among men and women whose grandparents and great-grandparents had scorned the title.

It must be stressed that the greatest advocates of Old Landmarkism were the preachers. For most Appalachian United Baptist church members, the Old Brethren legend, already extant and grounded in actual history, was quite enough, and if their ministers chose to interpret it in this new way, they of course must be right. Where the preachers were content to retain the name of United Baptist, so remained the associations; where they preferred Regular, that title was adopted, and there were even a few groups who used both names for a while. In his research in the preparation of this volume, this author has waded through a myriad of yellow, crumbling, half-literate pamphlets published years ago for distribution at association meetings by these well-intentioned but misled men, most stating incredible attempts to reconcile what they read in Semple's *Rise and Progress* with what they so desperately yearned to believe from the writings of Orchard, Graves, and Pendleton. These include claims that the Sandy Creek Association was given off as an "arm" of Opequon Creek Church; the Ketocton Association "gave off" the Holston Association in 1784 (two full years before it was actually organized), then within a year "gave off" central Kentucky's Elkhorn Association and had a "grandchild" by Elkhorn, the South Kentucky Separate Baptist Association, within two years following; and even that the Philadelphia Association was "armed off" from an eight-hundred-year-old church somewhere in the hinterlands of Wales, where of course the Apostle Paul brought the Gospel, though the Anglican Church–translated King James Bible makes no mention of it. Small wonder it is that even Appalachian scholars should be confused and misled when trying to research the subject of Appalachian mountain religious history using only folk memories and indigenous writings as their guides.

To return to the United Baptists, though, a stance such as was made by the North District in 1830 on the preservation of Baptist customs extant at the union of Regular and Separate Baptists in and of itself made for an environment in which traditionalism thrived and indeed continues to thrive even where Old Landmarker influences are not strong. All the Appalachian United Baptist associations that this author has observed maintain a high number of the customs Shubal Stearns introduced to the Carolina backcountry so many years ago, though there is considerable variation on small points between individual associations and association clusters. In more or less all, however, the practice of imposition after baptism is no longer extant, having virtually died out even in the years between the Virginia and Kentucky unions; that is, unless one counts the joyous exchange of hugs one always sees when a newly immersed individual steps out of the water. Likewise the custom of calling the elders' wives "eldresses" has long since disappeared, though the terms "deaconess" and "sister deacon" survive in some United Baptist clusters, and in a few instances one still sees these individuals called upon to lead public prayer much as Shubal Stearns employed his sister Martha and was so roundly criticized by the South Carolina Regular Baptists for doing. The practice of "devoting" children or "dry-christening" very nearly perished but has enjoyed a recent small revival among some groups in spite of the indignant statements of older members claiming that "the Baptist family never did such things." In addition, the old Stearns dress and hair length codes, time and social change having reversed their emphasis, at least until the early 1970s, to women's hair length rather than men's, are still stressed in a few small United Baptist associations and individual churches.

Perhaps the most variation one may observe between individual groups of United Baptists concerns three issues: "close" versus open communion, acceptance of "alien" immersions, and the styles of hymn singing employed. From the 1830s, most United Baptist churches and associations held to the policy established in Kentucky after the 1803 split that resulted in the formation of the Separate Baptists in Christ, that only those who are in direct "letter correspondence" may commune and wash feet with one another. Over time many also limited their acceptance of baptisms in the same way, but later, after observing the confusing tangles such policies inevitably produce, some reverted to the practice that originally defined close communion among Baptists: that only individuals baptized by immersion should partake, with self-examination under the guidelines of I Corinthians 11, and they have likewise once again enlarged the circle within which they will accept baptisms. As to the issue of music, one sees pianos and other instruments in a few churches and associations, but a great many Appalachian United Baptists restrict themselves to noninstrumental hymn singing. The styles range from "Shape-Note Harmony" as found in the hymnals such as are published by the Stamps-Baxter Company, "Christian Harmony," "Southern Harmony," and "Sacred Harp" (most of these singing styles are named for the hymnals that originally introduced them) to the old style brought by the Stearns family to the mountains: the evangelistic poetry of John Newton, Charles Wesley, Augustus Montague Toplady, and others set to ballad tunes popular during George Whitefield's and Shubal Stearns's own lifetimes, and now found in hymnals such as *The Sweet Songster* and the *Thomas Hymnal*. *The Sweet Songster* has been in publication since 1854, the *Thomas Hymnal* since 1876; the latter book was compiled expressly for use in Baptist churches, but *The Sweet Songster* appears to have been originally a Methodist hymnal borrowed and adopted by some Appalachian United Baptists, a fact that would cause great consternation to a few of the more conservative groups if it were emphasized, especially those most ardently subscribing to the claims of Old Landmarkism. Some Appalachian United Baptists even employ more than one style of singing in the same service.

The major doctrinal variation the author has observed among Appalachian United Baptist groups regards the issue of "perseverance of the saints." Most groups still hold essentially to the same principles found in the preamble of the 1756–1757 Abbott's Creek Church covenant, quoted in the third chapter of this work as reputed to have been penned by Shubal Stearns, of the Six Principles of the old General Baptists with the Calvinist assurance of perseverance thrown in. For example, the Bailey articles of faith subscribed to by most eastern Kentucky and western West Virginia United Baptists reflect this position. Interpretations on the fine points of the doctrine vary, however, often between individual preachers within a given group. Some stress individual accountability after the profession of an experience of conversion, allowing for the possibility of apostasy by conscious choice and action; others preach "once in grace, always in grace," a favorite maxim of some of the more conservative individuals and groups, but few if any take this to the extreme of a sanctificationist position.

All in all, there is much broad similarity among all the Appalachian United Baptist groups, but many small differences between certain associations and clusters of associations. Why, then, have the Appalachian United Baptists never lived up to the name they wear so proudly and exist as an organized denomination such as the Southern Baptists in a regional or even national association (which latter title at least one non–Appalachian United Baptist association somewhat presumptuously sports)? Many reasons could be given but they all boil down to one fact: when the Appalachian United Baptists took their stance apart from state Baptist conventions and associations as an entity in their own right in the wake of the Campbell Reform movement, on Baptist customs they perceived as having existed traditionally, they committed themselves to perpetuating every virtue and every fault that their old Goodly Fere, Shubal Stearns, had bestowed upon them. These United Baptist groups were, and are, literally small versions of the old Sandy Creek Association that kept—along with the faith, doctrines, and practices of the Separate Baptists that they prized so highly—the same limited small-community outlook and dependence on patriarchal, charismatic leaders around which the office of association moderator was and is hallowed. As is shown so painfully from Stearns's own experience between 1765 and 1771, they are simply not constructed to withstand either large growth and geographical spurts or dramatic social change without breaches and divisions, however minor their causes appear. Virtually all have the association constitutions the former Separate Baptists borrowed from the Regulars when the two groups united in the southeast, guaranteeing the protection of the rights of the local church from infringement by the association, and at least one privilege, the right of a local church to call for a presbytery of ministers to examine and ordain one of its number to the ministerial or diaconal office, is usually more or less respected. Had Shubal Stearns been willing to give on this one matter he could have saved himself one small part of the trouble he endured in the last years of his life. But in nearly all other matters Separate tradition, which Stearns borrowed from the old General Baptists and then hallowed with his own charisma, far outweighs Regular local-church principle. Most of the associations employ the same kind of central control over their churches, vested in the moderator's office (and at least since 1771 if not before, strengthened by the moderator's quasi-*Curia* on the "Arrangements Committee," which he handpicks at each annual association session) just as Stearns used his position more than two hundred years ago, now generally on the pretext of another constitutional article stating in various phrases that the association has the right to withdraw from any church it perceives as "acting in disorder." Given the usual United Baptist doctrinal stance that only "the old-time ways" are "orderly," this principle can be interpreted very narrowly depending on the outlook of individual association moderators. Although virtually all of the association divisions have been rooted broadly in positive versus negative response to some social change, their dynamics nearly always begin with a flare-up of the unresolvable controversy over the rights of individual churches versus the proper prerogatives of associations. Campaigning for both sides of a given issue follows, generally in the style old Robert Elkin, James French, and Jilson Payne of the North District Association would have understood and identified with completely, and finally, perhaps even inevitably given the heritage and the psychological context of the participants, the split occurs—of course always followed by a period of mourning on both sides of the division when much rhetoric is expended on how this whole thing wouldn't have happened if the Old Brethren had been there to guide them and how peaceful and loving everybody was in the Old Brethren's day. In truth one can hardly find two sequential decades in these associations' histories when one or more such splits did *not* occur somewhere within their ranks, but moderators who caused and/or participated in them have always shown great skill in de-emphasizing their effects and perpetuating the combination Old Brethren/Landmark legend. Thus we have the Paint Union, Old Paint Union, Original Old Paint Union, and "United"; Old Zion, New Zion, and Tri-State Zion; Bethlehem, Old Bethlehem, Union Bethlehem, Calvary (two factions), and Mt. Paran; Mt. Zion, Old Mt. Zion, and Ancient Christian; and Iron Hill, Old Iron Hill, and Mt. Carmel, Associations, to name only a portion, ostensibly all aspiring to reach the same destination but with many individuals among them either too stubborn or too cowed to admit that they are all in the same boat. To varying degrees this same tendency is shown in those United Baptist associations that later became Primitive and Old Regular Baptists, as well.

United Baptist groups as a rule have refrained from dividing over secular political issues and, for that matter, have kept away almost entirely from group secular political involvement. Though some local Appalachian historians have speculated otherwise, every evidence exists that they refused even to get involved in the issues of the Civil War, and United Baptists served in both Union and Confederate armies. Given the horrifying experiences of their ancestors in the faith during the Regulators' War, a certain skittishness toward the idea of group political involvement may have been subconsciously drummed into them long ago.

The rub, of course, lies in the small, internal community and social issues. "Double-married" converts seeking church membership (a term that, in the earliest instances dealt with by Appalachian churches, referred to the persistent problem of bigamy in a wilderness where men and women could move to new territories bringing no traces of their past lives with them, rather than divorcing before remarrying), varying singing styles, open versus close communion, Sunday schools, the extent of cooperation with other local religious groups, even personality clashes between prominent candidates for the moderator's office—all these issues and more have been the results of these dynamics and the causes of splits. The associations with the most reactionary moderators usually experience the most divisions. Their worlds become smaller and more insular with each breach of fellowship, and their association records from year to year fill up with more and more "orders" spelling out just exactly what churches and individual members may and may not do to remain in "correspondence" as well as acrimonious decrees of excommunication directed at those who have violated the rules.

Some members, and more often than not entire families, chafe under such restrictions when they become too onerous, and they depart reactionary ranks for other religious affiliations including, often, more moderate United Baptist groups with which the reactionaries were once affiliated. On the other side of the coin, there are all too frequent occasions in which individuals and families, when faced with the casting of a church or association order or decision they deem too liberal or otherwise unsatisfactory, drop churchgoing altogether because their church or association has gone "out of order" in their eyes, and yet they believe it is not proper for them to support or attend the services of any other extant religious body. Of those who remain in the extreme factions there are two general types: a few hardcore believers in the positions their moderators and associations have taken, and a majority of silent, complacent members who simply believe it is their duty to abide by what their association says with no questions asked, consequently refusing to address issues personally and acquiescing to association and moderator even at the expense of conscience and friendship. As has been demonstrated, this tendency to complacency was extant even in Shubal Stearns's time; it was part of his power as well as that of Robert Elkin, Jilson Payne, and James French, and it was the heartache of Daniel Williams, David Barrow, and Raccoon John Smith. Thus, ironically, these reactionary groups fulfill one aspect of the traditions of their forefathers perhaps more than they realize. In terms of their growth rates, some have already gone back farther than the Stearns tradition to that of the Rhode Island Yearly Meeting from which he drew his influences, and they are on the same slope of inexorable decline for essentially the same reasons the old body's power waned.

In fairness, though, the author must repeat here that not all Appalachian United Baptist groups are reactionary, though most are conservative, and the moderate groups are more and more inclined to view themselves as distinctively Appalachian United Baptist yet part of the bigger picture of Christianity. Too, in spite of the associations' self-imposed governmental limits, some association moderators labor in a genuinely dedicated, caring fashion like old Shubal Stearns at his best moments, to remain in close touch with the needs of both churched and unchurched in the communities where their associations are active—as well as trying hard to avoid further splits, in the process endeavoring to appease and manage fellow ministers and members who are by no means always easy to get along with. As a United Baptist preacher himself, the author hopes that there are and will be enough such moderators to keep the United Baptists, oddly and ironically titled though they are, alive as a vital part of the Appalachian religious scene for many years to come.

4. Appalachian Primitive Baptist Groups

The Primitive Baptist movement—or more properly, Predestinarian Baptist, since its doctrinal hallmark is the extreme Calvinist proposition that every individual in the human race is predestined even before birth for either heaven heaven or hell, with no choice in the matter—is no exclusively Appalachian phenomenon. At one time Primitive Baptist churches could be found in many of the settled areas of the United States, and they are still a viable presence in the lower Mississippi valley, the Midwest, Texas, the Deep South, and the Atlantic Coast as well as in Appalachia. Though we have already shown Kentucky's Licking Association to be the ideological forerunner of much Primitive Baptist thought, according to most historians the movement began with North Carolina's Kehukee Association in 1827 and Virginia's Ketocton Association shortly thereafter. By their reasoning both doctrinally and historically, the movement's origins can thus be traced to the Regular Baptists rather than the Separates, though many if not most of its strongest early ideologues, as has already been noted, were former Separates influenced by Regular Baptist thought.

The Primitive Baptist movement has likewise long been the subject of study for Appalachian scholars because of the early presence of nonmissionary hyper-Calvinistic Baptist churches in Appalachia that later took the name of Primitive Baptist, and to coin a term for lack of a better one, the already-discussed "Landmark Distortion Factor," along with Reformer propaganda like John Augustus Williams's hagiography of Raccoon John Smith, prompts many such scholars to identify the Primitive Baptist subdenomination as the "original" Appalachian Baptist church. But the Appalachian Primitives are, of course, themselves mostly of Separate ancestry, the exception being West Virginia's Primitive Baptists who truthfully can claim direct descent from the Philadelphia and Ketocton Associations. The origins of the Separate-descended Primitives' doctrinal stance have already been noted. Suffice it to repeat here that elements of Presbyterian Calvinism, Whitefield Methodism, and the practices and structure of the General Baptists' Rhode Island and Windham Yearly Meetings were all part of the amalgam the Stearns family brought to the Carolina uplands, and that after he became a Baptist Shubal Stearns himself never could be classified either as an outright Calvinist or Arminian. Among his followers no controversy over the scope and nature of the atonement was raised until at least four years after his death, and even then most Calvinistic Separate Baptists believed as much in evangelism as did the Arminians. The real bone of contention came when such Separates as William Marshall, John Price, Ambrose Dudley, John Tanner, and others came to study Regular Baptist Calvinism during the years of dialogue between the Ketocton, Kehukee, and Virginia Associations regarding the prospect of Baptist union in Virginia, and wound up "out-Calvining" both Baptists and Presbyterians. The tensions this ultra-Calvinistic minority came to generate in central Kentucky, evidenced by the formation of the Licking Association and culminating in its withdrawal from the General Union, have already been noted, and one might imagine that a similar minority came to exist in eastern Tennessee as the Separate Baptists under Tidence Lane's and William Murphy's care in the Holston Association began to try to dissect the Philadelphia Confession they had adopted for the sake of Baptist unity in 1786. This may have been the reason Murphy made his 1800 statement about the terms under which Holston's founders had accepted the Confession. For all we know, Raccoon John Smith's good old father George may have been a member of this Holston minority, but still, the claims Raccoon John made against the Baptists of his youth were merely patent and effective fodder for Alexander Campbell's press.

Back in North Carolina where the entire Separate movement began, though, it is doubtful that the Philadelphia Confession, at least in its complete form, was ever accepted by the decimated and later-recovered Sandy Creek Association. In fact statistics compiled by American Baptist registrar and chronicler John Asplund between 1790 and 1793 indicate that Sandy Creek, now dwarfed in comparison to the Yadkin Association to the west, Strawberry to the north, and Kehukee to the east, still retained more of the central-control policies of the Goodly Fere, probably under the leadership either of Elnathan Davis or Joseph Murphy, than did any of its neighboring "daughters" and "granddaughters." At the time, Sandy Creek was in direct correspondence evidently only with the Georgia Association old Daniel Marshall had helped to found, though Joseph Murphy was still one of the most popular and beloved preachers among Yadkin members as well, and one of its ministers, William Kendall, had recently "resigned ordination according to the rule of the Association"[54]—shades of the plight of the unfortunate John Newton. As an incidental note, the old historic Sandy Creek Church, numbering fourteen members in two congregations after the death of Shubal Stearns, now boasted a membership of twenty-five under the care of an unordained preacher, John Welborn, but by this time Abbott's Creek Church had been reorganized under the leadership of minister George Whitefield Pope and was once again growing rapidly.

By the late 1780s, though, every other association around Sandy Creek was concerned with Baptist union even though it seems to have taken the members of the older association a while to catch onto the idea themselves, and in 1793, three years after it was formally organized from the Strawberry Association, the Yadkin Association adopted a set of articles of faith apparently designed to please both Regular and Separate Baptist tastes. These articles will not be listed or examined in detail here, that chore having been already done by Howard Dorgan and other Appalachian scholars. Suffice it to say, they were brief in comparison to, and loosely based on at least some of the precepts of, the Philadelphia Confession. They were almost identical to a set of articles of faith found in Asplund's 1794 *Baptist Register* and were probably popular among American Baptists generally at the time. These articles of faith are nearly, if not completely, identical to those found in the annual published minutes of almost every Appalachian Primitive and Old Regular Baptist association that this author has seen, the only exceptions being a very few Primitive Baptist groups that have more recently adopted stricter articles, and therefore they have almost certain historical origins in the old Yadkin Association. This is why their precepts have already been studied, not from an historical standpoint but because the later associations that took the names of Primitive and Old Regular Baptist preserved them almost *in toto* and they were examined in connection with those groups.

However, when one examines the original records of these articles of faith, preserved on microfilm by the American Baptist Historical Society at Rochester, New York, one notable curiosity is observable. The article dealing with the subjects and scope of the atonement originally began thus: "We believe in the doctrine of particular election by grace." Yadkin's clerk evidently then blotted out the word "particular," but not so completely as to make it indecipherable.[55] This could be a strong indication that there was considerable disagreement on the subject among Yadkin's ministers and members even then, and the clerk removed the word "particular" simply to avoid conflicts on a subject still under thought and debate—or perhaps because a majority of the group demanded its removal. At any rate, as a rule in Primitive Baptist association articles of faith, the word "particular" is most often preserved while in those of the Old Regular Baptists it is left out.

With or without the presence of the adjective, the United Baptist associations of southwestern Virginia, western North Carolina, and even to some degree eastern Tennessee established themselves and grew on the basis of these articles of faith. The Yadkin Association organized the Mountain District Association from the churches in its northern territories in 1799; about five years before this, the Strawberry Association "gave off" another "daughter," the New River Association, in the territories to the Mountain District's northeast. New River was actually one of the few early United Baptist associations to represent a genuine Regular/Separate Baptist mix, the churches in its southern territories being former Strawberry Separates and those to the north in what is now West Virginia having been organized by John Alderson Jr. and Josiah Osburne from the Ketocton Association. This mix was lost, however, when Alderson and Osburne finally grouped the Regular-descended portion of the flock and organized their own Greenbrier Association in 1807. Further to the southeast, the Mayo Association was organized around 1808 partially from Yadkin churches and in part from some of the southern congregations of old Samuel Harris's beloved Roanoke Association. In the territories furthest southwest in Virginia, the Washington District Association was organized from Holston in 1811 though without the adoption of the Philadelphia Confession. In its turn, the Washington District re-connected with the Kentucky United Baptists by establishing correspondence with eastern Kentucky's New Salem Association, already mentioned as having been organized as an "arm" from the Burning Springs Association in 1825, and the loose affiliations continued northward with Burning Springs' relationships not only to the North District but the Regular-descended Teay's Valley Association in western West Virginia, formed in 1812 from John Alderson's and Josiah Osburne's Greenbrier Association, and its "daughter," the Ohio Association, in the territories of northeastern Kentucky and extreme southeastern Ohio. By the middle 1820s, the Ohio Association already belonged to the new Ohio State Baptist Convention; Teay's Valley, Greenbrier, Roanoke, and Strawberry to the General Association of Virginia Baptists; and even the Washington District had a tenuous relationship with the Virginia state association through the strong support for the organization of the Washington District's most prominent minister, Elder David Jesse. The others were still essentially "satellite" bodies around the more prominent groups, tied together by their proximity to one another and their correspondence relationships.

Such was the status of the Baptists in central Appalachia when the Campbell Reform began, and the event that most historians believe triggered the Primitive Baptist movement occurred within its context. The Kehukee Association's 1826–1827 rebellion against state Baptist conventions, Sunday schools, and the missionary movement in general caused it to assume initially the name of "Reformed Baptists," the title of "Primitive" not yet having been dreamed up, and Alexander Campbell gleefully wrote of the event in *The Christian Baptist* as if Kehukee were endorsing his principles rather than their own.[56] It is not known whether he ever published a retraction for this error, or for that matter whether he ever gave any sensible explanation for his own change of views on "the missionary business" later, when his paper had become the head of its own denomination and he recognized the utility of the institutions that he had once so roundly condemned. Nonetheless it is clear that Kehukee's leaders got much inspiration from at least this one aspect of Campbell's teaching, especially in light of the ironic fact that the association itself was converted from Paul Palmer General Baptist to Regular Baptist belief by the labors of Philadelphia and Charleston missionaries. Ketocton and a few other small associations and parts of associations in Virginia may have gotten similar inspiration, as their members joined the Kehukee camp with their Black Rock, Maryland, convention and the publication of *The Black Rock Address* in 1832.[57] Still, a few opponents to organized Baptist domestic and foreign missions had existed several years before Campbell had taken up his pen, but most of them, such as Kentucky's John Taylor, were former Separate Baptists who opposed missions not for any reasons involving Calvinism or fatalism of any sort but for the structured, arbitrary, impersonal manner in which they suspected the missions would be conducted and maintained. Thus for a brief while the Primitive Baptist movement was, at least outwardly, very similar to the United Baptist movement initiated by the minority faction of North District Association after the Campbell Reform: standing on its members' perceptions of the "old order" and opposed to "innovations," but yet with no real articuation of the hyper-Calvinistic, fatalistic beliefs that would become the hallmark of the Primitive Baptists in years to come.

On this basis, anti-missionary Baptist associations began to sprout up all over the United States about 1830 and thereafter, with little difference between them and Kentucky's United Baptist groups, which J.H. Spencer classified as "Go-Betweeners" on the issue, except the soon-to-be-titled Primitives' especial condemnation of missions.[58] In fact, these Baptists received the popular nickname of "hardshells" not for their developing ultra-Calvinistic doctrine, but because the moniker was the common early-nineteenth-century equivalent of tightwad or miser. In the Regular Baptist territories of what would become West Virginia were founded the Pocatalico, Indian Creek, and Elkhorn Associations (the latter of which has been mistaken by more than one religious scholar for the large Kentucky group, still active in the Kentucky Baptist Association and a member of the Southern Baptist Convention, which was instrumental in securing the 1801 Kentucky Baptist Union) from the pro-missionary Regular-based Greenbrier and Teay's Valley Associations. Interestingly the Greenbrier, Teay's Valley, and Ohio Associations are also the ancestors of the Southern Baptists in eastern Kentucky rather than the older associations of the Bluegrass or eastern Kentucky's oldest Separate-based Baptist groups, through Greenup (organized from Ohio Association in 1841), Enterprise (from Greenup in 1876), and Pike (from Enterprise in 1957) Southern Baptist Associations. Also of note is the fact that the division in Teay's Valley Association that created Pocatalico prompted at least one prominent Teay's Valley minister, Goodwin Lycans, to bring his Silver Creek Church into the organization of Kentucky's new Paint Union United Baptist Association rather than affiliate with either missionary or anti-missionary camps, and his subsequent involvement in the organization of Zion and Bethlehem United Baptist Associations brought, perhaps for the first time, a major Separate Baptist influence into what is now western West Virginia.

Meanwhile hyper-Calvinistic sentiments steadily grew among the anti-missionaries, the movement's fatalistic outlook causing its adherents to reassess not only the missionary concept but the theology of the New Birth in Christ, the idea of a personal knowledge of salvation, and the propriety of any effort to invite or bring sinners to Christ. The Separate-descended Baptists of southwestern Virginia, western North Carolina, and eastern Tennessee were drawn into the fray as well. Small Primitive Baptist associations split off both the old Sandy Creek and Yadkin confederacies to join the Kehukee circle of fellowship, and today there are both "missionary" and Primitive Baptist Sandy Creek and Abbott's Creek Churches, each faction claiming to represent the "original" congregations and both maintaining meetinghouses not far from one another. The more historically prominent early Primitive Baptist associations in western North Carolina that broke off Yadkin during the 1830s include the Roaring River, Fisher's River, and Senter Associations, and the Mountain District Association jumped into the movement between 1836 and 1838 with the wholehearted support of its leaders if not many of its members. Northward in southwestern Virginia, the Washington District Association finally ousted the much-beloved David

Jesse from its moderatorship in 1845 for his support of both the General Association of Virginia Baptists and the Holston Association, which had joined the newly formed State Baptist Association in Tennessee. Jesse and his followers, numbering about five hundred men and women in entire congregations and parts of churches, organized the Lebanon Baptist Association the next year, which became the premier voice of the Southern Baptists in southwestern Virginia; the Washington District broke off fellowship with Holston and threw in headlong with the Mountain District,[59] even to the adoption of the old Yadkin articles of faith that the Mountain District still maintained.

In spite of the fact that its oldest Baptist association joined forces with the Southern Baptists, east Tennessee was likewise subjected to its own share of divisions. Elder Daniel Parker, first of Tennessee and later of Texas, gained some adherents to his "Two-Seed-in-the-Spirit" theory, which he claimed to have picked up from an unnamed preacher somewhere in the east Tennessee mountains. For a while Parker's Two-Seed-in-the-Spirit Predestinarian Baptists even had a subdenomination of their own. (The number two seems to have a special significance with some Primitive Baptists, probably owing to the seeming dichotomy of foreordination and instances of free will in the Bible. Parker had his Two Seeds doctrine, Thomas P. Dudley of the Licking Association in central Kentucky preached and wrote about "Two Souls," and a more modern theory espoused by many non–Appalachian Primitive Baptists argues for "Two Salvations." The reader will be spared the theological subtleties.) In the northeastern corner of Tennessee, though, one breakoff group from the old Holston confederacy, first known as the Mulberry Gap Association of United Baptists and later as the Eastern District Association of Primitive Baptists, made no hard-line statements about predestination and was and is as evangelistic as its Separate Baptist ancestors. Having expanded northward to southwestern Virginia, eastern Kentucky, and, like all Appalachian Baptist subgroups, transplanted Appalachian communities in the industrial cities of the north, the Eastern District is possibly the largest Appalachian Primitive Baptist association extant.

The Primitive Baptist movement continued its expansion throughout Appalachia through the latter half of the nineteenth and the first half of the twentieth century, though slowly and almost always in a small way. The movement was not established in eastern Kentucky until after the Civil War with the espousal of Primitive Baptist principles by the

North District, Burning Springs, Red Bird, Sand Lick, and Mate's Creek Associations, and it did not reach some parts of northern Georgia until the early years of the twentieth century. Perhaps its last notable Appalachian manifestation occurred among the Paint Union and Zion United Baptist Associations with the establishment of the Big Sandy Valley Primitive Baptist Association, no longer extant, about the year 1925, not long after the Burning Springs Association finally changed its name from "Regular" to "Primitive." Even so, the movement was marked by backlashes all along, straining the credibility of its claim to be the "original" Baptist church. Most of the Primitive associations in North and South Carolina, Georgia, and Tennessee were themselves break-offs from the older associations, and those historically significant associations that adopted Primitive Baptist principles such as Mountain District, Washington District, North District, and Burning Springs, each experienced crippling splits of their own as the result of their actions. During and after the Civil War, the Mountain District lost many of its churches in North Carolina and southwestern Virginia, which formed associations of their own and are now known as Regular and "Union" Baptists; these associations have more in common both practically and doctrinally with the various United Baptist groups of eastern Kentucky and western West Virginia than they do with the North Carolina Primitives, even though these two different groups of Shubal Stearns's children in the faith have had no contact with one another for more than a century. They have been and continue to be much more prosperous than their more Calvinistic neighbors. The increasing hyper-Calvinism of the Washington District Association resulted in the formation of the Old Regular Baptists, who will be discussed in more detail in the next section. Still another example is the history of the Burning Springs Association in eastern Kentucky during its gradual move towards hyper-Calvinism. "Wallace" Bailey, the longstanding Burning Springs minister who drafted the articles of faith now used almost universally by United Baptist groups in the Levisa, Tug, and Guyandotte valleys of eastern Kentucky and western West Virginia, brought his Burning Springs Church from its namesake association into Paint Union in 1852, and the Burning Springs and Paint Union Associations dropped correspondence with one another in 1857. Burning Springs' annual association meetings were interrupted during the Civil War but at the first such meeting held afterward, in 1867, half its churches were not represented to vote on its adoption of the name of Regular Baptist. Two of these absent churches, Zion and

Low Gap, joined Paint Union Association and two years later, led the other Burning Springs absentees into the formation of the Mt. Zion United Baptist Association, which adopted the Bailey articles of faith and maintained fellowship with Paint Union and the other United Baptist associations within its connection for many years.

Even after this, Burning Springs was hardly uniform in doctrine. In gathering data for his *History of Kentucky Baptists* in the early 1880s J.H. Spencer obtained his information about Burning Springs from one of its more prominent ministers, Elder W.L. Gevedon of West Liberty in Morgan County, Kentucky, and made the following report about its condition at that time: "Its preachers are nearly all very illiterate, and are far from agreeing in doctrine or polity. Some of its older ministers are Hypercalvinists; but the younger are much divided in their views, some being inclined to Arminianism, some holding to Fuller's views of the atonement, and some teaching Parker's doctrine of the Two-Seeds. Some of them believe in making special efforts for the salvation of sinners, and go so far as to hold protracted meetings. This is a modern innovation in this fraternity, to which, however, it owes its recent prosperity."[60]

As might be expected, in little more than a decade Burning Springs split again, this time with Gevedon himself in the lead, over both differences in the doctrine of the atonement and the exacting system of "communion and footwashing with direct correspondence only" that had already thrown such a logjam into Appalachian Baptist relations. Gevedon led the formation of the Enterprise Association of Regular Baptists (not to be confused with the nearby Southern Baptist association of the same name) in 1894; this group spread rapidly over the northeast corner of Kentucky and into southern Ohio and is now doctrinally and practically similar in many ways to the mountain Free Will Baptists and/or the Church of God, other subgroups to be discussed in subsequent sections. In the twentieth century, Burning Springs quarrelled and lost fellowship with Rock Spring Association in Rowan and Carter Counties, Kentucky, which it had organized in 1887, over the younger group's less fatalistic outlook, and in the process it very nearly came to endorse the doctrine of absolute predestination. Finally in 1941 it split once more over open versus close communion, resulting in the existence of two Burning Springs Associations, each very small and one on each side of the question. As a side note, the "mother of all" eastern Kentucky Separate-descended Baptists, the North District Association, which had experienced similar schisms of its own since its assumption of Primitive

Baptist doctrine, mostly to the benefit of the nearby Boone's Creek Southern Baptist Association that it had organized in 1823, dwindled slowly and inevitably to three small churches in Clark and Estill Counties, Kentucky, and finally disbanded after its 1960 session. Two of North District's former churches, Goshen and Irvine, still exist as independent Primitive Baptist congregations. Likewise the Licking Association of Particular Baptists, which had pioneered hyper-Calvinism in the east central Bluegrass even before the Kehukee Association's 1827 actions in North Carolina, is no longer operating although at least one of its former churches, at Bryan's Station in Lexington, Kentucky, still exists as a "Landmark Missionary" Baptist church. The Red Bird Association has the unusual distinction of being organized as a General Union association in 1823, becoming a United and then a Primitive Baptist body and then disbanding about 1859; being reorganized as a Southern Baptist body a few years afterward, then again disbanding; and yet once again being reorganized as a Primitive Baptist association that, at least until this writing, still existed with two tiny churches in Clay County, Kentucky.

Generally speaking, the Primitive Baptists may now be divided into three distinct classifications both within and without central Appalachia: the "Regulars" who stress fatalism in regard to individual salvation, the "Absolutes" who preach the absolute foreordination and predestination of all things good and bad, and the "Progressives" such as Eastern District who are evangelical Separate-style mild Calvinists. A tiny fourth, exclusively Appalachian group, the Universalists or "No-Hellers," believe that the entire human race will eventually be saved by the predestination of God and were, historically, evidently an outgrowth of the same seedbed in southwestern Virginia that produced the Old Regular Baptists. Howard Dorgan, who studied this group extensively in the early 1990s, attempted to trace the historical evolution of its beliefs back through its ancestry; the only direct Appalachian parallel he could find, and that not even based in a Calvinistic context, was the Universalism preached for a short while by John Bailey in the old South Kentucky Association, and he was unable to connect Bailey by any historical link to the modern "No-Hellers." Neither has this author been able to find one, and certainly the testimonies of J.C. Swindall and Joseph Hall, ordained elders and church moderators in Three Forks of Powell's River Association, a "granddaughter" of the Washington District and one of the associations Dorgan studied in this connection, cast doubt that Universalism was preached in Three Forks of Powell's River before the early

1900s. When Swindall and Hall left the association in 1894 to join the Union Old Regular Baptist Association, which Swindall moderated successfully and with much acclaim for many years, the two wrote individual accounts of their departure from Three Forks of Powell's River that listed detailed descriptions of their perceptions of the association's doctrinal errors, mostly having to do with the group's espousal of absolute predestination. Swindall and Hall were certainly no Universalists and they never once mention this doctrine as being preached in Three Forks of Powell's River during their tenure there, but if it had been they certainly would have added it to their respective catalogues of complaints.[61] The question of the origins of Universalism among the central Appalachian Primitive Baptists must thus remain unanswered, and this author wonders if perhaps that the associations who embraced the doctrine simply might have gotten so fanatical about the concepts of eternal election and absolute predestination, over a period of several years, that—for lack of a better way to phrase it—they traveled all the way through the theological system that they had set up and came out on its other side, much as the original American Universalists did at the close of the eighteenth century.

Regular, Absolute, Progressive, and Universalist factions notwithstanding, the central Appalachian Primitive Baptists, in their desire to remain aloof from "innovations," have yet retained many of the worship modes they inherited from the Separate Baptists of many years ago, some of which—in a wryly amusing parallel found in the relations of the Southern and other "mainline" groups to the United and other traditional Appalachian Baptists—still make non-Appalachian Regular-descended Primitives squirm a bit. Most wash feet as a supplement to their communion services; some anoint the sick with oil; and in nearly all Shubal Stearns's New England Holy Tone is still used for preaching, though often in a more subdued way than that found in United and Old Regular Baptist groups. In common with the more conservative factions of the United Baptists as well as the Old Regular Baptists, most of the Regular and Absolute Primitives use either "Sacred Harp" singing or the old mountain style of *The Thomas Hymnal*, although they prefer their own volume, Goble's *Primitive Baptist Hymn Book*, which alters the lyrics of the old songs where necessary to reflect their own positions ("We might as well preach unsound doctrine as to sing it," they say). Like these other groups too, the Primitives of all factions have received a deep bite from the Landmark bug, and of course the twist that native central

Appalachian Baptist groups have always given to Landmarkism was undoubtedly the reference point by which they came to define themselves in the years of their development. Regulars, Absolutes, Universalists, and to some extent even the Progressives all claim that their doctrine and their ancestry is purely apostolic, calling each other and indeed all other denominations renegades who broke off from them and their pure belief at some point in time.

Like nearly all other native central Appalachian groups having sprung from the labors of Shubal Stearns, the Primitives have experienced—and brought upon themselves—association splits and divisions throughout their history generally on the same terms, and for the same nitpicky reasons, as those seen in the United and Old Regular Baptists. In fact these divisions have become so numerous that one sees more independent, unassociated Primitive Baptist churches than are found in any of the other traditional central Appalachian Baptist subdenominations. Nonetheless the Primitive Baptists, associated after the traditional manner or not, have, like Alexander Campbell, found the press and the periodical to be a great unifying force, and many Appalachian Primitive Baptist ministers and deacons are thus more aware of like-minded believers in other parts of the United States than are those of most of the region's other indigenous denominations. Primitive Baptist websites, many containing vociferous paeans to old G.H. Orchard's flawed, undependable *Baptist History*, flourish on the Internet as well, in an ironic mixture of traditionalistic dogma into the melting pot of the Information Age.

5. THE OLD REGULAR BAPTISTS

Long the subject of intensive study by Appalachian as well as other religious scholars as "the" definitive central Appalchian denomination, the Old Regular Baptists perhaps warrant no further detailed examination other than a slight clearing up of the muddy waters surrounding their historical origins, and a brief examination of their doctrines and practices in the context of these historical origins. In many if not most ways, they represent the results of a concerted, determined effort to maintain a high degree of both doctrine and practice traceable directly to Shubal Stearns in the face of the militant Primitive Baptist hyper-Calvinists of southwestern Virginia and western West Virginia, and given the context of the existence of their ancestors in the faith and the circumstances under which they developed, it was no mean effort.

Both the Twin Creek and Mountain Associations of the Old Regular Baptists have already been mentioned in connection with the North District Association and the formation of eastern Kentucky's United Baptists, but neither group is central to our discussion here; the former was, of course, only in existence eighteen years before merging with the North District, and the latter has been only marginally connected, and that in recent years, with the main body of the entity Appalachian scholars have recognized as Old Regular Baptists in southwestern Virginia, western West Virginia, and eastern Kentucky. The "old mother," as it were, of this group was and is New Salem Association, organized within the Kentucky General Union in 1825 of churches from Burning Springs Association in present Floyd, Pike, Knott, and Perry Counties, Kentucky. As was indicated in the previous section, New Salem enjoyed fellowship with the Washington District Association on its southern boundary, Paint Union to its north, and Burning Springs to its northwest. For a while it corresponded with Red Bird as well, its annual exchange of letters and delegates to this body apparently dropped when Paint Union Association, which was much closer geographically and which had the same annual meeting time as Red Bird, came into existence. To recapitulate briefly for the sake of clarity, New Salem's involvement in the Campbell Reform of the early 1830s seems to have been small, the body perhaps losing only one church, Mud Creek, to the Reformers, and at this point in time it identified itself, as did both Burning Springs and Paint Union to its north, as a United Baptist association according to the definition of that term established by the North District Association at the Lulbegrud and Goshen council meetings of 1830. The fact that these central Appalachian associations were still loosely connected with one another by direct and indirect correspondence relationships on the order of the structure of the old Kentucky General Union itself, however, still made for all the instability that has made the term United Baptist a misnomer in Appalachia, and of course more fights and divisions were still in store.

New Salem's fellowship with the Washington District Association was evidently still as cordial as its relations with its Kentucky sister associations, though the Washington District itself was for several years in a quandary about its own position in the General Association of Virginia Baptists. As long as the popular David Jesse retained the Washington District's moderatorship, matters appeared to be relatively stable. In fact in its early years, New Salem was perhaps as missionary-minded as the

Washington District itself before 1845: early association records show that James Fuller, a missionary visitor from the Teay's Valley Association in present West Virginia, was occasionally appointed to preach at New Salem association gatherings, and a few New Salem ministers, most notably Harvey G. Reynolds,[62] later became very vocal Southern Baptists. However, the dynamic of the old Kentucky General Union was still operative: just as the North District's leaders had discovered several years earlier, instability in any association was likely to spread to its direct correspondents, and when Jesse was ousted from the moderator's position in the Washington District in 1845 by the group's anti-missionary party, New Salem soon began to experience the ripple effect.

It must be reiterated here that the central Appalachian United Baptist associations were essentially on a Separate Baptist middle ground, strengthened by traditionalism, between both Southerns and Primitives. J.H. Spencer's nickname for them, "Go-Betweeners," has already been noted. New Salem, still maintaining the title of United Baptist, was neither quite Southern or Primitive Baptist in outlook, but increasingly over time it found its own middle ground between the reactionary Primitives of both the Washington District and Burning Springs Associations on one hand, and *both* United and Southern Baptists on the other. New Salem's association orders during this period were a patchwork of mixed messages to the increasingly divergent associations around them. In 1851 the body adopted the Washington District's association constitution and rules of decorum,[63] formally changed its name to "Regular United Baptist" in 1854,[64] and two years later made a decision to "reject all missionary baptisms from the year 1846 forward," particularly singling out Harvey G. Reynolds's Mt. Zion Church by requiring—in typical Shubal Stearns moderatorial style—that "Mt. Zion Church deliver Dillard Parsons and his wife the missionary letters that they laid in said church and also give a fair recommendation as to their moral walk, etc."[65] All these moves were clearly reactions to pressure from the Washington District over New Salem's acceptance of Virginia emigrants baptized by David Jesse and his followers in the Lebanon Southern Baptist Association, already noted as having broken from the Washington District and organized in 1846, the very year mentioned in the New Salem association order. The year after this, fifteen exclusions were noted in New Salem's minutes, almost double the number of the year before and more than triple the number of two years before, and neither

Reynolds nor Mt. Zion Church ever represented themselves in the New Salem Association again.

It is not known whether Mt. Zion joined the Lebanon Association in Virginia or the closest Southern Baptist association in Kentucky, which would have been Greenup, organized from the Ohio Association in 1841, but it is known that Harvey G. Reynolds and his family later moved to Johnson County where they were active in the Greenup Association as well as the Enterprise Southern Baptist Association, organized from Greenup in 1876. On the other hand, in 1854 New Salem had also accepted two new churches located in Russell County, Virginia,[66] an act that in that day and time both the Washington District and Lebanon (as well as the Stony Creek Association, organized in 1851 from Washington District and now also corresponding with New Salem) would likely have interpreted as an invasion by New Salem of their territories. Be that as it may, this move by the two Russell County churches lends credence to the idea that New Salem was establishing a reputation among Baptists of the Kentucky/Virginia border country as "middle-grounders" between the Primitives of Washington District and the Southern Baptists of Lebanon, and this tendency of southwestern Virginia Baptists to seek fellowship with New Salem rather than any of their "home" associations of either Primitive or Southern Baptist stamp continued until Union Association was organized, of both Kentucky and Virginia churches, by New Salem in 1859.

Besides this, when the Burning Springs Association, well on its way to becoming a Primitive Baptist group after Wallace Bailey's and Burning Springs Church's defection to the Paint Union Association in 1852, finally dropped correspondence with Paint Union in 1857, New Salem favored Paint Union over Burning Springs, accepting Paint Union's letter of correspondence and its delegates and rejecting Burning Springs'—but New Salem's "preaching committee" was careful to let both Wallace Bailey of Paint Union and James Fugate of Burning Springs preach during public worship at the stand after the Saturday association session. Correspondence was not renewed with Burning Springs until well after the Civil War was over and even then lasted only until 1890, but the Mate's Creek Association, which was organized by New Salem in 1849 from churches in eastern Pike County, Kentucky, and what is now Mingo County, West Virginia, for years maintained a stable relationship with the Zion United Baptist Association, which was apparently unaffected by either New Salem's, Paint Union's, or Burning Springs' troubles.

One may wonder what would have happened if the Civil War had not disrupted annual New Salem sessions between 1862 and 1868, but when the body reorganized itself in 1869, it still seemed to be seeking this same middle ground between Paint Union on one hand and the Washington District on the other. The body attempted to re-establish relations with both its northern and southern neighbors, but the next year when delegates came bringing letters from Paint Union and the Washington District, New Salem attempted to change its name to "Regular Primitive" Baptist or "Primitive Regular" Baptist, the titles apparently to be used interchangeably—a move that the Washington District itself did not make until 1876.[67] Even though New Salem reversed this decision only twelve months later, at that time opting for the title of "Regular Baptist Churches of Jesus Christ,"[68] apparently this name change was too much for the Paint Union delegates, because there is no record in the minutes of either association that correspondence between the two was renewed at this point or ever attempted again. Even so, the Zion United Baptist Association and Mate's Creek Association, now calling itself Regular Baptist as well, continued to enjoy their own separate, independent peace for several years more.

The 1870s continued to be years of upheaval within—and mixed messages from—New Salem Association and its correspondents. The Burning Springs Association reestablished fellowship with the body in 1873,[69] and in 1875 New Salem, perhaps under the usual pressure from Washington District and Stony Creek as well as the renewed influence from Burning Springs, made the following resolution: "The item to notice secret organizations was taken up and debated. *Resolved,* therefore, That we, as the Regular Baptist Association, known as the New Salem Association, do declare a non-fellowship with all modern institutions, called benevolent: such as Missionary, Bible and tract societies, Sunday School Union and Masonry, and all societies set on foot by men, whether secret or open, outside of the word of God."[70] The next year the Union Association, with both Kentucky and Virginia churches, filed an objection to New Salem for this harsh-sounding directive, but New Salem's only response was to repeat the order with the inclusion of the phrase "men or devils" and to withdraw correspondence from Union, accepting instead a letter from the newly organized Three Forks of Powell's River Primitive Baptist Association in Virginia. But then nine New Salem churches asked for letters of dismissal to organize the Sand Lick Association, and specified in their association articles of faith (based on the old Yadkin articles, which New Salem must have been discreetly using as well by this time though they did not appear in New Salem's minutes until 1885) the following:

12. We believe washing one anothers [*sic*] feet is a commandment of Christ, left on record with his disciples, and ought to be practiced by his followers.
13. We believe that any doctrine that goes to encourage, or indulge the people in their sins, or causes to settle down on anything short of saving faith in Christ for salvation, is erroneous, and all such doctrine will be rejected by us.
14. None of the above named articles shall be so construed, as to hold with particular election and reprobation, so as to make God partial either directly, or indirectly, so as to injure any of the children of men.[71]

In his assessment of the New Salem, Union, Mate's Creek, and Sand Lick Associations for his *History of Kentucky Baptists* in 1885, J.H. Spencer strongly criticized the group's ever-growing anti-missionary attitude and for this reason he appears to have been vilified by Old Regular Baptist history buffs ever since. He did praise the Sand Lick Association, though, for its stance on the articles of faith named above, although in one of the little ironies history always seems to favor, Sand Lick eventually repudiated its initial positions and became Primitive Baptist; and his criticisms of New Salem must be interpreted in light of the fact that he obtained his information on the association directly from Elder William Cook,[72] and it is easy to imagine that Cook, who himself was no reactionary hyper-Calvinist and who was described by Spencer as being "a man of fine and cheerful spirit . . . active and zealous in his holy calling," had long since grown tired of trying to satisfy the disparate factions in his association and simply let himself speak plainly to Spencer about his own gloomy assessment of New Salem's prospects.

Be that as it may, Primitives and moderates maintained an uneasy truce with one another in New Salem and its corresponding associations until the early 1890s, although several churches mostly in northern Floyd County, Kentucky, seem to have gotten discouraged with New Salem and abandoned it for membership in the Paint Union United Baptist Association. Adopting Paint Union's Bailey articles of faith over the Yadkin articles by now used evidently uniformly among New Salem and its correspondents, these churches were finally "armed off" from Paint Union and organized as the New Hope Association of United Baptists in 1919, though they have always maintained practices more common to New Salem than to even the most conservative United Baptist associations.

But to return to the story of New Salem itself, tensions between Primitive and non-Primitive factions finally came to a boiling point just about the time the body adopted the name of Old Regular Baptist in 1892. The body had dropped correspondence with the Burning Springs Association two years earlier, ostensibly over "secret orders"—that is to say, Freemasonry, which in its 1875–1876 directives it had equated with Sunday schools and missionary and Bible societies[73]—and this move turned out to be a permanent breach of fellowship between the two associations. Almost immediately afterward, queries began to be submitted by New Salem's churches, not about the severance of the Burning Springs correspondence but regarding doctrinal questions over the scope and nature of the atonement. The answer to one of these, given in 1892 and an obvious modification of an 1891 query answer that New Salem Primitives had protested, is regarded by Howard Dorgan as "the" definitive Old Regular Baptist doctrinal statement: "Resolved, that we drop the nineteenth item of our last year's minutes and advise our churches to cleanse, or abstain from the doctrine that God is the author of sin, or that He influences men thereto, and the doctrine of Arminianism that claims the work of the creature [man] to be essential to eternal salvation."[74]

Despite this still-conciliatory position, within a year splits began as if in a chain reaction. New Salem's Primitives left the association in high dudgeon the next year, evidently most or all joining the Sand Lick Association where they succeeded in driving the non-Primitive faction of Sand Lick away. These non-Primitive churches, still clinging to Sand Lick's original articles of faith, continued for some years as independent bodies meeting in a simple annual assembly for preaching, but they finally organized themselves into the Indian Bottom Association. In a move that has already been noted in the previous section in connection with Elders J.C. Swindall and Joseph Hall, the Three Forks of Powell's River Association kicked out its non-Primitives at about the same time Union Association split, with Swindall's large faction joining Union's non-Primitive side. The Mate's Creek Association split at very nearly the same time, resulting in the formation of the Sardis Old Regular

Baptist Association that for many years maintained fellowship with both the Zion United Baptist Association and other Old Regular Baptist groups, and to its northeast both the Elkhorn and Pocatalico Primitive Baptist Associations split as well, resulting in the organizations of the Pineville District and Mud River Associations. Eventually the Pineville District dissolved, combining with some Union Association churches to form the Friendship Association. With these schisms and regroupings, the Old Regular Baptists as a definitive, stable—relatively speaking—religious entity finally came into being.

Doctrinally, then, the Old Regular Baptists are what they were molded into during their formative years in the nineteenth century, a tightly knit hybrid of conservative United Baptist and Primitive Baptist belief. In terms of worship practice, they are in part this same hybrid, but like so many of the spiritual descendants of Shubal Stearns, they retain large distinctive portions of the Goodly Fere's teaching and example as virtual articles of their faith and perhaps advocate them more strongly and loudly than did Stearns himself. They preach a general atonement accessible by conscious choice to all whom God calls and do not hold with infant damnation, but they preach a "hope" of salvation rather than a personal knowledge of it and do not extend public invitations or altar calls of any sort other than simple exhortations for sinners to pray and "accept their call from God." Likewise, protracted "revival" services such as the six-day meeting at Haw River in the fall of 1765, of which Stearns wrote so happily to Noah Alden, disappeared among their churches due to Primitive Baptist influence long ago. Even so, they are enthusiastic worshipers who look for almost any opportunity to hold services, and their lack of protracted meetings is perhaps compensated in some part by the spate of "memorial" and "union" meetings scheduled by each church yearly—traditions they share with United Baptists as well as other Appalachian groups—as well as their custom of making funerals two-, three-, or four-service events.

Old Regular Baptist singing has been studied intensively by Appalachian scholars, and it is in essence the same hymnody the Stearns family brought with them from New England to the Carolinas: evangelistic Whitefield-era poetry set to Celtic-edged ballad tunes that have been passed down in an oral tradition from generation to generation. The Old Regulars have elevated the custom of "lining out" hymns, done from necessity in the days of few hymnals and few readers, almost to dogmatic status. Appalachian United and Primitive Baptists both practice lining with varying frequency depending upon the preferences of individual churches and associations, but nowhere is the custom maintained as passionately as it is in the Old Regular Baptists. *The Thomas Hymnal* and *The Sweet Songster* are both favored by the Old Regulars, but some ministers and members of their number have compiled and published their own hymnals as well, incorporating newer songs—some written by Old Regular and Primitive Baptists, the lyrics of others discreetly borrowed from the shape-note hymnals of other denominations—into the Old Regular Baptist tradition. One of the best-known examples in central Appalachia is *The New Baptist Song Book* (the author wonders with a bit of wry amusement how on earth the Old Regulars, Primitives, Uniteds, or other Baptists that use this hymnal could ever tolerate the word "New" in the title), for years published by the Ratliff family, Old Regular Baptists of Pike County, Kentucky, but now reprinted and edited regularly by Roland Conley, a United Baptist deacon of Magoffin County, Kentucky. Others include C.B. Smith's *Some of Our Favorite Songs* and Elder Baxter Osborne's *Old Regular Baptist Hymn Book*.

At least one more distinctively Old Regular Baptist practice can be traced directly back to Shubal Stearns and his family: that of the old dress and hair-length code, maintained in the Carolina Piedmont as well as many parts of central and eastern Virginia in the heyday of the Separate Baptist movement there. Men were required to forsake the fashion of the day and keep their hair short like the "Roundhead" chaplains of Oliver Cromwell, and both sexes were to attire themselves plainly and soberly. With the advancing social and style changes of the early twentieth century, the hair code's emphasis rapidly shifted from men to women; after the further upheavals of the 1960s and 1970s, it seems to have been stressed for both sexes, though perhaps somewhat more for the women. Some United Baptist associations, parts of associations, and individual churches likewise observe the old code and many more let a female member's conscience decide the issue, but the Old Regular Baptist Church is probably the only Stearns-descended denomination that observes the rule mostly strictly and uniformly and regards a female member's cutting her hair as an offense worthy of excommunication. Howard Dorgan dealt with this Old Regular Baptist characteristic extensively in his 1989 *Old Regular Baptists of Central Appalachia*, and he recounts stories both amusing and tragic as he writes of the Old Regulars' insistence on maintaining this tradition in a society that has lost track of the actual origins of the practice long ago.

As a professor of communications arts, Dorgan likewise extensively studied the preaching cant most commonly used by Old Regular Baptist ministers as well as others found within the Primitive Baptists, Regular Baptists of northwestern North Carolina, the mountain Free Will Baptists, and related groups. All show similarities to one another, and we have already seen from Morgan Edwards's notes on the Separate Baptists as they existed within a year of Shubal Stearns's death that they are undoubtedly variations, developed over time and distance, of Stearns's own exposition of the New England Holy Tone. Of course we cannot know exactly what this *Ur*-version of Appalachian preaching sounded like, but one is tempted to speculate that the common Old Regular mode, with its heavy dependence on singsong chant interspersed with elongated shouts and wails, appearing so similar to Edwards's description of the style that Philip Mulkey must have successfully parroted from Stearns, is the closet extant approximation. It is found among the other of Stearns's descendant groups but nowhere so uniformly as is found among the Old Regulars.

There are also points of interest concerning the Old Regulars' traditional anti-Masonic stance. Anti-Masonic flare-ups have occurred on occasion throughout American religious history in general, and recently, some modern fundamentalist television ministries have added their two cents' worth to the fray. Without entering into the dispute on the matter here, it may be said that it is decidedly odd that the Old Regulars, having always been very insular in terms of the influences they have allowed to affect their denominational lives, should have adopted an anti-Masonic stance simply because it was popular among the American religious community generally. The anti-Masonic attitude, at least to the degree it is exhibited among the Old Regulars, cannot be traced to any association within their direct correspondence at any time who did not itself become Old Regular Baptist during the battles of the 1890s. The North District Association did pass an anti-Masonic order in 1815,[75] but there is absolutely no evidence that Burning Springs ever followed suit even though it was in direct correspondence with North District at the time; indeed, the presence of "secret orders" was the ostensible reason New Salem dropped correspondence with Burning Springs in 1890, though the older group's increasingly "hardshell" stance may have been just as much a factor. Among the United Baptist descendants of Burning Springs, the matter of Masonic membership has traditionally been left up to the individual's conscience with the exception of the heavily

Old Regular–influenced New Hope Association. It is interesting to note, though, that one of the more obscure charges Herman Husbands leveled at the Orange County, North Carolina, courthouse ring during the worst of the Regulator troubles of the late 1760s and early 1770s was that Edmund Fanning, Sheriff Tyree Harris, Superior Court Justices Maurice Moore and Richard Henderson, and other officials used their connections within Freemansonry to abet one another in embezzlements and other crimes against the Piedmont farmers and backwoodsmen and to keep their bought-and-paid-for assemblymen in office to the exclusion of other candidates.[76] For all we know Husbands, who, it must be reiterated, was himself fast and loose with the truth whenever he found hyperbole to be expedient to advance his own ideas, very well may have been right in this case. One wonders if Husbands's agitation of so long ago might have been the original source for anti-Masonic sentiment within the families of those who later became Old Regular Baptists, and that the prejudice, like the old Stearns dress and hair-length practices, found its full expression in the Old Regular Baptists' orders.

In terms of governmental structure, the Old Regulars suffer the same fate as their United and Primitive Baptist cousins: their correspondence-linked associations, led by patriarchal moderators who are the successors to the role of Shubal Stearns and governed by an extremely strict central control in associations that loudly proclaim they do not "lord it over God's heritage," are not built to respond to either large or rapid growth or dramatic social change without schisms and a good deal of bitterness. In fact, such divisions are really a part of the Old Regulars' makeup even more than that of the United Baptists, as one of the first of their own divisions involved the break with the Uniteds to become the Regular Primitives and then the Regulars and Old Regulars. Even so, one Old Regular–United link was maintained in the correspondence of the Zion United Baptist and Sardis Old Regular Baptist Associations until the late 1920s, when simultaneous pressure from both the United Baptist correspondence cluster led by the Paint Union Association and the Old Regular cluster led by New Salem forced the two to sever relations. Up until that time, too, a small tradition of shape-note harmony singing had been maintained among a few Old Regular churches in the Tug valley, but these congregations affiliated themselves with Zion Association during that particular split and now the only singing tradition known among the Old Regulars is that of "lining the old songs." At the same time, however, the preaching of the Old Regular Baptists awakened in some United Baptists the idea that the Old Regular tradition was more ancient and more conservative and therefore better than their own, and the Old Regulars gained the Kyova and Philadelphia Associations as breakoffs from the Bethlehem and Iron Hill United Baptist Associations respectively. The Philadelphia Association, located in northeastern Kentucky, is still in the New Salem cluster of correspondence, but some years ago the leaders of the Kyova Association, which as its name bespeaks is located in the Kentucky/Ohio/West Virginia tri-state area, got the wild-haired idea that membership in the United Mine Workers of America should be forbidden along with the Masons as a "secret order," and that proved to be a little too much for the union miners of the other Old Regular associations to take. Kyova Association is still extant and independent, but according to Howard Dorgan it has now adopted a communion stance the other Old Regular associations classify as "open," and under such circumstances a reunion is unlikely.[77]

Still, the Old Regulars' interassociation correspondence has been somewhat more stable than that of the United Baptists; rather than fragmenting to the degree the Uniteds have, the Old Regulars exist in two major correspondence clusters with additional minor fragments. The larger is the New Salem cluster, composed of the New Salem, Union, Mud River, Old Friendship, Old Indian Bottom, Sardis, Philadelphia, and Northern New Salem Associations, and the other is built around the Thornton Union Association, a comparatively young group organized in the 1940s from the Union Association by an extremely charismatic moderator named G. Bennett Adams. Thornton Union was once in the New Salem correspondence cluster but was excluded for accusations of "liberal" tendencies including laxity on the hair-length ruling, and subsequently, under the leadership of Elder Wardie Craft, the Thornton Union established correspondence relations not only with the Mountain Association but also the Mt. Zion United Baptist Association (which had been kicked out of the Paint Union United Baptist cluster for similiary petty reasons), and several other fragments of the former New Salem cluster including one sizable faction of the Friendship Association. Craft's idea, which was indeed noble and visionary, was to unite all "Old Baptist" correspondence on the constitutional principles that each church "holds its own keys" and each association should handle its own affairs,[78] but unfortunately he was never able to elevate the ideals of his followers to his own vision. He was very much the Thornton Union's Goodly Fere even as Bennett Adams had been before him, and during his decline of health and after his death the associations he had brought together once again began to fight and to fragment. For a period of time Thornton Union Association elected a new moderator almost every year it met, bitterness increasing while the delegates searched for a replacement in their hearts for Craft, and at this writing the Thornton Union cluster's stability is yet questionable. In fact the New Salem cluster's sentiments toward correspondence and unity are in a state of flux as well; only time will tell if calm is to be established again—if indeed it ever was on a permanent basis.

Needless to say, the Appalachian twist of Graves's and Pendleton's Old Landmarkism has played just as large a hand in the reshaping of the history of this subdenomination within the minds of its members as it has those of the United and Primitive Baptists. Most Old Regulars and indeed many of the Appalachian scholars who have studied them and presented them to the public as the epitome of Appalachian mountain religion actually have no idea of how much the Old Regular Baptists may be identified with the original Separates and how little they truly have in common with those definitely known as Regular Baptists two hundred years ago. And of course, the stability implied, at least, in Old Landmarker philosophy has caused the Old Regulars, like most other Baptist subdenominations bitten by the Landmark bug, to discreetly and conveniently forget the upheavals and compromises in their past history and to present themselves to their adherents as a stable and unchanging unit throughout their existence. By 1912 the ministers of the New Salem Association seem to have forgotten or ignored so much of their history that they actually made the public claim that their heritage was both apostolic and independent of both General and Particular Baptist influence. Although this belief is now called into question within their ranks, their general assumption is still that they and all other American Baptists are descended from the so-called mother of us all, the Philadelphia Association, and from thence in a direct line backward to John the Baptist just like Graves and Pendleton said.[79] This author fully expects to be accused by some Old Regulars (as well as, perhaps, some members of his own denomination and others) of relating a great number of lies, errors, and misrepresentations in this book, but in response he can only quote King Lear's Fool: Truth's a dog must to kennel; he must be whipped out, while the Lady Brach may stand by the fire and stink.

Before the reader sighs once again over the lies told and perpetuated by well-intentioned men and women in the name of truth and purity, the author must state that the 1912 pronouncement (not quoted directly here due to permissions concerns of one of the copyright holders of the 1983 publication of New Salem Association's complete minutes), in spite of the glaring errors given by its Old Landmark slant, actually has a ring of authentic history. If the word *Separate* were used in all cases where *Regular* is employed and the Old Landmark garbage were cleared out of it altogether, one can see that in one way it is actually a pretty fair self-assessment by New Salem Association's leaders of their actual historical and theological heritage. In one more of the Old Regular Baptists' historical ironies, only the two tiniest associations within the New Salem Association's present circle of correspondence and only one in Thornton Union's, the Mud River and Old Friendship Associations in West Virginia in the New Salem circle and the slightly larger Friendship Association in the Thornton Union circle, can even truthfully claim descent from the original Regular Baptists, via the Pocatalico and Elkhorn Primitive Baptist associations that split from the Greenbrier and Teay's Valley Associations in the 1830s and 1840s. All the rest are of virtually pure Separate Baptist descent. In still another irony, one that would no doubt prove extremely disconcerting to the leaders of the New Salem and Union Associations, their neighboring Pike Association of Southern Baptists in Pike and Floyd Counties, Kentucky, can truthfully claim a more direct descent from the old Philadelphia Association than the subdenomination now known as Old Regular Baptist could ever hope for. But this is not to be ashamed of. Their history is much more understandable and compelling when it is examined in the light of their true heritage, and the fact that they are actually *Old Separate Baptists* both in ancestry and in spirit will always be a source of strength to them and their position in central and southern Appalachia.

6. The Mountain Free Will Baptists

The origins of the Free Will Baptists in both northern and southern United States have already been examined in earlier chapters. Neither northern or southern group was a native Appalachian denomination and of course neither can be traced directly to Shubal Stearns, although a good many of his former colleagues in New England joined up with Benjamin Randall when he organized the northern branch of the denomination in 1780. But as the small remnant of Palmerites from the southeastern coast and the Randall organization extended themselves into the Appalachians from eastern North Carolina and Ohio respectively into Kentucky, West Virginia, Tennessee, and Virginia, they came as a response to the needs of Stearns-descended Baptists who had gotten tired of the numerous rules, regulations, and restrictions that their associations and moderators had heaped upon them in the years following the Goodly Fere's death and who were looking for reform. Consequently the history of the Free Will Baptists in Appalachia is inextricably linked with that of Stearns's children in the faith. Although the denomination itself has no early Appalachian heritage, these Baptists of Separate descent took the Free Will Baptist Church, reshaped it to suit their own needs in the mountains, and made it a truly and uniquely Appalachian entity. The author uses the term Mountain Free Will Baptists to classify a distinct subgroup within (and in some cases, without) the denomination's national organization, headquartered in Nashville, Tennessee.

Like other Baptist groups, the National Association of Free Will Baptists puts something of its own spin on its history. Because Paul Palmer was, for a brief period, a member of the historic old Welsh Tract Church in Delaware that was one of the founding churches of the Philadelphia Association, some Free Will historians erroneously argue that their movement began in Wales, but thankfully this is one Baptist subdenomination that has never worried much about or had its perspectives altered by the claims of Old Landmarkism. As noted already, due to the loose, haphazard doctrinal and practical construction Palmer gave his North Carolina flock, only four or five small Palmerite churches resisted the reform efforts of Philadelphia and Charleston missionaries in the early 1750s, and one of these, Grassy Creek, became Separate Baptist under the leadership of Shubal Stearns and Daniel Marshall. From the remainder, mostly under the care initially of Joseph Parker,[80] the southern branch of the denomination slowly grew, and in the process its ranks were augmented more than a little by Separate Baptists who shied away from the quibblings over Calvinistic doctrine and church practice that occurred as Regulars and Separates united in North Carolina. Robert B. Semple believed that Jeremiah Walker joined this Free Will Baptist organization before his death,[81] and there were certainly others who did so. The Free Will Baptist General Conference is said to have been meeting in North Carolina as early as 1807 and to have framed a set of articles of faith in 1812, which came to be called a "treatise" as opposed to a confession or creed.[82] To the west in the North Carolina and eastern Tennessee mountains, the Toe River Association of Free Will Baptists was formed in 1850, possibly from a twenty-year-long quarrel over doctrine in the Holston Association's "daughter" French Broad River Association that was resolved to the dissatisfaction of a minority, disparagingly called "Freewillers," in 1848.[83] Tennessee Free Will historian Robert Picirilli frankly admits that the original Free Will Baptists in this region were rooted in the old Separate Baptist movement and that it is possible that they developed entirely from ex-Separates with no connection to either of the traditionally recognized northern and southern branches of the denomination.[84]

Be that as it may and from wherever Free Will Baptists may claim their origins, the development of the Tennessee Free Wills aptly demonstrates the niche the denomination found in the Appalachians. The French Broad River Association, like its parent Holston group, joined the East Tennessee State Baptist Association and the Southern Baptist Convention, and its development from that time forward demonstrated a concentrated effort on the part of its leaders to mold it to Southern Baptist standards; as with Baptists of Separate descent in this and every other corner of central and southern Appalachia, this move found grassroots resistance as individual clusters of Shubal Stearns's children in the faith strove to maintain the worship practices, the distinctive spirituality, and simply the general feeling and environment of church and association life that they held dear. We have already seen this tendency demonstrated in every group we have examined in this chapter so far, and of course the Primitive Baptists at this same time were already organizing and establishing themselves in east Tennessee, southwestern Virginia, and western North Carolina, as were the "Duck River and Kindred" Associations of the "Baptist Church of Christ" in southern Tennessee, northern Alabama, and northern Georgia. But to the east, for Tennessee Free Wills and indeed every other Appalachian former Separate Baptist group that assumed the denominational name, the operative word in their new title was *free*; not only did they strive to maintain their traditional Appalachian Baptist Christianity, but they sought to free themselves from the problems of inter- and intra-association fights and schisms that Stearns's pattern of government had made a part of their heritage by simply agreeing to disagree with each other on small issues and maintaining their fellowship through open communion. Thus, there were individual points of complaint that the old Goodly Fere probably would have had with their actions and their organization, but he undoubtedly would have loved their worship services.

Another good example of Appalachian Free Will development is the case of the origins of the eastern Kentucky Free Wills, and here some specific details of the Free Will reform can be examined. The Paint Union Association of United Baptists in eastern Kentucky at this writing exists in four shrinking fragments: Paint Union, Old Paint Union, Original Old Paint Union, and "United" Associations, the formations of all of which were the results of splits over nitpicky issues and petty personality clashes in the worst spirit of ex-Separate Baptist tradition. The four factions are not much different in doctrine, polity and spirit from one another, but they adamantly refuse to try to regroup. But in the mid-1870s and for many years thereafter Paint Union was the leader of a large cluster of United Baptist correspondence throughout the Kentucky/West Virginia border area. At this time, too, Paint Union was much more liberal than it would later become, some of its ministers preaching regularly in revival meetings with the pastors of local Methodist classes and the few Southern Baptist congregations nearby, and, in the case of one minister of which this author has learned (his great-great-grandfather, incidentally; the tendency to astigmatism where denominational names are concerned may be hereditary), with preachers of the Campbell Reform as well. There were even a few scattered Sunday schools in the association and its correspondents, though all four Paint Union factions at present preach against this institution. Still, despite the revivals with other denominations, which were almost always extremely successful, Paint Union as a whole maintained its stance on the old Baptist custom of close communion as it had developed over time, first in the Kentucky General Union and later in the United Baptists as that denomination had asserted its existence at the 1830 Lulbegrud and Goshen council meetings in the North District Association: communion and foot washing were only to be shared by members, churches, and associations that were in direct letter correspondence with one another. Since the 1830s, Burning Springs, New Salem, Paint Union, and the correspondence clusters they headed had not offered the sacraments to immersed Methodists, Reformers, or even in most cases Southern Baptists, and after the United Baptists began to fragment into Primitive and Old Regular factions, the three associations and their clusters no longer communed with each other either. The old Baptist principle of communion closed simply to those not baptized by immersion, though well documented in the writings of eighteenth-century Baptist ministers of both Regular and Separate stamp, seemed to have been long since forgotten.

A sizable number of members at the Tom's Creek United Baptist Church at present Tutor Key in Johnson County, Kentucky, one of Paint Union's oldest and at the time largest churches, saw this state of affairs as wrong. Very probably some others in the association (and certainly in its correspondents, as one of them, Bethlehem, split in 1882 over the communion issue) did as well, but took the politically prudent course of action of remaining quiet about it. The Tom's Creek faction, however, whose spokesman was a preacher named Eliphas VanHoose, was extremely vocal. Finally in 1875, because of the members' advocacy of open communion and probably due to pressure from the association as well (an order reiterating the association's stance on close communion and advising churches to exclude members who persisted in practicing it was passed by Paint Union that autumn), Tom's Creek Church excommunicated them, and they built a meetinghouse some miles up Tom's Creek from the older church and began holding services on their own. Local legend has it that at first this congregation tried to join the Paint Union Association but were refused because they were excommunicates from Tom's Creek Church. Even after this rebuff, they were not willing to try to maintain themselves as an independent church, but began to search for a group that practiced open communion and foot washing and preached general-atonement doctrine with which to ally themselves.

One wonders how eastern Kentucky's religious history might have been altered if the VanHoose group had been aware of the Separate Baptists in Christ in the south central portion of the state who had just that year implemented a decree that they had no right to bar any of God's children from the communion table, and had sought an affiliation perhaps with the South Kentucky or East Kentucky Associations. As it had happened, though, the flatlands and knobs of the central Bluegrass and Pennyroyal regions of the state had become almost a foreign country to eastern Kentuckians, and the VanHoose group found the affiliation they were looking for in the Ohio Yearly Meeting of Free Will Baptists,[85] part of the northern Randall group that had been a presence in the southern portion of that state since 1833. One William Calhoun was sent to pastor the new congregation, now calling itself the Tom's Creek Free Will Baptist Church, but characteristically, the eastern Kentuckians rapidly took their new denomination and made it their own. The leaders of the Ohio Yearly Meeting watched their new charges bring with them all the fire and fervor of New Birth preaching and the musical chant of the New England Holy Tone, which their own oldest preachers had all but forgotten since the end of the Great Awakening, and add to it Free Will inclusiveness and tolerance for small differences that made the eastern Kentucky Free Will Baptists a great power in their home region almost from the first. By 1879 enough new congregations in both Johnson and Lawrence Counties had grown from Tom's Creek's labors for the Ohio Meeting to form the Johnson County Quarterly Meeting as a subdivision of its own organization.

Since the schism between United Baptists and those who would become known as Old Regulars, there had arisen a sort of dividing line between United and Old Regular Baptist territories about halfway up the Levisa Fork of the Big Sandy River in Floyd County; correspondence between the Zion United and Sardis Old Regular Associations, as long as it lasted, softened the demarcation more in the Tug valley. The principle of close communion as interpreted by these Baptists had rapidly made them lose much contact with one another; ministers and members south of the line were becoming foreign to those north of it, an inevitable byproduct of the divisions the two groups had experienced. Of course, the growing number of young Free Will Baptist preachers recognized no such dividing line, or for that matter most of the issues that had wedged divisions among Appalachian Baptists in the first place including "alien immersion," "double marriage," Sunday schools, and the use of musical instruments in worship. As the Chesapeake and Ohio and Norfolk and Western Railroads laid track up both forks of Big Sandy, beginning in the 1880s, to accommodate the region's new and booming coal industry and the maintenance of company towns northern coal interests had built around their mines, the eastern Kentucky Free Wills—whose ministers, in Stearns tradition and like their neighboring United and Old Regular ministers, still took no pay for their services, and a great many supported themselves as miners—simply followed the trains upriver beginning at the railroad hub of Louisa in Lawrence County, Kentucky, and preached as they went. At the same time, of course, representatives of the growing coal interests imported their own Methodist, Baptist, Disciple, and other mainline denominational ministers and organized their own "company" churches, ostensibly for their workers' benefit. But among the workers and their families in general, their native United, Old Regular, Primitive, and of course Free Will preachers were by far the more popular and the more trustworthy to defend the miners' rights in the face of pious Christian businessmen who were wont to tell the miners coal dust was good for their lungs because it helped ward off colds. After many of these mainline ministers packed up and left the region, usually in tow of company officials abandoning towns after all the coal had been worked out around them, the Free Wills would reorganize congregations of those left behind, in meetinghouses the company men had built originally for their own faiths. Thus the Free Will Baptists became "The Miners' Church"[86] in the Levisa and Tug valleys, and in the heyday of the coal companies' presence in the region, Millard VanHoose, son of Tom's Creek's old open-communion spokesman and a preacher himself from the days of his youth until well into his ninth decade, was probably the closest thing to a Shubal Stearns figure that the eastern Kentucky Free Will Baptists ever had.

The Mountain Free Will Baptists (the author's classification of Appalachia's older Free Will exponents will be explained in more detail in a moment) provided a dose of moderation to Appalachian Baptist church life at a time one was desperately needed, in light of the fragmentation of the region's older native Baptist groups over what they considered the correct interpretations of the traditions of the Old Brethren. The philosophy of the founding ministers and members of the large Enterprise Association of Regular Baptists, noted beforehand as a split from the old Burning Springs group, owed much to Free Will influence, as did a shift toward moderate positions among several of the region's United and Progressive Primitive Baptist associations. Even so, Free Will influence made other United, Old Regular, and Primitive groups all the more vocally reactionary, and to this day there is bad blood between these reactionary groups and the Free Wills and those influenced by them—perhaps made worse by the fact that Free Will Baptist churches have often been the haven of those excluded from reactionary groups, as well as the church of choice for the sons and daughters of many reactionary members.

Like all other Baptists, though, the Free Wills and especially their mountain exponents have had their problems, and in good Stearns fashion most of these difficulties have occurred at the quarterly meeting and association level rather than in individual churches—or at least have been initiated at those levels before being introduced into the congregations. During the nineteenth century and the first decade of the twentieth, the northern Randall branch of the Free Will Baptist denomination, of which eastern Kentucky and West Virginia Free Wills were all a part, was headed by a General Conference composed of Yearly Meetings or associations, which were in turn composed of Quarterly Meetings or conferences. In 1910–1911, the great majority of northern Yearly Meetings in the General Conference opted for a merger with the mainline Northern Baptist Convention, at the time that region's equivalent of the Southern Baptist Convention and now known as the American Baptist Churches in the United States. In the process, the Randall branch of the Free Will denomination was decimated, but there remained a few Randall Free Wills who wished to retain independence from the Northern Baptists and to maintain their name and organization. Of this contingent, one of the most tenacious groups was that of the eastern Kentuckians and West Virginians who joined with the small remnant of southern Ohio Free Wills and organized their own Tri-State Yearly Meeting in 1919. As the Free Wills kept gaining ground, the individual Kentucky, West Virginia, and Ohio State Associations were organized from the older Tri-State Yearly Meeting; in the meantime and as more state associations came into being, contact was increasingly maintained between the Randall remnant and the southern branch of the denomination represented by the North Carolina and Tennessee Free Wills as well as states farther south. The northern and southern branches united to form the National Association of Free Will Baptists in Nashville, Tennessee, in 1935. So far so good, but once this level of organization was reached many of the state associations began to exhibit all of the tendency for central control over individual quarterly meetings or conferences shown by Shubal Stearns over his Sandy Creek Association two centuries beforehand. In turn the quarterly meetings began to try to exercise a similar control over the churches, in both cases using the modern twentieth-century style: not with one or more personable leaders who knew and loved everyone in their flocks and were known and loved in return, but with groups of oligarchs representing the monolithic institutions of the regional conference bodies and state associations.

It is difficult to assess just how much influence the National Association exercised over this tendency. In possibly the best-known case of power usurpation in Free Will Baptist history, a group of ministers leading the Western Conference of North Carolina Free Wills became deeply entangled in litigation involving a church that had split to factions in 1958; they recognized the minority party of the split over the majority as the legitimate faction of the church in question and then proceeded to try to help that minority gain legal title to and control over the church property. One of the documents used in court was an affadavit signed by these ministers claiming that "original" Free Will Baptist churches were not governed by majority rule but by a "connectional" form of government in which the rule of higher bodies superseded the rights of individual churches, in essence the same philosophy of power transference from churches to associations that Shubal Stearns learned from the New England General Baptists and on which Morgan Edwards heaped such scorn among the Separate Baptists in 1772. The North Carolina State Convention of Free Will Baptists supported the Western Conference ministers, but the National Association promptly removed from office in its own body the men who had signed the affadavit and requested that the North Carolina State Convention "repudiate any and all forms of connectional church government at its next session and reaffirm the position of our historical and established form of congregational church government."[87] Here the National Association appeared to be exercising the same checks-and-balances control for church protection envisioned by the Virginia United Baptists in their General Committee at the time of the Baptist union in 1787. But instead of complying, the North Carolina State Convention simply severed its fellowship with the National Association to style themselves as "Original" Free Will Baptists. Those North Carolina Free Wills who wished to remain connected to the national body were forced to form a new organization. The majority faction of the church in the center of the controversy, though, won its court case and was one of the first member churches of the newer North Carolina State Association affiliated with the national body.

On the other hand, in 1946 the Kentucky State Association—at the time composed of the central Appalachia-oriented Johnson, Lawrence, Floyd, Pike, Boyd, and possibly Letcher County Conferences but growing in areas that would soon include the non-Appalachian Blue Grass, Kosciusko (Indiana), Northern Ohio, and Green River Conferences as well as others—had passed a resolution to "withdraw" from any of its conferences "that uphold any minister or member who openly *or* indirectly opposes *any* work of faith which is adopted and practiced by the Kentucky State Association of Free Will Baptists" [emphasis added].[88] The broad language of this measure, which may have been taken in part to keep proselyted Free Will preachers of United, Primitive, and Old Regular Baptist backgrounds from preaching some of their former beliefs in Free Will churches and in that sense did contain some practical good for the group, makes it appear to be a harsh threat of excommunication for independent thinkers of any stamp. As such, it was an odd measure to be taken by a body supposedly founded upon the principle of open communion and certainly in direct contradiction to the philosophy of mutual tolerance over small matters that had been the catalyst for the Free Wills' rise to power in the mountains in the first place. In spite of the later stance it would take against the North Carolinans, the National Association evidently heartily approved of this resolution and very probably encouraged its introduction to the State Association's agenda. To be sure, the 1946 resolution caused no immediate difficulties for any Free Will church in either eastern or central Kentucky and probably few if any for the ministers who cared for them; but it must be remembered that its language was broad and inclusive and the outook reflected in its wording, shared or not by national, state, or local quarterly meeting officials, would have far-reaching consequences for Mountain Free Will churches and ministers.

For the specter of connectionalism still looms large over the Free Will Baptist denomination as a whole, or at least that part still affiliated with the National Association, and in the fifty-four-year interim between the 1946 Kentucky State Association resolution and this writing many of the the so-called works of faith endorsed by both that body and the National Association have more often than not put them at loggerheads with the Appalachian contingent that they no longer seem to recognize as one of their most important bases. Perhaps understandably, the National Association has come to live up to its name, as a national rather than a regional denomination, and, just like the Methodists, the Free Will Baptists at the national level have for several years de-emphasized and even ridiculed the native practices of their rural southeastern contingent as ignorance-based and detrimental to the national denomination's goals. Sadly, "shouting" Methodists of the type with which the United Baptists used to share revivals in the Appalachians are very nearly a thing of the past, if not completely extinct. The Mountain Free Wills, that portion of the denomination that still clings to traditional central Appalachian religious beliefs and worship practices, are of course still very much alive and active, but they are shrinking in number due to the persistent influence of the National Association to woo ministers, especially church pastors, and members away from the past and toward the goals of the denomination as its leaders perceive them. The author has heard ministers imported from Nashville to the mountains to pastor churches and/or spearhead various denominational goals within local quarterly conferences discourage the use of the New England Holy Tone among younger and even older ministers as foolish, superstition-based, and very nearly pagan, scathingly referring to the cherished mode of pulpit address as "the hillbilly hum" and "the preacher's bark." In many rural Appalachian conferences they and their local supporters have succeeded, if not in stamping out the use of the Tone entirely, at least in influencing their younger ministers to make themselves sound like someone they might hear on Trinity Broadcasting and thereby be accepted as keeping with current fashion. Admittedly, though, nowadays many young country preachers need little urging to adopt mannerisms they see on national religious broadcast networks, just as the young Separate preachers of the Carolina Piedmont two hundred years ago needed no prodding to try to sound like their beloved Goodly Fere. What once was fashion is now tradition; new fashions of today may make old traditions of tomorrow, if indeed the concept of tradition can survive in this day and age.

Along with the their efforts to change the pulpit mode of the mountains, the representatives of the National Association and their wheelhorses also seem to have produced a reassessment within some Appalachian Free Will Baptist circles of the traditional concept of the New Birth in Christ. The idea of patiently waiting on and praying with a penitent individual until he or she gives a voluntary and assured confession of heartfelt inner peace, whether accompanied by tears and/or shouts of joy or not, seems to have been grouped within some churches and conferences in the same category of anachronisms and superstitions as the New England Holy Tone. Going to an extreme of Arminianism actually very probably very like that which Paul Palmer must have preached on the North Carolina coast in the days before the Great Awakening, more than a few "progressive" Free Will ministers preach salvation as belief by nothing more than a conscious rational choice followed by an oral confession, and though this has become essentially standard mainline Protestant fare, it can achieve results simultaneously amusing and extremely disturbing when thrown into the pot of traditional Appalachian culture in which both local ministers and members have been raised. The author has known of many cases of penitents being peppered with relentless, frantic, staccato questions when they made nervous but positive responses to prayer invitations ("Do you believe? Do you believe? If you believe all you have to do is confess it with your mouth"), and in other cases being physically pulled up from altars of prayer with impatient words on the order of "Get up, you're all right now"—actions that the original Appalachian Free Wills would have considered, and the true Mountain Free Wills yet believe, to be reprehensible. As a side note, foot washing as well may be becoming another anachronism in progressive circles, even though the *Treatise on the Faith and Practice of the Original Free Will Baptists* (the Free Will equivalent of the Philadelphia Confession, published by the National Association's Randall House Publications and often mispronounced by rural Appalachian Free Will ministers as "The Treaty") still commands that the rite be maintained. Some "progressive" churches try to temper the custom to their ministers' and congregations' modern sensibilities by staging it in conjunction with an "Old Fashioned Day" in which all wear overalls, straw hats, long gingham dresses, and bonnets to church, a further reinforcement of the idea that the custom is obsolete.

Overlaying the whole, the National Association has of course embraced a long-term goal of attaining a formally educated and paid ministry as the standard for Free Will church pastors generally, New England Holy Tone and New Birth in Christ or not, and this too has had a great effect on the local conferences, some protagonistic and others extremely antagonistic. The Free Will Baptist Bible College in Nashville (the author does not know whether the denomination boasts a graduate theological seminary yet, but there was some talk of trying to establish one a few years ago) seems willing to offer off-campus classes within any local conference agreeing to finance a professor and a building to serve as a branch campus, and it is by this means that some of the more notable "Nashville imports" have come to the hills. In truth if the concept of money tithing is carefully studied with Scriptural references, it becomes an extremely debatable point both in Old and New Testaments; the entire law of the tithe as referred to in the Pentateuch involves a tither keeping back a tenth of the increase of his corn, wine, oil, and other produce, taking it to the house of God with him at specified times and then actually eating his own tithe himself with his family in a meal of thanksgiving. The only times the Levites were supposed to get their hands on any of these produce tithes were at the tables of these family feasts and every third year when they had to share it with widows and orphans.[89] All other Scriptural references to tithing are built around this Mosaic law, and as such tithing can be preached as an allegory of working and "saving" for the Lord during the week and eating and sharing the spiritual fruits with gladness in church on Sunday, with as much or greater validity than the established mainline Protestant tradition of money tithing for, among other things, paying the pastor. Yet "The Treaty" categorically states that this mainline Protestant concept is commanded in both Old and New Testaments, and it is maintained most vociferously in this context by those who come to the hills from Nashville. Being Arminians, some of them even stress that one must pay his or her tithes to maintain a state of grace and salvation, and arguments with "The Treaty" are not tolerated, although blind acceptance of any such creed—as Shubal Stearns and the Separate Baptists knew and proclaimed long ago—creates a mental and spiritual vacuity all its own. As a result, the number of tithe-collecting and pastor-paying Appalachian Free Will churches who demand preachers with at least a little formal Nashville training is on a steady increase, though this increase is accompanied by a good deal of resentment, often silent in the face of conference political pressure but sometimes not, within the traditionally oriented local churches.

Still, the National Association of Free Will Baptists has other notable differences from other mainline Protestant organizations. The true muscle and political strength that binds the denomination together is not in the head office or even at the state-association level but in the connectionalism of the local quarterly meetings, where power is exercised by the eight or ten (or in some cases, fewer) ministers within each quarterly meeting who control the committees that actually perform and oversee the conference's work. Free Will Baptists customarily do not ordain ministers in local churches but delegate that authority to the conferences; here licensing and ordination examinations, which nowadays can be both written and oral, take place in private with the candidates and the conference's "ordination committee" rather than in a public forum, and the committee members pretty much have free rein as to their treatment of candidates with reasonably good expectations that their report on each individual will be accepted without question by the business assembly of the conference. The attitude of this committee as a whole (or its at least its majority faction) towards the policies of the state and national associations and the dogmas contained in "The Treaty" essentially determines the entire outlook of an individual local quarterly meeting, and pressure on candidates for licensing and ordination to "line up" with whatever policies the committee endorses, with repeated refusals to ordain politically recalcitrant candidates or those hailing from recalcitrant churches, is probably the most powerful political tool the leaders of the conferences employ. The "business committee" of a conference is often very powerful in its own right as well. Customarily its members have, or at least exercise, the right to summarily dismiss any request or query sent by any church without airing the matter before the main business assembly of the conference and with no explanations required. Conversely, matters they deem important to the conference's agenda are introduced and stressed, and often rubber-stamped by the body. Under this connectional system "Mainline," "Mountain," and, to borrow Spencer's term, "Go-between" Free Will Baptist quarterly meetings exist in the Appalachians, and though ideologies may differ markedly from conference to conference, the manner in which they are maintained is very much the same.

To conclude, then, the Free Will Baptist denomination is in a transitional state, and although the time of the resolution of all its conflicts cannot be predicted with any certainty, when the day of stability comes, the odds seem to be stacked in favor of National Association ideals. There are, however, a few Free Will organizations in the mountains who have severed their ties with state and national bodies to exist independently, and the number of independent Free Will local churches is also on the increase despite the pontifications one often hears at National-affiliated quarterly conferences that "there is no such thing as an independent Free Will Baptist church." In Kentucky, the Pike County and, apparently, Letcher County Quarterly Meetings dropped their affiliation with the Kentucky State and National Associations long ago, and the churches in that area who wished to retain their state and national connections formed the Big Sandy Valley Conference.[90] The author has been informed by some Free Will ministers connected with State Association–oriented conferences that the Pike County Conference was a "renegade" group that left the State Association over the question of ordaining "double-married" ministers, but without either endorsing the "renegade" accusation or entering into debate over that particular question, it may be safely hypothesized that the Pike County leaders had other reasons, based in traditional concepts of worship, for leaving as well. The author has preached in times past in both Pike County and Big Sandy Valley Conference churches, and the difference in atmosphere is indeed palpable.

Some of these like-minded Mountain Free Will quarterly meetings, perhaps Pike and Letcher included, have in fact joined the only non-"Original" Free Will multi-conference association of which the author is aware that is not affiliated with the national body: the John-Thomas Association of Free Will Baptists, organized about 1921 or 1922 in southwestern Virginia and composed of churches in both Kentucky and Virginia as well as Appalachian outmigrant enclaves in Ohio and Indiana. In 1981 it boasted ninety-nine churches and 7,483 members.[91] Another similar group that has altered its name slightly is the Free Baptist Church, based in the Lawrence County, Kentucky/Wayne County, West Virginia, border area and composed of several congregations, and there are undoubtedly more like-minded Free Will offshoots as well. Besides these, the ranks of other native Appalachian denominations such as the moderate United and "Enterprise" Regular Baptists are periodically and perhaps even regularly strengthened in a small way by new members having departed the "Mainline" Free Wills, on occasion including very able ministers who have not been able to pass political muster at churches and/or quarterly conferences. Times have indeed changed; in the Appalachia of yesteryear, even as little as a quarter century ago as of this writing, this membership flux was going in exactly the opposite direction.

And yet even with the majority faction of Free Will churches that retain their connection with the National Association, one still thinks wryly of the proverb that the boy may be taken out of the country, but that doesn't mean that the country is taken out of the boy. Some years ago a congregation near the author's locality, one of the oldest Free Will Baptist churches in one of the oldest conferences in Appalachia in fact, asked for and was granted the privilege of hosting the annual Kentucky State Association, and a great crowd from all over the Bluegrass State and beyond descended on the church to participate in the event. Prominent at the first day's proceedings, which of course began with a worship service, was a Nashville minister who had been working for some time with churches in the vicinity and had actually gained some ground for National Association ideals and goals, as well as a stirring up a little ire, in the area; and when the delegates from the mountain conferences and many local members began showing their Stearns roots a little too loudly and a little too long to suit him, he stood up in the pulpit, impatiently waved his hand and loudly exclaimed, "Now, that's enough of that! We need to get down to business!" One would be hard put to find an occasion when a crowd became disenchanted with one individual quite so quickly and were still able to retain their religion and their manners; there but for the grace of God the minister might have been tarred and feathered. As it was he departed the hills for greener pastures and better fields of labor shortly thereafter, and the shouting of the children of the Goodly Fere continued—and still continues.

7. The Church of God (Cleveland, Tennessee) and its Offshoots

Though the author has not grouped the present-day Southern Baptists in this classification of the spiritual descendants of Shubal Stearns, it must be remembered that the denomination—at present considered to be the largest in the United States—would never have developed and progressed as it did without its Separate Baptist base. As a matter of fact, in his *Giving Glory to God in Appalachia,* Howard Dorgan tells of a few Southern Baptist churches in western North Carolina whose Separate roots are still very much visible, as well as independent "Missionary Baptist" (an old Appalachian name for Southern Baptist) congregations of identical makeup that have left the SBC's fold.[92] Besides these, it would appear that the western North Carolina/east Tennessee border area has more Southern Baptist churches and associations that retain their old title of United Baptist along with their SBC connection than is common for most other localities. Still, these are the exception rather than the rule for Southern Baptists generally, and in this section the author must be content with the hope that he has already given an adequate presentation in earlier chapters of how the Southern Baptists came to be formed from both Regular and Separate Baptist branches. Even so, considering the megalithic structure of the Southern Baptist Convention (to which Southern Baptist churches belong individually in addition to whatever local association affiliations they may maintain), the group's general embrace of Old Landmarkism as a very happy thought if not as accurate history, the politicking that has gone on at annual SBC meetings to produce some of the group's more recent pronouncements, and the typical Southern Baptist mind-set that whatever is Southern Baptist is good, one is tempted to speculate that one day history may come full circle with the assumption of power by an ultracharismatic SBC leader and that the Convention might truly assume its place in history as the largest heir of them all to the Sandy Creek Association. If such an event should occur, we must hope that the man of the hour is as kind and loving as Shubal Stearns but a bit wiser and more introspective, for he will have the potential and the opportunity to do a great deal of damage.

Here, though, our purpose is to discuss one more notable "family" of spiritual descendants of Shubal Stearns whose history merits attention, one that was born from a schism in a Southern-affiliated "United Missionary" Baptist church on the North Carolina/Tennessee border and that actually did grow into a national denomination under the direction of just such a charismatic leader: that of the Church of God (Cleveland, Tennessee) and its offshoots. The Church of God is considered by many to be the best-known national denomination with obvious roots in Appalachia and is perhaps accurately referred to by Deborah McCauley as "Appalachia for Export."[93]

In fact, McCauley's treatment of the origins of the Church of God and its offshoots in her *Appalachian Mountain Religion: A History* is so comprehensive and sympathetic that little else needs to be added to it, save the obvious and verifiable connection to the work, and the personality, of Shubal Stearns. The movement began in 1886 with an elder in the Holly Springs United Missionary Baptist Church at Turtletown, Tennessee, near both the North Carolina and Georgia borders, who had become disenchanted with the exclusivity his church and his denomination had assumed on accepting Old Landmark principles. A seventy-six-year-old preacher who had seen the Baptists come a long way since the days of his youth in eastern Tennessee, Richard Spurling initiated a society known as the Christian Union that met regularly in a small room attached to the gristmill by which he made his living. In McCauley's words, his purpose was "to give priority to the liberty of conscience of all of [the Christian Union's] members, thus returning to the full tradition of consensus-based, Holy-Spirit guided, priesthood-of-all-believers, free church polity that had shaped the church life of his Separate Baptist ancestors who had united with the Regular Baptists in Virginia in 1787."[94] Despite the fact that the personal influence of Stearns himself as well as all the rural mini-Stearnses who had come after him makes McCauley's assertion about the "free church polity" of the Separate Baptists open to question to a certain extent, in general she is undoubtedly correct, and Spurling's action was one more in a long series of attempts by Appalachian Christians to return to the spirit and the preaching of the Old Brethren. Though Spurling himself soon returned to Holly Springs Church and was restored to fellowship and preaching priviliges, his action possibly helping the "United Missionary" Baptist congregation soften its stance on Old Landmarkism somewhat, his preacher son Richard G. ("Green") Spurling remained independent and kept the Christian Union alive for about a decade essentially on Separate Baptist–based principles and interpretations of Scripture.

In 1896 Green Spurling began to work with William F. Bryant,

William Martin, and others of Cherokee County, North Carolina, who at the time were just beginning an independent movement of their own based on both Separate Baptist and Methodist principles. Bryant had fallen under the influence of Martin, a Methodist (not an ordained minister, though perhaps a "lay reader") who was preaching an extension of the old Wesleyan doctrine of sanctification as well as glossolalia, or the speaking of unknown tongues, as evidence of baptism by the Holy Ghost; in turn Martin himself had been heavily influenced by the preaching of Benjamin Irwin, a Pentecostal minister from the Midwest who had come into the mountains as an itinerant evangelist and had departed after initiating a successful revival. Martin defined sanctification as a life completely above sin in this present world and preached it as a second work of grace after salvation, the "baptism of the Holy Ghost"—that is, the ability to speak in unknown tongues—being a third work. Bryant's Baptist church taught the Separate principles that an individual was baptized in the Holy Ghost the moment he or she received the New Birth in Christ and that sanctification was the process by which a Christian grew in faith and knowledge of the Gospel, the individual never living above temptation to sin but always depending on the grace of God through Christ. They excluded Bryant and twenty-eight of his followers between 1896 and 1900 for "claiming that [they] were living free from sin." Bryant himself was excluded in 1899.[95] In the meantime, in Bryant's blunt words, Green Spurling's Christian Union had "went dead" in spite of Bryant's joining him occasionally to preach there,[96] and so Spurling, Bryant, another excluded Baptist preacher named Frank Porter, and M.S. Lemons, a former schoolteacher from Cleveland, Tennessee, and an early convert, continued holding meetings on their own with Martin's and others' help. Preaching in revivals and Methodist-style camp meetings almost continuously and making numerous converts to their combination of Separate Baptist and Wesleyan Methodist views and practices that soon received its own distinctive title of "Holiness," they finally formally organized the Holiness Church on Camp Creek in May 1902— roughly four years before the work of former Methodist William Joseph Seymour at the Asuza Street Mission in Los Angeles, who espoused essentially the same doctrines, would trigger the nationwide, and now nearly worldwide, Pentecostal movement.

There are some interesting parallels to be observed between the beginnings of Shubal Stearns's Sandy Creek Association in the pre-Revolutionary Carolina Piedmont and the later establishment of its descendant

Church of God in Tennessee. Exactly as the Separate Baptist movement was born with Valentine Wightman, Wait Palmer, Shubal Stearns, and others in New England, Spurling, Bryant, and their colleagues mixed established religious traditions of varying sects in their homeland and fused them with a spirit, and the phenomena, of religious revival to make a seemingly new entity. Just as Stearns's impressions of a great and extensive work waiting on him in "the west" must have been influenced by Joseph and Priscilla Breed's and then Daniel and Martha Marshall's earlier emigrations to Berkeley County, Virginia, causing him to lead nearly his entire family of wife, parents, brothers, sisters, nieces, and nephews to join them in the Shenandoah basin, so were Green Spurling and the remnant of his and his father's Christian Union drawn together to work with W.F. Bryant and "Billy" Martin, as much a visible result of time and chance as divine providence. Likewise, even as at first Stearns's "great work in the west" landed his clan in the wilderness of Hampshire County, Virginia, with virtually no neighbors whatsoever to preach to and convert, so the combined Spurling/Bryant movement remained very much a local one in its own little corner of the North Carolina/Tennessee/Georgia border. Neither group probably would have ever become more than obscure footnotes in local history had they not both experienced a catalyst to spur them to wider action. But here the similarity between the Stearns and Spurling/Bryant movements becomes almost eerie. For, just as the Maryland Quaker Herman Husbands must have talked Stearns and his family into settling on his North Carolina Piedmont lands in the hope of using them to bring about his own "Inner Light" induced vision of a New Jerusalem in the American backwoods, setting the stage for all that would follow until Stearns's own tragic death, so did an Indiana Quaker, A.J. Tomlinson, meet up with Bryant and Spurling, take control of their religious movement and make it the national and international entity that it is—all the while professing the reception of a characteristically Quaker, "Inner Light" induced divine revelation in which he claimed God Himself commanded him to do so.

Tomlinson came to the mountains in the first place as a home missionary and Bible distributor for the American Tract and American Bible Societies, representing northeastern interests making it their business to convert the supposedly benighted heathen of the Appalachians to Christianity. He first met W.F. Bryant in 1899 and Green Spurling not long thereafter, and although he came to the hills to save, he wound up being saved, as it were, himself. He was charmed with the work of Spurling,

Bryant, and their colleagues and evidently quickly became an active participant in both preaching and worship with them (though Bryant later said, with characteristic Appalachian self-deprecation, "Like myself, at that time he wasn't much of a preacher—you see, he had been a Quaker"[97]), but initially he was strenuously opposed to the formal organization of their first Holiness church. Apparently Tomlinson returned to Indiana from his home mission excursion and wrote back to Bryant from there reiterating his objections to the congregation's formal organization, and although Bryant himself had entertained some reservations himself due to the "confusion" he had seen both Baptists and Methodists experience as a result of their own structures, by 1902 he was in favor of organization and he and Green Spurling were "standing shoulder to shoulder" in agreement on the issue.[98] The Holiness Church on Camp Creek was thus duly organized in Tomlinson's absence, and the next summer he came back, perhaps with his family—if his wife and children had not been living with him during his Home Mission, certainly they joined him soon after—still objecting to its organization. As Bryant's houseguest, Tomlinson continued to state his objections and fears of formal organization, but seeing that Bryant was unmoved he stated that he wished to spend the night in prayer on the hill above Bryant's house, and Bryant promised him that when he was finished praying that his breakfast would be ready. The next morning—a Sunday, June 13, 1903—he returned from the hill in a state of joy approaching ecstacy, informing Bryant that he knew now that "the church is right" and that he intended to offer himself as a candidate for membership that day.[99]

Later, Tomlinson claimed that he had gotten a revelation from God that early morning on the hill at the end of his all-night prayer, in which God "revealed" the "True Church" to him and promised, or perhaps rather commanded him, that he was to be its "leader for life." Be that as it may, Tomlinson was not only accepted as a member but ordained as a minister and installed as pastor of the Camp Creek Holiness Church that day. McCauley believes that Spurling and Bryant ordained him and set him in as pastor of the church for, more than any other reason, the purpose of freeing them to continue their own itinerant evangelistic work. But for whatever reason, take the helm of the movement he did and with a vengeance. While Spurling, Bryant, Porter, Lemons, and their increasing number of ministerial colleagues preached, baptized converts, and "set churches in order" in the North Carolina/Tennessee/Georgia area,

Tomlinson moved to the valley town of Cleveland, Tennessee, and organized the growing number of churches into a General Assembly that first met there in January 1906, calling itself the Church of God. He also took a leaf from Alexander Campbell's notebook and established a periodical even before leaving for Cleveland. As soon as he was able to do so, he introduced his sons Homer and Milton to the work as preachers and leaders as well, and they gradually built an episcopal organization similar to that of the Methodists and installed Spurling, and evidently also Bryant, as bishops. The addition of the name of the town in which the denomination was headquartered to its title was the result of a similar Pentecostal/Holiness movement springing up in Anderson, Indiana, and likewise taking the name of Church of God.

But from the first, there were problems with Tomlinson's leadership role, especially felt by Spurling, Bryant, and M.S. Lemons. From their first days of preaching together in the Holiness movement, these "old hands" had experienced persecution not unlike that suffered by the Separate Baptists in pre-Revolutionary Virginia and perhaps the Campbell Reformers in antebellum Kentucky, though the latter situation might have involved as much give as take. But in the case of the Holiness preachers, the adherents of the older denominations rather than the legal authorities were cast in the role of persecutors. It is difficult to tell now just how much actual persecution the Holiness revivalists were actually subjected to, though it is probable that the most frequent charge levied against them, like the Virginia Separates before them, was disturbing the peace. But just like Herman Husbands in his conduct with the Regulators between 1768 and 1771, Tomlinson would run rather than maintain the ground he had stated he stood on. W.F. Bryant's wife Nettie told an interviwer years later that in these early days, "Brother Tomlinson was in and out. He would get scared out and go back to Culberson [North Carolina] twelve miles away where they were not fighting them."[100] Even so, M.S. Lemons later stated that they all felt that "the Lord had put [Tomlinson] in" as leader, perhaps more than any other reason for his degree of literacy that the mountain preachers (Lemons, a former schoolmaster, perhaps excepted) could not match.

The decade of 1910–1920 was a period of rapid growth for the Church of God as small and large Holiness movements swept across the different areas of the United States generally. It expanded up into Virginia and Kentucky and down through the states of the Old South, its growing cadre of preachers bringing sanctificationist and Holiness doctrine to new areas through tent meetings and other evangelistic endeavors overseen by the ever-centralizing head office of the denomination in Cleveland. In these years, W.F. Bryant, who, in spite of his reservations was still extremely attached to Tomlinson, moved to Cleveland from the mountains as well, but Green Spurling never left the hills except only rarely to preach for denominational functions, where his continuing rusticity gave ever-increasing embarrassment to the denomination's ostensible leader for life.

Especially in the period 1910–1914, the structure of the Church of God changed and was molded under Tomlinson's hand. McCauley records these brief and to-the-point observations from church historian Wade Phillips:

> Even the early "General Assemblies" were more or less fashioned according to Baptist association meetings and purposes. The local churches were still considered independent, and Assembly decisions and recommendations were held to be only advisory and informational. Everything—including missions—fell back to the local churches as a matter of principle. Not until A.J. Tomlinson gained preeminence in the organization (1910–1914) did changes begin to occur that little by little transformed the churches of God from Baptist-type independent republics into an authoritative and highly centralized episcopal system.
> ... Thus, through Tomlinson, primarily, the original Baptist-type concept of an Associational Moderator metamorphosed from 1906–1914 into the popish-type office of General Overseer; the Baptist practice of the Introductory Sermon was institutionalized in the prestigious Annual Address; committees became static authoritative councils, and councils ecclesiastical tyrannies; Pastors, once called by the churches (in the tradition of the Baptists), were soon appointed by the General Overseer, and later by state overseers when that office was created. As this episcopal hierarchy was little by little built down from the office of General Overseer, commensurately, the Baptist roots and legacy in the Church of God disappeared.[101]

Of course, we can see that the Church of God did not entirely depart *all* its Separate Baptist roots; after all, Tomlinson seems to have been accepted as a Goodly Fere figure would have been by Bryant,

Spurling, Lemons, and the other early Holiness ministers, and this was of course in keeping with their heritage as well. But this traditional context was that of Goodly Fere as the sort of spiritual big brother and community leader in which Stearns had envisioned himself, and of course Stearns, despite his faults, never (at least consciously) envisioned himself as a "leader for life" or took his bossiness to the impersonal level Tomlinson did. After 1913 Green Spurling ceased active participation in Church of God denominational life, even though Tomlinson had made him a bishop and was wont to mouth flowery platitudes about Spurling being his "spiritual father" in spite of the fact that he tried to alter the old man's rustic hill dress every time he visited Cleveland.[102] And by 1922 Lemons and Bryant, his oldest and once his staunchest supporters, had gotten their crawful, too. The old hill preachers brought charges in the General Assembly that year against Tomlinson for misappropriation of funds—odd considering all of them had professed to be living above sin in this present world, but then again, where would church history be without its scandals?—and Tomlinson resigned and withdrew with a following to found a competing Church of God group in Cleveland, known since 1952 as the Church of God of Prophecy and a major Appalachian Holiness denomination in its own right. After Tomlinson died in 1943, this organization's mantle of leadership passed to his son Milton, who held it until his own death in 1990, and the Church of God of Prophecy maintains "Prayer Mountain in Fields of the Wood," supposedly the site where Tomlinson got his revelation from God, as a sort of denominational shrine.

The Church of God (Cleveland, Tennessee) retains its episcopal structure and now boasts, among other amenities, a School of Theology in Cleveland, but it is highly likely that governmental practices are at least a little more democratic than they were in A.J. Tomlinson's time. Certainly its members have never allowed another General Overseer to assume as much power as Tomlinson did. But at the same time it was growing in Cleveland, its early preachers and their followers were still back in the hills, and along with the Church of God in the mountains there simultaneously arose other Pentecostal/Holiness denominations and independent churches of other names, simply because Green Spurling and other mountain preachers kept organizing them that way in spite of the control that Tomlinson tried to assume. Few of these Pentecostal churches are real schisms from the denominational Church of God. Many more are simply offshoots from the same stock and with the same original Spurling/Bryant/Martin mix of Separate and Wesleyan Methodist theology, which of course finds much in common with other Pentecostal movements originating elsewhere, and several even assume the same name as the major denomination. Others have joined outside Holiness denominations such as the Assemblies of God and younger regional groups like the International Pentecostal Churches of Christ.

One of Deborah McCauley's primary theses is that small independent Holiness churches represent the "true" typical Appalachian church of a kind that have always existed in the mountains, be they Baptist, Methodist, Reformer, or Holiness in sentiment. This is hard to prove. Neither Presbyterians, Methodists, nor the Separate Baptists who represented the Great Awakening mix of General Baptist practice with both beliefs and thus became the "original" native Appalachian church, brought a tradition of true congregational independency into the mountains, although the practice of holding home meetings wherever a crowd would gather and the services of a preacher could be secured was an Appalachian hallmark from the start. Regardless of the question's true answer, though, since the early work of Richard and Green Spurling, William F. Bryant, Frank Porter, Billy Martin, and, for that matter, even A.J. Tomlinson in the North Carolina/Tennessee border country, independent Holiness churches have become a true part of the Appalachian religious scene, and although they are not formally connected to one another, they have *still* managed to effect their splits from each other in the same fashion as all Shubal Stearns's other spiritual descendants. Nowadays the primary bone of contention between and within these independent churches is an obscure theological point about the nature of the Trinity, and in what form—Father and Son, or simply Father *as* Son—believers expect to see God when they get to heaven. Those that believe one way call themselves "Trinitarians," and the subscribers to the other school of thought are known as "Jesus Only" believers; and it is not even certain that either group completely understands exactly what the dispute is all about. This lack of knowledge is also in keeping with the good old central Appalachian tradition of splits.

Both "Jesus Only" and "Trinitarian" schools of thought have churches on an extreme fringe that takes the reference about serpents in Mark 16 as a literal commandment to handle the creatures as part of worship services and proof of believers' possession of the Holy Ghost. Unfortunately, this group has often been portrayed in the national media as the epitome of Appalachian mountain religion. As Pentecostals themselves rightly point out, snake handlers are represented in only a very small minority of their churches, and this movement now does not exist at all in several parts of Appalachia. Religious snake handling began with the preaching of one George Went Hensley, at the time a member and minister of the Tomlinson-led Church of God and actually one of Homer Tomlinson's converts, about 1910. Through bad times and good, one period of "backsliding" when he served time in prison for making moonshine, and numerous divorces and family scandals, Hensley traveled throughout Appalachia and beyond as an independent Holiness evangelist, preaching and demonstrating snake handling as well as fire handling and poison drinking. Perhaps at the time, his sanctificationist followers felt that as a man of God he was not really sinning in divorcing and remarrying so many times, moonshining, and trying to give his numerous (and often starving) children up for adoption but was somehow spiritually immunized from the stigma of deeds they would have condemned in others. Nowadays, though, some of his followers in the faith adamantly refuse to believe stories of his excesses.[103] After a long career during which he claimed to have been bitten 446 times, Hensley died in 1955 of his 447th snakebite while conducting services in a small blacksmith-shop-turned-Pentecostal church in Althea, Florida, but the movement he founded lives on in spite of media attention every time a believer gets bitten and dies. The snake handlers consider themselves to be the inheritors of the legal persecution once given to the Church of God and before them the Separate Baptists of more than two hundred years ago, and despite what reservations one may entertain about their doctrine and practices and the obvious health hazards for everyone involved in snake handling (most refuse medical attention when bitten, requiring court intervention to save lives but still sometimes resulting in deaths horrible to behold), when it comes down to brass tacks it must be admitted that in this particular, they have at least at times been correct. When we see snake handlers jailed, we do get a glimpse of the lives of the old Separate Baptist preachers in pre-Revolutionary Virginia, convicted for nothing more than the proclamation and free exercise of their beliefs. Handling dangerous serpents in a public place, however, does constitute more than a simple disturbance of the peace.

There is a famous picture of George Went Hensley taken while he was preaching on the grounds of the Hamilton County, Tennessee, court house in 1947 in the midst of one such court case brought against snake handlers in that area.[104] A small, spare, white-haired man, Hensley was caught by the photographer in an esctacy of preaching. His right hand is raised towards the sky, his left hand points to the Bible held in the hands of a follower directly beneath him and apparently holding it for him, his head is thrown back with his mouth open wide and his large, intensely bright eyes gaze in rapture at some unknown point on the unseen horizon, as if he could stare right through it and beyond.

Perhaps it is no wonder he garnered such a following to his peculiar interpretations of Scripture in Appalachia; he must have looked a lot like Shubal Stearns.

A Final Thought

At the end of one of the numerous written accounts of Raccoon John Smith's life, there is a rather maudlin scene in which we see old Raccoon John in Heaven, in company with Alexander Campbell and many other historically famous Reformers; if there are members of any other denomination in this vision of Heaven, the biographer does not portray them, not even Raccoon John's parents or his first wife. But according to the story line, Raccoon John and his great-grandson H. Leo Boles, who was also a famous preacher in the conservative faction of the Church of Christ, get to borrow wings and fly like angels over the earthly territories where Smith preached in life, clucking their tongues in sorrow over the hard-heartedness of the Baptists and other denominations as well as Campbell followers who they believed did not adhere to the Ancient and Scriptural order of things, evidently finally giving up on the old Reformer's stomping grounds as a hopeless field of confusion (all except for one particular type of church, of course, that still maintained the True Way) and flying home to Heaven, where things made sense, with hymns upon their lips.

In truth, Raccoon John deserved better than this two-dimensional pasteboard concept of Heaven, just as he deserves a more complete and accurate biography than has ever been written of him. No doubt Shubal Stearns likewise deserves a better telling of his life, times, and legacy than I have been able to give here, and perhaps one day a better and more scholarly one may be written. Since, as far as I have been able to determine, this is the first book devoted completely to a study of the life, the character, and the deeds of the little bright-eyed preacher who was so crucially important to the development of a distinct Appalachian religious culture, those that may follow will no doubt correct my mistakes and improve upon my style. But where do we leave Shubal Stearns? In the North Carolina grave where his tired, worn-out body was laid two hundred thirty-odd years ago in the aftermath of the Regulators' War and before the then-visible thunderclouds of the American Revolution burst forth upon America in both blood and bloody rhetoric, or in some obscene human conception of a flat pasteboard Heaven that, it seems, is about as high as our pitiful perceptions seem to rise? Which vision is better than the other?

And yet, as with the question of the Goodly Fere's political loyalties, the answer is hardly even relevant. For, though his name has been forgotten in Appalachia, Shubal Stearns has never really left us; though his body has long since mouldered back to dust in North Carolina, his followers nonetheless brought his spirit, still very much alive, with them to Tennessee, Virginia, Kentucky, South Carolina, and Georgia. The presence of this tyrannical and fatherly, superstitious and spiritual, noisy and musical, infuriating and lovable little man still haunts our churches, splintered from his original rootstock though they be and yet so strikingly similar at their hearts, as if it were a ghost. One can almost imagine a pair of large, piercing, spectral eyes, gleaming in fatherly pride as converts in countless backcountry Appalachian meetinghouses still respond to the Gospel of Jesus Christ articulated in the New England Holy Tone; snapping with anger or casting an expressive heavenward glance in disgust and resignation as the ghosts of poor old bumbling James Read and dissolute Philip Mulkey, and the poltergeist of Herman Husbands, every so often raise hell again and again in their own ways among his children in the faith; and perhaps crinkling a little in indulgent amusement and with a mischievous wink to the shades of Raccoon John Smith, Green Spurling, and Bill Bryant, as the ghosts of Alexander Campbell, A.J. Tomlinson, and James Robinson Graves exasperatedly try to convert him. Indeed Shubal Stearns is yet alive in the hearts and minds of Appalachian Christians and will always remain so as long as a distinctive Appalachian Christianity exists.

So rest in peace, Old Brother, Goodly Fere, but not apart from us; wherever God may keep your soul your spirit is still with us, not only in our virtues but in our many faults, and the faith in God you articulated for us will keep us going another mile—just as it always has.

Afterword

I, The Preacher

> And further, by these, my son, be admonished: of making many books there is no end; and much study is a weariness of the flesh.
> —Ecclesiastes 12:12, King James version

Whether good or bad, this work is the product of a ten-year hobby begun originally by a young Kentucky backcountry Baptist preacher with decided Old Landmarker leanings (of the peculiar twist to the belief so often found in Appalachia), and it was intended originally to trace the native Baptists in his locality back as far as possible historically in just one more reiteration of the Landmarker position. Needless to say, over the years he—I—was compelled to change my outlook, but the change did me no harm, I think, other than causing me to sigh repeatedly over Solomon's pronouncements on vanity every time I see historical truths twisted to make one Christian denomination look superior to another; and of course, never to accept any religious historical document with which I come into contact at face value, without checking it against all other available and relevant sources. "Where there is no vision, the people perish," says Proverbs, and much of Appalachia's—and indeed, America's—spiritual poverty has been due to well-meaning religious historians who have indeed often tried to put very thick blinders on their readers. But in the process of sifting through the truth and lies, the wheat and chaff of history, I managed to get acquainted with (to borrow David S. Dreyer's term) the "man who baptized the South," Shubal Stearns, and I've never regretted the acquaintance for a moment. Since the time I discovered his role in shaping the development and growth of the Baptist movement in the southeast, it's been a matter of continual wonder to me why some enterprising Appalachian scholar—or a Baptist historian with enough guts to challenge the SBC's view of Baptist history—hadn't penned his biography already. But who knows? Perhaps only now, at the beginning of the twenty-first century, can American

Christians or even Appalachian Christians themselves begin to understand his story.

During the course of my research and the writing of this work, I received assistance from many sources whom I doubt I'll ever be able to thank adequately. Miss Shirley Chafin, several years ago my—and currently my oldest daughter's—high school English teacher, kept after me with red ink until I learned how to write a coherent sentence and to not split my infinitives. My thanks to her for the grammar drill; although, like Raccoon John Smith, I can't quote one rule of grammar, at least I can look at a sentence and tell generally whether it is grammatical or not, and without her patience—*and* her impatience—I'd have never been able to write this book.

Speaking of grammar and patience, Ann Youmans, copyeditor for this work, has shown a great deal of both in her efforts to ready this volume for publication. I've enjoyed our written exchanges over the text, and I hope she has as well.

Patricia Patton, Esther Titlow, Lee and Wilma Pack, Mary Ann Runyon, and all the others at my local library, the Johnson County Public Library at Paintsville, Kentucky, patiently tried to fulfil my requests for rare books and microfilms on the Commonwealth's Interlibrary Loan Program for nearly a decade—and came through with flying colors each and every time. Likewise the staff at the Prestonsburg Community College Library at Prestonsburg, Floyd County, Kentucky, were equally generous in making the library's Special Collections Room, with many volumes dealing with local religious history, available for my frequent browsing, and if I did not wear their mimeograph machines out I certainly put some mileage on them. In addition, James R. Lynch, former director of the library at the American Baptist Historical Society at Rochester, New York, was a great help in allowing me to obtain microfilms and mimeographs from rare books and pamphlets, on an occasion or two even mailing me unsolicited material he considered germane to my research. Karen Sundland, also of ABHS, gave me invaluable assistance in tracing down one little-known author for a permissions request. I also need to thank Jo Sloan Philbeck and her research assistants of the library at the Southeastern Baptist Theological Seminary of Wake Forest University, Winston-Salem, North Carolina, for similar favors to a researcher not quite intent on presenting the Baptists of the American Southeast in the exact slant most ministers, or laypersons, in the region would expect. Thanks are also due to Clinton J. Holloway of the Disciples of Christ Historical Society in Nashville, Tennessee, who provided copies of rare papers and pamphlets on John Smith, Jilson Payne, and Buckner H. Payne, and Marsha Haithcock of the Randolph County Public Library, Asheboro, North Carolina, who supplied the photos of Sandy Creek Church. Loyal Jones, former professor of Appalachian studies at Berea College in Kentucky, read an early manuscript draft of this work and has provided consistent encouragement to me for its completion and publication since. For this, and especially for his too-kind foreword for this work, I owe much appreciation. David S. Dreyer, Palmer family genealogist and historian, read another early draft, offered several invaluable ideas on clarification, and generously shared materials from his own historical/genealogical collection with me. And Scotty Breed of the Stonington, Connecticut, Historical Library (a fellow Kentuckian, I might add, cold waters to a thirsty soul to converse with among all the dialects I encountered on the phone and in person while doing research), likewise sacrificed a good deal of time in research at the Stonington Library in my behalf. Thanks a lot, Scotty, and may ye hear the accents of your homeland more often.

I also wish to thank Terry Preston, Elders Blaine and Jeff Cooper, Ron Woodward, and the congregations of the Concord and Lexington, Kentucky, United Baptist Churches (how historically appropriately those church names come together in this section, and it's pure coincidence), for generously allowing me to view and take notes from the historical documents housed in their churches, as well as the families of the late D.J. Gambill and Raymond Benton, of Paint Union and Burning Springs Associations, respectively. Both these gentlemen were knowledgable and interested in local religious history and were very generous with their time in allowing me to examine and outline the documents under their care. I may never forget what Brother Benton said to me, after a long session I spent taking notes from the ancient South Fork Church record book he kept housed in his safety deposit box, when I asked if I owed him any compensation: "Why, you don't owe me a thing, but if I thought you were a Republican I'd charge you twenty dollars." (Fortunately for me at the time, I was not of that persuasion and evidently neither was Brother Benton, contrary to whatever Jerry Falwell and Ralph Reed may consider the necessary politics for a Christian to uphold.)

I'd like to thank my preaching colleagues and fellow church members of the Old Zion Association of United Baptists in eastern Kentucky, western West Virginia, and the Appalachian outmigrant enclave of Columbus, Ohio, as well as the association's moderator, Elder Jimmy Maynard of Lenore, West Virginia. He knew from experience the strengths and weaknesses of the native Appalachian Baptist system long before I ever researched its historical precedents as instituted by Shubal Stearns, and he, like the rest of us, tries to do the best he can under the system's limitations. The ministers I mentioned in the dedication at the beginning of this work—the "Goodly Feres" of my youth—are all gone to their rewards except for Brother Don Fraley who, at the time of this writing, has just completed his ninth decade. He no longer preaches much, but his voice in the pulpit is still considerably strong—good Lord, how I wish my voice boomed like that—and the preaching cant that he inherited from generations of mountain preachers before him and with which he taught me the principles of the Gospel years ago is still musical. I thank him for his inspiration to me and his indomitable sense of humor. And so, as Brother Don taught me to put it, Keithy, keep on a-harpin'.

Finally, once again I must thank the three "hopeful ladies of my earth"—my wife Sheila and my daughters Sarah and Amie. Perhaps I share a similar experience with some other fathers in the fact that Sarah, who was twelve years old when I purchased our first computer, taught her dad enough about Microsoft Works and WordPad to allow him to graduate from a very poor longhand to a PC. Otherwise all three have tolerated my hours over the keyboard—sandwiched in as best as I could manage between preaching, working, gardening, and so forth—with as much, and maybe more, good grace than they could be expected to exhibit under such circumstances. I daresay, though, that my undertaking any other writing of this sort will be the subject of much debate with all three—I can only hope, good-natured debate.

NOTES

ABBREVIATIONS FOR NOTES AND BIBLIOGRAPHY

ABHS = American Baptist Historical Society, Rochester, N.Y.
DCHS = Disciples of Christ Historical Society, Nashville, Tenn.
PBL = Primitive Baptist Library, Carthage, Ill.
SEBTS = Southeastern Baptist Theological Seminary, Wake Forest University, Winston-Salem, N.C.
SHL = Stonington Historical Library, Stonington, Conn.
SBTS = Southern Baptist Theological Seminary Library, Louisville, Ky.
UGL = University of Georgia Library, Athens, Ga.

INTRODUCTION: IN SEARCH OF THE GOODLY FERE

1. Loyal Jones, "Old-Time Baptists and Mainline Christianity," 120.

CHAPTER 1: THE COVENANT OWNERS

1. Stearns Family Genealogy Forum. Elder William Vaughan of Kentucky (1785–1876) noted this archaic pronunciation of the letter "e" in a recollection, passed on to his son, of his hearing the old Kentucky Indian fighter and Baptist Col. Robert Johnson "line out" a hymn when Vaughan was a boy: " . . . *Etarnal* are thy *marcies*, Lord . . . *Etarnal* truth abounds thy Word. . . ." See Vaughan, *Memoirs of Rev. William Vaughan*, 69–70.
2. Torbet, *A History of the Baptists*, 43.
3. Behling, "Twice Baked: the Story of Edward Wightman."
4. Torbet, 35.
5. Ibid., 66–67.
6. Knight, *A History of the General or Six Principle Baptists in Europe and America*, 320.
7. Elliott, "A History of the General Six Principle Baptists of North America," 166–67. ABHS.
8. *Minutes of the Philadelphia Baptist Association, 1707–1807*, ed. Gillette, 39.
9. Pingel, "History of the Town of Tolland."
10. Tull, *Shapers of Baptist Thought*, 57.

11. Ibid., 58.

Chapter 2: Rude Awakening

1. Dodds, *Marriage to a Difficult Man*, 87.
2. Torbet, 218; also Benedict, *A General History of the Baptist Denomination*, 686.
3. Torbet, 214–20; also Spencer, *History of Kentucky Baptists 1769–1885*, 1:97.
4. Stout, *The Divine Dramatist*, 70–71.
5. Isaac, *The Transformation of Virginia 1740–1790*, 148–49, quoting Morris's written statement.
6. Dodds, 86–87.
7. Ibid., 91–92.
8. Ibid., 94.
9. Ibid., 89, using a quote from New England lawyer William Livingston.
10. Backus, *A History of New England*, 2:231.
11. Tull, 60.
12. Torbet, 222.
13. Semple, *Rise and Progress of the Baptists in Virginia*, 15.
14. McCauley, *Appalachian Mountain Religion*, 214–15.
15. Dodds, 86.
16. Taylor, *Virginia Baptist Ministers*, 1:23.
17. Ibid., 1:19.
18. Patterson, "In Memoriam: Elder Shubal Stearns," 2.

Chapter 3: The "Garding in Closed"

1. Edna Hewitt Tryon, "From Congregational Records," in *First Baptist Church of North Stonington, Connecticut: The Papers and Addresses Delivered at the Dedication of a Granite Memorial on the Site of the First Church Edifice*, 42–47; also Rev. Albert Palmer, "A Discourse Delivered at the One Hundredth Anniversary of the Organization of the First Baptist Church in North Stonington, September 20, 1843," in ibid., 98. The only place this author has found the full name of Rev. Waitstill ("Wait") Palmer is in the original deed of the Stonington Church, a copy of which is in this volume. From the collection of Palmer genealogist David S. Dreyer, Indianapolis, Ind.
2. Elliott, 66–68.
3. Records of the Rhode Island Yearly Meeting, ABHS.
4. Knight, 307; Elliott, 67–68.
5. Benedict, 469–76; Elliott, 66, 219.
6. Annual Report of the 307th General Six Principle Baptist Conference of Rhode Island, ABHS.

7. Tull, 70.
8. Palmer, "Discourse," in *First Baptist Church, North Stonington*, 112–13.
9. Backus, 1:519.
10. Rites listed were compiled within a year of Stearns's death by Morgan Edwards in his manuscript *Materials Toward a History of the Baptists in America;* microfilm, ABHS. Hereinafter this document will be referred to as "Edwards, *Materials.*"
11. Paschal, *History of North Carolina Baptists*, 1:311n.
12. Ibid., 1:403; evidently taken directly from the church's record book.
13. Gewehr, *The Great Awakening in Virginia*, 109n.

CHAPTER 4: CHANCE AND PROVIDENCE

1. Cirillo, "Descendants of Joseph Breed"; also Wheeler, *History of the Town of Stonington*, 244–45. SHL Collection.
2. Taylor, 1:19, quoting Abraham Marshall.
3. Cirillo, "Descendants of Joseph Breed."
4. Taylor, 1:19.
5. Will of Shubal Stearns.
6. Stearns Family Genealogy Forum.
7. Semple, 377; also Taylor, 1:24.
8. Semple, 394.
9. Spencer, 1:93.
10. Backus, 2:530.
11. Powell, *The War of the Regulation and the Battle of Alamance*, 8; also Mark Jones, "Herman Husbands," in the *Dictionary of North Carolina Biography*, 3:242.
12. Mark Jones, "Herman Husbands," 3:242.
13. Robinson, *The Five Royal Governors of North Carolina*, 32.
14. Bernheim, *A History of the German Settlements and of the Lutheran Church in North and South Carolina*, 154; see also Edwards, *Materials.*
15. Rouse, *Some Interesting Colonial Churches in North Carolina*, 46. See also Edwards, *Materials.*
16. Robinson, 38.
17. Mark Jones, "Herman Husbands," 3:242.
18. Robinson, 38.
19. Mark Jones, "Herman Husbands," 3:242.
20. Patterson, 2.
21. Ibid., 5.
22. Taylor, 1:19.
23. Tull, 67.
24. Ahlstrom, *A Religious History of the American People*, 319; also Semple, 16; Benedict, 684–85.

25. Edwards, *Materials*, in this instance quoted in Paschal, *History of North Carolina Baptists*, 1:286–7. See also Burnett, *Sketches of Tennessee's Pioneer Baptist Preachers*, 318–22.

26. Edwards, *Materials*, quoted in Paschal, *History of North Carolina Baptists*, 1:287–88.

27. Edwards, *Materials*.

28. Ibid.

29. Paschal, *History of North Carolina Baptists*, 2:42–43.

Chapter 5: Chamomile

1. Hamilton, "Hermon [*sic*] Husbands," in the *Dictionary of American Biography*, 5:427.

2. Mark Jones, "Herman Husbands," 3:243.

3. Semple, 394.

4. Paschal, *History of North Carolina Baptists*, 1:290–91.

5. Data taken from the March 7, 1757, entry in the journal of Rev. John Newton, Special Collections, UGL.

6. Paschal, *History of North Carolina Baptists*, 1:266.

7. Rouse, 47.

8. David Benedict erroneously identifies the minister in question here as Rev. Nicholas Bedgegood, who subsequently did serve as pastor of Pee Dee Church; however, at this period Bedgegood, a former employee of George Whitefield at his Georgia orphanage, was still a member of the Church of England, not joining the Regular Baptists until 1757 and not being ordained as a minister until 1759. Edwards, *Materials*.

9. Robinson, 39.

10. Edwards, *Materials*.

11. Semple, 16; Benedict, 684.

12. Edwards, *Materials*.

13. Reference to Taylor, 1:20.

14. Paschal, *History of North Carolina Baptists*, 1:300.

15. Edwards, *Materials*.

16. Ibid.

17. Ibid.

18. Benedict, 2:156.

19. Paschal, *History of North Carolina Baptists*, 1:383. Edwards listed Philip Mulkey's surviving children in 1772 in his *Materials*.

20. Spencer, 1:377–8.

21. Paschal, *History of North Carolina Baptists*, 1:308.

22. Ibid., 1:311n.

23. Ibid., 1:310.

24. Edwards, *Materials*.
25. Paschal, *History of North Carolina Baptists*, 1:404.
26. Ibid., 1:406n., quoting Sandy Creek historian G.W. Purefoy.
27. Ibid., 1:283, quoting the manuscript of Elder James Read.
28. Ibid., 1:397.
29. Edwards, *Materials*.
30. Paschal, *History of North Carolina Baptists*, 1:284, quoting David Benedict and Robert B. Semple.
31. Ibid., 1:398; also Edwards, *Materials*.
32. Edwards, *Materials*.
33. Ibid.
34. Paschal, *History of North Carolina Baptists*, 2:101–2, quoting General William Lenoir. Mulberry Fields Church began as an arm of another congregation Joseph Murphy had gathered, at a place then evidently known as Shallow Ford but that Paschal identifies as Timber Ridge.
35. Edwards, *Materials*.
36. Paschal, *History of North Carolina Baptists*, 2:38–39n.
37. Edwards, *Materials*. See also Burnett, 318–22.
38. Edwards, *Materials*.
39. Ibid.
40. Paschal, *History of North Carolina Baptists*, 1:399.
41. Ibid., 1:297, quoting the letter from Stearns that had been given by Noah Alden to Isaac Backus.

CHAPTER 6: MESHECH

1. Edwards, *Materials*.
2. Ibid. The author is informed by the Special Collections Department of the University of Georgia Library, where John Newton's manuscript journal is housed, that there is no substantial reference in the journal to this matter whatsoever. Newton may have been so upset and hurt by the conflict, and Stearns's treatment of him, that he could not even bear to write about it.
3. Paschal, *History of North Carolina Baptists*, 1:279, quoting Benedict and Semple.
4. Ibid., 1:280, quoting Benedict and Semple.
5. McCauley, 190–95, 221.
6. Johnson, *The Frontier Camp Meeting*, 27–28.
7. McCauley, 221.
8. Benedict, 2:396–97.
9. Semple, 156.
10. Spencer, 1:29.
11. Edwards, *Materials*. G.W. Paschal could find no court records substan-

tiating Edwards's claim and was inclined to disbelieve it; however, Edwards must have been told of the experience, which had occurred only five years or so before, in one or more instances during his travels in North Carolina and was therefore undoubtedly speaking with participants and eyewitnesses.

12. Edwards, *Materials*. Fristoe had just been ordained at a new Ketocton church known as Chappawamsick.
13. *Minutes of the Philadelphia Baptist Association*, 205.
14. Spencer, 1:89.
15. Edwards, *Materials*.
16. Semple, 107–8, paraphrasing all that author's obvious prejudice against Arminianism. In the pithy style of the rural lawyer that he was, Semple fumed, "It is probable that few men could make gewgaws look more like jewels than Jeremiah Walker. His was a sweetened dose."
17. Spencer, 1:16.
18. Taylor, 1:35.
19. Paschal, *History of North Carolina Baptists*, 1:276.
20. Ibid., 1:399–400.
21. Edwards, *Materials*.
22. Powell, 6–7.
23. Mary Claire Engstrom, "Edmund Fanning," in *Dictionary of North Carolina Biography*, 3:181.
24. Ibid. 3:182.
25. Robinson, 55; Powell, 11.
26. Price, *Not A Conquered People*, 8.
27. Edwards, *Materials*.
28. Semple, 37.
29. Paschal, "Editorial notes on Morgan Edwards's *Materials*," 365–99.
30. Edwards, *Materials*; Paschal, *History of North Carolina Baptists*, 1:365.
31. Edwards, *Materials*; Paschal, "Editorial Notes."
32. Powell, 11.
33. Ibid., 12.
34. Powell, 7; Robinson, 56.
35. Powell, 14–15.
36. Edwards, *Materials*; Paschal, *History of North Carolina Baptists*, 1:361–63.
37. Semple, 29–30.
38. Edwards, *Materials*.
39. Hamilton, "Hermon [sic] Husbands," 5:427–8.
40. Robinson, 58; Powell, 14.
41. Powell, 16.
42. Semple, 489, quoting the manuscript journal of Elder John Williams.
43. Ibid., 490, from John Williams's journal.
44. Semple, 68.

45. Edwards, *Materials*.
46. Ibid.
47. Ibid.
48. Ibid.
49. Semple, 68.
50. Powell, 16.
51. Edwards, *Materials*.
52. Paschal, *History of North Carolina Baptists*, 1:391, 471–73.
53. Ibid., 1:470–71.
54. Semple, 24.
55. Johnson, 27.
56. Powell, 16.
57. Semple, 68–69, quoting Elijah Craig.
58. Ibid., 69.
59. Ibid., 72.
60. Edwards, *Materials*.
61. Paschal, *History of North Carolina Baptists*, 1:302.
62. Ibid., 2:67.
63. Price, 8.
64. Powell, 17.
65. Ibid., 19.
66. Price, 8.
67. Powell, 19.
68. Ibid., 21.
69. Ibid., 23.
70. Ibid.
71. Ibid., 23–24.
72. Edwards, *Materials*; Paschal, *History of North Carolina Baptists*, 2:72–73.
73. Paschal, *History of North Carolina Baptists*, 2:73.
74. Ibid., 1:382.
75. Powell, 26.
76. Last Will and Testament of Shubal Stearns.

Chapter 7: Requiem

1. Mark Jones, "Herman Husbands," 3:243.
2. Slaughter, *The Whiskey Rebellion*, 276n.
3. Hamilton, "Hermon [*sic*] Husbands," 5:428.
4. Cirillo, "Descendants of Joseph Breed."
5. Paschal, *History of North Carolina Baptists*, 1:393.
6. Semple, 72.
7. Paschal, *History of North Carolina Baptists*, 1:302–3.

8. Ahlstrom, 319.
9. Semple, 59.
10. Spencer, 1:107–10.
11. Edwards, *Materials*; see also the obituary of Elder Robert Elkin, Minutes of the North District Association of Baptists, 1822, SBTS.
12. Spencer, 1:45–47; see also *Descendants of Rev. Robert Elkin, 1745–1822*. Spencer, in one of a few unintentional mistakes within two volumes containing many deliberate obfuscations, identifies Elkin as a Regular rather than a Separate Baptist.
13. Burnett, 321–22; also Minutes of the Holston Baptist Association, ABHS.
14. Spencer, 2:80–81.
15. Ibid., 1:339
16. Ibid., 1:546.
17. Ibid., 1:532.

Chapter 8: The Legacy of the Goodly Fere

1. Spencer, 1:599.
2. *Minutes of the North District Baptist Association*, SBTS.
3. Minutes of the North District Association, 1803–1804. SBTS; also Everett Donaldson, *Raccoon John Smith*, 83–85.
4. Minutes of the Elkhorn Baptist Association, 1802. SBTS.
5. Ibid.
6. *Minutes of the North District Association*, 1803.
7. *Minutes of the North District Association*, 1804.
8. *Minutes of the North District Association*, 1805; see also *Minutes of the North District*, 1813; Spencer, 2:240, 249.
9. Spencer, 2:83; 89.
10. Spencer, 1:80; 2:127.
11. Tull, 67, quoting Isaac Backus; also Spencer, 1:546. It is possible, however, that at its organization in 1771, the Rapidan Association in Virginia initially forbade its members from communing with Ketocton and Kehukee churches, although of course by the time of Kentucky's General Union any such obstacles had long since been cleared away.
12. *Minutes of the North District Association of Baptists*, 1805 and 1806.
13. Spencer, 2:140.
14. Ibid., 2:143.
15. Dorgan, *In the Hands of a Happy God*, 13.
16. Donaldson, *The Legacy of Raccoon John Smith*, 258; 272.
17. Spencer, 1:584, quoting the July 4, 1823, (first) issue of *The Christian Baptist*.

18. Donaldson, *Legacy of Raccoon John Smith*, 116–17, 186; Williams, *Life of Elder John Smith*, 579.

19. Garrett, *The Stone-Campbell Movement*, 410. This volume was, and perhaps still is, a standard textbook of Campbell Reformation history and was written by an elder in the conservative, nonmusical Church of Christ.

20. Donaldson, *Legacy of Raccoon John Smith*, 62; Williams, 579.

21. Spencer, 2:214.

22. Garrett, 282.

23. Williams, 88–89.

24. Ibid., 568.

25. Donaldson, *Raccoon John Smith: Frontiersman and Reformer*, 83–84.

26. Donaldson, *Legacy of Raccoon John Smith*, 31.

27. Williams, 206–7; see also Donaldson, *Legacy of Raccoon John Smith*, 170.

28. Spencer, 2:249.

29. Donaldson, *Legacy of Raccoon John Smith*, 170.

30. Donaldson, *Raccoon John Smith: Frontiersman and Reformer*, 78–79.

31. Donaldson, *Legacy of Raccoon John Smith*, 103; see also 287.

32. Ibid., 47–48.

33. Williams, 180–90; see also *Minutes of the North District Association*, 1827.

34. Williams, 180–81.

35. Williams, 217–21.

36. Ibid., 341–43, quoting James Mason's letter as it appeared in *The Millennial Harbinger*, May 1830.

37. Ibid., 291–92.

38. Ibid., 358–59.

39. Spencer, 1:636.

40. Williams, 568.

41. Garrett, 388–99.

42. Dorgan, *In the Hands of a Happy God*, 19.

43. Grammich, *Appalachian Atlas*, 38–39.

44. Spencer, 2:122–24; Minutes of the Lulbegrud and Goshen Council Meetings, 1830. SBTS.

45. Minutes of the North District Association (French faction), 1831. ABHS.

46. Minutes of North District Association (French faction), 1834.

47. Minutes of the North District Association (Smith faction), 1830 (the Reformers completely omitted the name "Baptist" from this entire report).

48. The author has pieced together his case on this point, which admittedly contains some circumstantial albeit logical evidence, with the help of numerous sources. One was an extremely rare copy of the 1834 Burning Springs Association minutes in the possession of the American Baptist Historical Society; Hanna, Kash, and other eastern Kentucky Reformers were present and participating,

and the entire document is of a decidedly Reformer slant. Besides the 1836 Burning Springs minutes, of which several copies exist in the libraries of ABHS, the Southern Baptist Theological Seminary, the Southern Baptist Historical Commission, and numerous local private collections, other sources include the recollections of the late Elder B.C. Ferguson, for many years the moderator of both the Paint Union Association of United Baptists and the Concord Church, later reorganized and relocated to Thealka and then Thelma, Kentucky; the research of Everett Donaldson of Mount Sterling, Kentucky, who assisted the author in tracing Raccoon John Smith's movements in eastern Kentucky in the early 1830s; and the recollections of Elder Walter Akers, assistant clerk of the New Salem Old Regular Baptist Association, whose father, W.L. Akers, assisted Burning Springs Association several years ago in recompiling their early records from copies made by the first clerk of both Burning Springs and New Salem Associations, Elder Alexander Lackey. The stories of Raccoon John Smith in eastern Kentucky are part of the folklore of Morgan and Wolfe Counties, especially around the community of Hazel Green in eastern Wolfe County; additional information taken from the *Low Gap United Baptist Church Record Book, 1814–1860*, courtesy of Lexington United Baptist Church, Lexington, Ky.

49. Spencer, 2:125.

50. Record Book of the Paint Union Association of United Baptists, 1838–1993, courtesy of the late D.J. Gambill of Thelma, Kentucky, longtime association recording secretary. At least one locally published work intent on establishing the legitimacy of the Primitive Baptists claims that Paint Union's articles of faith were modified to reflect this general-atonement outlook in 1865, asserting this as the reason for the breach of fellowship between the Burning Springs and Paint Union Associations, but in combing the record book carefully, this author determines that the articles written by Bailey when the body was organized have been changed only once since, and that in 1989 to advocate the use of the King James version of the Bible and no other.

51. Minutes of the North District Association, 1855–1856; Spencer, 2:616–17.

52. Spencer, 2:246; 604–5.

53. Tull, 135–37.

54. Asplund, *Universal Register of the Baptist Denomination in America*, statistics for North Carolina, 1794; Paschal, *History of North Carolina Baptists*, 2:559–70.

55. Minutes of the Yadkin Baptist Association, 1794.

56. Spencer, 1:609.

57. McCauley, 203.

58. Spencer, 1:645.

59. Sutherland, *Regular Primitive Baptist Washington District Association*, 15–16.

60. Spencer, 2:286.
61. J.C. Swindall, "Reminiscence," in *History of Regular Baptist*, ed. Rufus Perrigan et al., 195–97; also Joseph Hall, "Circular Letter," in ibid., 198–201.
62. Dixon and Akers, eds., *Minutes of the Burning Springs Association of Baptists, 1813–1824 and Minutes of the New Salem Association of Old Regular Baptists, 1825–1983*, 1:New Salem Minutes, 1–20; 72, 74, 79, 82, et al.
63. Dixon and Akers, 1:69.
64. Ibid., 1:86.
65. Ibid., 1:90–91.
66. Ibid., 1:79.
67. Sutherland, 19.
68. Dixon and Akers, 1:121.
69. Ibid., 1:129.
70. Spencer, 2:395.
71. Spencer, 2:643–44.
72. Ibid., 1:8; 2:397.
73. Dixon and Akers, 1:212.
74. Dorgan, *The Old Regular Baptists of Central Appalachia*, 37.
75. Minutes of the North District Association, 1815.
76. Paschal, *History of North Carolina Baptists*,1:372.
77. Dorgan, *The Old Regular Baptists of Central Appalachia*, 12, 250n.
78. Ibid., 232–33.
79. Dixon and Akers, 1:350; also, telephone interview on October 20, 2000, with Elder Walter Akers of Honaker, Kentucky, assistant clerk of New Salem Association and one of the copyright holders of New Salem's complete published version of its *Minutes* from 1825 until 1983.
80. Paschal, *History of North Carolina Baptists*,1:202, 223.
81. Semple, 106–9.
82. Ronald Creech, "North Carolina State Association," in *History of Free Will Baptist State Associations*, ed. Robert E. Picirilli, 72–73.
83. Robert E. Picirilli, "Tennessee State Association," in *History of Free Will Baptist State Associaions*, 94; Paschal, *History of North Carolina Baptists*, 2:426–33.
84. Picirilli, in *History of Free Will Baptist State Associations*, 94–95.
85. Spencer, 1:670–71.
86. McCauley, 23.
87. Creech, in *History of Free Will Baptist State Associations*, 74–75.
88. Mrs. E.O. Griffith, "Kentucky State Association," in *History of Free Will Baptist State Associations*, 47.
89. Deuteronomy 12:17–19; 14:22–29, King James version.
90. Griffith, in *History of Free Will Baptist State Associations*, 46.
91. Dorgan, *Giving Glory to God in Appalachia*, 38.

92. Dorgan, *Giving Glory to God in Appalachia*, 41–44.
93. McCauley, 277–78.
94. McCauley, 289.
95. Ibid., 282.
96. Ibid., 283.
97. Ibid., 285.
98. Ibid., 284.
99. Ibid., 285.
100. Ibid., 298.
101. Wade H. Phillips, "Richard Spurling and the Baptist Roots of the Church of God," 39–40; quoted in McCauley, 300.
102. McCauley, 299.
103. Kimbrough, *Taking Up Serpents*, 5.
104. Ibid., 129.

SELECTED BIBLIOGRAPHY

Ahlstrom, Sydney E. *A Religious History of the American People.* New Haven: Yale Univ. Press, 1972.
Allen, Albert. "Reminiscences of Eld. John Smith, of Kentucky." *The Millennial Harbinger* 7, 4th ser. (March 1857): 276-82. DCHS.
Annual Report of the 307th General Six Principle Baptist Conference of Rhode Island, September 9–11, 1977. ABHS.
Asplund, John. *Universal Register of the Baptist Denomination in America, 1790–1794.* 1794. Reprint, New York: Arno Press, 1980. ABHS.
Backus, Isaac. *A History of New England, etc.* Ed. David Weston. 2 vols. 1777–1796. Reprint, Newton, Mass.: Backus Historical Society, 1871.
Behling, Suzanne. "Twice Baked: the Story of Edward Wightman." World Wide Web, 1997. http://homepages.rootsweb.com/~sam/edw.html.
Benedict, David. *A General History of the Baptist Denomination.* New York: Sheldon, Lamport, and Blakeman, 1855.
Bernheim, G.D. *A History of the German Settlements and of the Lutheran Church in North and South Carolina.* Reprint, Bowie, Md.: Heritage Books, 1990.
Biblical Recorder: Journal of the Baptist State Convention of North Carolina. World Wide Web. "At Abbott's Creek . . ." http://biblicalrecorder.org/opinion/9_18_98/abbotts.html. "Mocksville's Eatons Church Marks 225th Anniversary." http://www.biblicalrecorder.org/news/Eatons10–24.shtml.
Burnett, J.J. *Sketches of Tennessee's Pioneer Baptist Preachers.* Reprint, Johnson City, Tenn.: Overmountain Press, 1985.
Campbell, Alexander. "Address to the Readers of the Christian Baptist." *The Christian Baptist* 1, no. 8 (March 1, 1824): 276-82. DCHS.
Cirillo, Lotus Dale. "Descendants of Joseph Breed." World Wide Web. http://www.butterfly.net/lotus/archives/r-jos-breed1.txt.
Cochran, Louis. *Raccoon John Smith.* New York: Duell, Sloane, and Pierce, 1961.
Descendants of Rev. Robert Elkin, 1745–1822. Winchester, Ky.: privately printed, n.d. Clark County Public Library, Winchester, Ky.
Dixon, Dexter, and Walter Akers, eds. *Minutes of the Burning Springs Association of Baptists, 1813–1824 and Minutes of the New Salem Association of Old Regular Baptists, 1825–1983,* 2 vols. Pikeville, Ky.:Executive Printing, 1983.
Dodds, Elisabeth D. *Marriage to a Difficult Man: the "Uncommon Union" of Jonathan and Sarah Edwards.* Philadephia: Westminster Press, 1971.
Donaldson, Everett. *The Legacy of Raccoon John Smith.* Mt. Sterling, Ky.: North Ridge Publishing, 1995.

———. *Raccoon John Smith: Frontiersman and Reformer.* Lexington, Ky.: Wind Publications, 1993.

Dorgan, Howard. *In the Hands of a Happy God.* Knoxville: Univ. of Tennessee Press, 1997.

———. *Giving Glory to God in Appalachia: Worship Practices of Six Baptist Subdenominations.* Knoxville: Univ. of Tennessee Press, 1987.

———. *The Old Regular Baptists of Central Appalachia: Brothers and Sisters in Hope.* Knoxville: Univ. of Tennessee Press, 1989.

Dreyer, David S. *The Palmer Saga: The History of a Family of Baptist Preachers and Their Descendants.* Author, 1984.

Edwards, Morgan. *Materials Toward a History of the Baptists in America 1772–1795.* Microfilm, ABHS.

Elliott, Nelson R. "A History of the General Six Principle Baptists of North America." Master's thesis, Southwestern Baptist Theological Seminary, 1958. Microfilm, ABHS.

Engstrom, Mary Claire. "Edmund Fanning." In *Dictionary of North Carolina Biography*, ed. William S. Powell. Chapel Hill: Univ. of North Carolina Press, 1993.

First Baptist Church, North Stonington, Connecticut: The Papers and Addresses Delivered at the Dedication of a Granite Memorial on the Site of the First Church Edifice. Westerly, R.I.: Utter, 1936.

Garrett, Leroy. *The Stone-Campbell Movement.* Joplin, Mo.: College Press, 1981.

Gewehr, W.M. *The Great Awakening in Virginia, 1740–1790.* Gloucester, Mass.: Peter Smith, 1965.

Grammich, Clifford A., Jr. *Appalachian Atlas: Maps of the Churches and People of the Appalachian Region.* Knoxville: Commission on Religion in Appalachia, 1990.

———. *Local Baptists, Local Politics.* Knoxville: Univ. of Tennessee Press, 1999.

Hamilton, J.G. de R. "Hermon [sic] Husbands." In *The Dictionary of American Biography*, ed. Dumas Malone and Allen Johnson. New York: Charles Scribner's Sons, 1929.

Handy, Elder W.W. *United Baptist Churches: Who Are They?* Piedmont, Mo.: Author, 1973.

History of Free Will Baptist State Associations. Ed. Robert E. Picirilli. Nashville: Randall House Publications, 1976.

History of Regular Baptist. Ed. Rufus Perrigan et al. Haysi, Va.: Rufus Perrigan, 1961.

Ice, Thomas. "Morgan Edwards: Another Pre-Darby Rapturist." World Wide Web. http://www.novia.net/~todd/tt3.html.

Isaac, Rhys. *The Transformation of Virginia 1740–1790.* Chapel Hill: Univ. of North Carolina Press, 1982.

Ivey, Elder Michael. "A Welsh Succession of Primitive Baptist Faith and Prac-

tice." World Wide Web. http://www.pb.org/pbdocs/chhist5.html.
Johnson, Charles A. *The Frontier Camp Meeting: Religion's Harvest Time*. Reprint, Dallas: Southern Methodist Univ. Press, 1985.
Jones, Loyal. *Faith and Meaning in the Southern Uplands*. Urbana: Univ. of Illinois Press, 1999.
———. "Old-Time Baptists and Mainline Christianity." In *An Appalachian Symposium: Essays in Honor of Cratis D. Williams*. Ed. J.W. Williamson. Boone, N.C.: Appalachian State Univ. Press, 1977.
Jones, Mark H. "Herman Husbands." In *Dictionary of North Carolina Biography*, ed. William S. Powell. Chapel Hill: Univ. of North Carolina Press, 1993.
Kimbrough, David L. *Taking Up Serpents*. Chapel Hill: Univ. of North Carolina Press, 1995.
Knight, Richard. *A History of the General or Six Principle Baptists in Europe and America*. Providence, R.I.: Smith and Parmenter,1827.
Last Will and Testament of Shubal Stearns, October 24, 1771. Guilford County, North Carolina, Will Book A, 329.
McCauley, Deborah Vansau. *Appalachian Mountain Religion: A History*. Urbana: Univ. of Illinois Press, 1995.
Mead, Frank S. *Handbook of Denominations in the United States*. New York: Abingdon Press, 1961.
Miller, Perry. *Jonathan Edwards*. New York: William Morrow and Co., 1949.
Minutes of the Burning Springs Association of United Baptists in eastern Kentucky, years 1834 and 1836. ABHS.
Minutes of the Concord United Baptist Church, Thelma, Johnson County, Kentucky, 1857–1940. Courtesy of Terry Preston, church clerk, Thelma, Kentucky.
Minutes of the Elkhorn Baptist Association, 1785–1813. Microfilm, SBTS.
Minutes of the Holston Baptist Association, 1786–1807. Microfilm, ABHS.
Minutes of the Low Gap United Baptist Church, Magoffin County, Kentucky, 1814–1860. Manuscript courtesy of the Lexington United Baptist Church, Lexington, Kentucky.
Minutes of the Lulbegrud and Goshen Council Meetings, 1830. Microfilm, SBTS.
Minutes of the North District Association of Baptists/United Baptists/Old Baptists/Primitive Baptists. Microfilm. 1802–1952, STBS; 1831 and 1834, ABHS.
Minutes of the North District Association at Spencer Creek Church, 1830. Microfilm, SBTS.
Minutes of the Paint Union Association of United Baptists, 1837–1994. Unpublished record book. Courtesy of D.J. Gambill, associational recording secretary, Thelma, Johnson County, Kentucky.

Minutes of the Philadelphia Baptist Association, 1707–1807. Ed. A.D. Gillette. Reprint, Ortonville, Mich.: Baptist Book Trust, 1976.
Minutes of the Red Bird Association of Primitive Baptists, 1980–1990. PBL.
Minutes of the Regular Primitive Baptist Mates Creek Association, various years. PBL.
Minutes of the South Fork Primitive Baptist Church, Morgan County, Kentucky, 1808–1838. Manuscript courtesy of Raymond Benton, West Liberty, Kentucky.
Minutes of the Teays' Valley Baptist Association of West Virginia, 1827, 1830, and 1834. ABHS.
Minutes of the Yadkin Baptist Association. 1790–1805. Microfilm, ABHS.
Newton, Rev. John. Unpublished journal. Special Collections, UGL.
"Our Baptist Heritage." A Landmarker document. World Wide Web. http://www.aaces.com/tlbc/heritage.htm.
Paschal, G.W. "Editorial notes on Morgan Edwards' *Materials.*" *North Carolina Historical Review* 7, 3 (1930): 365–99. ABHS.
———. *History of North Carolina Baptists.* 2 vols. Raleigh: North Carolina Baptist State Convention, 1930.
Patterson, A.J. "In Memoriam: Elder Shubal Stearns" Liberty, N.C.: author, 1902. ABHS.
Payne, Buckner H. (Ariel, pseud.). *The Negro: What is His Ethnological Status?* Cincinnati, author, 1867. DCHS.
Phillips, Rev. Wade H. "Richard Spurling and the Baptist Roots of the Church of God." Unpublished manuscript.
Pingel, Linda. "History of the Town of Tolland." World Wide Web. http://freepages.genealogy.rootsweb.com/~tollandct01/TollandHistory.html.
Pound, Ezra. *Personae: The Collected Shorter Poems of Ezra Pound.* New York: New Directions, 1926.
Powell, William S. *The War of the Regulation and the Battle of Alamance.* Reprint, Raleigh: North Carolina Department of Cultural and Historical Resources, 1975.
Price, William S., Jr. *Not A Conquered People: Two Carolinans View Parliamentary Taxation.* Raleigh: North Carolina State University Graphics, 1975.
Records of the Rhode Island Yearly Meeting of General or Six Principle Baptists held at Providence on June 23, 1758. Microfilm, ABHS.
Robinson, Blackwell P. *The Five Royal Governors of North Carolina.* Reprint, Raleigh, N.C.: State Department of Archives and History, 1968.
Rouse, J.K. *Some Interesting Colonial Churches in North Carolina.* Kannapolis, N.C.: privately printed, 1961. North Carolina Baptist Historical Collection, SEBTS.
Semple, Robert B. *Rise and Progress of the Baptists in Virginia.* Reprint, Lafayette, Tenn.: Church History Research and Archives, 1976.

Slaughter, Thomas P. *The Whiskey Rebellion: Frontier Epilogue to the American Revolution.* New York: Oxford Univ. Press, 1994.
Spencer, J.H. *History of Kentucky Baptists 1769–1885.* 2 vols. Cincinnati: Author, 1886.
Stearns Family Genealogy Forum. World Wide Web. http://genforum.genealogy.com/stearns/index.html.
Stout, Harry S. *The Divine Dramatist: George Whitefield and the Rise of Modern Evangelicalism.* Grand Rapids, Mich.: Eerdmans, 1991.
Sutherland, Elihu J. *Regular Primitive Baptist Washington District Association.* Elon College, N.C.: Primitive Baptist Publishing House, 1952.
Taylor, James B. *Virginia Baptist Ministers.* 2 vols. Philadelphia: Lippincott, 1859.
Torbet, Robert G. *A History of the Baptists.* Valley Forge, Penn.: Judson Press, 1969.
Tull, James E. *Shapers of Baptist Thought.* Valley Forge: Judson Press, 1972.
Vaughan, Thomas M. *Memoirs of Rev. William Vaughan.* Louisville: Caperton and Cates, 1878.
Wheeler, Richard Anson. *History of the Town of Stonington, County of New London, Connecticut.* Reprint, Mystic, Conn.: Lawrence Verry, 1966.
Williams, John Augustus. *Life of Elder John Smith.* Cincinnati: R.W. Carroll and Co., 1870.
Young, Robert A., D.D. *The Negro: A Reply to Ariel.* Nashville: J.W. McFerrin, 1867. DCHS.

INDEX

Page numbers for photographs are in italics.

Abbott's Creek Church, 59, 74–79, 88, 90, 91, 95, 96, 97, 100, 104–5, 107, 137, 158, 176, 235, 241, 245. *See also* Stephens' Creek Church (S.C.)
Act of Toleration (1689), 5, 30
Adams, G. Bennett, 262–63
Ahlstrom, Sydney, 89
Akers, Walter, 304n. 48, 305n. 79
Akers, W.L., 304n. 48
Alamance Creek, Battle of, 170–74, 175
Albigenses. *See* Cathars
Alden, Noah, 47, 51, 54, 62, 108, 110, 258, 299n. 41
Alderson, John, Jr., 53, 116, 243
Alderson, John, Sr., 53, 116–19
"alien" immersion. *See* baptism
American Baptist Churches in the United States. *See* Northern Baptists
American Baptist Historical Society, 242, 303–4n. 48
American Bible/American Tract Societies, 282
American Revolution, xix, 54, 73, 96, 134, 135, 136–37, 156, 157–58, 181–82, 184, 186–87, 188, 189, 196, 290
Ammen, Thomas, 193
Anabaptists, 4, 5, 36. *See also* German Baptists, Mennonites
Ancient Christian Association, 237. *See also* Mt. Zion Association
Anglican Church, xvi, 3–4, 5, 11, 14, 17–18, 21, 22–23, 55, 58, 60, 69, 85–87, 101, 107, 116–17, 119, 123, 141, 153, 193, 196, 234, 298n. 8
anointing of the sick, 5, 44, 90, 250
"Arians." *See* Christian Church (Stone Movement)

Arminianism, 5, 6, 17, 37, 40, 84, 126, 188, 189, 240, 248, 274, 276, 300n. 16
Arminius, Jacobus. *See* Arminianism
Ashe, John, 170–71
Asplund, John, 241–42
Assemblies of God, 287. *See also* Pentecostalism
Avery, Priscilla (Mrs. Joseph Breed), 49, 50, 53, 98, 104, 105, 107, 132, 282

Backus, Isaac, xix, 36, 37, 39, 43, 48, 55, 63, 299n. 41
Bailey, Cornwallis ("Wallace"), 231, 235–36, 247–48, 254, 256, 304n. 50
Bailey, John, 207–9, 249
Bailey, Wallace. *See* Bailey, Cornwallis
Baker, Desolate, 20, 40, 49, 53
Baker, George, 230
Bald Eagle Church (Ky.), 206, 218–19, 220
baptism: by affusion (pouring), 4; by immersion, 4, 6, 35–36, 40, 44, 221, 223, 234–35, 269; by sprinkling, 4, 35–36, 37, 40. *See also* devoting children, practice
Baptist History. See Orchard, G.H.
Baptists. *See* "Duck River and Kindred" Associations; Enterprise [Regular Baptist] Association (Ky.-Ohio-Ind.); Enterprise [Southern Baptist] Association; Free Baptists; Free Will Baptists; General Baptists; German Baptists; "Independent Baptists" of Virginia; Northern Baptists; Old Regular Baptists; Primitive Baptists; Regular (Particular) Baptists; Regular

314   Index

("Union") Baptists; Separate Baptists; Separate Baptists in Christ; Sabbatarian (Seventh Day) Baptists; Southern Baptists; United Baptists
Barrow, David, 201, 203, 206, 208, 219–20, 222, 239
Barth, Karl, 185
Bedgegood, Nicholas, 298n. 8
Benedict, David, xv, 48, 54, 55, 79, 83–84, 89, 92, 107, 111, 121, 186–87, 232, 298n. 8
Berkeley County, Virginia (present W.Va.). *See* Opequon Creek Church
Bethel Association (Mo.), 228
Bethel Association (S.C.), 188, 194
Bethel Church (Ky.), 216, 217–18
Bethlehem Association (W.Va.), 231, 237, 245, 262, 268; Calvary subgroup, 237; Mt. Paran subgroup, 237; Old Bethlehem subgroup, 237; Union Bethlehem subgroup, 237
Big Sandy Valley Association (Ky.), 247
Big Sandy Valley Quarterly Meeting (Ky.), 277
Billingsley, James, 105, 107, 137, 139, 150–51, 155, 158, 176
Black River Church, 87, 95, 105, 111, 114
Black Rock Address, 244
Blackwater (Holston-Staunton) Church (Va.), 104, 165, 173, 188, 192
Blaine Union Association (Ky.), 231
Bledsoe, Joseph, 193
Bledsoe, Moses, 204
Bloodworth, Timothy, 184
Blue Grass Quarterly Meeting (Ky.), 272
Blue Licks, Battle of, 182
Blue Run Church (Va.), 165. *See also* Craig, Elijah
Boles, H. Leo, 289
Boone, Daniel, 72, 100, 135, 161, 178, 220
Boone, George, 100
Boone, Sarah, 72
Boone, Squire, Jr., 100, 178, 193, 203
Boone, Squire, Sr., 72, 73, 100
Boone, Thomas, 220, 226, 229–30
Boonesborough settlement, 100, 178, 192, 203, 207
Boone's Creek Association (Ky.), 249

Boyd County Quarterly Meeting (Ky.), 272
Bracken Association (Ky.), 201, 203, 206
Bradford, David, 184
Breed, Joseph: death, 187; migration to South Carolina, 104, 105, 107, 132; possible kinship to Waitstill ("Wait") Palmer, 49; preaching in North Carolina, 63, 70, 74–76, 79; preaching in Virginia, 49, 50, 53–54, 98, 282
Bristol Baptist College, 10, 64
Broad Run Church (Va.), 116
Brown, Eleazar, 41
Brown, Simeon, 41
Bryan's Station Church (Ky.), 249
Bryant, Nettie, 284
Bryant, William F., 280–87, 290
Buis, W.M., 77
Bullen (Bowling), John, 158
Burleigh Church (Va.), 19–20
Burning Springs Association (Ky.), 206–7, 230–31, 243, 247–48, 252–57, 260, 267, 270, 303–4n. 48
Burning Springs Church (Ky.), 247, 254
Burruss, John, 147, 159
Bush, William, 192
Butler, William, 137, 138, 139, 140, 142–43, 151–52, 161–62

Cacapon River, Va. (present W.Va.), 48, 53–54, 61, 107
Caldwell, David, 171, 184
Calhoun, William, 268
Calvinism, 2, 5, 9, 12, 17, 23, 24–25, 32, 35, 37, 39–40, 45–46, 64, 77, 84, 96, 126, 189, 190, 201, 203–6, 211, 217, 235, 240, 244, 265. *See also* hyper-Calvinism
Calvin, John, xx, 2, 224. *See also* Calvinism, hyper-Calvinism
Campbell, Alexander. *See* Campbell Reform movement
Campbell, Thomas. *See* Campbell Reform movement
Campbell Reform movement, 210–28, 229–31, 232, 236, 241, 243–44, 251, 252, 267, 284, 287, 289–90, 303–4nn. 19, 48

Index   315

Camp Creek Holiness Church (N.C.), 281–84
Cane Springs Church (Ky.), 222, 223
catechisms, 10, 190
Cathars (Albigenses), 9, 232
Catholics. *See* Roman Catholic Church
Chappawamsick Church (Va.), 300n. 12
Charles I. *See* English Civil War
Charles II, 5
Charleston Association (S.C.), 39, 59, 77, 86, 88, 98, 128, 188, 189, 244
Charleston Church (S.C.), 98, 113, 265
Chenault, David, 222–23, 226, 229–30
Cherokee Indians, 57, 98, 100, 104, 142, 178
Childs, James, 119, 122, 157, 159
Christadelphians, 227
Christian Baptist, The, 211–14, 223, 226, 244
Christian Church (Stone Movement), 120–21, 194, 201, 213, 216–17
Christian Churches, "Independent," 210, 214, 227. *See also* Campbell Reform movement
"Christian Harmony." *See* hymnody
Christian Standard, The, 215
Christian Union (Spurling movement), 280–82. *See also* Church of God (Cleveland, Tenn.)
Christian Unity Association (N.C.-Va.), 209
Churches of Christ (Campbell movement), 210–28, 303n. 19
Church of England. *See* Anglican Church
Church of God (Anderson, Ind.), 284
Church of God (Cleveland, Tenn.), xvii, 248, 279–90
Church of God of Prophecy, 286
Civil War (American), 238, 247, 248, 255
Clark, Edy (Mrs. Henry Ledbetter), 79
Clarke, John, 10
"close" communion. *See* communion
Cochran, Louis, 215–16, 228
Coffee, Jesse, 230
Coffee, William, 230
communion (Lord's Supper), 44, 75, 100, 208–9, 221, 234–35, 238, 266–68, 272–73
Concord Church (Ky.), 230, 304n. 48
Congaree Association (S.C.), 165, 187–88, 194
Congaree Church (S.C.), 105, 111–16, 128, 148, 165
Congregationalists. *See* Independents (Puritan)
Conley, Roland, 259
Connagogig, PA, 50, 51
Cook, William (Old Regular Baptist), 256
Cook, William (Separate Baptist), 158
Cotton, John, 10, 190
covenant-owning rite (Puritan), 12, 19, 92
Craft, Wardie, 262–63
Craig, Elijah, 117–20, 122, 124–25, 127, 147, 149, 162–63, 165, 188, 189, 190, 202, 301n. 57
Craig, Joseph, 118, 121–22, 126
Craig, Lewis, 118, 122, 148, 159, 189, 192
Craven, Peter, 137, 139, 143
Creath, Jacob, 163
Cromwell, Oliver, 5, 9, 46, 259
Cumberland Presbyterians, 120–21, 194, 195
Cunerad, Sarah, 180

Dan River Church (Va.), 103, 104, 119, 122, 128, 165, 188, 192
Davenport, James, 25
Davies, Samuel, 23, 116
Davis, Elnathan, 65–66, 67, 74, 107, 109, 120, 155, 156–58, 164, 166, 176, 241
Declaratory Act, 116, 134, 181
Deep Creek Church (N.C.), 191
Deep River Church (N.C.), 82–83, 84, 88, 91, 95, 98, 104–5
devoting children, practice of, 44–45, 234
Dillard, Ryland T., 202
Disciples of Christ, xvi–xvii, 210, 214, 227, 269. *See also* Campbell Reform movement
Disciples of Christ Historical Society, 215

316 Index

Dobbs, Arthur, 57, 60, 62, 77, 131, 133
Donaldson, Everett, 215, 217, 220, 227, 304n. 48
Donatists, 4
Dorgan, Howard, xvi–xvii, 68, 69, 209–10, 228, 242, 249–50, 257, 259–60, 262, 279
Dorsett, Francis, 137
Dow, Lorenzo, 208
Dreyer, David S., 291, 293, 296n. 1
"dry-christening." *See* devoting children, practice of
"Duck River and Kindred" Associations (N.C., Ga., Ala.), 229, 266
Dudley, Ambrose, 202, 240
Dudley, Jeptha, 202
Dudley, Thomas P., 246
"Dunkards." *See* German Baptists
Dunmore, Lord (John Murray), 169

Eastern District Association (Tenn-Va.-Ky.-Ohio), 246
East Kentucky Association (Ky.), 209, 268
Eaton, Isaac, 96
Edmondson, James, 226, 229–30
Edwards, Jonathan, 18–19, 24–25
Edwards, Joshua, 77–78, 97
Edwards, Morgan, xix, 48, 49, 54, 55, 64–70, 75, 76, 78, 79, 80, 83, 84–85, 88–89, 96, 98, 100, 101–3, 105, 107, 109–11, 112, 114–15, 123, 124–26, 135–37, 138, 141, 148–54, 157, 164, 173, 174, 175, 178, 186–87, 259, 272, 297n. 10, 300n. 11
Elkhorn Association (Ky.), 190, 193, 194, 199, 201–2, 203–6, 221, 229, 234, 245
Elkhorn Association (W.Va.), 245, 258, 264
Elkin, Richard, 192
Elkin, Robert, 104, 192, 193–94, 203, 205–6, 218, 237, 239, 302n. 12
Ellicott, Andrew, 182
emancipationism, 7, 201, 206, 220
English Baptists, xvi–xviii, 4–5. *See also* General Baptists, Regular (Particular) Baptists, Sabbatarian (Seventh Day) Baptists

English Civil War, 5, 6, 11
"Eno [River], Battle of the," 142
Enterprise [Regular Baptist] Association (Ky.-Ohio-Ind.), 248, 270, 278
Enterprise [Southern Baptist] Association (Ky.), 245, 248, 254
Episcopal Church. *See* Anglican Church
Errett, Isaac, 215
Erskine, Ebenezer and Ralph, 16, 18, 27, 29
Evans, Anna, 176
Evans, Christmas, 68
Evans, James, 176

Fairforest Church (S.C.), 104, 112, 113
Fall Creek Church (Va.), 104, 128, 149, 191
Fan for Fanning, A (Husbands), 174
Fanning, Edmund, 131–32, 137–43, 155–56, 161–62, 167, 169, 173–74, 175, 183, 261
Fanning, William, 131, 141
Faulkner, William, 208
feast of charity. *See* love feasts
Ferguson, B.C., 304n. 48
Fields, Jeremiah, 137, 161
Fifth Monarchy movement. *See* Sabbatarian (Seventh Day) Baptists
First London Confession, 9, 45
Fisher's River Association (N.C.), 245
Fiske, Daniel, 36, 37–38, 41, 44, 90
Floyd County Quarterly Meeting (Ky.), 272
foot-washing rite, 5, 40, 44, 75, 90, 100, 190, 235, 250, 256, 275
Franklin, Benjamin, 1, 2, 14, 15, 55, 56, 134
"Franklin," state of, 176–78, 216
Free Baptists, 278
Freemasonry, 255, 257, 260–61, 262
Free Will Baptist Bible College, 275–76
Free Will Baptists, 21, 40, 59, 248, 260, 264–78. *See also* Free Will Baptists, General Conference of (extinct); Free Will Baptists, National Association of; "Original" Free Will Baptists (N.C.)
Free Will Baptists, General Conference of (extinct), 265, 270–71

Index   317

Free Will Baptists, National Association of, 21, 40, 265, 271–78. *See also* "Original" Free Will Baptists; *Treatise on the Faith and Practice of the Original Free Will Baptists* ("the Treaty")
Frelinghuysen, Theodorus, 18
French and Indian War, 54
French Broad River Association (Tenn.), 266
French, James, 203–6, 208, 217, 218, 221–23, 225, 226, 229–30, 237, 239
Friends, Society of. *See* Quakers
Friendship Association (Va..-W.Va.), 258, 262, 264; Old Friendship subgroup, 262, 264
Fristoe, Daniel, 124–25, 300n. 12
Fugate, James, 254
Fuller, Andrew, 218, 248
Fuller, James, 253

Gallatin, Albert, 183
Gambill, D.J., 304n. 50
Gano, John, 96–99, 100, 104, 191, 202, 204–5
Garrard, James, 200–201
Garrard (Garret), John, 50, 53, 116–19, 127
Garrett, Leroy, 215, 303n. 19
Garrick, David, 83
General Baptists: early history in England and America, 5–8, 10, 11, 58, 59, 244, 263, 272; and formation of the Separate Baptists, 34–37, 44, 47, 53, 76, 77, 78–79, 89–90, 92–93, 186, 230, 235, 237, 240, 287; rejection of the Separate Baptists/Congregationalists, 37–38; and Shubal Stearns/Appalachian Christianity, 44–47, 49, 64, 123, 141, 196; subsequent history, 38–39, 41
George II, 60
George III, 140, 156
Georgetown College, 202
Georgia Association, 188, 194, 241
German Baptists, xvi–xvii, 58, 59, 77
Gevedon, W.L., 248
Gilbert, John, 230

Gilbert's Creek Church (Ky.), 192, 193
Gill, John, 11, 35
Glorious Revolution, 5
glossolalia, 281
Gorton, Stephen, 8, 34, 38
Goshen Church (Ky.), 225, 229, 249, 252, 267
Granville, Lord (John Carteret), 57, 60, 70, 74
Grassy Church [Disciples of Christ] (Ky.), 230
Grassy Creek Church (N.C.), 59, 80, 90, 98, 118, 119, 125, 127, 155, 160, 162–65, 166–67, 178, 188
Grassy Lick Church (Ky.), 208, 216, 217–18, 224–25, 265
Graves, James Robinson, 232–33, 263, 290
Great Awakening, 14, 15–31, 34–40, 46. *See also* Whitefield, George
Great Cohara Church (N.C.), 87, 176
Greenbrier Association (Va., present W.Va.), 243, 245, 264
Green River Association (Ky.), 194, 228
Green River Quarterly Meeting (Ky.), 272
Greenup Association (Ky.), 245, 254
Groton Church (Conn.), 7–8, 19, 36, 38, 41, 44, 46, 49, 76
Groton Union Conference (Conn.), 40

Haggard, Rice, 216
hair length codes. *See* Stearns/Separate Baptist dress and hair length codes
Halfway Covenant, 12–13, 25, 26, 89
Hall, Joseph, 249–50, 257
Hamilton, Alexander, 183–84
Hamilton, Ninian Bell, 137, 139, 143
Hanna, Samuel, 230–31, 303–4n. 48
Hargitt, Thomas, 146
Harris, Howell, 16, 18, 27, 28, 68
Harris, Samuel: background and conversion, 101–4, 107; as a later Virginia Baptist leader, 123, 188–92, 243; ordination as a minister, 149; and the Tidewater Baptist revival, 117–20, 121–28, 141–42, 145, 148, 153, 155, 159, 160, 164–67, 197
Harris, Tyree, 132, 138–39, 144, 261

Hart, Oliver, 98, 113, 114
Hatch, Jeremiah, 13
Hatch, Joseph, 13, 51
Haw River Church (N.C.), 98, 105, 107, 108, 120, 156–58, 163, 164, 165–66, 176, 178, 258
Heaton, Samuel, 49, 53, 116
Henderson, Richard, 100, 135, 161–62, 167, 169, 178, 261
Hensley, George Went, 287–89. *See also* snake-handling
Hill Cliffe Church (Wales), 9
Hillsboro, N.C. (formerly Orange Court House and Corbinton), 58, 59, 132, 133, 138–43, 145, 150, 151, 161–62, 166, 169, 170, 173
"Holiness." *See* Pentecostalism
Holliman, Ezekiel, 6
Holly Springs Church (Tenn.), 280
Holston Association (Tenn.-Va.), 193–94, 201, 216–17, 233–34, 241, 243, 246, 266
Hooper, William, 135, 161–62
Hovey, Alvah, 63
Howard, Martin, 123, 135, 141, 142, 169, 173
Howard's Creek (Providence) Church (Ky.), 192, 193
Howard's Upper Creek Church (Ky.), 229
Howell, Rednap, 137, 140, 142, 151–52, 161–62
Hunter, Ezekiel, 87, 98, 107
Hunter, James, 137, 138, 140, 142, 151–52, 161–62, 167, 170
Husbands, Amy (*née* Allen), 73, 184
Husbands, Herman: and the American Revolution, 182–83; birth and ancestry, 55; death, 184, 290; earlier N.C. activities, 56–61, 63, 69–71, 76; later career, 72–74; New Birth conversion, 55; probable meeting with Shubal Stearns in Virginia, 61–62, 282 ; and the Quakers, 56–61, 72–74, 134, 282; and the Regulators' War, 134–72, 174, 175, 183, 202, 261, 284; and the Whiskey Rebellion, 183–84; youth, 55

Husbands, Mary (*née* Kinkey), 55
Husbands, Mary (*née* Pugh), 72
Husbands, William, 55
hymnody, 5, 8, 22, 44, 91, 235, 238, 250, 258–59, 261, 269
hyper-Calvinism, 201–2, 206, 216, 218, 228, 231–32, 239–51, 253–58
hywl, 28, 68–69, 76, 78. *See also* New England Holy Tone

imposition, 5, 44, 90, 234
"Independent Baptists" of Virginia, 189
"Independent" Christian Churches. *See* Campbell Reform movement
Independents (Puritan), 2, 4, 8, 13, 24–25, 87, 181–82, 186. *See also* Puritans
Indian Bottom Association (Ky.), 257; Old Indian Bottom subgroup, 262
Indian Creek Association (Va., present W.Va.), 245
infant damnation, preaching of, 206, 222, 227–28, 258
International Pentecostal Churches of Christ, 287. *See also* Pentecostalism
Ireland, James, 125, 190
Iron Hill Association (Ky.), 231, 237, 262; Old Iron Hill and Mt. Carmel subgroups, 237
Irvine Church (Ky.), 249
Irwin, Benjamin, 281

Jacobs, Wightman, 38, 43, 44, 46, 90. *See also* General Baptists; Windham County Yearly Meeting (Conn.)
James, Elizabeth (Mrs. George Whitefield), 18
James I, 5. *See also* King James translation
Jarratt (Garret), Devereux, 69, 116
Jefferson, Thomas, 191
Jersey Settlement, Rowan County, N.C., 59, 75, 76–77, 78, 96–97, 98–99, 100, 137
Jesse, David, 243, 245–46, 252–53
"Jesus Only"/"Trinitarian" controversy, 287. *See also* Pentecostalism
Jeter, J.B., 232
Johnson, Charles A., 120, 122
Johnson, Robert, 295n. 1

Index 319

Johnson County Quarterly Meeting (Ky.), 269–70, 272
Johnston Riot Act, 168, 169, 174, 178
Johnston, Samuel, 135, 168
John-Thomas Association (Ky./Tenn./Va.), 278
Jones, Ambrose, 206
Jones, Erasmus, 28
Jones, Loyal, xv–xvi, 293
Jones, Richard, 19
Jones, Samuel, 219

Kash, Caleb, 231, 303–4n. 48
Keel, James, 192, 194
Kehukee (Quehuky) Association (N.C.), 40, 88, 128, 148, 176, 188–89, 192, 201, 240, 241, 243–44, 245, 249, 302n. 11
Kendall, William, 241
Kentucky General Union. *See* United Baptists
Kentucky (Southern) Baptist Association/Convention, 202, 228, 245
Kentucky State (Free Will Baptist) Association, 271, 272–73, 277, 278
Ketocton (Catoctin) Association (Va.), 40, 116, 124–25, 127–28, 148–49, 190, 233, 240, 243, 244, 300n. 12, 302n. 11
Ketocton Church (Va.), 53, 116
King James translation, 109, 199, 234
Kinkey, Herman, 55
Knight, Richard, 36
Kosciusko Quarterly Meeting (Ind.), 272
Kyova Association (W.Va.), 262

Lackey, Alexander, 304n. 48
Lane, Dutton, 100–101, 103, 107, 114, 119, 127, 159, 160, 163, 165, 188, 189, 191
Lane, Esther, 101, 176
Lane, Richard, 101
Lane, Tidings ("Tidence"), 65, 67, 74, 100, 101, 107, 109, 155, 158, 164, 176, 179, 180, 192–93, 198, 241
Laurel River Association (Ky.), 230
Lawrence County Quarterly Meeting (Ky.), 272

Leatherman, Daniel, 58
Lebanon Association (Va.), 246, 253–54
Ledbetter, Henry, 78–79
Lee, Henry, 183
Leland, John, 189
Lemons, M.S., 281, 283, 284, 285–86
Lenoir, William, 99, 298n. 34
Letcher County Quarterly Meeting (Ky.), 272, 277
Lick Creek Church (Ky.), 230
Licking Association (Ky.), 201–2, 206, 219, 220, 240–41, 249
Licking-Locust Association (Ky.), 201. *See also* emancipationism
Lilly, Edmund, 158
Lindsay, Marcus, 208
"lining out." *See* hymnody
Little River Church (N.C.), 98–99, 107, 137, 158, 163, 173, 175
Lockwood's Folly Church (N.C.), 87
Lollards, 4, 9
London Confessions. *See* First London Confession; Second London Confession
Long Parliament, 11
Loveall, Henry. *See* Baker, Desolate
love feasts, 5, 128
Low Gap Church (Ky.), 248, 304n. 48
Lulbegrud Church (Ky.), 203–6, 208, 216–18, 220, 221, 225, 229, 252, 267. *See also* Smith, John ("Raccoon"); Williams, Daniel; Vardeman, Jeremiah
Luther, Martin, xx, 212
Lutheran Church, xvi, 58. *See also* Virginia "Lutheran" Movement
Lycans (Lykins), Goodwin, 245
Lynch's River Church (S.C.), 78–79

MacCalla, W.L., 211, 227
Madison, James, 183
Major, Richard, 127
Manning, James, 39
Markland, Charles, 87, 107
Marks, John, 53, 116
Marshall, Abraham, 50, 79, 188
Marshall, Daniel: birth and early life, 30–31; later ministry and death, 188;

marriage to Martha Stearns, 30; migration to and ministry in South Carolina, 105, 107, 111–12, 114, 149; migration to Georgia, 187, 241; migration to Virginia, 48–51, 282; ministry with Shubal Stearns, 49, 53, 63, 69, 74–80, 83, 84–87, 92, 95, 97, 98, 99, 101, 127, 265; Presbyterian mission to the Mohawks, 31, 43, 51. *See also* Stearns, Martha (Mrs. Daniel Marshall); Stearns, Shubal
Marshall, Hannah (*née* Drake), 31
Marshall, John, 126
Marshall, Mary (*née* Drake), 30
Marshall, Thomas, 30
Marshall, William, 126–27, 147, 240
Martin, Alexander, 184
Martin, Josiah, 169, 173
Martin, William, 281–87
Mary I ("Bloody Mary"), 3
Mash (Marsh), Robert, 157
Mash, William, 119
Mason, James, 224–25, 303n. 36
Mate's Creek Association (Ky.-Va.-W.Va.), 247, 254–55, 256–58
Mayo Association (Va.-N.C.), 243
McCauley, Deborah Vansau, xvi–xvii, xx, 18, 92, 120–21, 195–96, 210, 280, 283, 285, 287
McGready, James, 120–21, 196
McRoberts, Archibald, 69, 116
Mennonites, 4, 5, 6, 36
Merrill, Benjamin, 137, 150–52, 169, 170, 173, 175, 180, 183
Merrill, Jemima, 175
Methodists, xvi, xvii, 14, 15, 17, 21, 22, 23, 86, 91, 120–21, 193, 195, 196, 217, 220, 235, 240, 267, 269, 273, 281, 283, 284, 286–87
Milk for Babes. See catechisms
Millennial Harbinger, The, 211–14, 224, 226, 227, 230, 303n. 36
Miller, Benjamin, 59, 75, 76, 77, 88, 96
moderator, associational, office of, 92–96, 238
Mohawk Indians, 31, 43, 49, 50, 51
Mohegan Indians, 12

Moore, Maurice, 131, 133, 135, 167, 169, 261
Moore's Creek Bridge, Battle of, 60, 137
Moravian Church, xvi, 58
Mormon movement, 227
Morris, Samuel, 23, 26, 32, 101
Morse, Joshua, 38, 39, 41, 43, 90
Mountain Association (Ky.), 232, 252, 262
Mountain District Association (N.C.-Va.), 242–43, 245–46, 247
Mount Olive Association (Tenn.), 209
Mount Sterling Church (Ky.), 219, 220–21, 225–26
Mt. Zion Association (Ky.), 231, 237, 248, 262; Ancient Christian Association subgroup, 237; Old Mt. Zion subgroup, 237
Mt. Zion Church (Ky.), 253–54
Mud Creek Church (Ky.), 230–31, 252
Mud River Association (W.Va.), 258, 262, 264
Mulberry Fields meetinghouse (N.C.), 99–100, 158, 298n. 34
Mulberry Gap Association. *See* Eastern District Association (Tenn.-Va.-Ky-Ohio)
Mulkey, John Newton, 84
Mulkey, Jonathan (John), 84, 192, 194, 216–17
Mulkey, Philip, Jr., 84, 192, 194
Mulkey, Philip, Sr.: conversion of, 80–82; downfall of, 83–85, 187–88, 290; North Carolina ministry, 82–85, 87, 89, 92, 95, 98; preaching of, 82–85, 217, 260; South Carolina ministry, 104–5, 107, 114, 132, 149, 187
Mullen, Thomas, 119
Munster tragedy, 135–36
Murphy, Joseph, 98–100, 101, 107, 112, 113, 114, 137, 155, 158, 173, 175, 178, 191, 241, 298n. 34
Murphy, William, 98–99, 100, 101, 107, 114, 119, 127, 155, 159, 163, 165, 173, 188, 189, 191–93, 198, 241

"National" Association of United Baptists, 236

Index 321

New Baptist Song Book, The, 259
New England Holy Tone, 27–28, 37, 44, 50, 53, 63, 67–69, 75–76, 95, 97, 98, 108, 180, 189–90, 217, 250, 259, 268–69, 273–74, 275, 290. See also *hywl*
New Hope Association (Ky.), 231, 257, 261
New London Church (Conn.), 8, 38, 43
New River Association (Va.), 242–43
New River Church (eastern N.C.), 87
New Salem Association (Ky.), 230–31, 243, 252–64, 267, 304n. 48, 305n. 79
Newton, John (hymnist), 22, 91, 235
Newton, John (minister): censure by Shubal Stearns and aftermath, 114–16, 127–28, 145, 148–49, 165, 187, 188, 197, 241, 299n. 2; conversion and early ministry, 76; evangelization of Philip Mulkey, 80–82, 84; North Carolina preaching career, 76, 79, 84, 85, 87, 95, 97; ordination, 111–13; South Carolina preaching career, 105, 107
Newton, Philip, 85
"No-Hellers." *See* Universalism
Nolynn Association (Ky.), 209
Nordin, Robert, 19
North Carolina Gazette, 167
North Carolina General Conference (Free Will Baptist State Convention), 272
North Carolina State Association (Free Will Baptists), 272
North District Association (Ky.), 194, 200, 201, 202–7, 208, 217–28, 229–32, 234, 237, 243, 244, 247, 248–49, 252, 253, 260, 267
Northern Baptists, 271
Northern New Salem Association (Ky.-Ohio), 262
Northern Ohio Quarterly Meeting (Ohio), 272
Nutbush Address, The, 133
Nutbush Creek, N.C., 57, 59, 62, 162

Ohio Association (Ky.-Ohio), 243, 245, 254

Ohio State Association of Free Will Baptists, 271
Ohio State Baptist Convention, 243
Ohio Yearly Meeting (Ohio), 268–69
Oldcastle, Sir John, 9
Old Landmark movement, xviii, xix, 8–9, 35, 36, 40, 68, 136, 195, 215, 217, 230, 232–34, 235, 240, 249, 250–51, 263–64, 265, 279–80. *See also* Graves, James Robinson; Orchard, G.H.; Pendleton, James M.
Old Regular Baptist Hymn Book (Osborne), 259
Old Regular Baptists, 221, 229, 232, 238, 242, 247, 249–50, 251–64, 267, 269–70, 272
"Old School" Baptists. *See* Old Regular Baptists, Primitive Baptists, Regular ("Union") Baptists, United Baptists
Olive Association (Ky.), 231
Onnaquaggy, Penn. (Mohawk settlement), 31, 50, 51
Opequon Creek Church (Va.), 20, 40, 48, 49–53, 59, 96, 98, 107, 116, 233
Orange Presbytery (N.C.), 120
Orchard, G.H., 232–33, 251
"Original" Free Will Baptists (N.C.), 271–72
Osborne, Baxter, 259
Osburne, Josiah, 243

Paint Union Association (Ky.), 231, 237, 245, 247–48, 252–55, 256–57, 261, 262, 267–68, 304n. 50; Old Paint Union subgroup, 237, 267; Original Old Paint Union subgroup, 237, 267; "United" subgroup, 237, 267
Palmer, Albert, 41–42
Palmer, Paul, 8, 19–21, 36, 40, 41, 49, 59, 60, 78, 86, 88, 96, 188–89, 244, 264–65, 274
Palmer, Waitstill ("Wait"), 33, 34–35, 36, 41–44, 77, 90, 282, 296n. 1
Parker, Daniel, 246, 248
Parker, Joseph, 265
Parsons, Dillard, 253–54
Particular Baptists. *See* Regular (Particular) Baptists

Paschal, George W., 76, 84, 89, 92, 96–97, 108, 111, 112, 134, 135, 136–37, 138, 141, 142, 153, 157–58, 170, 173, 175, 299–300n. 11
Patterson, A.J., 62
Payne, Buckner H., 220
Payne, Henry, 205–6
Payne, Jilson, 203–6, 208, 217–18, 221, 237, 239
Pee Dee Church (S.C.), 59, 77–78, 97, 98, 113, 298n. 8
Pendleton, James M., 232–33, 263
Penn, William, 5
Pentecostalism, xvii–xviii, 47, 220, 279–90. *See also* Church of God (Cleveland, Tenn.)
Perry, James, 157
"perseverance of the saints," 45–46, 235–36
Person, Thomas, 137, 143, 155
Philadelphia Association (Penn-N.J.-Del.), 11, 39–40, 49, 59, 63, 76, 79, 86, 88, 95, 116, 125, 204, 233–34, 240, 244, 263–64, 265
Philadelphia Confession, 39, 45, 47, 63, 113, 125–26, 148, 188, 190, 193–94, 199, 203–4, 206, 211, 212, 218–19, 223, 241–42, 243, 275
Philadelphia [Old Regular Baptist] Association (Ky.), 262
Philips, Wade H., 285, 306n. 101
Picirilli, Robert, 266
Pierce, Benjamin, 36
Pietists, 5, 44, 196
Pike Association (Ky.), 245, 264
Pike County Quarterly Meeting (Ky.), 272, 277
Pineville District Association (W.Va.), 258
Plain Truth, The, 213
Pocatalico Association (Va., present W.Va.), 245, 258, 264
Polk (Paulk), Jonathan, 13, 51, 104, 132
Pope, George Whitefield, 105, 241
Porter, Frank, 281, 283, 287
Portsmouth Association (Va.), 192, 201
Potok, Chaim, 67
Potts, Joshua, 76

Pound, Ezra, 70, 94, 195
Powell, Nathaniel, 105, 107, 137, 139, 150–51, 156
Powell, William S., 138, 144, 155, 170–71, 178
Pratt, Parley P., 227
"Prayer Mountain in the Fields of the Wood" (Camp Creek, N.C.), 286
Presbyterians, xvi–xvii, 2, 4, 11, 13, 18, 21, 22, 23–25, 26, 31–32, 34, 43, 44, 50, 55, 57, 58, 69, 89, 91–92, 120–21, 141, 145, 153, 181–82, 186, 195, 196, 211, 221, 240–41, 287. *See also* Cumberland Presbyterians
Price, John, 202, 204–6, 240
Primitive Baptist Hymn Book (Goble), 250
Primitive Baptists, xv, 9, 201, 221, 229, 231, 238, 239–51, 253–59, 260, 261, 263–64, 266, 267, 269–70, 272, 304n. 50
Pugh, Evan, 98, 113, 114
Purefoy, G.W., 92, 299n. 26
Puritans, 2–5, 9, 12–13, 49, 87, 92, 190, 196; and dissenters, 2–13, 25–30. *See also* Independents (Puritan); Presbyterians; Separatists

Quakers, 4, 41, 56, 58–59, 60, 61, 72–73, 134, 141, 153, 167, 171, 282, 283
Quesenberry, James, 193, 229

Randall, Benjamin, 41, 264, 268, 270–71
Rapidan Association (Va.), 164–65, 188–91, 194, 240, 302n. 11
Read, James: career as a Virginia evangelist, 118–23, 125, 127, 141, 155, 189; early preaching, 79, 80, 91–92, 98, 114, 227, 299n. 27; restoration and later years, 188; scandal and downfall, 159–61, 163–64, 166–67, 178, 290
Red Bird Association (Ky.), 230, 247, 249, 252
Red River Church (Ky.), 230
Redstone Association (PA), 211
Reese, Joseph, 111–16, 128, 149
"Reformers." *See* Campbell Reform

Index   323

Movement; Churches of Christ (Campbell movement); Disciples of Christ
Regular (Particular) Baptists, 8–11, 19, 21, 35, 36, 39–40, 41, 44, 47, 49, 53, 59, 60, 61–62, 74–79, 87–88, 95, 96–98, 100, 116–19, 124–28, 189–90, 191–94, 199–202, 209, 211, 215, 218–19, 223, 232–34, 236–37, 240, 241–44, 263–64, 265, 267, 280, 298n. 8. *See also* Charleston Association (S.C.); Kehukee Association (N.C.); Ketocton Association (Va.); Northern Baptists; Southern Baptists
Regular ("Union") Baptists (N.C.-Va.), 247, 260
Regulators, North Carolina, 129–80, 186, 192, 195, 197, 238
Regulators, South Carolina, 105, 107, 133–34
Regulators' War. *See* Regulators, North Carolina
"Republican Methodists." *See* Christian Church (Stone movement)
Revolutionary War. *See* American Revolution
Reynolds, Harvey G., 253–54
Rhode Island Yearly Meeting, 6–8, 11, 19–20, 35–39, 41, 44, 46, 90, 135, 239, 240. *See also* General Baptists
Rice, John, 208
Rigdon, Sidney, 227
Roaring River Association (N.C.), 245
Robinson, Blackwell P., 57
Robinson, William, 23
Roanoke Association (Va.), 192, 243
Rock Spring Association (Ky.), 248
Rocky River Church (N.C.), 157
Roman Catholic Church, 5, 202, 207, 232
Rush, Benjamin, 184

Sabbatarian (Seventh Day) Baptists, 8, 10
Sacred Harp singing. *See* hymnody
Salem Association (Ky.), 190, 193, 194, 199
Salisbury, N.C., 70, 74, 77, 169–70

Saltonstall, Gurdon, 7
Saluda Church (S.C.), 165
Sand Lick Association (Ky.), 247, 255–57
Sandy Creek Association (N.C.-S.C.-Va.), 87–98, 107–8, 109–16, 119, 122–23, 127–28, 131, 135, 145, 146–55, 156, 162–67, 170, 174–78, 180, 187, 188, 191, 192–93, 194, 196–97, 216, 233, 236, 241–42, 245, 272, 279, 281–82
Sandy Creek Church (N.C.), 63, 64–65, 74–77, 79–80, 82, 87, 88, 90, 91, 93, 104, 105, *106*, 107, 120, 146, 158–59, 168, 176, 180, 192, 193, 241, 245. *See also* Tolland Church (Conn.)
Sandy Creek, N.C., 59, 61, 63, 72–74, 94, 132, 133–34, 162, 168, 170, 173
Sardis Association (Ky.-W.Va.), 257–58, 261, 262, 269
Saybrook Platform, 12–13, 25, 26, 34, 41, 89
Schneerson, Menachem Mendel, 67
Scotch-Irish settlers, 58
Scott, Walter, 221
Scottish Highlanders, xvi–xvii, 58, 141
Second London Confession, 10–11, 45
Semple, Robert B., xix, 27, 48, 54, 55, 79, 89, 107, 108, 111, 119, 121–22, 148–49, 153, 162–63, 165, 186–87, 190, 233, 265, 300n. 16
Senter Association (N.C.-Va.), 245
Separate Baptists: formation, 34–37, 41, 89, 287 (*see also* General Baptists); growth in New England, 35–36, 43–47, 88, 92; merge with Regular (Particular) Baptists in the north, 39–41; merge with Regular (Particular) Baptists in the south, 124–28, 187–95, 199–209, 211, 241, 244–45, 248, 265, 280; and northern Free Will Baptists, 41, 264, 266, 272. *See also* Sandy Creek Association (N.C.-S.C.-Va.); Sandy Creek Church (N.C.); Separate Baptists in Christ; Stearns, Shubal; Tolland Church (Conn.)
Separate Baptists in Christ, 199–210, 235, 268

Separate Congregationalists: development, 25, 89, 90; extinction, 40–41; limitations of, 32, 35–36; rise to prominence, 26–28, 35, 44, 88, 123
Separatists (Puritan), 3, 5
Seventh Day Baptists. *See* Sabbatarian (Seventh Day) Baptists
Seymour, William Joseph, 281
Shaftesbury Association (N.Y.), 43
shape-note harmony. *See* hymnody
Shallow Fords (Timber Ridge) Church (N.C.), 100, 158, 173, 175–76, 298n. 34
Silver Creek Church (Va., present W.Va.), 245
Sims, George, 133
Sinners in the Hands of an Angry God (Edwards), 25
Six Principle Baptists. *See* General Baptists
slavery. *See* emancipationism
Smith, C.B., 259
Smith, George, 241
Smith, James, 207
Smith, John ("Raccoon"), 215–28, 229–31, 239, 240, 241, 289–90, 304n. 48
Smith, Jonathan, 219, 220
Smith, Joseph, 227
Smith, Michael, 86–87
Smith and Lynville's Creek Church (Va.), 53, 116
snake-handling, xv, 287–89
Society for the Propagation of the Gospel, 60. *See also* Anglican Church
Some of Our Favorite Songs (Smith), 259
Sons of Liberty, 133, 134
Southampton Church (PA), 76
South Carolina Association. *See* Congaree Association (S.C.)
South District Association (Ky.), 194, 200, 202, 207–9
Southern Baptist Convention. *See* Southern Baptists
Southern Baptists, 8, 90, 112, 194–95, 201, 209, 215, 228–29, 232, 236, 245, 246, 249, 250, 253–54, 264, 266, 267, 269, 271, 279, 304n. 48
"Southern Harmony." *See* hymnody

South Kentucky Association (Ky.), 193–94, 199–210, 229, 234, 249, 268
Southwest West Virginia Association (W.Va.), 209
Spencer, John Henderson, 35, 84, 111, 119, 126–27, 195, 199, 207, 209, 220, 244, 248, 253, 256, 276, 302n. 12
Spencer Creek Church (Ky.), 216, 217–18, 225, 229–30
Spurling, Richard, 280, 287
Spurling, Richard G. ("Green"), 280–87, 290
Stamp Act controversy, 116, 131, 133, 134, 135
Stamps-Baxter Publishing Company. *See* hymnody
Stearns, Anna (*née* Field), 13, 51
Stearns, Charles (great-grandfather), 2
Stearns, Ebenezer (brother), 13, 30, 104, 107, 132, 179
Stearns, Elizabeth (Mrs. Enos Stinson, sister), 13, 30, 51, 104, 107, 132, 179
Stearns, Elizabeth (*née* Young), 13
Stearns, Hannah (*née* Stinson, sister-in-law), 13, 51
Stearns, Hephzibah (niece), 51, 107, 153
Stearns, Isaac (ancestor or uncle), 1–2
Stearns, Isaac (brother), 13, 51, 107, 153, 179
Stearns, John (uncle), 11
Stearns, Martha (Mrs. Daniel Marshall), 13, 30–31, 43, 48, 50, 51, 53, 74–76, 79–80, 98, 99, 104, 107, 132, 179, 187–88, 209, 234, 282
Stearns, Mary (Mrs. Joseph Hatch, sister), 13, 51
Stearns, Mary (*née* Upton, grandmother), 2
Stearns, Peter (brother), 13, 30, 104, 107, 132, 179
Stearns, Rebecca (*née* Gibson, great-grandmother), 2
Stearns, Rebecca (*née* Johnston, sister-in-law), 13, 51
Stearns, Rebecca Ruth (Mrs. Jonathan Polk, sister), 13, 30, 51, 104, 107, 132, 179

Index   325

Stearns, Rebecca Sanford *(nee'* Lariby, mother), 2, 46, 51, 93, 104
Stearns, Sarah (Mrs. Jeremiah Hatch, sister), 13
Stearns, Sarah *(née* Johnston, wife), 13, 30, 48, 51, 64, 107, 132, 153, 179, 180, 192
Stearns, Shubael (father), 2, 12, 46, 51, 93, 104
Stearns, Shubael (first American ancestor), 1–2
Stearns, Shubael (grandfather), 2, 13
Stearns, Shubal: birth, probable pronunciation of name and ancestry, 1–2, 295n. 1; decline of health and death, 174–80; early life, 11–14; immersion and ordination as Separate Baptist minister, 43–47; migration to North Carolina, 48, 55–63; migration to Virginia, 48, 50–55; New Birth conversion, 29; North Carolina ministry, 63–71, 72–108, 109–16, 120–21; phenomena associated with preaching, 63–71, 153–54; and the Regulators' War, 129–80, 186, 290; relationships to present American and Appalachian denominations, 65, 87–94, 107–8, 119–21, 185–87, 189–90, 195–98, 199, 204, 208–10, 211, 214–15, 216, 218–19, 220, 223–24, 227, 228–29, 230, 231–33, 234–39, 240, 241, 246, 247, 249, 250–51, 258–64, 265–66, 267, 270–78, 279–90; "revelations," 48–62, 109–11, 112, 115, 143, 145–46, 164, 165, 167, 174–75; Separate Congregational ministry, 29–33; and the Tidewater Baptist revival, 116, 122–28
Stearns/Separate Baptist dress and hair length codes, 46, 99, 148, 234, 259, 261
Steel, Stephen, 12, 29, 30, 166
Stephens' Creek Church (S.C.), 105, 113
Steward, John, 65–66
Stweart, James, 137, 150–51, 173, 175
Stinson, Enos, 13, 51, 104, 132
Stockton, Robert, 104
Stockton's Valley Association (Ky.), 216–17

Stoddard, Solomon, 12, 18, 24, 93
Stone, Barton W. *See* Christian Church (Stone movement)
Stonington Association (Conn.), 39
Stonington Church (Conn.), 34–35, 36, 41–43, 44, 46
Stony Creek Association (Va.), 254, 255
Strawberry Association (Va.-N.C.), 191, 192–93, 194, 241–43
Sunday schools, 10, 238, 243, 255, 257, 267, 269. *See also* catechisms
Sweet Songster, The, 235, 259
Swift, Thomas, 180
Swindall, J.C., 249–50, 257
Sycamore Church (Ky.), 203, 205–6. *See also* Williams, Daniel

Talcott, Joseph, 7
Tanner, John, 240
Tate's Creek Association (Ky.), 194, 205–6, 207–8, 217
Tate's Creek Church (Ky.), 203
Taylor, John, 126, 244
Teague, Elijah and Alice, 77
Teay's Valley Association (Va., now W.Va.), 243, 245, 253, 264
Tennant, Gilbert, 22, 24, 25, 55
Tennant, William, 18, 22, 55
Tennessee State Baptist Association, 246, 265–66
Terms of General Union, 194, 200, 208, 212, 231
Tharp, William, 205
Thomas, David, 116–19, 124
Thomas, John, 227–28
Thomas, Owen, 19
Thomas, Richard, 206, 218–19
Thomas Hymnal, The, 235, 250, 259
Thompson's Meetinghouse (Va.), 165
Thornton Union Association (Ky.-Ohio-Ind.), 262–64
Three Forks of Powell's River Association (Va.), 249–50, 255
tithing, 275–76
Toe River Association (N.C.), 265–66
Tolland, Conn., 11, 13–14, 29, 30, 31, 32, 48, 51, 52
Tolland Church (Conn.), 29–32, 43–47,

51, 77, 90, 107; practices and origins, 44–47. *See also* Sandy Creek Church (N.C.)
Tomlinson, A.J., 282–88, 290
Tomlinson, Homer, 284, 288
Tomlinson, Milton, 284, 286
Tom's Creek Church (Ky.), 268–69, 270
Toplady, Augustus Montague, 22, 91, 235
Torbet, Robert, 7
Toulmin, Harry, 200
Town Fork Church (Ky.), 204–6
"Transylvania" colony. *See* Boonesborough settlement; Henderson, Richard
Transylvania University, 200, 204–5
"Traveling Church." *See* Craig, Lewis; Gilbert's Creek Church (Ky.); Upper Spotsylvania Church (Va.)
Treatise on the Faith and Practice of the Original Free Will Baptists ("the Treaty"), 275–76
Trent River Church (N.C.), 87
Tribble, Andrew, 119, 191, 193, 203
Tri-State [Free Will Baptist] Yearly Meeting (Ky.-W.Va.-Ohio; extinct), 271
Tryon, William, 131–32, 133, 136, 138, 139–43, 145, 153, 156, 162, 167–75, 183
Tull, James, 12, 89
Turner, James, 87, 107
Twin Creek Association (Ky.), 232, 252
"Two Salvations" doctrine, 246
"Two-Seed-in-the-Spirit" theory. *See* Parker, Daniel
"Two Souls" doctrine. *See* Dudley, Thomas P.

Ulster Scots. *See* Scotch-Irish settlers
Uncas, Joshua, 12
Union Association (Ky.-Va.), 250, 254, 255–56, 257–58, 262, 264
"Union" Baptists. *See* Regular ("Union") Baptists
Unitarians, 200–201
United Baptists, xvii, 189, 190–94, 199–209, 228–39, 241–45, 247–48, 249, 250, 251, 252–55, 256–57, 258–63, 267–70, 272, 273, 278, 279–80
Universalism, 207–9, 249–50
Upper Spotsylvania Church (Va.), 127, 192

VanHoose, Eliphas, 268, 270
VanHoose, Millard, 270
Vardeman, Jeremiah, 208, 217–18, 222, 226
Vaughan, Thomas M., 215–16
Vaughan, William, 215, 295n. 1
Vestry Act (N.C.), 60–61, 70, 74
Virginia Association (1771). *See* Rapidan Association (Va.)
Virginia Baptists, General Association of, 243, 246, 252–53. *See also* Rapidan Association (Va.)
Virginia "Lutheran" Movement, 23–24, 25, 26, 32, 43, 101, 116. *See also* Whitefield, George

Waddell, Hugh, 169–70, 172, 173, 174, 183
Waldensians, 4, 9
Walker, Jeremiah, 119, 125–26, 127, 149, 159, 189, 201, 265, 300n. 16
Walker, John, 170–71
Waller, John, 119–20, 122, 126, 147, 159, 160, 189
Wallingford Church (Conn.), 8
War of 1812, 183, 184–85
Warren Association (R.I.), 39, 47, 51
Washington, George, 54, 183–84, 191
Washington District Association (Va.), 243, 245–46, 247, 249, 252–58
Watchman, The, 209
Watchtower, The, 213
Watts, Isaac, 22, 91, 122, 125
Weatherford, John, 119
Welborn, John, 241
Welsh Baptists, xvi, 76. *See also* Regular (Particular) Baptists
Welsh Tract Church (DE), 19, 78, 265
Wesley, Charles, 16–17, 22, 91, 235
Wesley, John, 16–17
Western Free Will Baptist Conference (N.C.), 271–72. *See also* Free Will Baptists

Westminister Confession (Presbyterian), 11, 32, 45
West Virginia State Association (Free Will Baptist), 271
Whiskey Rebellion, 183–84
Whitefield, George: birth and early life, 15–17; death, 28, 161; establishment of "living" and ordination, 17–18, 21; New Birth conversion, 17; preaching in New England's/America's Great Awakening, 14, 24–29, 34, 35, 49, 55–56, 58, 63, 68, 74, 89, 92, 110, 166, 196, 235, 240, 298n. 8; repudiation of the work of Shubal Stearns, 16, 86; and "St. Margaret's affair," 21–22, 24; and Virginia "Lutherans," 23–24, 43; and the Wesleys, 17–18
White Oak Church (Ky.), 230
Wightman, Edward, 5, 7
Wightman, Timothy, 36, 38, 41, 42, 90
Wightman, Valentine, 7–8, 19, 33, 34, 36, 37, 38, 41, 43, 49, 90, 282
Williams, Daniel, 72, 203–7, 208, 222, 230, 231, 239
Williams, Edward, 72, 203, 207
Williams, Jeremiah Vardeman, 208
Williams, John (attorney), 161–62
Williams, John Augustus, 215–18, 220, 225–26, 240

Williams, John (minister), 146–48, 189, 300nn. 42, 43
Williams, Roger, 5, 6
Windham County Yearly Meeting (Conn.), 38, 44, 46, 90, 240. *See also* Jacobs, Wightman
Wolf Hills (Abingdon, Va.), 192
Wolf Hills Church (Va.). *See* Howard's Creek (Providence) Church (Ky.)
Woods, Archibald, 205
Woods, Peter, 205
Wyley, Allen, 116–17

Yadkin Association (N.C.), 192, 194, 241–43, 245–46, 256–57
York, Jeremiah, 180
York, Seamore, 107, 137, 155, 176, 179, 186
Yorktown, Battle of, 182
Younger, James, 59, 75, 77–78, 79, 97, 99, 105, 176

Zion Association (Ky.-W.Va.-Ohio), 231, 245, 247, 254–55, 258, 261, 269; New Zion subgroup, 237; Old Zion subgroup, 237; Tri-State Zion subgroup, 237
Zion Church (Ky.), 247–48

www.ingramcontent.com/pod-product-compliance
Lightning Source LLC
Chambersburg PA
CBHW020330240426
43665CB00043B/198